TREES
of
ILLINOIS

Linda Kershaw
with contributions by

Christopher Dunn & Clem Hamilton

Lone Pine Publishing International

Distributed by Lone Pine Publishing
1808 B Street NW, Suite 140
Auburn, WA, USA 98001

Website: www.lonepinepublishing.com

Publisher's Cataloging-In-Publication Data
(Prepared by The Donohue Group, Inc.)

Kershaw, Linda, 1951–
  Trees of Illinois / Linda Kershaw ; with contributions by Christopher Dunn & Clem Hamilton.

  p. : ill., maps ; cm.

  Includes bibliographical references and index.
  ISBN-13: 978-1-55105-475-9
  ISBN-10: 1-55105-475-2

  1. Trees—Illinois—Identification. 2. Trees—Illinois—Pictorial works. I. Dunn, Christopher Paul, 1954– II. Hamilton, Clement Wilson. III. Title.

QK484.I3 K47 2007
582/.1609/773

The photographs in this book are reproduced with the generous permission of their copyright holders. A full list of photo credits appears on p. 6, which constitutes an extension of this copyright page.

Disclaimer: This guide is not intended to be a "how to" reference guide for food or medicinal uses of plants. We do not recommend experimentation by readers, and we caution that a number of woody plants in Illinois, including some used traditionally as medicines, are poisonous and harmful.

PC: P14

Contents

List of Keys

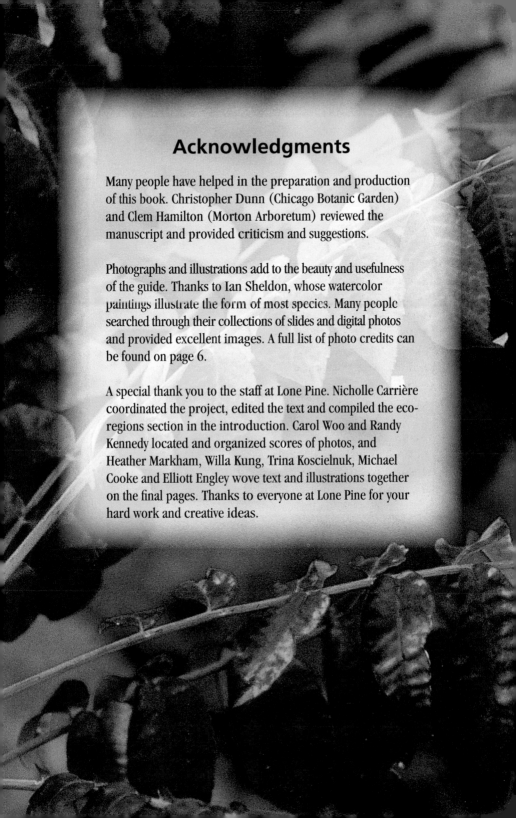

Acknowledgments

Many people have helped in the preparation and production of this book. Christopher Dunn (Chicago Botanic Garden) and Clem Hamilton (Morton Arboretum) reviewed the manuscript and provided criticism and suggestions.

Photographs and illustrations add to the beauty and usefulness of the guide. Thanks to Ian Sheldon, whose watercolor paintings illustrate the form of most species. Many people searched through their collections of slides and digital photos and provided excellent images. A full list of photo credits can be found on page 6.

A special thank you to the staff at Lone Pine. Nicholle Carrière coordinated the project, edited the text and compiled the eco-regions section in the introduction. Carol Woo and Randy Kennedy located and organized scores of photos, and Heather Markham, Willa Kung, Trina Koscielnuk, Michael Cooke and Elliott Engley wove text and illustrations together on the final pages. Thanks to everyone at Lone Pine for your hard work and creative ideas.

Photo Credits

Photos are by Linda Kershaw, except the following:

Ralph Arvesen: 182b

Wasyl Bakowsky: 24a, 28b, 29c, 69b, 77b, 84a, 85a, 116b, 125b, 150b, 190a, 214a, 222a, 237a, 265b

Steve Baskauf: 70, 95a, 95b, 98a, 98c, 102b, 102c, 123, 131, 132b, 134, 181, 205, 207, 238

Bill Cook: 94c, 94b, 99a, 105b, 127c, 129b, 143c, 174a, 237b, 271b

Bill Crins: 71b, 171a, 183a, 190b, 197b, 198b, 203b

Tamara Eder: 20

Troy Evans: 96

Mary Gartshore: 101a, 107b, 202a, 261a, 264

Erich Haber: 72a, 76b, 94a, 103, 112a, 117a, 127b, 137c, 138b, 140b, 165b, 239a, 242a, 262c

Alex Inselberg: 5

W.S. Justice, Smithsonian Institution: 211b

Dawn Loewen: 83c

Glen Lumis: 32a, 33a, 33b, 33c, 84b, 112b, 113, 121a, 124a, 126c, 138c, 174b, 203c, 217b, 232a, 237c, 239b, 242b, 246b, 254b, 255c, 259a, 273a, 273b, 274b, 274c, 276c, 276a

Tim Matheson: 25b

Robert Mohlenbrock: 195a, 204, 268b

Morton Arboretum (Lisle, IL): 21b, 80b, 86, 92b, 92c, 95c, 98b, 102a, 119, 120, 122b, 126b, 128b, 130, 132a, 133b, 142b, 146a, 149b, 156b, 158, 170, 178a, 182a, 185, 189, 195b, 200, 203a, 206, 208, 209, 210a, 210c, 213a, 216b, 219, 221a, 221c, 223b, 224b, 225, 226a, 226b, 227, 229b, 240, 241a, 244, 245b, 245c, 252, 257a, 257b, 258c, 268a, 272a, 275, 278b, 279b, 279c

Fred Nation: 154

Ozarks Regional Herbarium, Missouri State University (Springfield, MO): 110b, 110c

Allison Penko: 19

Tony Presley: 211a

Anton Reznicek: 97b

Robert Ritchie: 202c

Anna Roberts: 157b

Royal Botanical Gardens (Ontario, Canada): 71c, 109b, 109c, 183b, 183c, 186b, 235a, 266b

Guy Sternberg: 23a, 110a

Don Sutherland: 83b, 117b, 186a

Pictorial Guide

NEEDLE LEAVES

Eastern white pine
p. 68

Red pine
p. 69

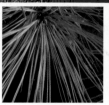

Loblolly pine
p. 70

Pitch pine
p. 71

Scots pine
p. 72

Jack pine
p. 73

Tamarack
p. 74

Black spruce
p. 75

Norway spruce
p. 76

Eastern red-cedar
p. 77

Eastern white-cedar
p. 78

Southern bald-cypress
p. 79

ALTERNATE BROAD LEAVES

Small-flower tamarisk
p. 80

Tulip-tree
p. 82

Cucumber-tree
p. 83

Pawpaw
p. 84

Sassafras
p. 85

Spicebush
p. 86

American sycamore
p. 87

American witch-hazel
p. 88

Pictorial Guide

ALTERNATE BROAD LEAVES

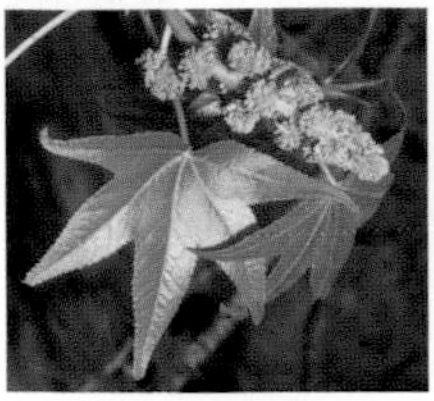
Sweetgum
p. 89

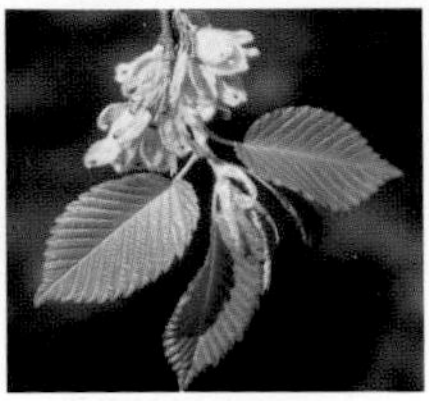
American elm
p. 91

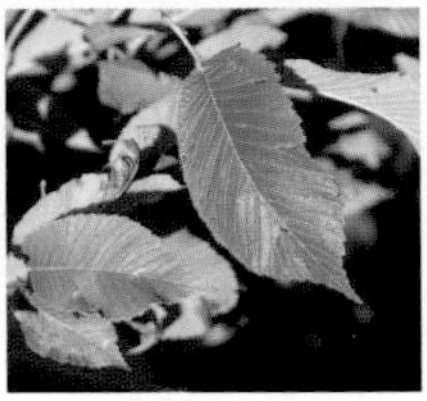
Slippery elm
p. 92

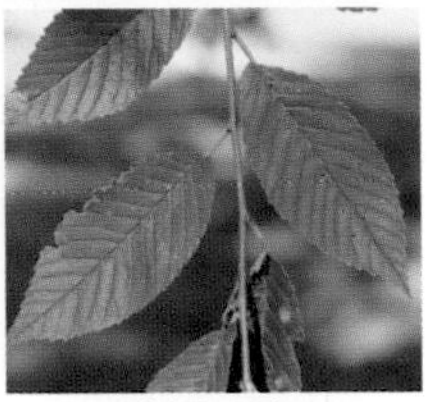
Siberian elm
p. 93

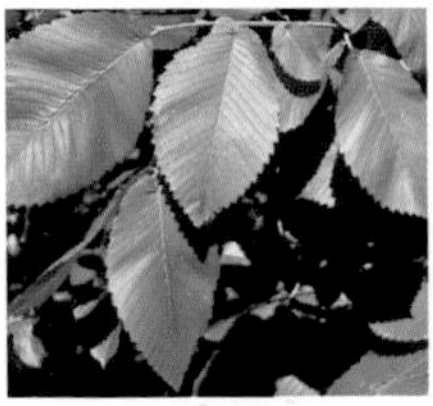
Rock elm
p. 94

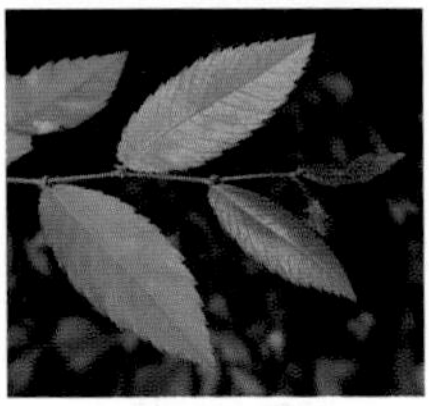
Winged elm
p. 95

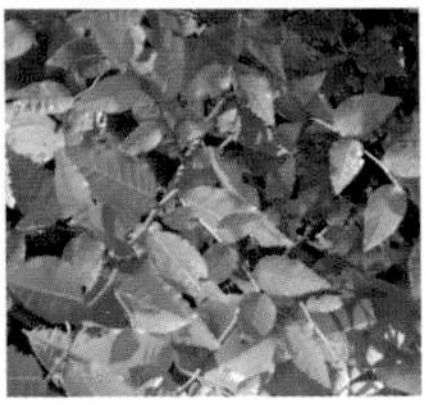
Planertree
p. 96

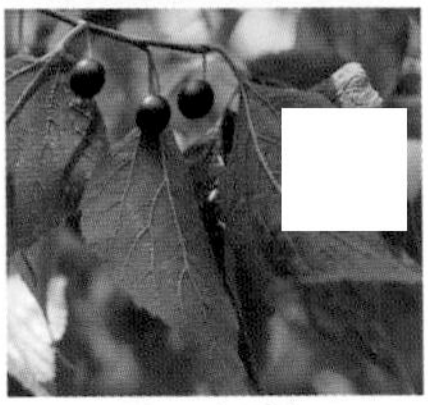
Common hackberry
p. 97

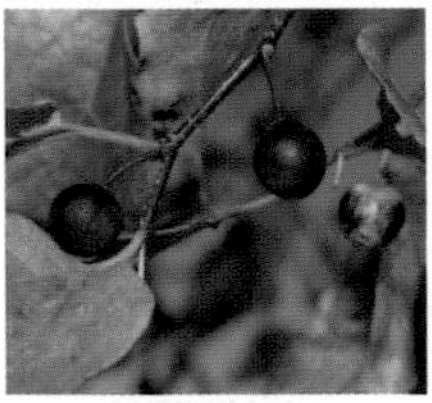
Sugarberry
p. 98

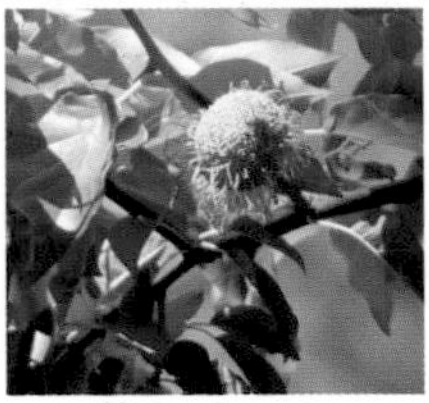
Osage-orange
p. 99

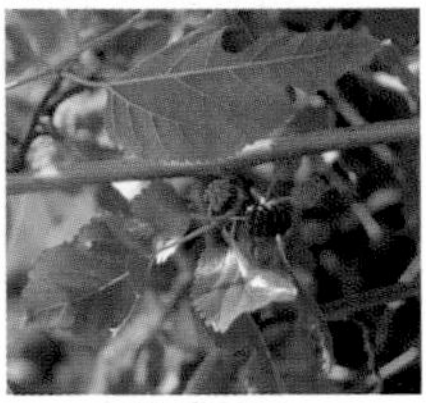
Mulberries
pp. 100–101

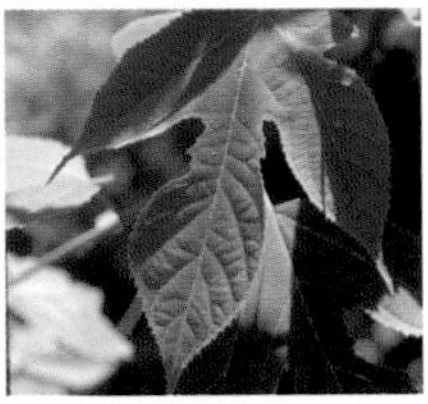
Paper-mulberry
p. 102

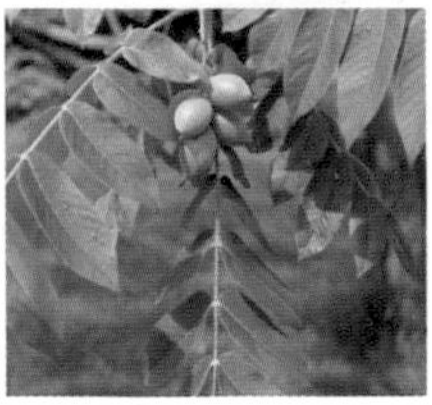
Butternut
p. 105

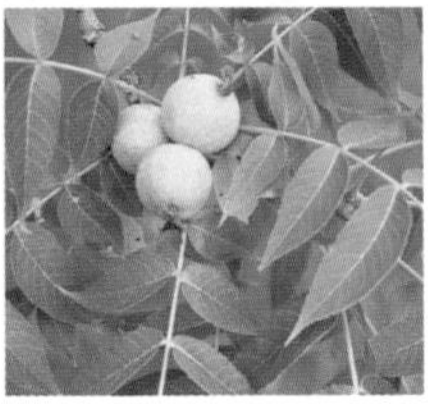
Black walnut
p. 106

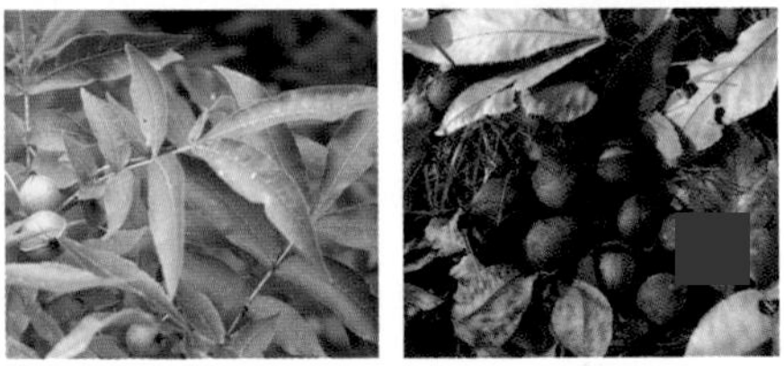
Hickories
pp. 107–112

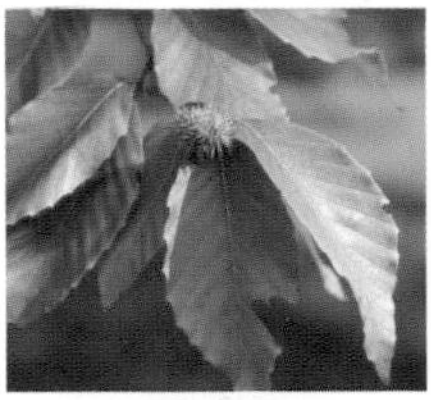
American beech
p. 116

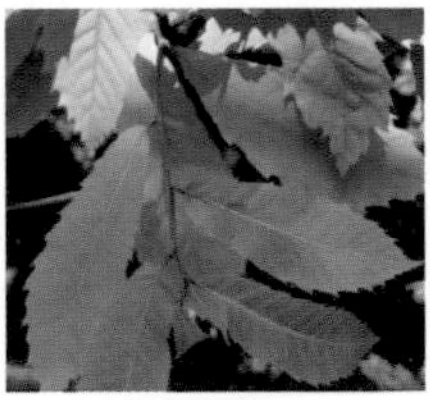
American chestnut
p. 117

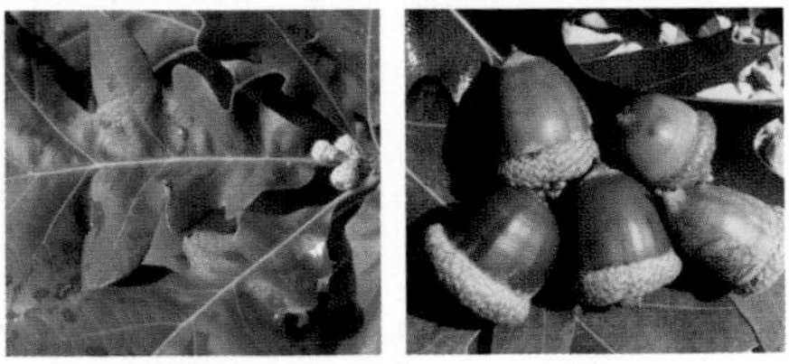
Oaks
pp. 118–134

Pictorial Guide

Hop-hornbeam
p. 137

Blue-beech
p. 138

American hazelnut
p. 139

Yellow birch
p. 140

Paper birch
p. 141

European white birch
p. 142

Speckled alder
p. 143

Black alder
p. 144

White poplar
p. 149

Large-toothed aspen
p. 150

Quaking aspen
p. 151

Balsam poplar
p. 152

Cottonwoods
pp. 153–154

Willows
pp. 155–166

Cherries
pp. 174–176, 178–179

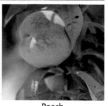
Peach
p. 177

9

Pictorial Guide

| Plums | | Common pear | Quince |
| pp. 180–183 | | p. 184 | p. 185 |

| Wild crabapple | Siberian crabapple | Common apple | Prairie crabapple |
| p. 186 | p. 187 | p. 188 | p. 189 |

| Mountain-ashes | | Hawthorns | |
| pp. 190–191 | | pp. 192–201 | |

| Serviceberries | | Southern-buckthorns | |
| pp. 202–203 | | pp. 204–205 | |

| Sourwood | Tree farkleberry | Rose-of-Sharon | Common persimmon |
| p. 206 | p. 207 | p. 208 | p. 209 |

Pictorial Guide

Mountain silverbell
p. 210

Bigleaf snowbell
p. 211

Yellow-wood
p. 212

Black locust
p. 213

Eastern redbud
p. 214

Honey-locust
p. 215

Water-locust
p. 216

Kentucky coffee-tree
p. 217

Hercules-club
p. 218

Staghorn sumac
p. 220

Winged sumac
p. 221

Poison-sumac
p. 222

European smoketree
p. 223

Common winterberry
p. 224

Deciduous holly
p. 225

American holly
p. 226

Common mountain-holly
p. 227

Tree-of-heaven
p. 228

Mimosa-tree
p. 229

Goldenrain-tree
p. 230

11

Pictorial Guide

Common hop-tree
p. 231

Russian-olive
p. 232

American basswood
p. 233

Littleleaf linden
p. 234

Black tupelo
p. 235

Water tupelo
p. 236

Glossy buckthorn
p. 237

Carolina buckthorn
p. 238

OPPOSITE BROAD LEAVES

European buckthorn
p. 239

Dahurian buckthorn
p. 240

Alternate-leaf dogwood
p. 242

Gray dogwood
p. 244

Cornelian-cherry dogwood
p. 245

Eastern flowering dogwood
p. 246

Eastern wahoo
p. 247

European spindle-tree
p. 248

American bladdernut
p. 249

Horsechestnut
p. 250

Ohio buckeye
p. 251

Red buckeye
p. 252

Pictorial Guide

OPPOSITE BROAD LEAVES

Maples
pp. 254–260

Ashes
pp. 262–266

Common lilac
p. 267

Eastern swamp-privet	European privet	Empress-tree	Northern catalpa
p. 268	p. 269	p. 270	p. 271

Buttonbush	Nannyberry	Smooth blackhaw	Wayfaring-tree
p. 272	p. 274	p. 275	p. 276

   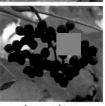

American highbush-cranberry, p. 277	Amur honeysuckle p. 278	Common elderberry p. 279	Amur corktree p. 280

Illinois would be a very different place without trees. Each spring, trees are among the first plants to bring a flush of green, often accompanied by sprays of fragrant flowers. In summer, trees shade our parks and yards, giving shelter from hot sun or drenching downpours and providing homes for birds and squirrels. In autumn, the red and golden leaves of some trees create a beautiful patchwork of color, and the fruits of others provide delicious treats. In winter, evergreen trees shelter us from wind and snow and add color to a drab landscape.

Trees are our largest plants, and they dominate many ecological systems. Some plants require the shelter of a forest canopy for survival, while others need the partial protection of open-grown trees in sunnier sites to become established. Beneath the canopy, light levels are lower, humidity is higher and the immediate impacts of wind and rain are muted.

Trees are also important ecosystem producers. They create large quantities of carbohydrates and oxygen, and they store huge amounts of nutrients in their massive trunks and branches. Their leaves, flowers, fruits, bark and twigs provide food for insects, birds and mammals, and their trunks and boughs provide shelter and nesting sites.

Carya ovata, shagbark hickory

Through the ages, trees have been important to human survival. Bark was used for covering canoes, roofs and walls, for tanning leather, for making dyes and even for producing soft fibers that could be woven into blankets and clothing. Sap provided food, glue, caulking and waterproofing. Fruits and nuts are still an important source of food, and many parts of different trees have been used as medicines. Fine roots were split and spun to make thread and cord, and the knees and elbows of some larger roots were highly valued in shipbuilding. Most notably, however, trees have provided wood. This strong, light, versatile material is still widely used for building homes and other structures; for making boats, tools, utensils and other small items; for carving works of art; for producing paper, cellophane, turpentine, charcoal and countless other products; and for fuel. Without the food, shelter and fuel provided by trees, settlement in Illinois would have been difficult at best.

Many collections of trees have been established in parks and gardens throughout Illinois. An **arboretum** is a place where trees and other plants are cultivated for their beauty and for scientific and educational purposes. If you would like to learn more about trees by viewing living specimens, try visiting some of the collections listed in the appendix (p. 281).

Plants can also be studied using dried, pressed specimens. A **herbarium** is a large collection of such specimens that have been mounted, labelled and filed systematically. See the appendix (p. 281) for the names and locations of herbaria in Illinois.

What Is a Tree?

Most of us have a fairly clear idea of what a tree is. Trees are tall, long-lived plants with stout, woody trunks and spreading canopies. A giant sugar maple or perhaps a towering spruce might come to mind with the word "tree." Many small trees, however, fall into the gray area between trees and shrubs. Robust specimens might be considered trees, but younger or less robust individuals would be called shrubs. These species have also been included in this guide in an effort to include all plants that could possibly be viewed as "trees."

For the purposes of this guide, a **tree or tall shrub** is defined as an erect, perennial, woody plant reaching **over 13'** in height, with a distinct crown and with a trunk (one or more of the trunks on a multi-stemmed specimen) reaching at **least 3" in diameter**. The trunk diameter is the DBH (diameter at breast height), measured 4^{1}/$_{4}$' from the ground.

Some definitions stipulate that a true tree must have a single trunk that divides into branches well above the ground, so that the tree has a clearly defined bole (main stem). However, many trees, such as some willows, have trunks that divide at or near the ground. Other species, such as the birches and native chestnuts, often coppice (form bushy clumps from sprouting stumps).

Trees are our longest lived and largest organisms. Most live about 100–200 years, but some survive much longer. For example, southern baldcypress can live for over 1000 years. Smaller trees are usually shorter-lived, typically surviving about 60–80 years. Most trees reach 50–80' in height, but some grow even taller. For example, eastern white pine can reach 100' and American sycamore, tulip-tree and white oak may tower to 115'. At the other end of the spectrum, pussy willow, mountain maple and poison-sumac rarely exceed 15'.

In order to support the large trunks and branches of a tree, many cells are gradually transformed into non-living supportive tissues, such as wood and cork. These dead cells account for about 80% of a mature tree, and the remaining 20% are live cells that maintain vital functions.

Trunks

The sturdy, woody trunk of a tree supports the weight of the aboveground mass, and it supplies the living tissues with water and nutrients from the ground and with food from the leaves. A trunk is made up of several distinct layers, each with a different function.

The outermost layer is the bark. Tree bark forms a protective, waterproof layer that can shield the tree from fire damage, insect or fungal attack and the stress of sudden temperature changes. Not all types of bark offer the same protection. For example, trees with thick, corky bark may survive a fire that would seriously damage or kill trees with thin, papery bark.

All bark has small, round or vertically or horizontally elongated pores called lenticels, which

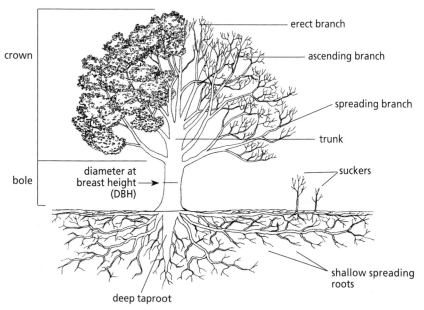

crown

bole

diameter at breast height → (DBH)

deep taproot

erect branch

ascending branch

spreading branch

trunk

suckers

shallow spreading roots

Trunk cross-section

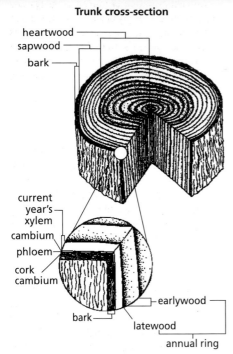

heartwood
sapwood
bark

current
year's
xylem
cambium
phloem
cork
cambium

bark
latewood
earlywood
annual ring

To the inner side of the cork cambium lies the **phloem** or bast. This thin, inconspicuous layer of cells is very important to the tree because it carries the food (carbohydrates) produced by the leaves to all other living tissues. Trees are killed by "girdling," i.e., removing or cutting through the bark, cork cambium and phloem in a complete band around the trunk. The roots of a girdled tree no longer receive food, and the tree eventually dies. Some roots may persist for a time using stored reserves, but the final effect of girdling is inevitable.

On the inner side of the phloem lies an even narrower ring of cells, too thin to see, called the **cambium**. The cambium is responsible for increases in the diameter of a trunk or branch. Cambium cells produce phloem cells along the outer surface of the ring and xylem cells along the inner surface. The **xylem** transports water and nutrients up from the roots to the branches and leaves, where the tree produces food and energy. The thick-walled, cylindrical cells of the xylem join end to end, forming thousands of capillary tubes that extend up the trunk like tiny, elongated drinking straws. The xylem cells soon die, but their firm hollow tubes continue to function, often for many years.

Within its bark, then, the trunk of a tree has a thin outer ring of living tissue composed of the phloem and cambium, and a narrow ring of living xylem. Most of the rest of the trunk, which we call **wood**, is made up of dead xylem cells. With time, these may gradually become plugged with resins, tannins and other compounds and eventually cease to transport fluids altogether, but by then many younger xylem cells have been laid down around them to take their place. As long as xylem cells continue to transport fluids, they are part of the tree's **sapwood**, but once they clog and cease to function, they become part of the **heartwood**. Heartwood is often darker and harder than sapwood because of the resins and other compounds that fill its cells. Heartwood helps support the trunk but otherwise is not important to the general health of the tree. A tree's heartwood can burn or rot away almost completely, leaving a hollow trunk, while the branches and leaves continue to flourish.

allow the trunk to breathe. Lenticels are often difficult to see, but in some trees they are very conspicuous and distinctive, with raised edges that roughen the bark. Often, trees with thin, smooth bark (e.g., birches, cherries) have large, conspicuous lenticels.

Bark is sometimes very distinctive (e.g., in beeches and sycamores), but often it is not a useful identifying feature. Bark characteristics can also change greatly with age. Young bark is usually smooth, with visible pores, but as a tree ages, its bark becomes thicker and rougher, and the pores are obscured in many corky layers.

Bark cells grow from a special thin layer of living cells on the inner side of the bark, called the **cork cambium** or bark cambium. Each year, the cork cambium lays down another successive layer of bark to cover the ever-expanding trunk or branch. As growth continues, the oldest, outermost layers of bark are forced either to split into corky ridges or scales (as in maple bark) or to peel away from the tree (as in birch bark).

Trees growing in temperate regions, where there are definite seasonal changes in growth, develop patterns in their wood called **annual rings**. Each year, after the first flush of spring growth, the trees set down large, relatively thin-walled, light-colored xylem cells. As the season progresses, growth slows and the xylem cells become smaller and thicker-walled. Eventually, trunk growth stops almost completely in late summer, as trees begin to store nutrients for the coming winter and following spring. Consequently, the ring of wood that is laid down each year gradually changes from pale, large-pored **earlywood** or springwood to harder, darker, small-pored **latewood** or summerwood. The following spring, a new layer of pale springwood is laid down, often in sharp contrast with the darker adjacent summerwood of the previous season. As a result, each year's growth forms a distinct annual ring. The rings can be observed as concentric circles across a log or stump when a tree is cut down, or as a series of light and dark bands along a cylinder when a core is taken from the trunk.

Close examination of annual rings reveals much about the history of a tree. Because a new ring is created each year, counting the rings reveals the age of the tree. We can also learn much about the tree's health and environment because many factors affect the growth rate and subsequent ring widths of a tree. Droughts, unusually cold years, ash deposits from volcanic eruptions, insect infestations, diseases and pollution can all make a tree produce narrow annual rings. Alternatively, increased light (perhaps as a result of an opening in the canopy), influxes of nutrients and unusually warm years can result in wider annual rings. Scars from forest fire or avalanche damage may eventually be overgrown by new wood but will remain hidden in the trunk as a permanent record of the event.

Branches and Twigs

Branches develop the same woody structure as trunks. In young twigs, however, the soft central core of early growth, called the **pith**, is more obvious. In some trees, the pith is quite distinctive. For example, in pawpaw twigs, the pith is marked with horizontal bands, and in hackberry twigs, it has a series of horizontal chambers; both patterns are visible in longitudinal section (cut lengthwise down the middle of the twig). In oaks, the pith is five-pointed when viewed in cross-section (cut across the twig).

Unlike the trunk, branch tips and twigs grow lengthwise as well as widthwise. The history of recent growth can often be observed through a series of leaf or bud scars on young branches. Each summer, small branches produce buds along their lengths and (usually) at their tips. By autumn, each bud contains all of the rudimentary cells necessary to produce a new structure. The **tip bud** or terminal bud is often much larger than the lower **side-buds** or lateral buds, and it produces a new extension of the shoot the following year. Most side-buds produce leaves and sometimes flowers, but a few send out new branches.

Buds develop gradually over the summer. Usually they are covered by one or more tough, overlapping **bud scales**, which protect the tender, developing tissues from insect and fungal attacks

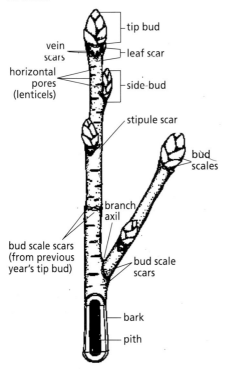

vein scars

horizontal pores (lenticels)

tip bud

leaf scar

side-bud

stipule scar

bud scales

branch axil

bud scale scars (from previous year's tip bud)

bud scale scars

bark

pith

and from drying out. A few trees have **naked buds**, which lack bud scales.

Each bud contains embryonic tissues of the part that it will produce the following year. These tissues remain dormant over winter, but in spring rapid growth resumes, and the new shoots, leaves and flowers expand to emerge from their buds. As the buds open, the scales are shed, but scars remain to show where the scales were attached to the branch. Buds at the twig tips are encircled by scales, which leave a ring of scars around the twig; each successive ring or **annual node** along a branch indicates one year's growth.

Leaves

Leaves come in all shapes and sizes, from the tiny, simple scales on cedar boughs to the giant, compound leaves almost a metre long on the Kentucky coffee-tree. (See pp. 36–41 for further discussion of leaf shapes, structures and arrangements.)

Leaves house the food factories and breathing devices of the tree. A leaf produces food by first capturing the sun's energy with the green pigment **chlorophyll**, which is concentrated in the outer leaf tissues. The leaf then uses the trapped energy in a process called **photosynthesis** to combine carbon dioxide and water and produce sugars (the direct or indirect source of energy for animals) and oxygen (also essential to animal life).

Most trees that have needle-like leaves are **evergreen**, shedding leaves gradually throughout the year but always retaining some green needles for photosynthesis. In Illinois, most trees have broad, **deciduous** leaves, which are produced each spring and shed each autumn.

Leaves breathe through many tiny pores called **stomata**. During the day, leaves take in carbon dioxide and give off moisture and oxygen through their stomata. At night, photosynthesis stops, but the tree continues to respire, expelling carbon dioxide. On broad, deciduous leaves, stomata are usually concentrated on the lower surface of the leaf, and a thin, waxy coating called the **cuticle** protects the upper surface and reduces water loss. On evergreen needles, all sides of the leaf are coated with a cuticle, and the stomata are scattered over the needle surface or concentrated in bands or lines on the lower side. The more extensive cuticle of evergreen needles helps to reduce water loss in winter, when water supply is limited by below-freezing temperatures.

Reproductive Structures

Most tree species reproduce sexually, but the reproductive structures are not always present on every tree. Male and female structures are produced on mature trees in cones or in flowers. In **cones** these parts are hidden behind protective scales, but in most Illinois trees male and/or female structures are readily visible in flowers.

Flowers may consist of several series of structures. Usually the female organs, or **pistil**(s), are at the center, surrounded by a ring of male organs, or **stamens**, and then rings of floral leaves (petals and sepals). **Petals**, which collectively form the **corolla**, are usually much larger

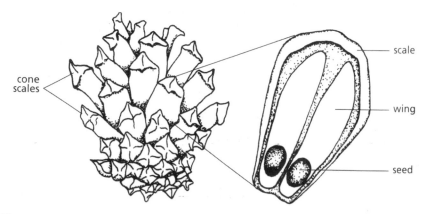

cone scales

scale

wing

seed

and showier than sepals. Most showy tree flowers in Illinois have white petals, but some are brightly colored or marked with contrasting spots or stripes. **Sepals**, which collectively form the outer ring or **calyx**, tend to be small and green, serving primarily to protect immature flowers in much the same way as bud scales. Sometimes the petals and sepals look alike and all are then called **tepals**.

When all four sets of organs are present, the flower is called **complete**, but in most cases, one or more are absent. **Bisexual** or perfect flowers have both female and male organs (pistils and stamens), unisexual, flowers have either male or female parts. Unisexual flowers of each sex may be borne on the same **(monoecious)** or separate **(dioecious)** trees.

A flower's main function is to transfer viable **pollen** from its **anthers** (pollen-producing organs of the stamens) to the receptive **stigma** (pollen-receiving organ of the pistil) of another flower, preferably on another plant. When transfer to another plant succeeds, **cross-pollination** occurs.

Malus cultivar, crabapple

Many tree flowers are small, greenish and inconspicuous, with minute petals or no petals at all. These flowers usually appear early in the year and are wind pollinated (the pollen is carried from one flower to another by the wind). Other trees have insect-pollinated flowers, with showy petals that attract insects and sometimes provide them with handy landing platforms. Often flowers also have special glands called **nectaries**, which produce a sugary liquid **(nectar)** that attracts numerous insects. Many flowers also produce strong odors. Usually these are sweet and fragrant, attracting bees and other nectar-seeking insects, but sometimes flowers have a fetid odor that is irresistible to flies in search of carrion. When an insect visits a flower it is first directed over the stigma, where it deposits pollen from the previous flower, and then

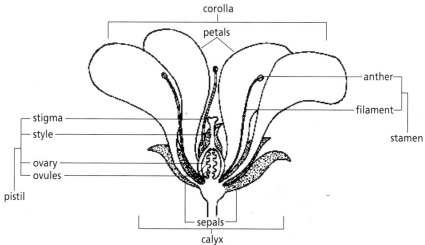

corolla

petals

anther

filament

stamen

stigma

style

ovary

ovules

pistil

sepals

calyx

19

Acer ginnala, Amur maple

and rich in sugars. These fruits attract fruit-eating birds and mammals that swallow the seeds along with the flesh and later deposit the seeds in their droppings at new sites. Similarly, many animals eagerly seek the oil-rich meat of **nuts** (e.g., walnuts, butternuts, hickory nuts, acorns). In fleshy fruits, the edible part is outermost, enclosing one or more seeds that are often protected by woody or bony structures (e.g., cores or stones). In nuts, the edible part of the fruit is encased in a hard shell, and the seed within lacks a protective inner covering.

Many animals also feed on non-fleshy fruits, but these fruits often have special structures that promote seed dispersal without animal assistance. Trees such as ashes, maples and elms produce **samaras** with broad wings that help to carry the seeds through the air or on water to new sites. **Capsules** (e.g., willows, American witch-hazel, common lilac), and **legumes** (e.g., redbud, honey-locust, Kentucky coffee-tree, black locust) are all dry fruits with protective coverings that eventually dehisce (split open) to release the seeds.

Seeds vary greatly in size from one species to the next, but all have a dry, often hard covering, the **seed coat**, which protects the developing **embryo** and its food reserves. Seeds with thin, papery seed coats usually germinate as soon as they are shed, whereas those with thick, hard seed coats may persist for several years before developing. Many Illinois trees have seeds that must experience a cold, dormant period before they can germinate. Once germination begins, food reserves in the seed sustain the seedling while it develops roots and leaves for producing its own food. Large seeds, such as those of chestnuts and oaks, may have enough stored energy to allow the seedling to survive for many days. Small seeds have limited reserves, so the seedlings must develop quickly.

Although trees may produce many thousands of seeds each year, very few survive predation and disease, and even fewer find their way to suitable sites where they can grow into new trees.

past the anthers, where it picks up pollen to carry to the next blossom.

When pollen fertilizes an **ovule** in a female cone or flower, the ovule develops into a **seed**. In conifers, the seeds are naked but remain protected behind the scales of the cones. Other trees produce flowers with ovules in **ovaries**, which develop into **fruits**. Fruits generally have a protective outer skin, but the inner layer surrounding the seeds can vary from thick and fleshy to dry and fibrous or even hard and bony. In most cases, **simple fruits** are produced from the fertilization of a single ovary. However, in some trees (e.g., tulip-tree), dense clusters of many fertilized ovaries produce **aggregate fruits**. Occasionally, compact flower clusters produce very dense clusters of fruits (e.g., mulberries). These **multiple fruits** resemble aggregate fruits, but each part of the group is produced by an individual flower.

Fruits can serve many functions, including protecting the seeds, aiding in seed dispersal and providing moisture and nutrients for the developing seedlings. Fleshy fruits such as **drupes** (e.g., cherries, plums, nannyberries), **pomes** (e.g., apples, serviceberries, mountain-ash fruits) and true **berries** (e.g., pawpaw fruits) are often juicy

Illinois Forests

Although Illinois is known as the "Prairie State" today, at the end of the last ice age, about 12,000 years ago, it was almost completely forested, though the forests were quite different than those of the present-day. The climate was cooler, and the most common tree species were pines and spruces, characteristic of the boreal forest found in more northern climates. Over time, as the climate became warmer and drier, prairie evolved in the central plains area of the state and deciduous hardwoods, primarily oaks and hickories, replaced the conifers. Forest and parkland predominated near water, on hills and uplands and in areas protected from fire, especially in the Shawnee Hills in the south, in the area of land between the Mississippi and Illinois Rivers and in the unglaciated northwestern corner of the state. Cypress swamps similar to those found in the southern states occured in the southernmost part of Illinois.

Prior to European settlement, which began early in the 19th century, nearly 14 million acres (38%) of the state was forested, while the remaining area was prairie. Settlers avoided farming on the prairies, preferring forested areas because of the erroneous belief that the lack of trees meant the prairie soil was infertile. Settlers cleared bottomlands along watercourses and upland forests for agriculture. Tree species in forests changed, and some forests vanished altogether as large, old-growth trees were felled and livestock grazing destroyed the forest understory.

As more settlers arrived looking for land to farm, the need for wood for fuel and building material increased. From 1830 to 1880, deforestation occurred at a rate of about 1% per year. Only about 6 million acres of forest remained by 1870, with some areas completely deforested. By 1920, Illinois had only 22,000 acres of undisturbed forest left (about 0.15% of the original forested area).

In the 1930s, people began to realize the value of preserving natural areas and efforts were made to conserve what remained of the state's forests and to reforest marginal areas of pasture and cropland. The government began to buy land in 1933, creating forest preserves such as Shawnee National Forest, which came into being in 1938. Today, 4.4 million acres (12%) of Illinois is forested, with 425,000 of those acres in urban areas. The state ranks 49th among all the states in the percentage of land that retains its original vegetation.

Fagus grandifolia, American beech

Quercus stellata, post oak

Illinois Ecoregions

- Driftless Area
- Southwestern Wisconsin Till Plains
- Central Corn Belt Plains
- Interior Plateau
- Interior River Valleys and Hills
- Mississippi Alluvial Plain

Illinois Ecoregions

Many of the dominant plants in Illinois's natural vegetation are trees, and as such, trees help to define most biological zones in the state. Broadleaf deciduous species are predominant, dominating 97% of the state's forests, while the remaining 3% are composed primarily of conifers.

The principal forest types are:
- oak-hickory (53% of forests; 6.4% of state)
- elm-ash-cottonwood (22% of forests; 2.5% of state)
- maple-beech (20% of forests; 2.4% of state)
- conifers, mostly pine (3% of forests; 0.3% of state)
- oak-gum-cypress (2% of forests; 0.2% of state)

Slippery elm is the most common tree species, and white oak is the state tree.

Illinois can be divided into six ecoregions, which are shown on the map above: the Driftless Area, the Southwestern Wisconsin Till Plains, the Central Corn Belt Plains, the Interior Plateau, the Interior River Valleys and Hills and the Mississippi Alluvial Plain (Woods et al., 2006). Each ecoregion is characterized by particular geographic, topographic and edaphic (soil) conditions.

DRIFTLESS AREA

The Driftless Area, in the extreme northwest corner of Illinois, remained unglaciated in the last ice age, and this is reflected in its topography, which has the greatest relief in the state. This ecoregion is characterized by rolling uplands and deeply dissected hills. Today there is a mixture of agriculture and forest, though forests are more widespread here than in adjacent ecoregions. Agricultural areas are found in lowland areas and on flatter hilltops. Upland forest can be found on steeper slopes, with black oak and white oak dominating in drier areas, and basswood, red oak and sugar maple more common in areas with greater soil moisture. American elm, green ash and silver maple are the most common trees in floodplain forests.

SOUTHEASTERN WISCONSIN TILL PLAINS

The Wisconsin Till Plains region is found in the northernmost part of the state. It is composed of flat glacial till and outwash plains and hilly moraines. This ecoregion supports a mosaic of vegetation types and is a transitional area between the hardwood forests and oak savannas to the west and the tallgrass prairie that originally dominated farther south. Before settlement, maple-basswood, oak-hickory and oak savanna forests were likely common on moraines, in uplands and along watercourses, while prairie species covered flatter, more level terrain. Today, white oak, swamp

Carya texana, black hickory

Acer ginnala, Amur maple

white oak and American elm forests persist in morainal areas, but most of the Till Plains are used for agriculture.

CENTRAL CORN BELT PLAINS

The Central Corn Belt Plains was the largest area of prairie habitat in the state at the time of settlement in the early 19th century. This region was dominated by tallgrass prairie. Trees occurred in isolated groves scattered across the prairie and were mostly oaks such as white oak, post oak, bur oak and black oak. Scrub oak forests of black oak and blackjack oak mixed with hickories grew on sandy ridges. Marshy areas, now mostly drained for agriculture and urban development, supported trees such as pin oak and swamp white oak. This region is now primarily agricultural.

INTERIOR PLATEAU

The Interior Plateau, a small region in southern Illinois, includes the Northern and Southern Shawnee Hills. Though some of the area is agricultural, much of the original forest remains, mostly within the Shawnee National Forest. Uplands support a variety of oaks and hickories, while cooler, shaded ravines are forested with red oak, beech and sugar maple.

Quercus velutina, black oak (above), *Acer saccharum*, sugar maple (below)

Floodplain forests of sycamore, black walnut, Kentucky coffee-tree, sugarberry and honey-locust are found in bottomland areas.

INTERIOR RIVER VALLEYS AND HILLS

As the name implies, this ecoregion includes major rivers, river valleys, hills and river bluffs, as well as till plains. Before settlement, native vegetation in poorly drained areas and bottomlands, included hardwoods such as pin oak, bur oak, Shumard oak and swamp white oak, and swamps supported water-tupelo and bald-cypress. Beech-maple forests predominated in ravines and uplands with good drainage had a mosaic of oak-hickory forest and prairie. Cropland and pastureland are now predominant in this ecoregion and floodplains have been largely drained or ditched for agriculture.

MISSISSIPPI ALLUVIAL PLAIN

This small region at the southernmost tip of the state historically supported southern floodplain forest species at the northern limit of their range, including bald-cypress and water-tupelo. Today, much of the region has been cleared and drained for agriculture and only a few remnants of bottomland forest and swamp remain.

Threatened and Endangered Trees

Some of Illinois' native tree and tall shrub species are considered threatened or endangered in the state and/or in the United States, but the status of rare species is continually changing. Up-to-date information about rare, threatened and endangered species is available from Center for Biodiversity at the Illinois Natural History Survey in Champaign, Illinois.

Acer saccharum, sugar maple

Acer rubrum, red maple

25

Introduction

Threatened and Endangered Trees and Tall Shrubs in Illinois

Scientific Name	Status	Family	Common Name
Alnus incana	endangered	*Betulaceae*	speckled alder
Amelanchier interior	endangered	*Rosaceae*	inland serviceberry
Amelanchier sanguinea	endangered	*Rosaceae*	round-leaf serviceberry
Amorpha nitens	endangered	*Fabaceae*	smooth false indigo
Betula alleghaniensis	endangered	*Betulaceae*	yellow birch
Carya aquatica	threatened	*Juglandaceae*	water hickory
Carya pallida	endangered	*Juglandaceae*	pale hickory
Castanea dentata	extirpated	*Fagaceae*	American chestnut
Cladrastis kentukea	endangered	*Fabaceae*	yellow-wood
Corylus cornuta	endangered	*Betulaceae*	beaked hazelnut
Halesia tetraptera	endangered	*Styracaceae*	mountain silverbell
Larix laricina	threatened	*Pinaceae*	tamarack
Malus angustifolia	endangered	*Rosaceae*	narrow-leaved crabapple
Pinus banksiana	endangered	*Pinaceae*	jack pine
Pinus echinata	endangered	*Pinaceae*	shortleaf pine
Pinus resinosa	endangered	*Pinaceae*	red pine
Planera aquatica	endangered	*Ulmaceae*	planertree
Populus balsamifera	endangered	*Salicaceae*	balsam poplar
Quercus montana	threatened	*Fagaceae*	rock chestnut oak
Quercus phellos	threatened	*Fagaceae*	willow oak
Quercus texana	endangered	*Fagaceae*	Texas red oak
Salix serissima	endangered	*Salicaceae*	autumn willow
Sambucus racemosa ssp. *pubens*	endangered	*Caprifoliaceae*	red-berried elderberry
Sideroxylon lanuginosum	endangered	*Sapotaceae*	woolly southern-buckthorn
Sorbus americana	endangered	*Rosaceae*	american mountain-ash
Styrax americana	threatened	*Styracaceae*	storax
Styrax grandifolius	endangered	*Styracaceae*	bigleaf snowbell
Tilia americana var. *heterophylla*	endangered	*Tiliaceae*	white basswood
Ulmus thomasii	endangered	*Ulmaceae*	rock elm
Viburnum molle	threatened	*Caprifoliaceae*	arrowwood

(Source: 2006 Endangered and Threatened Species List, Illinois Department of Natural Resources, Office of Resource Conservation, http://dnr.state.il.us/espb/datelist.htm.)

How to Use This Guide

This guide includes all of Illinois's native trees as well as many introduced species that have escaped cultivation and therefore could be mistaken for wild trees. If a tree is introduced, its country or region of origin is noted under the heading "Distribution." Assume that each species is native to Illinois unless otherwise specified.

When identifying a tree, be sure to look carefully for all available clues, both on the tree and on the ground nearby. Large features such as tree size and shape, bark patterns and leaf dimensions may be clearly visible at a glance, but a 10x hand lens can come in handy for examining smaller features such as leaf hairs, flower structures and bud scales.

The main information sources used for compiling the species descriptions in this guide are Gleason and Cronquist (1991), Holmgrem (1998), Mohlenbrock (2002), Elias (1989), Little (1996), Voss (1972, 1985, 1996). Additional sources of information are included in the reference list (pp. 290–291).

Keys

The guide presents several illustrated keys to each genus based on different tree features such as leaves (pp. 36–41), flowers and young cones (pp. 42–46), fruits and mature cones (pp. 47–51) and winter characteristics (twigs and buds, pp. 52–56). These keys are followed by a broader, conventional key (pp. 57–64) that uses combinations of characteristics (e.g., leaves and fruits) to identify all families and some genera. Throughout the rest of the book, large families are prefaced with a key for identifying each genus, as well as keys to the species for large genera. (The terms family, genus and species are discussed in the next section, "Organization.")

If you are a novice botanist, don't feel intimidated by any of the keys. Once you have used keys a few times, they become invaluable aids to identification. You may want to start with the illustrated keys, which are more user-friendly for beginners. All of the keys in this book are **dichotomous**—that is, they provide mutually exclusive, paired descriptions (e.g., 1a and 1b). Each choice leads either to another dichotomy or to the name of the group (family, genus or species)

tree shape

leaf and flower detail

bark colour and texture

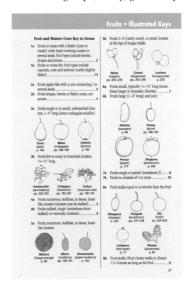

27

Gymnosperms (conifers or softwoods)

Angiosperms (flowering trees or hardwoods)

alternate branching   opposite branching

to which the tree belongs. Whenever possible, keys use everyday language and focus on readily recognizable features. Consult the glossary (pp. 282–289) for explanations of any unfamiliar terms.

Organization

Trees can be divided into two main groups—the gymnosperms in Division Pinophyta and the angiosperms in Division Magnoliophyta.

Gymnosperm trees are also called **conifers** or **softwoods**, because they produce cones rather than flowers and fruits, and because their wood is typically softer than that of the flowering trees. The name gymnosperm ("naked seed") refers to the bare seeds produced at the base of protective scales in cones. All gymnosperms in Illinois have needle-like leaves and most are evergreen. Some people mistakenly use "conifer" and "evergreen" interchangeably, but larches (p. 74) are conifers with deciduous leaves.

All of the **angiosperm** trees in Illinois bear **deciduous** leaves with broad, flat blades—hence the name **broad-leaved trees**. Broad-leaved evergreens grow elsewhere in the world (e.g., arbutus trees in western North America) but are not now part of the Illinois flora. Angiosperm ("enclosed seed") trees are also called **flowering trees** or **hardwoods**. All species in this large, highly variable group produce flowers with ovules (immature seeds) protected by ovaries, which eventually develop into fruits. In a few cases, the flowers are reduced to tiny structures behind protective scales in cone-like clusters, but most flowers have visible petals and/or sepals as well as stamens and/or pistils. Although broad-leaved trees produce the hardest, heaviest wood, the general label 'hardwood' can be misleading, because the wood of many angiosperms (e.g., willows, poplars, basswoods) is softer than that of some softwoods (e.g., some pines).

The families, genera and species in this guide have been organized in a roughly systematic order, in an attempt to place the most similar, closely related species together. Minor deviations from the taxonomic sequence allow the angiosperms to be divided into two convenient groups: species with **alternate branching** (only one leaf or branch at each node) and those with **opposite branching** (two leaves or branches at each node).

Within the three broad groups—needle-leaved, alternate broad-leaved and opposite broad-leaved—trees are further divided into a hierarchy of taxonomic groups, beginning with **families**, such as the rose family (Rosaceae; look in the keys or index for the Latin equivalents of all family names). Families are then divided into **genera** (plural of genus); for example, the rose family is made up of several genera including *Amelanchier* (serviceberries), *Prunus* (cherries, plums) and *Sorbus* (mountain-ashes). Genera, in turn, are divided into **species**; for example, the mountain-ash genus, *Sorbus*, includes species such as *Sorbus aucuparia* (European mountain-ash) and *Sorbus decora* (showy mountain-ash).

Some species can be divided further into forms, varieties and subspecies, but these taxa are not usually described in this guide. Species in some groups of plants (e.g., spruces, poplars, willows, ashes) frequently cross-pollinate to produce **hybrids** with characteristics of both parents. In some cases (e.g., hawthorns), hybridization is so common and the characteristics of offspring are so variable that much of the genus might be best described as a highly variable complex. This guide mentions a few hybrids, but they are not described in separate entries. Similarly, horticultural variants or **cultivars**, developed by plant breeders, are also mentioned in some species accounts but are not described separately.

NEEDLE LEAVES

ALTERNATE BROAD LEAVES

OPPOSITE BROAD LEAVES

FAMILY
e.g., Rose Family (Rosaceae)

GENERA

Sorbus
mountain-ash

Malus
apple

SPECIES

Sorbus decora
showy mountain-ash

Sorbus aucuparia
European mountain-ash

29

Introduction

Species Entries

NAMES

Each species entry provides the scientific name (usually derived from Latin or Greek and always italicized), as well as one or more common names. The preferred or most common name in each category is presented first, but additional common names and scientific **synonyms** (earlier names for the same species) can be found under the heading "Also Called."

Although common names may seem easiest to use at first, they can present problems. Most species have many different common names, some unique to different regions. Because common names originate through local usage, it is also possible for the same name to apply to different trees in different regions.

Scientific names, on the other hand, are much less confusing. All must be published in taxonomic works, which clearly describe the plant being named. If the study of a group results in a taxonomic revision, and the name of a species is changed, this change must be justified and published before the existing name can be replaced by a new one. Theoretically, a species can have only one accepted scientific name, but taxonomists, like most scientists, have been known to disagree, and in some cases different groups of botanists recognize different names. However, because all name changes must be published, it is possible to trace synonyms and reduce confusion.

Though unfamiliar to the ear, scientific names are much more consistent than common names and provide a reference point for finding and exchanging information in Illinois and around the world. The scientific names used in this guide follow treatments of the Integrated Taxonomic Information System (ITIS 2003), Gleason and Cronquist (1991) and the Kartesz and Meacham (1999).

A full scientific name is properly followed by the name, often abbreviated, of the **authority** (person or persons) who specified it. In this book, authorities can be found in the index.

NOTES

The paragraph at the top of each entry provides special points of interest for each species. The content of the notes varies from one species to the next. Ethnobotanical information is usually provided,

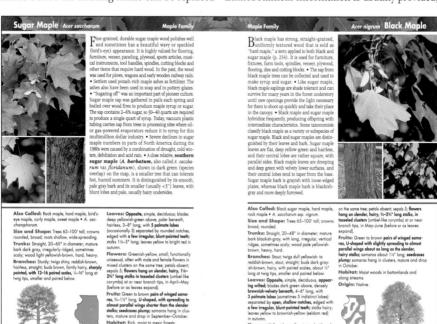

Sugar Maple *Acer saccharum* — Maple Family

Fine-grained, durable sugar maple wood polishes well and sometimes has a beautiful wavy or speckled (bird's-eye) appearance. It is highly valued for flooring, furniture, veneer, paneling, plywood, sports equipment, musical instruments, tool handles, spindles, cutting blocks and other items that require hard wood. In the past, the wood was used for plows, wagons and early wooden railway rails. • Settlers used potash-rich maple ashes as fertilizer. The ashes also have been used in soap and in pottery glazes. • "Sugaring off" was an important part of pioneer culture. Sugar maple sap was gathered in pails each spring and boiled over wood fires to produce maple syrup or sugar. The sap contains 2–6% sugar, so 30–40 quarts are required to produce a single quart of syrup. Today, vacuum plastic tubing carries sap from trees to processing sites where oil- or gas-powered evaporators reduce it to syrup for this multimillion dollar industry. • Severe declines in sugar maple numbers in parts of North America during the 1980s were caused by a combination of drought, cold winters, defoliation and acid rain. • A close relative, **southern sugar maple** (*A. barbatum*, also called *A. saccharum* var. *floridanum*), shown in dark green (species overlap) on the map, is a smaller tree that can tolerate hot, humid summers. It is distinguished by its smooth, pale gray bark and its smaller (usually <3") leaves, with blunt lobes and pale, usually hairy undersides.

Also Called: Rock maple, hard maple, bird's-eye maple, curly maple, sweet maple • *A. saccharophorum.*
Size and Shape: Trees 65–100' tall; crowns rounded, broad; roots shallow, wide-spreading.
Trunks: Straight, 20–60" in diameter; mature bark dark gray, irregularly ridged, sometimes scaly; wood light yellowish-brown, hard, heavy.
Branches: Sturdy; twigs shiny, reddish-brown, hairless, straight; buds brown, faintly hairy, **sharply pointed, with 12–16 paired scales**, ⅛–¾" long at twig tips, smaller and paired below.
Leaves: Opposite, simple, deciduous; blades deep yellowish-green above, paler beneath, hairless, 3–8" long, with **5 palmate lobes** (occasionally 3] separated by rounded notches, edged with **a few irregular, blunt-pointed teeth**; stalks 1½–3" long; leaves yellow to bright red in autumn.
Flowers: Greenish-yellow, small; functionally unisexual, often with male and female flowers in mixed clusters on the same tree; petals absent; sepals 5; flowers hang on slender, hairy, 1½–2¾" long stalks in tasseled clusters (umbel-like corymbs) at or near branch tips, in April–May (before or as leaves expand).
Fruits: Green to brown pairs of winged samaras, ¾–1½" long, with spreading to almost parallel wings other than the slender stalks; seedcases plump; samaras hang in clusters, mature and drop in September–October.
Habitat: Rich, moist to mesic forests.
Origin: Native.

Maple Family — *Acer nigrum* **Black Maple**

Black maple has strong, straight-grained, uniformly textured wood that is sold as "hard maple," a term applied to both black and sugar maple (p. 254). It is used for furniture, fixtures, farm tools, spindles, veneer, plywood, flooring, dies and cutting blocks. • The sap from black maple trees can be collected and used to make syrup and sugar. • Like sugar maple, black maple saplings are shade tolerant and can survive for many years in the forest understory until new openings provide the light necessary for them to shoot up quickly and take their place in the canopy. • Black maple and sugar maple hybridize frequently, producing offspring with intermediate characteristics. Some taxonomists classify black maple as a variety or subspecies of sugar maple. Black and sugar maples are distinguished by their leaves and bark. Sugar maple leaves are flat, deep yellow-green and hairless, and their central lobes are rather square, with parallel sides. Black maple leaves are drooping and deep green with velvety lower surfaces, and their central lobes tend to taper from the base. Sugar maple bark is grayish with loose-edged plates, whereas black maple bark is blackish-gray and more deeply furrowed.

Also Called: Black sugar maple, hard maple, rock maple • *A. saccharum* ssp. *nigrum.*
Size and Shape: Trees 65–100' tall; crowns broad, rounded.
Trunks: Straight, 20–48" in diameter; mature bark blackish-gray, with long, irregular, vertical ridges, sometimes scaly; wood pale yellowish-brown, heavy, hard.
Branches: Stout; twigs dull yellowish- to reddish-brown, stout, straight; buds dark grayish-brown, hairy, with paired scales, about ¼" long at twig tips, smaller and paired below.
Leaves: Opposite, simple, deciduous, appearing wilted; blades dark green above, densely brownish-velvety beneath, 4–6" long, with 3 palmate lobes (sometimes 5 indistinct lobes) separated by open, shallow notches, edged with a few irregular, blunt-pointed teeth; leaves yellow to brownish-yellow (seldom red) in autumn.
Flowers: Yellowish, small; unisexual with male and female flowers mixed or in separate clusters on the same tree; petals absent; sepals 5; **flowers hang on slender, hairy, ¾–2¾" long stalks, in tasseled clusters (umbel-like corymbs) at or near branch tips, in May–June (before or as leaves expand).**
Fruits: Green to brown pairs of winged samaras, U-shaped with slightly spreading to almost parallel wings about as long as the slender, hairy stalks; seedcases plump; samaras hang in clusters, mature and drop in October.
Habitat: Moist woods in bottomlands and along streams.
Origin: Native.

254

255

indicating how a tree has been and is important to people. You may also find points of historical interest and notes about propagating and cultivating certain species. Trees are very important components of natural systems, and ecological factors such as common diseases and pests, and the importance of trees to wildlife, may be noted here. Also look for the derivation (etymology) of common and scientific tree names. Names often have an interesting history that can help you to understand and remember them. Finally, one or more secondary species closely related to the primary species may be described in this section. Taxonomic problems may also be addressed, particularly if the trees are sterile or frequently hybridize, and tips are provided to help distinguish commonly confused species.

ILLUSTRATIONS

Each primary species is illustrated with one or more color photos or drawings showing diagnostic characteristics. Secondary species mentioned in the notes section may also be illustrated with photos, in which case a caption can be found at the end of the notes section. A watercolor silhouette at the bottom of the page shows the primary species' overall shape.

DESCRIPTIONS

The lower section of each account presents a detailed description of the tree and its parts. Diagnostic or key features are highlighted in bold text. Descriptions include size ranges based on information from Illinois or occasionally from elsewhere in the North America. Most trees that you come across in the field should fall within these ranges.

Tree characteristics are described under the following headings:

Size and Shape. In addition to describing the size and shape of the tree as a whole, this section may also include the depth and expanse of the roots.

Trunks. Here you will find information on trunk shape, diameter and orientation, as well as bark characteristics. Because bark can change dramatically with age, young bark and old bark are often presented separately. Bark descriptions usually focus on color, texture and thickness. Although

Gymnocladus dioicus, Kentucky coffee-tree

bark is not always a reliable feature for identifying trees, some groups of trees (e.g., birches, sycamores, beeches) have very distinctive bark, and in some genera (e.g., the ashes), bark characteristics can be useful in distinguishing species.

The wood of different species may be recognizably distinct under a compound microscope, but wood is seldom used for identifying trees in the field. Many people, however, consider wood the most important part of the tree. Wood descriptions usually include color, hardness, weight and strength. In this book, some of these features may be mentioned, along with a discussion in the notes section of how the wood has been used.

Branches. This section begins with a description of the size, orientation and arrangement of the main branches. Spines or thorns are important diagnostic features for some species. Twigs are often very different from the larger branches and can provide helpful clues for identifying a tree. Twig descriptions usually include color, texture, hairiness and occasionally pith characteristics (when viewed in cross- or long-section) or general twig shape (e.g., round or square). Buds can help you

31

Prunus pensylvanica, pin cherry

Juglans nigra, black walnut

identify a tree during the winter, when leaves, fruits and flowers are absent (see the illustrated twig key, pp. 52–56). Important bud characteristics vary with the species, but they may include color, texture, hairiness, size, number of scales, arrangement of buds and their scales and the presence of sticky or fragrant resins.

Leaves. Of all the parts of a tree, the leaves are most widely used for identifying species (see the illustrated leaf key, pp. 36–41). The leaf descriptions in this guide usually begin with the arrangement of leaves on the branch (opposite, whorled, alternate, spiral) and the type of leaf (simple or compound; deciduous or evergreen). In some cases, care must be taken not to confuse compound and simple leaves. The long, firm central axes of some large compound leaves (e.g., Kentucky coffee-tree) could be mistaken for a small branch and the leaflets for simple leaves. Leaflets of a compound leaf are always attached to a herbaceous (non-woody) main stalk that lacks buds. Most branchlets, on the other hand, have developed buds in the leaf axils by midsummer. Definitions and illustrations of leaf shapes and arrangements are presented in the glossary (pp. 282–289).

Leaf characteristics can vary greatly with age and environment, so when choosing a representative sample for identification, look for healthy, mature leaves on normal branches in full sun. Disease, insect infestations, adverse climatic conditions (e.g., drought, late frost), low light levels and rapid growth spurts can all produce abnormal leaves. Some trees are more changeable than others. The hawthorns are extremely variable, but aberrations are greatest on vegetative shoots, so choose leaves from flowering or fruiting shoots.

The most obvious part of a leaf is the blade. Important blade characteristics include size, color (above and beneath), texture (thin, leathery, fleshy), shape (linear, oblong, round, widest above or below the middle) and edges (smooth, toothed, lobed). Leaf stalks are described separately,

Amelanchier laevis, smooth serviceberry

because they are often quite different from the blades in color and hairiness. Some leaf stalks have distinctive characteristics such as unusual shapes (e.g., distinctly flattened), lengths (e.g., as long as the blade) or glands (usually near the junction with the blade); others have stipules at the stalk base. Leaf scars can also be useful diagnostic features, especially when identifying trees in winter (see twig key, pp. 52–56). Important leaf scar characteristics include shape, size and arrangement on the branch, and the number and arrangement of vein scars within the leaf scars.

The leaf section may also contain a few notes about seasonality (e.g., leaf color in fall).

Reproductive structures. Cones, flowers and fruits are usually much less variable than vegetative parts such as leaves and branches, and consequently reproductive parts are more reliable features for identifying trees. Unfortunately, not all

Viburnum lantana, wayfaring-tree

trees have reproductive structures at any given time. Many species don't begin to produce seed until they are 30 years old, and even then, they may not flower every year. Diseases, insect infestations, droughts and other environmental stresses can all prevent trees from flowering. In most cases, only healthy, mature trees have the reserves necessary to produce abundant seed crops.

Cones are the reproductive structures of the first trees in the guide—the gymnosperms (see the illustrated keys on pp. 42–51). Although male cones and female cones usually appear on the same tree, they are very different in appearance and position, so they are described separately. Male (pollen) cones are small and soft, whereas

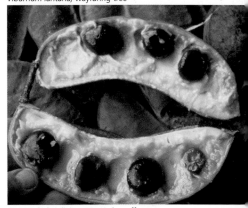

Gymnocladus dioicus, Kentucky coffee-tree

female cones are relatively large and woody when mature. Important characteristics include color, texture, shape, size and arrangement on the branches. The scales of female cones are sometimes also described. The cone section ends with a short description of seasonality (the timing of cone growth and changes at maturity).

Most Illinois tree species produce flowers and fruits. Flowers can be very distinctive and can provide essential clues to a tree's identity (see the illustrated flower key, pp. 42–46). Unfortunately, most flowers appear for short periods only and then fade or develop into fruit. Occasionally, the structure of a faded flower can be reconstructed through careful observation of parts that persist on the fruits. The flower section of the tree description indicates color, texture, shape, size, fragrance and sexuality (e.g., bisexual or unisexual). Many flowering trees in Illinois have unisexual flowers, so male flowers and female flowers and their clusters are often described separately. Diagnostic flower parts such as petals, sepals, stamens and stigmas are sometimes described in detail, but in many cases these components are too small or are not sufficiently distinctive to warrant description. The flower section also describes the arrangement of flowers and types of **inflorescences**, or flower clusters (e. g., racemes, panicles, corymbs, umbels; see glossary, pp. 282–289), and the timing of their development (seasonality).

Fruits are usually more useful than flowers in tree identification, because they tend to last longer. Many fruits can be found throughout the year, either on branches or on the ground nearby, providing valuable clues to the identity of the tree (see the illustrated fruit key, pp. 47–51). The fruit section describes the color, texture, shape, size and type of fruit (e.g., drupes, capsules, nuts, samaras; see glossary, pp. 282–289). The number, size and shape of the seeds are usually described separately. The fruit section also describes the arrangement of the fruits (hanging vs. erect; cluster shape and size) along with the characteristics of mature fruit (e.g., color changes, dehiscence).

Habitat. This section describes the types of sites where a tree species is usually found. Habitat information, combined with the distribution (see next section), gives a general idea where to look for the tree. Almost all trees grow best on rich, deep, well-drained soils with adequate moisture, but some also do well on open, disturbed sites and others require the shade and humidity of an established forest. Trees that move in to colonize recently disturbed areas are often called **pioneer species**, and those that require the protection of a forest canopy are sometimes called **climax species**. In the absence of repeated disturbances, sun-loving pioneer species are gradually replaced by shade-tolerant climax species, which eventually create relatively stable, self-perpetuating ecosystems. Usually, however, the equilibrium is upset by disturbances such as fire, windfall or insect attacks, and then the canopy opens and the cycle begins again.

Distribution

The distributions of native tree species are presented graphically in maps. These range maps are based on information from published sources, mainly Mohlenbrock and Ladd (1978). The range of the primary species discussed on each page is shown in bright green, and if an additional native species is mentioned in the notes section, its range may be shown on the same map in pink (where sufficient information is available). Areas where the two species overlap are indicated in dark green. A third species may appear on the map in dark pink. The countries or regions that make up the native ranges of introduced species' are also noted under the heading "Distribution."

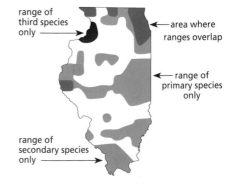

range of third species only →

← area where ranges overlap

← range of primary species only

range of secondary species only →

Illustrated Keys

IT'S EASY TO IDENTIFY TREES using the 4 illustrated keys based on leaf, flower, fruit and twig features. Simply work your way through a key, choosing between paired alternatives. Try the leaf key with a red maple, for example. The leaves have broad blades, so at lead **1** choose **1b**. This takes you to **4**. Your leaf is simple, so choose **4b** and go to **10**. Toothed edges take you to **10a, 11a, 12b, 15b** and finally **17b**. This brings you to the end of your search—a group of illustrations. Choose the best fit, and go to the page or pages indicated for more information.

Leaf Key to Genus

1a   Leaves narrow, either needle-like or scale-like **2**
1b   Leaves broad, with definite blades **4**

2a   Leaves needle-like **3**
2b   Leaves scale-like

Juniperus   **Thuja**   **Tamarix**
(red-cedar)   (white-cedar)   (tamarisk)
p. 77   p. 78   p. 80

3a   Needles in pairs, whorls, tufts or bundles

Juniperus   **Larix**   **Pinus**
(red-cedar)   (larch)   (pine)
p. 77   p. 74   pp. 68–73

3b   Needles single, alternate

Taxodium   **Picea**
(bald-cypress)   (spruce)
p. 79   pp. 75–76

4a   Leaves divided into leaflets (compound)....**5**
4b   Leaves simple...**10**

5a   Leaves pinnately compound **6**
5b   Leaves palmately compound or trifoliate

Ptelea   **Staphylea**   **Aesculus**
(hop-tree)   (bladdernut)   (buckeye)
p. 231   p. 249   pp. 250–252

6a   Leaves 2–3 times divided into leaflets **7**
6b   Leaves once divided **8**

7a   Tip leaflets present at branch tips

Aralia   **Aralia**   **Koelreuteria**
(angelica-tree)   (Hercules-club)   (goldenrain-tree)
p. 218   p. 218   p. 230

7b   Tip leaflets absent at branch tips

Gleditsia   **Gymnocladus**   **Albizia**
(honey-locust)   (coffee-tree)   (mimosa-tree)
pp. 215–216   p. 217   p. 229

8a   Leaves alternate..**9**
8b   Leaves paired (opposite)

Fraxinus   **Acer**   **Phellodendron**   **Sambucus**
(ash)   (maple)   (corktree)   (elder)
pp. 262–266   pp. 254–260   p. 280   p. 279

9a Leaf edges smooth, without teeth or with 1–2 basal lobes

| *Toxicodendron* (poison-sumac) p. 222 | *Robinia* (locust) p. 213 | *Ailanthus* (tree-of-heaven) p. 228 |

| *Cladrastis* (yellow-wood) p. 212 | *Rhus* (sumac) pp. 220–221 | *Gleditsia* (water-locust) pp. 215–216 |

9b Leaf edges toothed or many-lobed

| *Sorbus* (mountain-ash) pp. 190–191 | *Juglans* (walnut) pp. 105–106 | *Rhus* (sumac) pp. 220–221 | *Carya* (hickory) pp. 107–112 |

10a Leaf edges toothed or lobed **11**
10b Leaf edges smooth, without teeth or lobes ... **29**

11a Leaves lobed, with or without teeth........... **12**
11b Leaf edges toothed but not lobed **18**

12a Leaves pinnately lobed **13**
12b Leaves palmately lobed **15**

13a Lobes pointed, edged with sharp teeth **14**
13b Lobes blunt, smooth or edged with rounded teeth

| *Hibiscus* (rose-of-Sharon) p. 208 | ⌐ *Quercus* ¬ (oak) pp. 118–134 | *Populus* (poplar) pp. 149–154 |

14a Lobes cut more than halfway to the midvein

| *Crataegus* (hawthorn) pp. 192–201 | ⌐ *Quercus* ¬ (oak) pp. 118–134 |

14b Lobes cut less than halfway to the midvein

| *Crataegus* (hawthorn) pp. 192–201 | *Corylus* (hazelnut) p. 139 | *Alnus* (alder) pp. 143–144 |

  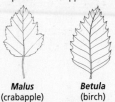

| *Acer* (maple) pp. 254–260 | *Malus* (crabapple) pp. 186–189 | *Betula* (birch) pp. 140–142 |

15a Lobes smooth- or wavy-edged, without teeth **16**
15b Lobes toothed... **17**

16a Lobe tips pointed

| *Sassafras* (sassafras) p. 85 | *Liriodendron* (tulip-tree) p. 82 | *Quercus* (oak) pp. 118–134 |

| *Acer* (maple) pp. 254–260 | *Viburnum* (viburnum) pp. 274–277 | *Malus* (crabapple) pp. 186–189 |

16b Lobe tips blunt

Populus
(poplar)
pp. 149–154

Acer
(maple)
pp. 254–260

17a Lobes deeply incised, usually cut more than halfway to the midvein

Morus
(mulberry)
pp. 100–101

Acer
(maple)
pp. 254–260

Broussonetia
(paper-mulberry)
p. 102

Liquidambar
(sweetgum)
p. 89

17b Lobes shallow, cut less than halfway to the midvein

Platanus
(sycamore)
p. 87

Acer
(maple)
pp. 254–260

Viburnum
(viburnum)
pp. 274–277

Crataegus
(hawthorn)
pp. 192–201

Hibiscus
(rose-of-Sharon)
p. 208

18a Leaves alternate **19**
18b Leaves opposite or whorled

Euonymus
(euonymus)
pp. 247–248

Viburnum
(viburnum)
pp. 274–277

Rhamnus
(buckthorn)
pp. 239–240

Forestiera
(swamp-privet)
p. 268

Broussonetia
(paper-mulberry)
p. 102

19a Leaf bases symmetrical **20**
19b Leaf bases clearly asymmetrical

Celtis
(hackberry)
pp. 97–98

Hamamelis
(witch-hazel)
p. 88

Tilia
(basswood)
pp. 233–234

Ulmus
(elm)
pp. 91–95

Planera
(planertree)
p. 96

20a Leaf blades broad, mostly less than twice as long as wide **21**
20b Leaf blades narrower, mostly at least twice as long as wide **26**

21a Leaf blades approximately as long as wide, broadly rounded to squared or notched at the base **22**

21b Leaf blades ovate to broadly elliptical, longer than wide, rounded to wedge-shaped at the base..**25**

22a Leaf blades rounded to heart-shaped........**23**
22b Leaf blades roughly triangular with squared bases

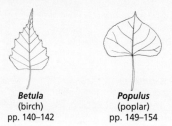

Betula	Populus
(birch)	(poplar)
pp. 140–142	pp. 149–154

23a Teeth coarse and/or double......................**24**
23b Teeth fine, single

Populus	Pyrus
(poplar)	(pear)
pp. 149–154	p. 184

Prunus	Broussonetia
(cherry, etc.)	(paper-mulberry)
pp. 174–183	p. 102

24a Teeth single

Populus	Morus	Tilia	Celtis
(poplar)	(mulberry)	(basswood)	(hackberry)
pp. 149–154	pp. 100–101	pp. 233–234	pp. 97–98

24b Teeth double

Crataegus	Corylus	Betula
(hawthorn)	(hazelnut)	(birch)
pp. 192–201	p. 139	pp. 140–142

25a Leaves finely and regularly toothed

Amelanchier	Malus	Pyrus
(serviceberry)	(crabapple)	(pear)
pp. 202–203	pp. 186–189	p. 184

Prunus	Halesia	Populus	Salix
(cherry, etc.)	(silverbell)	(poplar)	(willow)
pp. 174–183	p. 210	pp. 149–154	pp. 155–166

25b Leaves sharply and irregularly toothed

Alnus	Betula	Crataegus	Malus
(alder)	(birch)	(hawthorn)	(crabapple)
pp. 143–144	pp. 140–142	pp. 192–201	pp. 186–189

26a Leaf edges more finely toothed.................**27**
26b Leaf edges coarsely toothed, usually 1 tooth per vein

Castanea	Fagus	Quercus
(chestnut)	(beech)	(oak)
p. 117	p. 116	pp. 118–134

(continued on next page)

26b (continued)

Ilex	*Nemopanthus*	*Nyssa*
(holly)	(mountain-holly)	(tupelo)
pp. 224–226	p. 227	pp. 235–236

27a Leaf edges with finer or more rounded, relatively regular teeth **28**

27b Leaf edges sharply, often irregularly saw-toothed

Ulmus	*Betula*	*Carpinus*
(elm)	(birch)	(blue-beech)
pp. 91–95	pp. 140–142	p. 138

Ostrya	*Oxydendrum*	*Vaccinium*
(hop-hornbeam)	(sourwood)	(farkleberry)
p. 137	p. 206	p. 207

28a Blades widest above the middle

Prunus	*Ilex*
(cherry, etc.)	(holly)
pp. 174–183	pp. 224–226

28b Blades widest at or below the middle

Prunus	*Salix*	*Halesia*	*Populus*
(cherry, etc.)	⌐ (willow) ⌐	(silverbell)	(poplar)
pp. 174–183	pp. 155–166	p. 210	pp. 149–154

29a Leaf blades broad, clearly less than twice as long as wide **30**

29b Leaf blades narrower, usually at least twice as long as wide **32**

30a Leaves alternate **31**

30b Leaves opposite

Catalpa	*Cornus*	*Syringa*
(catalpa)	(dogwood)	(lilac)
p. 271	pp. 242–246	p. 267

Cephalanthus	*Paulownia*
(buttonbush)	(princesstree)
p. 272	p. 270

31a Leaf tips blunt

Cydonia	*Cotinus*
(quince)	(smoketree)
p. 185	p. 223

31b Leaf tips pointed

Cercis	*Celtis*	*Sassafras*
(redbud)	(hackberry)	(sassafras)
p. 214	p. 97–98	p. 85

Styrax	*Cornus*	*Nyssa*
(snowbell)	(dogwood)	(tupelo)
p. 211	pp. 242–246	pp. 235–236

32a Leaves elliptical to ovate **33**
32b Leaves narrowly oblong to linear

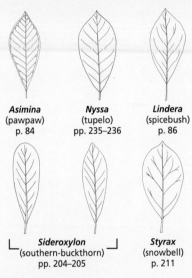

Salix
(willow)
pp. 155–166

Elaeagnus
(oleaster)
p. 232

Quercus
(oak)
pp. 118–134

33a Leaf blades widest at or below the middle.. **34**
33b Leaf blades usually widest above the middle

Asimina
(pawpaw)
p. 84

Nyssa
(tupelo)
pp. 235–236

Lindera
(spicebush)
p. 86

Sideroxylon
(southern-buckthorn)
pp. 204–205

Styrax
(snowbell)
p. 211

34a Leaf tips pointed **35**
34b Leaf tips blunt

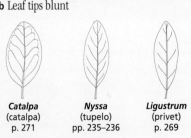

Catalpa
(catalpa)
p. 271

Nyssa
(tupelo)
pp. 235–236

Ligustrum
(privet)
p. 269

35a Leaves mostly 1¹/₂–3" long

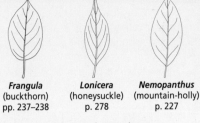

Frangula
(buckthorn)
pp. 237–238

Lonicera
(honeysuckle)
p. 278

Nemopanthus
(mountain-holly)
p. 227

35b Leaves mostly 3–7" long or longer

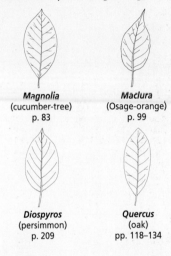

Magnolia
(cucumber-tree)
p. 83

Maclura
(Osage-orange)
p. 99

Diospyros
(persimmon)
p. 209

Quercus
(oak)
pp. 118–134

Flower and Young Cone Key to Genus

1a Reproductive parts tiny, concealed in cones; male cones soft and relatively small; female cones usually with larger, firmer scales.......**2**
1b Reproductive parts in true flowers...............**3**

2a Female flowering cones small, <³/₈" long

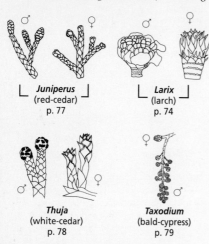

Juniperus		Larix
(red-cedar)		(larch)
p. 77		p. 74

Thuja	Taxodium
(white-cedar)	(bald-cypress)
p. 78	p. 79

2b Female cones larger, >³/₈" long

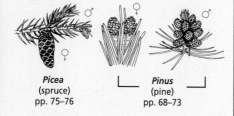

Picea	Pinus
(spruce)	(pine)
pp. 75–76	pp. 68–73

3a Flowers short-stalked or stalkless, tiny, inconspicuous, usually greenish, in dense clusters.......................................**4**
3b Flowers clearly stalked, usually larger (>¹/₄" across) and showier **9**

4a Flowers unisexual; male and female flowers in separate clusters......................................**5**

4b Flowers bisexual, with both male and female parts

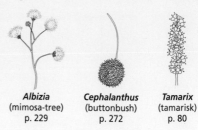

Albizia	Cephalanthus	Tamarix
(mimosa-tree)	(buttonbush)	(tamarisk)
p. 229	p. 272	p. 80

5a Flowers (at least male flowers) in spherical clusters...**6**
5b Flowers (at least male flowers) in elongated clusters (catkins)...**7**

6a Flower clusters short-stalked or stalkless

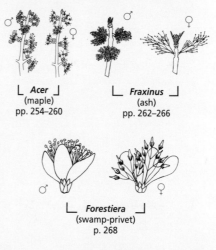

Acer	Fraxinus
(maple)	(ash)
pp. 254–260	pp. 262–266

| Forestiera |
| (swamp-privet) |
| p. 268 |

6b Flower clusters clearly stalked, often hanging

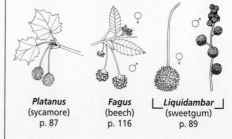

Platanus	Fagus	Liquidambar
(sycamore)	(beech)	(sweetgum)
p. 87	p. 116	p. 89

6b (continued)

Maclura
(Osage-orange)
p. 99

Nyssa
(tupelo)
pp. 235–236

7a Male and female flowers on the same tree ...**8**
7b Male and female flowers on separate trees

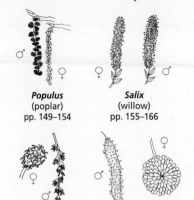

Populus
(poplar)
pp. 149–154

Salix
(willow)
pp. 155–166

Morus
(mulberry)
pp. 100–101

⌐ **Broussonetia** ⌐
(paper-mulberry)
p. 102

8a Female flowers few, in small, inconspicuous clusters of 1–7

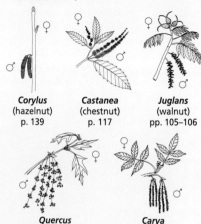

Corylus
(hazelnut)
p. 139

Castanea
(chestnut)
p. 117

Juglans
(walnut)
pp. 105–106

Quercus
(oak)
pp. 118–134

Carya
(hickory)
pp. 107–112

8b Female flowers numerous, usually 15 or more per cluster

Alnus
(alder)
pp. 143–144

Betula
(birch)
pp. 140–142

Carpinus
(blue-beech)
p. 138

Morus
(mulberry)
pp. 100–101

Ostrya
(hop-hornbeam)
p. 137

9a Flowers small, <³/₄" across, inconspicuous or in showy clusters **10**
9b Flowers large and showy, usually >1" across **21**

10a Flowers small, inconspicuous, greenish or yellowish, single or in small, usually tassel-like clusters; petals tiny or absent **11**
10b Flowers relatively showy, with noticeable petals or petal-like sepals **13**

11a Flower stalks unbranched **12**
11b Flowers in branched, often elongated clusters

Acer
(maple)
pp. 254–260

Ulmus
(elm)
pp. 91–95

Ilex
(holly)
pp. 224–226

12a Flowers single

Celtis
(hackberry)
pp. 97–98

Nemopanthus
(mountain-holly)
p. 227

43

12b Flowers in tassel-like clusters

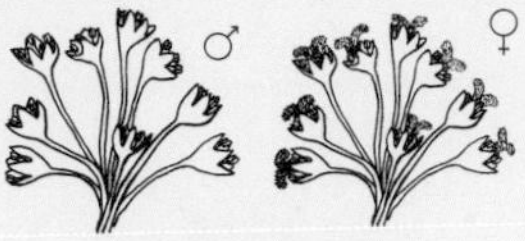

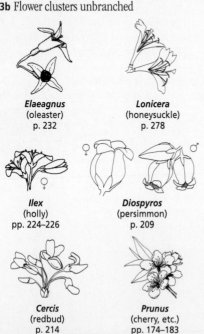

Ulmus
(elm)
pp. 91–95

Frangula
(buckthorn)
pp. 237–238

Rhamnus
(buckthorn)
pp. 239–240

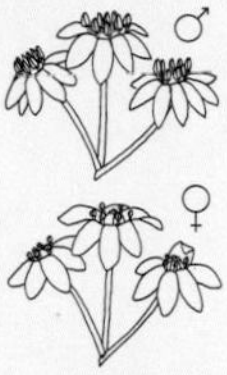

Ilex
(holly)
pp. 224–226

Lindera
(spicebush)
p. 86

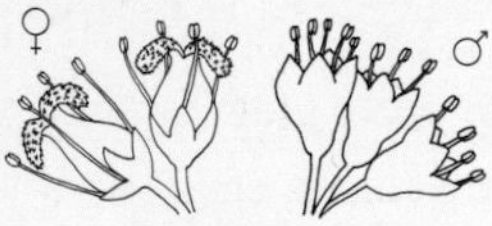

Planera
(planertree)
p. 96

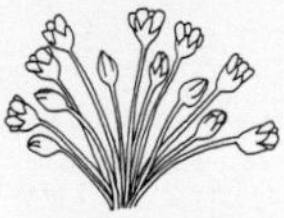

Sideroxylon
(southern-buckthorn)
pp. 204–205

13a Flower clusters branched **14**
13b Flower clusters unbranched

Elaeagnus
(oleaster)
p. 232

Lonicera
(honeysuckle)
p. 278

Ilex
(holly)
pp. 224–226

Diospyros
(persimmon)
p. 209

Cercis
(redbud)
p. 214

Prunus
(cherry, etc.)
pp. 174–183

14a Flower clusters flat-topped or rounded
(corymbs, cymes, umbels) **15**
14b Flower clusters more elongated, clearly
longer than wide (panicles, racemes) **17**

15a Flowers bisexual **16**
15b Flowers unisexual, greenish, about $1/4$–$1/2$"
across, in rounded clusters

Ptelea
(hop-tree)
p. 231

Sassafras
(sassafras)
p. 85

Acer
(maple)
pp. 254–260

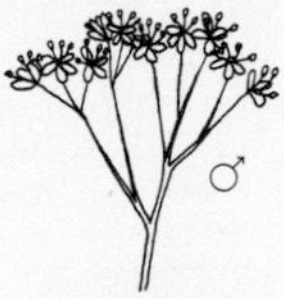

Ilex
(holly)
pp. 224–226

Phellodendron
(corktree)
p. 280

16a Flowers small (mostly <$3/8$"), white, in
showy, many-branched clusters 2–6" across

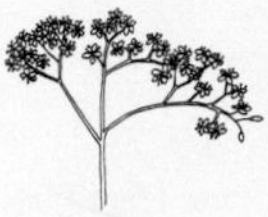

Cornus
(dogwood)
pp. 242–246

Sorbus
(mountain-ash)
pp. 190–191

Viburnum
(viburnum)
pp. 274–277

Acer
(maple)
pp. 254–260

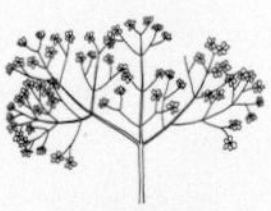

Sambucus
(elder)
p. 279

Aralia
(Hercules-club)
p. 218

16b Flowers at least ³/₈" across, usually in tassel-like or few-branched clusters

| *Tilia* (basswood) pp. 233–234 | *Euonymus* (euonymus) pp. 247–248 | *Prunus* (cherry, etc.) pp. 174–183 |

| *Crataegus* (hawthorn) pp. 192–201 | *Viburnum* (viburnum) pp. 274–277 |

17a Flower clusters roughly cylindrical, with an unbranched main axis (central stalk) **18**
17b Flower clusters widest near the base, with some side-branches again divided............ **19**

18a Flowers star-like, with 5 similar and clearly separate petals

| *Acer* (maple) pp. 254–260 | *Prunus* (cherry, etc.) pp. 174–183 | *Gleditsia* (honey-locust) pp. 215–216 |

| *Gymnocladus* (coffee-tree) p. 217 | *Amelanchier* (serviceberry) pp. 202–203 |

18b Flowers pea-like or bell-shaped, with petals dissimilar or not clearly separate

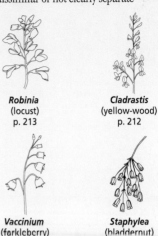

| *Robinia* (locust) p. 213 | *Cladrastis* (yellow-wood) p. 212 |

| *Vaccinium* (farkleberry) p. 207 | *Staphylea* (bladdernut) p. 249 |

19a Flowers white, pink or purple.................... **20**
19b Flowers yellow to greenish-yellow

| *Rhus* (sumac) pp. 220–221 | *Ailanthus* (tree-of-heaven) p. 228 |

| *Toxicodendron* (poison-sumac) p. 222 | *Koelreuteria* (goldenrain-tree) p. 230 |

20a Flowers 4-petaled, funnel-shaped and fragrant

| *Syringa* (lilac) p. 267 | *Ligustrum* (privet) p. 269 |

45

20b Flowers 5-petaled, star- or urn-shaped

Gymnocladus
(coffee-tree)
p. 217

Sambucus
(elder)
p. 279

Aralia
(Hercules-club)
p. 218

Cotinus
(smoketree)
p. 223

Oxydendrum
(sourwood)
p. 206

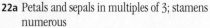

21a Flowers (or flower-like clusters) single or in clusters of 2–3 .... **22**
21b Flowers in clusters of 4 or more **23**

22a Petals and sepals in multiples of 3; stamens numerous

Asimina
(pawpaw)
p. 84

Magnolia
(cucumber-tree)
p. 83

Liriodendron
(tulip-tree)
p. 82

22b Petals, petal-like bracts and sepals in multiples of 4 or 5; stamens various **23**
23a Petals and sepals 5; stamens numerous

Hibiscus
(rose-of-Sharon)
p. 208

Cydonia
(quince)
p. 185

23b Petals, petal-like bracts and sepals 4; stamens 4–16

Cornus
(dogwood)
pp. 242–246

Halesia
(silverbell)
p. 210

Hamamelis
(witch-hazel)
p. 88

23a Flowers bell-, trumpet- or pea-shaped, variously colored **24**
23b Flowers cupped to star-shaped, with 5 showy, white or pinkish petals

Amelanchier
(serviceberry)
pp. 202–203

Malus
(crabapple)
pp. 186–189

Pyrus
(pear)
p. 184

Prunus
(cherry, etc.)
pp. 174–183

Crataegus
(hawthorn)
pp. 192–201

24a Flowers radially symmetrical (circular), bell-shaped, with 4 or 5 equal petals

Styrax
(snowbell)
p. 211

Halesia
(silverbell)
p. 210

24b Flowers bilaterally symmetrical (2-sided), with a distinct lower lip

Aesculus
(buckeye)
pp. 250–252

Catalpa
(catalpa)
p. 271

Robinia
(locust)
p. 213

Paulownia
(princesstree)
p. 270

Fruit and Mature Cone Key to Genus

1a Fruits or cones with a fleshy (juicy to mealy) outer layer covering a stone or several seeds; fruit types include berries, drupes and pomes......................... **2**

1b Fruits or cones dry; fruit types include capsules, nuts and achenes (rarely slightly fleshy) **13**

2a Fruits apple-like with a core containing 1 to several seeds................................ **3**

2b Fruits drupes, berries or fleshy cones; not pomes... **4**

3a Fruits single or in small, unbranched clusters, 1–4" long (some crabapples smaller)

Pyrus (pear) p. 184 | **Malus** (crabapple) pp. 186–189 | **Cydonia** (quince) p. 185

3b Fruits few to many in branched clusters, 1/4–1/2" long

Amelanchier (serviceberry) pp. 202–203 | **Crataegus** (hawthorn) pp. 192–201 | **Sorbus** (mountain-ash) pp. 190–191

4a Fruits numerous, stalkless, in dense, head-like clusters (clusters may be stalked) **5**

4b Fruits stalked, single (sometimes short-stalked) or variously clustered.................... **6**

5a Fruits numerous, stalkless, in dense, head-like clusters

Maclura (Osage-orange) p. 99 | **Morus** (mulberry) pp. 100–101 | **Broussonetia** (paper-mulberry) p. 102

5b Fruits 2–6 (rarely more), in small clusters at the tips of longer stalks

Nyssa (tupelo) pp. 235–236 | **Cornus** (dogwood) pp. 242–246 | **Lonicera** (honeysuckle) p. 278

6a Fruits small, typically 1/4–5/8" long (sometimes larger in domestic cherries) **7**

6b Fruits large (1–4" long) and juicy

Asimina (pawpaw) p. 84 | **Prunus** (plum) pp. 180–183

Prunus (peach) p. 177 | **Diospyros** (persimmon) p. 209

7a Fruits single or paired (sometimes 3) **8**

7b Fruits in clusters of 4 or more **10**

8a Fruit stalks equal to or shorter than the fruit

Elaeagnus (oleaster) p. 232 | **Frangula** (buckthorn) pp. 237–238 | **Ilex** (holly) pp. 224–226

Juniperus (red-cedar) p. 77 | **Planera** (planertree) p. 96

8b Fruit stalks (fruit cluster stalks in *Nyssa*) 1.2–4 times as long as the fruit.................. **9**

9a Fruits containing a single stone

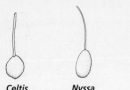

Celtis
(hackberry)
pp. 97–98

Nyssa
(tupelo)
pp. 235–236

Elaeagnus
(oleaster)
p. 232

9b Fruits containing 2–5 stones

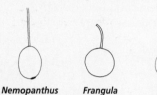

Nemopanthus
(mountain-holly)
p. 227

Frangula
(buckthorn)
pp. 237–238

Ilex
(holly)
pp. 224–226

10a Fruit clusters elongated, longer than
wide... **11**

10b Fruit clusters rounded or flat-topped,
usually as wide as long.............................. **12**

11a Fruit clusters with a main central stalk and
few or no side-branches

Prunus
(cherry, etc.)
pp. 174–183

Vaccinium
(farkleberry)
p. 207

11b Fruit clusters with branched side-branches

Rhus
(sumac)
pp. 220–221

Toxicodendron
(poison-sumac)
p. 222

Sassafras
(sassafras)
p. 85

11b (continued)

Ligustrum
(privet)
p. 269

Sambucus
(elder)
p. 279

12a Fruit stalks nearly equal, unbranched, in
small, usually tassel-like clusters

Frangula
(buckthorn)
pp. 237–238

Rhamnus
(buckthorn)
pp. 239–240

Prunus
(cherry)
pp. 174–183

Sideroxylon
(southern-buckthorn)
pp. 204–205

Lindera
(spicebush)
p. 86

Forestiera
(swamp-privet)
p. 268

12b Fruit stalks varied, branched, in relatively
large, spreading clusters

Cornus
(dogwood)
pp. 242–246

Viburnum
(viburnum)
pp. 274–277

Aralia
(Hercules-club)
p. 218

12b (continued)

Phellodendron	*Sambucus*
(corktree)	(elder)
p. 280	p. 279

13a Fruits in dense cones or cone-like clusters of firm, overlapping scales or scale-like fruits..**14**

13b Fruits not in cone-like clusters.................**16**

14a Cones or cone-like fruits composed of overlapping scales that cover seeds or seed-like fruits..**15**

14b Cones composed of overlapping fruits (samaras or follicles)

Liriodendron	*Magnolia*
(tulip-tree)	(cucumber-tree)
p. 82	p. 83

15a Cone scales thick and firm, woody, leathery or somewhat fleshy

└─ *Pinus* ─┘	*Alnus*
(pine)	(alder)
pp. 68–73	pp. 143–144

Taxodium	*Juniperus*
(bald-cypress)	(red-cedar)
p. 79	p. 77

15b Cone scales relatively thin and pliable

Thuja	*Larix*	*Picea*
(white-cedar)	(larch)	(spruce)
p. 78	p. 74	pp. 75–76

16a Fruits stalkless or short-stalked, in dense, head-like or cylindrical clusters (clusters may be stalked)......................................**17**

16b Fruits stalked, single or loosely clustered.**18**

17a Fruit clusters round

Platanus	*Liquidambar*	*Cephalanthus*
(sycamore)	(sweetgum)	(buttonbush)
p. 87	p. 89	p. 272

17b Fruit clusters roughly cylindrical, clearly longer than wide

Carpinus	*Ostrya*	*Betula*
(blue-beech)	(hop-hornbeam)	(birch)
p. 138	p. 137	pp. 140–142

Populus	*Salix*	*Tamarix*
(poplar)	(willow)	(tamarisk)
pp. 149–154	pp. 155–166	p. 80

18a Fruits without wings **19**
18b Fruits winged nutlets (samaras)

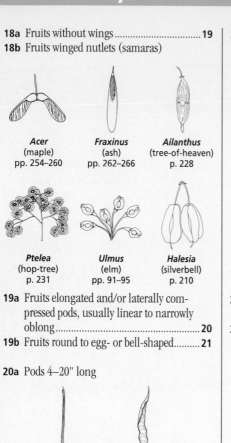

| Acer (maple) pp. 254–260 | Fraxinus (ash) pp. 262–266 | Ailanthus (tree-of-heaven) p. 228 |

| Ptelea (hop-tree) p. 231 | Ulmus (elm) pp. 91–95 | Halesia (silverbell) p. 210 |

19a Fruits elongated and/or laterally compressed pods, usually linear to narrowly oblong **20**
19b Fruits round to egg- or bell-shaped **21**

20a Pods 4–20" long

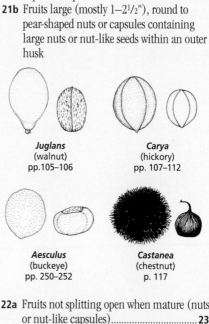

| Catalpa (catalpa) p. 271 | Gleditsia (honey-locust) pp. 215–216 |

| Albizia (mimosa-tree) p. 229 | Gymnocladus (coffee-tree) p. 217 |

20b Pods 1–4" long

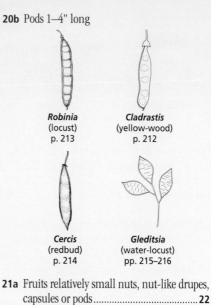

| Robinia (locust) p. 213 | Cladrastis (yellow-wood) p. 212 |

| Cercis (redbud) p. 214 | Gleditsia (water-locust) pp. 215–216 |

21a Fruits relatively small nuts, nut-like drupes, capsules or pods **22**
21b Fruits large (mostly 1–2$\frac{1}{2}$"), round to pear-shaped nuts or capsules containing large nuts or nut-like seeds within an outer husk

| Juglans (walnut) pp.105–106 | Carya (hickory) pp. 107–112 |

| Aesculus (buckeye) pp. 250–252 | Castanea (chestnut) p. 117 |

22a Fruits not splitting open when mature (nuts or nut-like capsules) **23**
22b Fruits splitting open when mature to release nutlets or seeds **24**

50

23a Fruits single or in compact, short-stalked clusters of 2–5

| *Planera* (planertree) p. 96 | *Corylus* (hazelnut) p. 139 | *Quercus* (oak) pp. 118–134 |

23b Fruits few to many in elongated, often branched clusters

| *Tilia* (basswood) pp. 233–234 | *Cotinus* (smoketree) p. 223 | *Styrax* (snowbell) p. 211 |

24a Mature capsules woody, tipped with a single point (before opening) **25**

24b Mature capsules membranous, 3–4-lobed, inflated and hollow, or with seeds embedded in a fleshy aril

| *Euonymus* (euonymus) pp. 247–248 | *Staphylea* (bladdernut) p. 249 |

Koelreuteria (goldenrain-tree) p. 230

25a Fruits single or paired

| *Hamamelis* (witch-hazel) p. 88 | *Fagus* (beech) p. 116 | *Hibiscus* (rose-of-Sharon) p. 208 |

25b Fruits numerous, in branched clusters panicles)

| *Oxydendrum* (sourwood) p. 206 | *Paulownia* (princesstree) p. 270 |

Syringa (lilac) p. 267

Winter Key to Genus
(excluding characteristics of persistent fruits)

1a Leaves evergreen needles **2**
1b Leaves deciduous, absent in winter **3**

2a Leaves small, flat-lying scales

Juniperus
(red-cedar)
p. 77

Thuja
(white-cedar)
p. 78

2b Leaves needle-like

Juniperus   **Picea**   **Pinus**
(red-cedar)   (spruce)   (pine)
p. 77   pp. 75–76   pp. 68–73

3a Branches and bud scars opposite **4**
3b Branches and bud scars alternate **7**

4a Buds covered by 3 or more scales **5**
4b Buds covered by 1 or 2 scales, naked (with
exposed, immature leaves), or embedded in
bark and too tiny to see

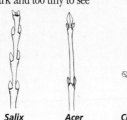

Salix   **Acer**   **Cornus**
(willow)   (maple)   (dogwood)
pp. 155–166   pp. 254–260   pp. 242–246

Phellodendron   **Viburnum**   **Cephalanthus**
(corktree)   (viburnum)   (buttonbush)
p. 280   pp. 274–277   p. 272

5a Leaf scars small, with 1–3 dots (vein scars),
or absent **6**
5b Leaf scars large, often horseshoe-shaped,
usually with several dots (vein scars)

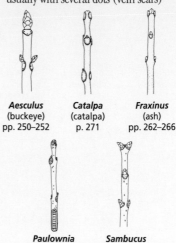

Aesculus   **Catalpa**   **Fraxinus**
(buckeye)   (catalpa)   (ash)
pp. 250–252   p. 271   pp. 262–266

Paulownia   **Sambucus**
(princesstree)   (elder)
p. 270   p. 279

6a Leaf scars with 3 dots (vein scars)

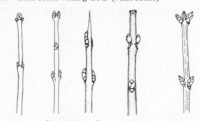

Acer   ⌐ **Rhamnus** ⌐   **Staphylea**   **Lonicera**
(maple)   (buckthorn)   (bladdernut)   (honeysuckle)
pp. 254–260   pp. 239–240   p. 249   p. 278

6b Leaf scars with a single dot (vein scar)

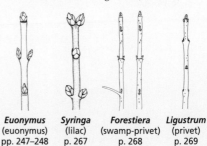

Euonymus   **Syringa**   **Forestiera**   **Ligustrum**
(euonymus)   (lilac)   (swamp-privet)   (privet)
pp. 247–248   p. 267   p. 268   p. 269

7a Branches armed with thorns or spine-tipped twigs **8**

7b Branches lacking spines or thorns **9**

8a Branches armed with true thorns

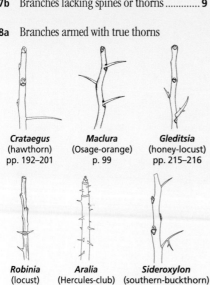

Crataegus	*Maclura*	*Gleditsia*
(hawthorn)	(Osage-orange)	(honey-locust)
pp. 192–201	p. 99	pp. 215–216

Robinia	*Aralia*	*Sideroxylon*
(locust)	(Hercules-club)	(southern-buckthorn)
p. 213	p. 218	pp. 204–205

8b Branches armed with spine-tipped branches or sharp, dwarf side-branches

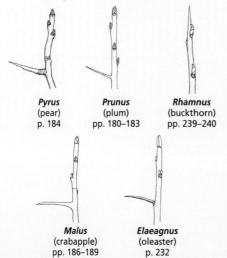

Pyrus	*Prunus*	*Rhamnus*
(pear)	(plum)	(buckthorn)
p. 184	pp. 180–183	pp. 239–240

Malus	*Elaeagnus*
(crabapple)	(oleaster)
pp. 186–189	p. 232

9a Bruised twigs with a noticeable odor **10**

9b Bruised twigs with no noticeable odor **11**

10a Bruised twigs or inner bark sweet-smelling

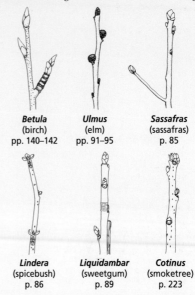

Betula	*Ulmus*	*Sassafras*
(birch)	(elm)	(sassafras)
pp. 140–142	pp. 91–95	p. 85

Lindera	*Liquidambar*	*Cotinus*
(spicebush)	(sweetgum)	(smoketree)
p. 86	p. 89	p. 223

10b Bruised twigs or inner bark foul-smelling

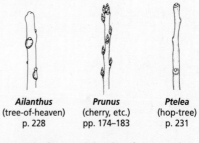

Ailanthus	*Prunus*	*Ptelea*
(tree-of-heaven)	(cherry, etc.)	(hop-tree)
p. 228	pp. 174–183	p. 231

11a Pith of twigs solid and uniform, not chambered or banded **12**

11b Pith of twigs chambered or banded

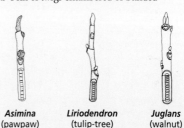

Asimina	*Liriodendron*	*Juglans*
(pawpaw)	(tulip-tree)	(walnut)
p. 84	p. 82	pp. 105–106

(continued on next page)

11b (continued)

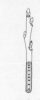

Celtis
(hackberry)
pp. 97–98

Nyssa
(tupelo)
pp. 235–236

Halesia
(silverbell)
p. 210

12a Buds clearly visible on twigs.................... **13**
12b Buds tiny and difficult to see, often embedded in bark

Albizia
(mimosa-tree)
p. 229

Hibiscus
(rose-of-Sharon)
p. 208

Tamarix
(tamarisk)
p. 80

Taxodium
(bald-cypress)
p. 79

13a Buds protected by scales.......................... **14**
13b Buds without scales, so immature leaves exposed

Hamamelis
(witch-hazel)
p. 88

Frangula
(buckthorn)
pp. 237–238

Rhus
(sumac)
pp. 220–221

Cladrastis
(yellow-wood)
p. 212

Styrax
(snowbell)
p. 211

14a Buds with 1 or 2–6 equal (not overlapping) scales or scales too tiny to see clearly....... **15**
14b Buds with 3 or more overlapping scales... **17**

15a Buds covered by 2–6 scales...................... **16**
15b Buds covered by 1 scale or buds embedded in the twig, tiny and difficult to see

Magnolia
(cucumber-tree)
p. 83

Platanus
(sycamore)
p. 87

Salix
(willow)
pp. 155–166

16a Terminal bud absent at the twig tip

Tilia
(basswood)
pp. 233–234

Alnus
(alder)
pp. 143–144

Diospyros
(persimmon)
p. 209

16b Terminal bud present at the twig tip

Carya
(hickory)
pp. 107–112

Castanea
(chestnut)
p. 117

Cornus
(dogwood)
pp. 242–246

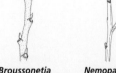

Broussonetia
(paper-mulberry)
p. 102

Nemopanthus
(mountain-holly)
p. 227

17a Buds arranged in 2 opposite, vertical rows; twigs somewhat zigzagged, lacking a true terminal (tip) bud (sometimes with a pseudo-terminal bud very near the tip)...**18**
17b Buds arranged in 3 or more vertical rows; twigs tipped with a bud............................**20**

18a Leaf scars with 1–3 dots (vein scars).......**19**
18b Leaf scars with 4 or more dots (vein scars)

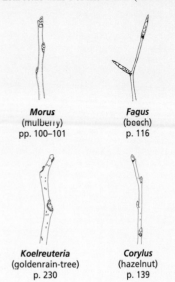

| *Morus* (mulberry) pp. 100–101 | *Fagus* (beech) p. 116 |

| *Koelreuteria* (goldenrain-tree) p. 230 | *Corylus* (hazelnut) p. 139 |

19a Leaf scars with 3 dots (vein scars)

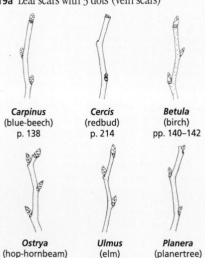

| *Carpinus* (blue-beech) p. 138 | *Cercis* (redbud) p. 214 | *Betula* (birch) pp. 140–142 |

| *Ostrya* (hop-hornbeam) p. 137 | *Ulmus* (elm) pp. 91–95 | *Planera* (planertree) p. 96 |

19b Leaf scars with 1 dot (vein scar)

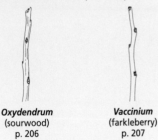

| *Oxydendrum* (sourwood) p. 206 | *Vaccinium* (farkleberry) p. 207 |

20a Twigs lacking short, dwarf side-branches...**21**
20b Twigs with short, dwarf side-branches tipped with leaf, cone or flower buds

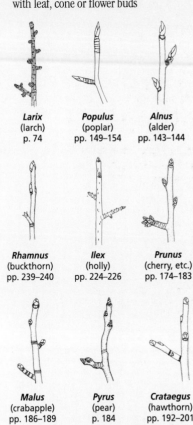

| *Larix* (larch) p. 74 | *Populus* (poplar) pp. 149–154 | *Alnus* (alder) pp. 143–144 |

| *Rhamnus* (buckthorn) pp. 239–240 | *Ilex* (holly) pp. 224–226 | *Prunus* (cherry, etc.) pp. 174–183 |

| *Malus* (crabapple) pp. 186–189 | *Pyrus* (pear) p. 184 | *Crataegus* (hawthorn) pp. 192–201 |

21a Leaf scars with 1 or 3 dots (vein scars)

21b Leaf scars with 5 to many dots

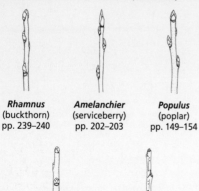

Rhamnus
(buckthorn)
pp. 239–240

Amelanchier
(serviceberry)
pp. 202–203

Populus
(poplar)
pp. 149–154

Toxicodendron
(poison-sumac)
p. 222

Gymnocladus
(coffee-tree)
p. 217

Quercus
(oak)
pp. 118–134

Crataegus
(hawthorn)
pp. 192–201

Ilex (1 dot)
(holly)
pp. 224–226

Sorbus
(mountain-ash)
pp. 190–191

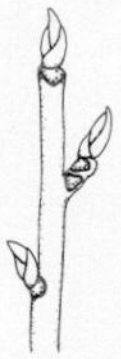

Alnus
(alder)
pp. 143–144

Carya
(hickory)
pp. 107–112

The easiest way to identify a tree is by using a key. It takes a long time to flip through every page in this guide, and many trees look very similar at first glance. A key provides you with a logical way to evaluate the most important characteristics of a tree and to rapidly narrow your choices.

This guide contains several different keys. All are dichotomous—that is, they present you with pairs of descriptions, only one of which will apply to your specimen. Simply work your way through the key choosing one of the two alternatives and then moving to the next set of choices, as indicated by the number at the end of the line. When the line ends in a name (rather than a number), you have found the name of your tree or the group to which it belongs.

The key below will help you identify the major groups (families and genera) of trees in Illinois. It may appear a bit long and intimidating at first, but remember, you don't have to read every pair of choices. For example, choice **1b** takes you to lead **5**, **5b** takes you to lead **21**, and **21b** takes you to lead **33**, nearly halfway through the key. For large families, you may be directed to other keys farther along in the guide. For example, **4a** leads you to the pine family and genus keys on pp. 66–67.

1a	Leaves reduced to needles or scales, usually evergreen **2**
1b	Leaves broader, not needle-like, deciduous **5**

2a Trees producing true (though very tiny) flowers; seeds borne in small ($1/8$" long) capsules that split in 3–4 parts to release many tiny seeds; leaves scale-like, deciduous, forming feathery sprays
. . . . **Tamaricaceae, Tamarisk Family (*Tamarix*, tamarisk, p. 80)**
2b Trees not producing true flowers; seeds borne in cones; leaves various **3**

3a Female cones small (<⅝"), sometimes berry-like, with whorled or paired scales; leaves usually scale-like, opposite or whorled . . . .**Cupressaceae, Cypress Family**
 i Cones dry, about $1/2$" long, with thin, woody or leathery scales, spreading to open at maturity; branchlets flattened, forming horizontal sprays . . . . . . **Thuja, white-cedar** (p. 78)
 ii Cones berry-like, $1/8$–$1/4$" long, with fleshy scales fused together at maturity; branches scarcely flattened, if at all. . . . .***Juniperus*, red-cedar** (p. 77)
3b Female cones usually larger, never berry-like; leaves needle-shaped, bundled, spirally arranged or alternate, but sometimes twisted into 2 opposite rows **4**

4a Leaves evergreen or, if deciduous, borne in compact tufts (larch, *Larix*); cones usually oblong to ovoid, woody, with a thin bract behind each scale
. . . . **Pinaceae, Pine Family** (keys to genera and species, pp. 66–67)
4b Some leaves shed with their twigs each autumn; cones spherical, leathery, without bracts
. . . . **Taxodiaceae (*Taxodium*, bald-cypress, p. 79)**

Pine Family   Cypress Family

| Scots pine p. 72 | jack pine p. 73 | eastern red-cedar p. 77 | eastern white-cedar p. 78 |

Key to Families and Genera

5a Leaves divided into leaflets (compound) **6**
5b Leaves smooth-edged, toothed or lobed, but not divided into leaflets (simple) **21**

6a Fruits winged samaras. **7**
6b Fruits not winged samaras **10**

7a Leaves alternate; samaras with the seed near the center **8**
7b Leaves opposite; samaras with the seed near one end **9**

8a Leaves with 3 leaflets (trifoliate); samaras round and flat
. . . .**Rutaceae, Rue Family (*Ptelea*, hop-tree**, p. 231)
8b Leaves pinnately divided into 11–41 leaflets; samaras oblong, twisted, with a seed near the center
. . . . **Simaroubaceae, Quassia Family (*Ailanthus*, tree-of-heaven**, p. 228)

9a Samaras single . . . .**Oleaceae, Olive Family** (keys to genera and species, p. 261)
9b Samaras paired . . . . .**Aceraceae, Maple Family (*Acer*, maple**, key to species, p. 253)

10a Fruits thick-husked capsules containing a nut or large, nut-like seed. **11**
10b Fruits otherwise **12**

11a Leaves opposite, palmately divided into 5–9 leaflets . . . .
Hippocastanaceae, Horsechestnut Family (*Aesculus*, buckeye, pp. 250–252)
11b Leaves alternate, pinnately divided into 11–23 leaflets
. . . . . .**Juglandaceae, Walnut Family** (keys to genera and species, pp. 103–104)

12a Fruits plump to dry capsules or pods **13**
12b Fruits somewhat fleshy pomes or drupes **18**

13a Fruits inflated, thin-walled, 3-pointed pods that persist well into winter. **14**
13b Fruits otherwise **15**

14a Leaves opposite, divided into 3 finely toothed leaflets; flowers greenish-white, in small, unbranched clusters (racemes); capsules pale green to yellowish-brown
. . . . . **Staphyleaceae, Bladdernut Family (Staphylea, bladdernut**, p. 249)
14b Leaves alternate, once or twice pinnately divided into 10 or more, irregularly coarse-toothed leaflets; flowers bright yellow, numerous, in large, branched clusters (panicles); capsules lime green to reddish
. . **Sapindaceae, Soapberry Family (*Koelreuteria*, goldenrain-tree**, p. 230)

15a Fruits small, round, red capsules containing 1–2 shiny, black seeds
. . . .**Rutaceae, Rue Family (*Zanthoxylum*, prickly-ash**, p. 222)
15b Fruits elongated, pea-like pods **16**

Maple Family	Walnut Family	Cassia Family	Rose Family

silver maple p. 257 — shagbark hickory p. 108 — honey-locust p. 215 — European mountain-ash p. 191

16a Leaves once-divided . . . . **Fabaceae, Pea Family**
   i Twigs spiny . . . . *Robinia*, **locust** (p. 213)
   ii Twigs slender, without spines . . . . *Cladrastis*, **yellow-wood** (p. 212)
16b Leaves twice-divided **17**

17a Flowers bisexual, with long, showy anthers extending beyond 5 inconspicuous petals, forming fluffy, tassel-like heads 1–2" in diameter in broad, branched clusters
         . . . .**Mimosaceae, Mimosa Family** (*Albizia*, **mimosa-tree,** p. 229)
17b Flowers unisexual, pea-like, with 5 showy petals, borne in elongated, branched clusters
         . . . . **Caesalpiniaceae, Cassia Family**
   i Branches usually thorny; leaflets up to $1/2$" wide; flowers in compact, elongated clusters (racemes) . . . . *Gleditsia*, **honey-locust** (pp. 215–216)
   ii Branches without thorns; leaflets $1/2$–$11/2$" wide; flowers in widely branched clusters (panicles) . . . . *Gymnocladus*, **coffeebean** (p. 217)

18a Fruits small pomes (like tiny apples) in rounded to flat-topped clusters (corymbs)
         . . . . **Rosaceae, Rose Family** (keys to genera and species, pp. 167–173)
18b Fruits fleshy drupes **19**

19a Leaves opposite; drupes 5-seeded
         . . . .**Rutaceae, Rue Family** (*Phellodendron*, **corktree,** p. 280)
19b Leaves alternate; drupes 1-seeded **20**

20a Leaves once-pinnate **Anacardiaceae, Cashew Family** (keys to genera and species, p. 219)
20b Leaves twice-pinnate . . . . **Araliaceae, Ginseng Family** (*Aralia*, **aralia,** p. 218)

21a Leaves and branches paired (opposite) or whorled **22**
21b Leaves and branches single (alternate) **31**

22a Fruits pairs of winged keys; leaves palmately veined and lobed
         . . . .**Aceraceae, Maple Family** (*Acer*, **maple,** key to species, p. 253)
22b Fruits and leaves otherwise **23**

23a Fruits tiny capsules in dense, elongated clusters (catkins); buds covered by a single scale
         . . . . **Salicaceae, Willow Family** (keys to genera and species, pp. 145–148)
23b Fruits and scales otherwise **24**

24a Leaves toothed **25**
24b Leaves smooth-edged (not toothed) **27**

25a Fruits 4-lobed capsules
         . . . **Celastraceae, Staff-tree Family** (*Euonymus*, **burning-bush,** pp. 247–248)
25b Fruits berries or berry-like drupes **26**

26a Flowers 5-parted; flowers and fruits paired in leaf axils or numerous, in branched clusters at branch tips . . **Caprifoliaceae, Honeysuckle Family** (keys to genera and species, p. 273)
26b Flowers 4-parted; flowers and fruits few, in small, unbranched clusters (umbels) from leaf axils
         . . . . **Rhamnaceae, Buckthorn Family** (*Rhamnus*, **buckthorn,** pp. 239–240)

27a Flowers large ($^1/_2$–$2^3/_4$" long), funnel-shaped, numerous, in showy, branched clusters
(panicles); fruits not juicy and berry-like; leaves heart-shaped **28**

27a Flowers small (up to $^1/_4$" long), whitish, 4-parted; leaves elliptical to oval **30**

28a Fruits bean-like pods about 12" long
. . . . . . **Bignoniaceae, Trumpet-creeper Family (*Catalpa*, catalpa,** p. 271)

28b Fruits short ($^1/_2$–2" long), pointed, leathery to woody capsules **29**

29a Flowers large ($1^1/_2$–$2^3/_4$" long), 2-lipped, violet purple; leaves 6–12" long, gray-velvety
beneath with star-shaped, branched hairs
. . . **Scrophulariaceae, Figwort Family (*Paulownia*, empress-tree,** p. 270)

29b Flowers small (about $^1/_2$" long), with 4 spreading lobes (not 2-lipped), purple, blue or white;
leaves 2–5" long, hairless beneath or with a few hairs on the veins
. . . . **Oleaceae, Olive Family (Syringa, lilac,** p. 267)

30a Flowers with petals separate; fruits juicy, berry-like drupes $^1/_4$–$^3/_4$"; flowers/fruits in open,
branched clusters or in compact heads surrounded by showy bracts (pseudanthia)
. . . . **Cornaceae, Dogwood Family, (*Cornus*, dogwood,** key to species, p. 241)

30b Flowers with petals fused into a funnel shape; fruits reddish-green to brownish, pyramidal
capsules, $^1/_4$" long; flowers/fruits in long-stalked, spherical heads
. . . . **Rubiaceae, Madder Family (*Cephalanthus*, buttonbush,** p. 272)

31a Leaves smooth-edged (not toothed). **32**

31b Leaves toothed **49**

32a Flowers single, large and showy; fruits large (>$^3/_4$") berries or fleshy pods in cone-like clusters
. . . . **33**

32b Flowers usually in clusters of 2 or more, relatively small; fruits small (<$^3/_4$") drupes
(occasionally forming large, round masses), berries, pods, capsules or nuts **35**

33a Flowers $^3/_8$–$^3/_4$" long, in leaf axils; petals 4, fused in a tube or bell; fruits large (1–2"), pale
orange berries with thick, persistent sepals at the base
. . . . **Ebenaceae, Ebony Family (*Diospyros*, persimmon,** p. 209)

33b Flowers large (1–3" long) at branch tips; petals 6, separate; fruits not as above **34**

34a Flowers dull purple; fruits large, sweet-pulpy berries with many large seeds; leaves widest above the
middle, not dotted . . . **Annonaceae, Custard-apple Family (*Asimina*, pawpaw,** p. 84)

34b Flowers yellowish-green, often with yellow or orange markings; fruits numerous, forming dense,
cone-like clusters; leaves with tiny, transparent dots . . . **Magnoliaceae, Magnolia Family**
   i Leaves broad and squarish, usually 4-lobed; fruits dry, winged nutlets (samaras),
      not splitting open . . . . ***Liriodendron*, tulip-tree** (p. 82)
   ii Leaves oblong to elliptical, never lobed; fruits fleshy pods (follicles), splitting open to release
      seeds. . . . . ***Magnolia*, cucumber tree** (p. 83)

35a Fruits small, fleshy, numerous, in large (4–$5^1/_2$"), round, pulpy aggregates resembling
lumpy oranges; branches thorny with milky juice
. . . . **Moraceae, Mulberry Family (*Maclura*, Osage-orange,** p. 99)

35b Fruits and branches otherwise. **36**

36a Fruits fleshy berries or drupes **37**

36b Fruits dry capsules, pods, nuts, nutlets or dry drupes **44**

37a Leaf surfaces silvery above and below with dense, star-shaped hairs; drupes silvery, mealy
. . . . **Elaeagnaceae, Oleaster Family (*Elaeagnus*, oleaster,** p. 232)

37b Leaves and fruits not silvery; fruits crimson, dark blue or purplish-black **38**

38a Flowers small (<¼"), white bells tipped with 5 shallow lobes, numerous, in elongating clusters;
fruits shiny, black berries containing 8–10 seeds
. . . . **Ericaceae, Heath Family (*Vaccinium*, farkleberry,** p. 207)

38b Flowers not bell-shaped, with petals separate or joined at the base only, clustered or single; fruits
drupes with juicy or mealy flesh enclosing a single, hard, stone. **39**

39a Flowers ¼–³⁄₈" across, yellow, 6-lobed; bark, twigs and wood spicy-fragrant
. . . . **Lauraceae, Laurel Family**

    i Leaves unlobed, ovate, pinnately veined; flower/fruit clusters stalkless, scattered along
branchlets; fruits red . . . . **Lindera, spicebush** (p. 86)

    ii Leaves typically 2–3-lobed, palmately veined; flower/fruit clusters on stalks at branch tips;
fruits blue . . . . **Sassafras, sassafras** (p. 85)

39b Flowers tiny (about ⅛" long), greenish to cream, with 3–5 sepals and petals (sometimes lacking
petals); leaves not lobed; trees not spicy-fragrant. **40**

40a Flowers borne on long, slender stalks, single or in tassel-like clusters from leaf axils; fruits 1 per
stalk **41**

40b Flowers in dense clusters at the tips of long stalks; fruits usually 2 or more per stalk **43**

41a Flowers unisexual, single from leaf axils; winter buds with scales
. . . . **Aquifoliaceae, Holly Family (*Nemopanthus*, mountain-holly,** p. 227)

41b Flowers bisexual, in small, tassel-like clusters from leaf axils **42**

42a Winter buds with protective scales; sap milky; leaves elliptical to lance-shaped, usually widest
toward the tip; fruits shiny, black berries with 1 seed . . . .
Sapotaceae, Sapodilla Family (*Sideroxylon*, southern-buckthorn, pp. 204–205)

42b Winter buds lacking scales; sap clear; leaves broadly elliptical to ovate, often widest toward the
tip; fruits purplish-black drupes with 2–4 stones . . . .
Rhamnaceae, Buckthorn Family (*Frangula*, glossy buckthorn, pp. 237–238)

Beech Family	Dogwood Family	Holly Family	Willow Family

bur oak p. 121	gray dogwood p. 244	common mountain-holly p. 227	pussy willow p. 165

43a Flowers bisexual, with 4 stamens and 4 petals; sepals minute; fruits fleshy, red to purplish-black
. . . . . **Cornaceae Dogwood Family (*Cornus*, dogwood,** key to species p. 241)

43b Flowers unisexual, with 5 evident sepals and 5–8 minute petals; fruits oily, blue-black, plum-like drupes . . . . **Nyssaceae, Sourgum Family (*Nyssa*, tupelo,** pp. 235–236)

44a Fruits acorns (1-seeded nuts with the base enclosed in a distinctive cup of overlapping bracts)
. . . . **Fagaceae, Beech Family (*Quercus*, oak,** key to species, pp. 113–115)

44b Fruits otherwise **45**

45a Flowers showy, with well-developed petals **46**

45b Flowers tiny, without obvious petals. **48**

46a Flowers pink, pea-like, in small, tassel-like clusters along branches; fruits flattened pods (legumes); leaves heart-shaped . . . . .**Caesalpiniaceae, Cassia Family (*Cercis*, redbud,** p. 214)

46b Flowers white bells in branched and/or elongated clusters. **47**

47a Flowers large (1" wide), bell-shaped, in elongating clusters (racemes) up to 5" long at branch tips; fruits dry, round, densely short-hairy drupes
. . . . **Styracaceae, Snowball Family (*Styrax*, snowbell,** p. 211)

47b Flowers small (<¹/₄" wide), urn-shaped in large (6–8" long) branched clusters (panicles) at branch tips; fruits egg-shaped capsules; leaves oblong to narrowly ovate
. . . . **Ericaceae, Heath Family (*Oxydendrum*, sourwood,** p. 206)

48a Flowers/fruits in compact, elongated clusters (catkins); fruits short-stalked capsules containing many fluffy-parachuted seeds; leaves not aromatic
. . . . **Salicaceae, Willow Family** (keys to genera and species, pp. 145–148)

48b Flowers/fruits in airy, many-branched clusters (panicles); fruits dry drupes on long, slender stalks with many feathery hairs; leaves aromatic, smelling of orange peels. . . . .
. . . . **Anacardiaceae, Cashew Family (*Cotinus*, smoketree,** p. 223)

49a Branches spiny or thorny **50**

49b Branches without spines or thorns **51**

50a Flowers relatively large (>¹/₂"), with showy, white to pink petals; fruits various; leaves alternate
. . . . **Rosaceae, Rose Family** (keys to genera and species, pp. 167–173)

50b Flowers tiny, with petals about ¹/₃₂" long, borne in tassel-like clusters (fascicles) arising from leaf axils; fruits small, berry-like drupes; leaves often opposite
. . . . **Rhamnaceae, Buckthorn Family (*Rhamnus*, buckthorn,** pp. 239–240)

Holly Family	Elm Family	Witch-hazel Family	Beech Family

common winterberry p. 224	American elm p. 91	American witch-hazel p. 88	American beech p. 116

51a Flowers and fruits in small, flat-topped clusters on slender stalks from the middle of strap-like, membranous bracts; leaves usually unevenly heart-shaped
. . . . **Tiliaceae, Linden Family** (*Tilia*, **basswood,** pp. 233–234)

51b Fruits, flowers and leaves not as above **52**

52a Flowers tiny, without petals or sepals, unisexual; male flowers numerous, in dense heads or catkins **53**

52b Flowers not in dense heads or catkins. **58**

53a Male and female flowers in spherical heads; leaves palmately lobed **54**

53b Male flowers (and sometimes female also) in elongated clusters (catkins) **55**

54a Leaves with 3–5 broad, shallow, coarsely toothed lobes; fruits tiny, club-shaped, 1-seeded nutlets forming dry, finely dimpled heads
. . . . **Platanaceae, Plane-tree Family** (*Platanus*, **sycamore,** p. 87)

54b Leaves with 5–7 slender-tipped, deeply cut, finely toothed lobes; fruits woody capsules tipped with 2 points, forming spiny heads
. . . . . **Hamamelidaceae, Witch-hazel Family** (*Liquidambar*, **sweetgum,** p. 89)

55a Fruits tiny, short-stalked capsules in catkins; seeds tipped with a tuft of long, silky down; buds often covered by 1 scale
. . . . **Salicaceae, Willow Family** (keys to genera and species, pp. 145–148)

55b Fruits otherwise, seeds not tipped with silky hairs; buds never 1-scaled **56**

56a Fruits large, single nuts seated in a scaly cup or in a bristly husk
. . . . **Fagaceae, Beech Family** (keys to genera and species, pp. 113–115)

56b Fruits small, numerous, in dense clusters **57**

57a Fruits tiny, winged nutlets, protected by dry bracts in scaly or woody catkins
. . . . **Betulaceae, Birch Family** (keys to genera and species, pp. 135–136)

57b Fruits tiny nutlets, each surrounded by fleshy, swollen sepals, forming compact, often blackberry-like clusters . . . . **Moraceae, Mulberry Family**

i Bark flaky to furrowed; leaves hairless or short-hairy (not velvety), with hairless to flat-hairy, short (<1¹⁄₈") stalks, fruit clusters oblong. . . . . . . *Morus*, **mulberry** (pp. 100–101)

ii Bark smooth; leaves velvety beneath, with silky, long (>1¹⁄₈") stalks; fruit clusters round . . . . *Broussonetia*, **paper mulberry** (p. 102)

58a Leaves asymmetrical, with one edge longer than the other at the base **59**

58b Leaves with symmetrical bases **60**

59a Flowers showy, with 4 slender, yellow petals, appearing in autumn; fruits woody, 2-seeded capsules; leaves wavy-toothed
. . . **Hamamelidaceae, Witch-hazel Family** (*Hamamelis*, **witch-hazel,** p. 88)

59b Flowers inconspicuous, greenish, lacking petals, appearing in spring; fruits round, winged samaras or red to blackish drupes; leaves sharply toothed
. . . . **Ulmaceae, Elm Family** (keys to genera and species, p. 90)

60a Flowers white, pink, blue or violet, relatively large (>1/2") and showy, with 5 petals (4 in silverbell) and 10 or more stamens (8 or 16 in silverbell); fruits various, but drupes 1-seeded. **61**

60b Flowers yellowish-green, <1/4" across, with 4–8 petals and 4–10 stamens; fruits various, but drupes 2–5-stoned. **63**

61a Flowers large (21/4–4" across), broadly trumpet-shaped, with an anther-dotted tube at the center tipped with a 5-branched stigma; fruits egg-shaped, 1/2–3/4" capsules containing numerous fringed seeds . . . . .**Malvaceae, Mallow Family (*Hibiscus*, rose-of-Sharon**, p. 208)

61b Flowers smaller (<21/4" across), bell-shaped, cupped or saucer-shaped, usually white or pinkish; fruits various. **62**

62a Flowers bell-shaped, with fused petals; fruits dry drupes with 1–4 stones
. . . . **Styracaceae, Snowball Family**
  i Fruits distinctive, corky, 4-winged drupes; flowers with 4 petals, 4 sepals and 8 or 16 stamens; flowers/fruits in tassel-like clusters from leaf axils . . . . ***Halesia*, silverbell** (p. 210)
  ii Fruits dry, round, densely short-hairy drupes; flowers with 5 petals, 5 sepals and 10 stamens; flowers/fruits in elongating clusters at branch tips . . . . . ***Styrax*, snowbell** (p. 211)

62b Flowers cupped or saucer-shaped, with separate petals; fruits various, usually fleshy, 1-seeded if drupes . . . . **Rosaceae, Rose Family** (keys to genera and species, pp. 167–173)

63a Flowers white bells tipped with 5 shallow lobes, bisexual; petals fused; fruits berries or capsules
. . . . **Ericaceae, Heath Family**
  i Flowers abundant, in large, branched clusters (panicles); fruits 5-sided, woody capsules
. . . . ***Oxydendrum*, sourwood** (p. 206)
  ii Flowers less numerous, in elongating, unbranched clusters (racemes); fruits shiny, black berries. . . . . ***Vaccinium*, farkleberry** (p. 207)

63b Flowers not bell-shaped, often unisexual; petals separate of fused at the base only; fruits berry-like drupes **64**

64a Flowers unisexual with male and female flowers on separate plants or bisexual; bisexual flowers with a long, slender style tipped with a stigma; unisexual flowers with split styles and 2 stigmas
. . . . **Rhamnaceae, Buckthorn Family**
  i Winter buds protected by scales; flowers bisexual, with undivided styles
. . . . ***Rhamnus*, buckthorn** (pp. 239–240)
  ii Winter buds lacking scales; flowers unisexual, with styles split 1/3 of their length
. . . . ***Frangula*, glossy buckthorn** (pp. 237–238)

64b Flowers unisexual, with male and female flowers on separate plants; styles short, the stigmas almost sessile . . . . **Aquifoliaceae, Holly Family**
  i Flowers white, with petals joined at the base; leaves lacking a short, sharp point at the tip, edged with teeth (coarse and spiny to shallow and rounded) . . . . ***Ilex*, holly** (pp. 224–226)
  ii Flowers yellow, with separate petals; leaves tipped with a short, sharp point, smooth-edged or with a few small, sharp teeth . . . . ***Nemopanthus*, mountain-holly** (p. 227)

Needle
Leaves

Key to Genera in the Pine Family (Pinaceae)

1a Needles in clusters of 2 or more; branches with dwarf shoots 2

1b Needles single, spirally arranged; branches lacking dwarf shoots
. . . . *Picea*, **spruce** (pp. 75–76)

2a Needles drop each autumn (deciduous), numerous, in dense clusters at the tips of stubby dwarf branches . . . . *Larix*, **larch** (p. 74)

2b Needles evergreen, in bundles of 2–5 along branches
. . . .*Pinus*, **pine** (key to species, p. 67)

Pinus banksiana, jack pine

Key to the Pines (Genus *Pinus*)

1a Needles soft and slender, in bundles of 5; seed cone scales thin and flexible, without spiny, thickened tips **2**

1b Needles firmer, thicker, in bundles of 2–3; seed cone scales thickened and rather woody . **3**

2a Needles 2–5" long; cones 3–6" long . . . . . *P. strobus*, **eastern white pine** (p. 68)

2b Needles mostly >5" long; cones <6" long
. . . .*P. walichiana*, **Himalayan white pine** (p. 68)

3a Needles 5½–10" long, in bundles of 3 . . . . *P. taeda*, **loblolly pine** (p. 70)

3b Needles shorter, in bundles of 2 or 3 . . . . **4**

4a Seed cone scales tipped with a prickle **5**

4b Seed cone scales lacking spines or with a tiny, reflexed, flat-lying spine **7**

5a Needles 1½–3½" long; seed cone scales with stout, triangular, ¼" long spines
. . . . *P. pungens*, **Table-Mountain pine** (p. 71)

5b Needles 2½–5" long; seed cone scales with slender, 1/16–1/8" long spines **6**

6a Needles about 1/32" wide, in bundles of 2 or 3; twigs pale with a whitish bloom
. . . . *P. echinata*, **shortleaf pine** (p. 70)

6b Needles about 1/16" wide, mostly in bundles of 3; twigs brown, without a whitish bloom. . .
. . . . *P. rigida*, **pitch pine** (p. 71)

7a Needles 3–6" long, straight. **8**

7b Needles ¾–2¾" long, usually twisted lengthwise or with spreading pairs **9**

8a Needles 3½–6¼" long, stiff, snapping readily when bent in half; seed cones reddish-brown, stalkless when shed; buds chestnut brown . . . . *P. resinosa*, **red pine** (p. 69)

8b Needles flexible, not snapping when bent in half; seed cones shiny, brown, shed with stalks; buds with whitish resin . . . . *P. nigra*, **Austrian pine** (p. 72)

9a Needles 1½–4" long, spirally twisted (both sides visible at once), not noticeably spreading; bark of older branches orange-brown . . . . *P. sylvestris*, **Scots pine** (p. 72)

9b Needles ¾–1½" long, slightly twisted (only 1 side visible), spread in a "V"; bark of older branches not orange-brown . . . . *P. banksiana*, **jack pine** (p. 73)

This majestic soft pine is one of eastern North America's most commercially valuable trees. Before the arrival of the Europeans, white pine stands contained an estimated 900 billion board feet of lumber, but most were cut from the 1700s through the 1800s. The tall, straight trunks made excellent ship masts • Eastern white pine trees live about 200 years and seed regularly after 20–30 years. Seed production fluctuates, with good crops every 3–5 years and little or no production in between. Seedlings can persist in the understory for up to 20 years. The bark of this fire-dependent tree resists fire well, and after forest fires, surviving trees readily shed their seed over freshly exposed ground. • This attractive, fast-growing tree has been used in landscaping and reforestation projects. • The wood is moderately strong and easily worked, with uniform texture and low shrinkage. It has been used in construction, interior and exterior finishing, furniture, cabinets and carvings. • **Himalayan white pine (*P. wallichiana*)**, shown in pink on the map, introduced from Asia, occasionally grows wild in Unions County. It is distinguished from white pine by its longer (usually 5" or more), gray-green (not blue-green) needles and its larger (6" or more) cones.

Also Called: Northern white pine, Weymouth pine, soft pine.

Size and Shape: Coniferous trees 65–100' tall; crowns conical when young, becoming irregular (often lopsided) with age in open sites; roots wide-spreading, very wind-firm.

Trunks: Tall, straight, 24–40" in diameter; young bark grayish-green, thin, smooth; mature bark dark grayish-green, ¾–2" thick, with broad ridges of purple-tinged scales; wood pale brown, soft, lightweight, straight-grained.

Branches: Stout, irregular, horizontal to ascending; twigs flexible and rusty-hairy (1st year) to brownish and hairless (2nd year); buds slender, ¼–½" long, red- to yellow-brown, with overlapping scales.

Leaves: Light **bluish-green, soft, slender, straight, flexible, evergreen needles bundled in 5s** and sheathed with membranous scales at the base; **needles 2–6" long,** 3-sided, finely toothed; needles persist 1–4 years.

Cones: Male and female cones on the same tree; male cones yellow, small, clustered at the base of current year's growth in midcrown; female cones light brown and woody when mature, **cylindrical,** often curved, **3–10" long,** hanging on ¾" long stalks at branch tips in upper crown; scales 50–80, exposed portions thin, rounded, lacking prickles; seeds mottled reddish-brown, about ¼" long with a ½–¾" wing, 2 per scale; seed cones mature in 2–3 years, drop soon after shedding seeds.

Habitat: Dry to wet, wooded sites; does best on cool, humid sites with well-drained soils.

Origin: Native.

This tree lives about 200 years. It is slow growing at first, but once established, it can shoot up at a rate of 12" per year. Most red pine trees produce seed consistently at 15–25 years of age, with good crops every 3–7 years. • Red pine requires sunny sites, and it grows well on open sites with thin, infertile soils, where its deep roots help it withstand strong winds. Natural stands usually establish when fire removes competing plants and insect pests, leaving an open seedbed for the wind-borne seeds. • This tree is an important timber and pulp tree, extensively planted in eastern North America, but native populations in Illinois are so rare that this species is considered endangered. The moderately hard wood readily absorbs preservatives, making it useful for structural beams, bridges, piles and railroad ties. • Red pine has relatively little genetic variation, so it has a fairly consistent form and growth rate. It is often used in reforestation projects, tree plantations, parks and windbreaks. • Many songbirds, especially red crossbills, pine grosbeaks, and pine siskins, eat red pine seeds. Red squirrels harvest the ripening cones from the trees, and chipmunks, mice and voles gather seeds on the ground.

Also Called: Norway pine (possibly from Norway, Maine).

Size and Shape: Coniferous trees 65–100' tall; crowns conical when young, **rounded and irregular with age.**

Trunks: Tall, straight, 24–32" in diameter; young bark reddish to pinkish-brown, scaly; **mature bark reddish, flaky, with broad, scaly plates,** 1–1½" thick, fire-resistant; wood pale to reddish-brown, lightweight, close-grained.

Branches: Spreading or drooping (lower) to upcurved (upper), in annual false-whorls; twigs stout, ridged; **buds resinous,** ½–¾" long, red-brown, with white-fringed scales.

Leaves: Shiny, dark green, evergreen needles **bundled in 2s,** with persistent membranous sheaths; crowded toward branch tips; **needles straight, 4–7" long, brittle** (snap easily), finely sharp-toothed; needles persist 4–5 years.

Cones: Male and female cones on the same tree; male cones small, purple to yellow, clustered at the base of new shoots; female cones light chestnut brown, woody, 1½–2¾" **long,** stalkless, hanging at upper branch tips; **scales only slightly thickened, concave,** tipped with a **spineless bump;** seeds mottled chestnut brown, with a ⅜–⅝" wing, 2 per scale; seed cones mature in 2–3 years, shed seeds in autumn, usually drop within the year.

Habitat: Dry, acidic woods; grows best in dry to moist areas with light, sandy loam but out-competed by hardwoods.

Origin: Native.

Loblolly pine is native to the southeastern U.S. Its range extends north to Illinois, where it is probably limited by low temperatures and relatively lower rainfall. Native populations are rare in this state, but this tree is widely planted and often escapes to thrive in abandoned fields and other disturbed areas. These fast-growing trees usually begin to produce seed at 30–40 years of age. Frequent, abundant seed crops provide important food for many rodents and birds, including squirrels, chipmunks, mice, bobwhite quail and wild turkeys. • New shoots and needles expand in April–May, about 10 days before the male cones mature. Female cones develop next, typically producing 50–60 seeds. Pollen is rarely carried to trees more than 1000' away, and seeds seldom fly more than 1000' from the parent tree. • The wood is sold commercially for general construction and pulp. • **Shortleaf pine** (*P. echinata,* also called yellow pine), shown in pink/dark green (species overlap) on the map, is another southeastern species, rare in Illinois but often grown in plantations. It is a tall tree of sandy or rocky sites that has slender, relatively short (2¹/₂–5" long) needles in bundles of 2–3. It is also distinguished by its short (¹/₈") cone spines and the pale grayish bloom on its twigs.

Size and Shape: Coniferous trees 80–120' tall; crowns dense, rounded.

Trunks: Straight, long, 20-40" in diameter; mature bark bright red-brown, ¾–1¼" thick, with broad, flat plates, flaky with age; wood light brown, coarse grained, brittle.

Branches: Thick, stout; twigs brownish yellow to reddish brown, rough; buds red-brown, not resinous, <⅝" long at twig tips, covered in overlapping scales with free tips.

Leaves: Slender, light yellowish-green, **evergreen needles,** slightly twisted, **in bundles of 3** (rarely some 2s), **5½–10" long;** sheaths ⅝–1" long when young, persistent; needles persist 3 years.

Cones: Male and female cones on same tree, spreading; male cones yellow, ¼–½" long, clustered at branch tips; **female cones light reddish-brown, oblong to cone-shaped, ¼–½" long,** pointing outward; **scales thick, triangular tip with a short, spreading to reflexed spine** at the center; seeds dark brown or mottled with black markings, angular, 4-sided, with a ¼" long seed and a ¾–1" long wing, 2 per scale; cones single or in small groups, produced in April–May, mature and shed seed in October, dropped the next year.

Habitat: Moist, sandy soil.

Origin: Introduced from the southeastern U.S.

This hardy tree has been used to reforest bare, sandy soil and "worn-out" land. It takes about 5 years to establish but then grows rapidly on very poor soils. • Pitch pine can live 200 years and survive fires that would eliminate other trees. In fact, it depends on fire for success. Large natural stands establish only after fire has removed competing plants and diseases. Many cones remain closed on trees for decades, but open and shed seeds immediately after a fire. Mature trees also recover quickly from fires, using dormant buds in their bark. These buds sprout quickly when the tree's needles are killed, producing new shoots and needles almost immediately. On seedlings and small trees, hidden buds often lie protected in crooks near the ground. • Pitch pine wood resists decay, so colonists in the eastern U.S. used it in shipbuilding. • Another species, which is native to regions farther east and occasionally escapes from cultivation in Illinois, is **Table-Mountain pine (*P. pungens*,** also called prickly pine), shown in dark green (species overlap) on the map. This small (up to 33' tall), often crooked tree has short (1½–3½") needles in bundles of 2 (rarely 3). Its heavy, 2½–3½" long cones have been likened to medieval caltrops, bristling with stout, ¼" long spines (1 per scale). These distinctive cones are easily identified and persist for many years.

Size and Shape: Coniferous trees 50–65' tall; crowns rounded, irregular (open-grown) to regular (forest-grown).

Trunks: Short, twisted (open-grown) to tall, straight (forest-grown), up to 1' in diameter; young bark reddish-brown; mature bark dark gray, with loose, irregular plates; wood pale reddish-brown, soft, coarse-grained.

Branches: Irregular, numerous, gnarled (open-grown), sometimes **stubby, clustered and cone-bearing** (cones appear to grow from trunks); twigs stout, hairless, ridged; **buds chestnut brown,** resinous, about ⅝" long, with loose, fringed scales.

Leaves: Stiff, shiny, **yellowish-green,** evergreen needles, **bundled in 3s** (usually) with membranous sheaths; **needles 2½–5" long,** blunt, 3-sided, twisted, minutely sharp-toothed; **growing from trunks, branches and twig tips;** persisting 2–3 years.

Cones: Male and female cones on same tree; male cones yellow, ⅝–¾" long, clustered below new shoots; female cones light brown, **woody, 2–3½" long,** clustered near branch tips; **scales flat** with thick, ridged tips bearing a **curved, 1/16–⅛" spine;** seeds dark, ⅛–3/16" long with a ½–¾" wing; female cones mature in 2–3 years, open irregularly (some immediately, others only after fire), persist many years.

Habitat: Dry, rocky or sandy sites.

Origin: Introduced from the eastern U.S

S cots pine is the world's most widely distributed pine and was one of the first exotic trees introduced to North America. Its great variability reflects genetic and habitat differences as well as damage from diseases and pests. In the northern and mountainous regions of Europe, Scots pine is commonly tall and straight-trunked with high-quality wood. In contrast, trees from southern Europe tend to have crooked trunks with numerous, spreading branches and poor-quality wood. Unfortunately, these are the trees that were first to arrive in North America, owing in large part to poor seed selection when the species was introduced. Because of its inferior wood quality, Scots pine was often abandoned in favor of other species for lumber, shelterbelts and erosion control. • Scots pines are widely planted as ornamentals and as Christmas trees. Old plantations sometimes appear to be stands of native trees. • Another introduced species, **Austrian pine (*P. nigra*)**, shown in dark green (species overlap) on the map, is a 2-needle pine with straight (not spirally twisted), dark green (not blue-green) needles. This tall (to 100'), attractive tree has long (3–6"), flexible needles that are not easily snapped. A European introduction, Austrian pine is widely planted as an ornamental and rarely escapes to grow wild.

Also Called: Scotch pine.

Size and Shape: Coniferous trees 35–60' tall, often shrubby; crowns cone-shaped when young, rounded and irregular with age; roots widespreading, with a distinct taproot when young.

Trunks: Short and crooked with large branches, rarely straight and branch-free, 8–20" in diameter; **young bark orange-red, papery,** peeling in strips; mature bark grayish-brown to orange-brown, in irregular, loose plates; inner bark brownish-red; wood reddish-brown, strong, light, straight-grained.

Branches: Irregular, spreading; twigs reddish- to grayish-brown, hairless, ridged; buds red-brown, sharp-tipped, ¼–½" long, with some loose-tipped lower scales.

Leaves: Slender, **stiff, spirally twisted, dark blue-green, evergreen needles, bundled in 2s** with persistent, membranous sheaths about ¼" long; **needles 1½–3" long,** sharp-pointed, finely toothed; needles persist 3–4 years.

Cones: Male and female cones on the same tree; male cones small, yellow, clustered at the base of new shoots; female cones in 2s or 3s, woody, yellowish- to purplish-brown, 1–3" long, often asymmetrical and **bent backward on the branch; scales flattened, tipped with a 4-sided, spineless bump;** seeds dark reddish-brown, about ⅛" long, ⅜–¾" wing soon lost, 2 per scale; seed cones mature in second autumn, shed seeds over winter and spring, often long-persistent.

Habitat: Upland sites and pine plantations, preferably with sandy loam soils.

Origin: Introduced from Europe.

A lthough jack pine is widespread across Canada and the northeastern U.S., it is an endangered species in Illinois. Trees occasionally escape from plantings, but native populations are very rare. • Jack pine is a slow-growing tree that lives for about 150 years. Mature cones can remain closed on the tree for many years, until heat from fire, or from sunlight on hot days, melts the resin that seals the scales shut, allowing the cones to pop open and release their seeds. Fire produces a favorable seedbed, free of competing plants and disease. However, repeated burns at intervals of less than 15 years will destroy the seed supply. Jack pine can also colonize exhausted sandy sites, where soil conditions are very poor and competition from other plants is limited. • White tailed deer browse on new growth, snowshoe hares eat the seedlings, and porcupines often eat the bark. Intensive browsing can deform trees, particularly young trees. Red squirrels, chipmunks, white-footed mice and songbirds such as goldfinches, grackles and robins eat large quantities of fallen seeds. • In the north, where jack pine is very common, the wood is used widely for pulp and paper, mine timbers, railway ties, poles, pilings, lumber and wood fiber.

Also Called: Black pine, Banksian pine, scrub pine, gray pine, Hudson Bay pine • *P. divaricata.*

Size and Shape: Small coniferous trees, usually 35–50' tall; crowns cone-shaped, open.

Trunks: Straight, 8–12" (rarely up to 28″) in diameter; young bark reddish- to grayish-brown, thin, flaky; mature bark dark brown, ⅜–1" thick, with irregular, narrow, rounded ridges; wood light brown, soft, close-grained.

Branches: Spreading to ascending, often arched; twigs yellowish-green to purplish-brown, slender, flexible, ridged; buds cinnamon brown, resinous, ¼–½" long.

Leaves: Stout, stiff, yellowish-green, evergreen needles ¾–1½" long, **straight or slightly twisted,** sharp-pointed, finely toothed, **bundled in 2s** with spreading tips and sheathed bases; needles persist 2–3 years.

Cones: Male and female cones on the same tree; male cones yellow, ½–¾" long, clustered at the base of new shoots; female cones yellowish-brown when mature, shiny, woody, usually **asymmetrical,** 1–3" long, **pointing toward branch tips,** mostly in 2s and 3s near branch tips; scales serotinous (glued shut with resin), their **tips thick, smooth or with a tiny spine;** seeds dark, ⅛" long with a pale, ⅜" wing, 2 per scale; seed cones mature in 2–3 years but most remain closed for many years or until fire.

Habitat: Dry, infertile, acidic, often sandy soils.

Origin: Native.

73

Tamarack usually survives about 150 years, with peak seed crops at 50–75 years of age. In cold, nutrient-poor environments, tamarack often becomes stunted and produces small needles and narrow-scaled cones. • Tamarack wood is not valued for lumber but has been used occasionally in rough construction and as poles, piers and railway ties and can also make beautiful paneling. • Tannin-rich tamarack bark was used traditionally for tanning leather. • In early fall, red squirrels strip off the cones and eat the seeds. Chipmunks, mice and red crossbills also gather the seeds. White-tailed deer browse on young shoots, and porcupines often kill tamarack trees by stripping off the outer bark to feed on the sweeter inner bark. • Tamarack is relatively free of serious infection by fungal diseases, but its foliage is sometimes damaged severely by larch sawfly (*Pristiphora erichsonii*). • **European larch (*L. decidua*** or *L. europaea*) shown in pink/dark green (species overlap) on the map, often planted in eastern North America as an ornamental or for forestry purposes, and it occasionally escapes cultivation near parent stands. It is readily distinguished by its large ($3/4$–$1^3/8$" long) cones, which have more than 30 finely hairy scales.

Also Called: American larch, hackmatack, eastern larch, Alaska larch.

Size and Shape: Coniferous trees 40–65' tall, roughly cone-shaped, irregular with age; roots shallow, wide-spreading.

Trunks: Usually straight, 12–24" in diameter; young bark gray, smooth, thin; mature bark light reddish-brown, with narrow, peeling scales; **newly exposed bark reddish-purple;** wood heavy, strong, durable.

Branches: Of 2 types: long, **slender, spreading branches** with scattered leaves, often gracefully curved; and **stubby, dwarf side-branches** (spur-branches) elongating slowly over many years; buds brown to dark red, hairless or ringed by hairs.

Leaves: Bright green, **soft, slender, deciduous needles** $3/4$–1" long; tightly spiraled in clusters of 10–20 or more at tips of stubby side-shoots; needles yellow when shed each autumn.

Cones: Male and female cones on the same tree; male cones small, yellow; female cones yellow-green or reddish when young, pale brown and not very woody when mature, $3/8$–$3/4$" **long,** on short, curved stalks at tips of leafless, stubby side-branches; **scales 10–20, stiff, hairless, longer than wide;** seeds light brown, $1/8$" long with a $1/4$" wing; seed cones mature in mid-August, soon shed seeds, often persist through the year.

Habitat: Usually cold, wet sites such as bogs and muskeg, but grows best on moist, well-drained upland sites.

Origin: Native.

The range of this small conifer extends north to the edge of the Arctic tundra and south barely into northeastern Illinois. In the far north, shallow roots allow black spruce to grow in the thin, seasonally thawed layer over permanently frozen ground. However, trees often tilt precariously and are susceptible to damage from high winds, flooding and fire. The buds open late as a safety measure against late spring frosts. • These trees live up to 100 years. Healthy trees are prolific seed producers from about 10 years of age, with good crops every other year. Cones can persist for many years in dense clusters on uppermost branches. Fire stimulates cones to open and shed seeds onto newly exposed soil. • When lower branches touch the ground, they often develop roots and send up shoots. This process, called "layering," produces small clumps of young trees around parent trees. In habitats where seed success is limited (e.g., cold, wet, acidic sites), layering is often the main means of regeneration. • Black spruce is used across North America for pulp and fuel. • Red squirrels nip the tips off cone-bearing branches to gather the cones and eat the seeds. This pruning can result in a dense mass of branches in the upper crown with a bare stretch of trunk immediately underneath.

Also Called: Bog spruce, swamp spruce, water spruce • *P. nigra, Abies mariana.*

Size and Shape: Coniferous trees, **columnar** and often stunted on poorly drained sites, cone-shaped and up to 50' tall on upland sites; **crowns dense, often club-shaped;** roots shallow.

Trunks: Straight, 4–12" in diameter; mature bark dark grayish-brown with thin, irregular scales; **newly exposed bark olive- or yellowish-green;** wood yellowish-white, soft, light.

Branches: Short, spreading to drooping, upturned at tips; **twigs dull orange- to yellowish-brown,** with peg-like, leaf-bearing bumps; **new twigs minutely reddish-hairy;** buds gray-brown, hairy, blunt, ⅛–¼" long, with **grayish, finely hairy, slender-pointed scales projecting beyond the tips.**

Leaves: Stiff, **straight, 4-sided, evergreen needles;** needles grayish-green, ¼–¾" **long,** short-stalked, spirally arranged, spreading in all directions, some curved upward; needles persist 7–10 years.

Cones: Male and female cones on the same tree; male cones red to yellow, about ½" long, numerous; female cones woody, dull grayish- to **purplish-brown,** rigid, ¾–1⅛" **long,** hanging on scaly, curved, **short stalks** near branch tips; scales thin, stiff, brittle, roughly toothed, close-fitting and firmly attached; seeds about ⅛" long with a ⅜–½" wing, 2 per scale; seed cones mature in first September, **shed seeds over 1–2 (up to 30) years** or quickly after fires.

Habitat: Cool, damp sites such as bogs.

Origin: Introduced from the northeastern U.S.

75

This spruce has 2 forms: the "brush" form, with bunched shoots typical of spruce trees; and the "comb" form, with sparser, upcurved branches from which smaller side branches hang in lines, like teeth on a comb. • Norway spruce is one of the most important timber trees in central and northern Europe. The timber, known as "whitewood" or "deal," is used in roofing, in house interiors and as a source of pulp. In Britain, Norway spruce is the traditional Christmas tree, and in Germany, turpentine is extracted from the trunks for use in tanning leather. • Norway spruce is widely planted as an ornamental tree and windbreak in temperate North America. It has also been cultivated in North America for Christmas tree purposes and has been used in many reforestation projects in eastern Canada and the northeastern U.S. The trees are hardy enough to survive in regions north of Lake Superior, but they are often stunted by winter frosts near their northern limit. • Plant breeders have developed more than 100 cultivars of Norway spruce, in many shapes and sizes, but only a few are commonly cultivated.

Also Called: Common spruce • *P. excelsa.*

Size and Shape: Coniferous trees 50–80' tall; crowns cone-shaped.

Trunks: Tall, 12–40" in diameter; young bark reddish-brown, smooth to shredding; mature bark dark purplish-brown with small, rounded scales; wood white, strong, fine-grained.

Branches: Drooping; twigs hairless, creamy green to **light orange-brown,** rough with small peg-like, leaf-bearing bumps; buds pale to reddish-brown, ¼–⅜" long, blunt, not resinous.

Leaves: Dark green, 4-sided, evergreen needles ½–1" long, **sharp-pointed;** spirally arranged but curved upward and forward; needles persist 5–7 years.

Cones: Male and female cones on the same tree; male cones red to yellow, ¾–1" long; female cones woody, grayish- or reddish-brown when mature, **cylindrical,** tapered at the tip, **4–7" long,** hanging near branch tips; scales thin, flat, tapered to a slightly toothed tip; seeds ⅛" long, long-winged, 2 behind each scale; seed cones drop in first autumn to winter.

Habitat: Varied, but prefers shaded or partially shaded sites with deep, rich, moist soils.

Origin: Introduced from northern and central Eurasia; occasionally grows wild near parent stands.

This tree is the most widespread and drought-resistant conifer in eastern North America. It is becoming increasingly common as more and more forests are removed or disturbed by human activities. Breeders have developed many cultivars for use in landscaping. • Eastern red-cedar lives about 200–350 years. Mature females produce some seed every year but bear large crops every 3 years or so. • The French name for this tree, *baton rouge*, or "red stick," was given to the capital city of Louisiana. • The beautiful, reddish wood resists decay, is easily worked and takes a fine finish. It has been used for interior trim, sills and posts. Its aromatic oils repel insects, so cedar chests have traditionally been used for storing woolens. Cedar oil, distilled from the wood, has been used as perfume. • Many birds use eastern red cedar for food and cover. Game birds such as quail, grouse, pheasant and wild turkey as well as many songbirds feed on the "berries." Seed-eating birds (especially cedar waxwings) readily disperse the seeds, so that trees often grow in isolated places along bird migration routes. • The name "red-cedar" is also used for the western tree *Thuja plicata*.

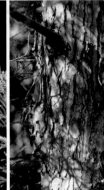

Also Called: Red-cedar juniper.

Size and Shape: Small, coniferous trees up to 35' (rarely to 100') tall; crowns conical to almost cylindrical, irregular with age, highly variable; roots very fibrous and deep.

Trunks: Irregular, often buttressed at base, 8–12" in diameter, branched to near base; bark light reddish-brown, ⅛–¼" thick, peeling in long, narrow strips; wood reddish, aromatic, brittle, weak, fine-grained.

Branches: Spreading to ascending; twigs light green to reddish-brown, slender, 4-sided.

Leaves: Evergreen, dark bluish-green (yellowish-brown in winter), of **2 types:** on mature branches, **flat-lying scales** ⅛" long, convex, **in overlapping pairs;** and on young branches, **sharp needles** ¼–½" long, spreading to erect; both leaf types sometimes on one branch; needles persist 5–6 years.

Cones: Male and female cones usually **on separate trees;** male cones yellowish, ⅛" long; **female cones berry-like, deep blue with a whitish bloom when mature,** ⅛–¼" long, firm, resinous, aromatic, not splitting open, short-stalked at twig tips; scales thick, fleshy, eventually fused; seeds 1–2 per "berry" (seed cone), light brown, grooved, pitted, about ⅛" long; **"berries" ripen first autumn.**

Habitat: Dry, open, rocky or sandy sites and abandoned fields.

Origin: Native.

Eastern white-cedar is threatened in Illinois, but common farther north in eastern Canada and the U.S. • Eastern white-cedar has maximum cone production at 75–150 years of age, with large crops every 3–5 years. • This attractive, versatile species provides dense growth in foundation plantings, hedges and windbreaks on both wet and dry sites. Many cultivars are available. • Although the wood is known for its resistance to rot, the trunks of living trees are often hollow from heart-rot. Eastern white-cedar wood is commonly used for construction in and near water, in cedar-strip canoes, boats, fence posts, shingles and dock posts. It also splits easily and has provided rails for many split-rail fences. • Red squirrels eat the buds in spring and later store cone-laden branches in winter caches. The plentiful seeds provide food for pine siskins, goldfinches, redpolls and other winter finches. These trees provide cover and shelter for white-tailed deer, who also favor the tender branch tips as winter food. In the north, however, reproduction has been virtually halted in the wild because of intensive browsing by white-tailed deer. • Native peoples used northern white-cedar to prevent scurvy and taught this practice to French settlers, giving rise to the name "arborvitae," or "tree of life."

Also Called: Eastern arborvitae, northern white-cedar, eastern thuja, swamp-cedar, tree-of-life, white arborvitae.

Size and Shape: Coniferous trees 35–50' tall; crowns steeple-shaped, compact and "neatly trimmed" (open-grown) to irregular (forest), often browsed to an even height by deer, producing a curtain-like effect; roots shallow, spreading.

Trunks: Often buttressed, knobby and/or curved, 12–24" in diameter; mature bark reddish-brown to gray, ¼–½" thick, shredding in narrow, flat strips; wood pale yellowish-brown, fragrant, lightweight, soft.

Branches: Short, wide-spreading, gradually upturned; twigs many, soft, forming **flat, fan-shaped sprays;** buds tiny, protected by leaves.

Leaves: Dull yellowish-green (sometimes bronze in winter), **scale-like,** evergreen; leaves near branch tips **about ⅛" long, gland-dotted,** overlapping, **opposite, in 4 longitudinal rows** with side leaves folded lengthwise and upper/lower leaves flattened; leaves on older branches lance-shaped, about ¼" long, glandless; needles persist 1–2 years.

Cones: Male and female cones on the same tree; male cones yellowish, ¹⁄₁₆" long; female cones dry, pale red-brown, ¼–½" long, upright at branch tips; **scales in 4–6 overlapping pairs,** middle ones producing 2–3 seeds; seeds light brown, about ⅛" long, with 2 narrow wings about ½ as long as the body; seed cones produced in April–May, release seeds that autumn, drop over several months.

Habitat: Swampy ground to dry limestone outcrops; prefers cool, humid sites with calcium-rich soils.

Origin: Native.

S outhern bald-cypress is the state tree of Louisiana and a universal symbol of the southern swamp. It provides important food and shelter for many animals, especially geese, ducks and other waterfowl. • These majestic trees are usually slow-growing, but in their native swamps, they can live for over 1000 years—the oldest trees in eastern North America. However, bald-cypress can be very difficult to age because of its false growth rings. • Bald-cypress is a very attractive ornamental tree in parks and large gardens, especially around ponds and lakes. These tall trees are moderately shade tolerant and extremely wind-firm, and can be grown successfully as far north as southern Canada. • The durable, easily worked wood is very resistant to decay. A natural preservative called cypressene builds up in the heartwood over many decades, making the wood very resistant to decay once it has aged for a century or two. Despite this, most old trees

are damaged or hollow. • Bald-cypress wood has been used to make many different items, including barrels, caskets, shingles, railroad ties and bridge beams. • The drainage of hundreds of acres of swamp coupled with overly zealous logging has led to a decline in bald-cypress populations. Fortunately, a few large stands still remain in parks and forest reserves.

Size and Shape: Coniferous trees 65–130' tall; crowns irregular with age; roots shallow, spreading, in water developing emergent cone-shaped "cypress knees" up to 14' tall and 1' thick.

Trunks: Tapered, fluted to conspicuously **buttressed at the base,** about 3–5' wide; **bark light red-brown, fibrous, peeling** in long strips; wood hard, straight-grained, durable.

Branches: Short, often wide-spreading with **drooping tips,** alternate, dimorphic (some persisting, others shed with leaves); leafy twigs horizontal, flexible; buds tiny, spherical.

Leaves: Alternate, **deciduous needles,** soft, **flat,** yellow-green, ⅜–⅝" long, in 2 opposite rows on small, leaf-bearing shoots, ⅜" long and scale-like on larger, fertile branches; leaves dull orange in late autumn, **leaf-bearing branches drop with leaves attached,** other leaves dropping singly.

Cones: Male and female cones on same tree; male cones, tiny, in drooping, branched clusters (panicles) ⅜–⅝" long at branch tips, form in late autumn, shed pollen in April; **female cones like tiny soccer balls,** ⅝–1⅜" across, leathery green and wrinkled at first, brown and woody when mature; seeds brown, resinous, 2 per scale; female cones 1 to several, hanging on short stalks near year-old branch tips, appear in March–April, mature and disintegrate in October–December.

Habitat: Swamps and edges of rivers and lakes.

Origin: Native.

79

Tamarisks are easily recognized as a group, but species classification is complex and often controversial. Of the deciduous tamarisks introduced to North America, trees with 5-parted flowers belong to a complex of several salt-cedar species (generally called *T. ramosissima*). Trees with 4-parted flowers (the only ones growing wild in Illinois) are *T. parviflora*. • These hardy, attractive shrubs have been widely planted as ornamentals for their unusual foliage and springtime haze of profuse flowers. Tamarisks are also hardy as windbreaks and in erosion control. They are relatively long-lived, spreading rapidly via massive quantities of seeds and sprouting stem fragments. Once established, they tolerate drought and saline soils (though small-flower tamarisk is less salt tolerant). Such hardy, prolific trees can become aggressive invaders, especially where human activities have altered flooding, salinity, soil texture and vegetation. In the western states, up to one million acres have been invaded by tamarisk. Tamarisk escapes only occasionally in Illinois, but it should be carefully monitored. • Many species (not *T. parviflora*) exude sugary sap when punctured by insects. This sweet gum is believed to be the Biblical manna. It can be gathered by shaking branches over sheets and is used as a sweetener.

Also Called: French tamarisk, salt-cedar • *T. gallica.*

Size and Shape: Tall shrubs or small trees 10–20' tall; crowns broad to sprawling; deep taproot.

Trunks: Clumped, slender; mature bark brown to dark purplish with horizontal pores (lenticels).

Branches: Few, arching, twiggy, **feathery** in appearance; **twigs purple, as fine as thread and very wiry,** completely covered by scale-like leaves.

Leaves: Alternate, deciduous, scale-like, lance-shaped, about ⅛" long, with thin, membranous edges, **overlapping, sheathing,** forming feathery sprays; leaves faded green to yellow in fall.

Flowers: Pale pink, bisexual, tiny; 4-parted (4 sepals, 4 petals, 4 stamens); petals separate, about 1⁄16" long, often persistent on fruits; ovaries single, with the stamens, nectary disc, petals and sepals attached at the base; flowers in enormous numbers, borne in elongated clusters (racemes) ¾–2" long, **grouped in feathery, branched clusters** (panicles), appear in early May–early June (may be found at any time of year in some regions).

Fruits: Cone-shaped capsules, about ⅛" long, splitting into 3–4 parts (valves), fairly inconspicuous; seeds numerous, tiny, **tipped with a tuft of tiny, 1-celled hairs;** capsules faded green to slightly yellow in autumn.

Habitat: Low areas near lakes, rivers, and wetlands.

Origin: Introduced from the northeastern Mediterranean region.

Alternate
Broad
Leaves

This large, fast-growing, attractive tree is occasionally used in landscaping well outside its natural range. It needs plenty of open space to flourish. • Tulip-tree lives about 150 years and usually begins producing flowers and seed when it is 15–20 years old. • Tulip-tree is a valuable hardwood timber tree in the U.S. The easily worked wood has been used for interior finishing, cabinet making, construction, pulp and paper; and for making furniture, musical instruments and plywood. • Native peoples used the tall, straight trunks to make large canoes, some capable of carrying 20 people or more, and the sharp-tasting roots to treat rheumatism and fevers. • Bees gather considerable amounts of nectar from the large flowers. Quail, finches, cardinals, rabbits, red squirrels, gray squirrels, mice and deer eat the abundant seeds. White-tailed deer and rabbits browse on saplings and young trees. • This massive hardwood is sometimes called "Apollo-of-the-woods." Its flowers resemble those of tulips, hence the common name "tulip-tree" and the scientific name *Liriodendron*, from the Greek *leirion*, "lily," and *dendron*, "tree." The specific epithet *tulipifera* means "tulip-bearing."

Also Called: Tulip-poplar, yellow-poplar, tulip-magnolia, whitewood, Apollo-of-the-woods.

Size and Shape: Trees 50–115' tall; crown compact, cone-shaped; roots deep, spreading.

Trunks: Tall, straight, 24–48" in diameter, ⅔ or more branch-free; young bark with conspicuous, white vertical pores (lenticels); mature bark ash gray to brown, with intersecting, rounded ridges; wood pale yellow, fine-grained, lightweight.

Branches: Stout; twigs smooth, brittle; **buds dark red, flat, duckbill-shaped,** with 2 scales meeting at the edges, **about ½" long** at twig tips (smaller below), powdery.

Leaves: Alternate, simple, deciduous; blades bright green above, paler beneath, **2¾–6" long,** with **squared, notched tips** and 2–3-lobed sides; stalks often longer than blades; stipules large (in spring), leaving a thin scar encircling the twig; leaves yellow in autumn.

Flowers: Showy, tulip-shaped, 1½–2" wide, single at branch tips, bisexual; petals 6, **pale greenish-yellow with orange bases,** erect, each 1½–2⅜" long and ¾–1⅛" wide; sepals 3, large, green; stamens many, flattened; carpels pale yellow, numerous, in a "cone" at the flower's center; flowers in May–June (after leaves expand).

Fruits: Dry, **green to straw-colored,** long-winged, 1–2-seeded nutlets (samaras), 1⅛–2" long, overlapping in **cone-like clusters 2–3" long;** most fruits drop in autumn, leaving erect central stalks at branch tips.

Habitat: Sheltered woods with rich, moist but well-drained soils.

Origin: Native.

Cucumber-tree is the only magnolia that grows wild in Illinois and is the largest, hardiest and most widespread magnolia in North America. This shade-intolerant, fast-growing tree can live 125–150 years, but may not flower until it is 25–30 years old. Once mature, cucumber-trees produce seed each year, with good crops every 3–5 years. • Magnolia wood is fairly durable and has been used to make boxes, crates, cabinets, inexpensive furniture and paneling. Otherwise, cucumber-tree has little economic importance. Its yellow-green blooms are relatively inconspicuous, and though showier cultivars have been developed, they are planted only occasionally. The relatively hardy roots provide stocks for grafting fragile exotic magnolias that would otherwise die in winter. Most common orna-

mentals, including **saucer magnolia (*M.* x *soulangiana*)** and **star magnolia (*M. stellata*)**, come from Asia. • Many birds and rodents eat magnolia seeds. • The generic name *Magnolia* commemorates Pierre Magnol (1638–1715), director of the botanical garden in Montpellier, France. The common name reflects a fancied resemblance between the green fruit clusters and a small cucumber.

Photo, bottom right: *M. stellata*

Also Called: Cucumber magnolia, pointed-leaved magnolia.

Size and Shape: Trees to 80' tall, broadly cone-shaped.

Trunks: Straight, up to 2½' in diameter; mature bark dark gray-brown, with narrow ridges, **aromatic;** wood pale, lightweight, close-grained.

Branches: Spreading or drooping to ascending; twigs brittle, hairless, **aromatic; buds dark red, 1-scaled, silvery-hairy,** ⅝–¾" long at twig tips (smaller below).

Leaves: Alternate, simple, deciduous; blades dark green, shiny above, paler and finely hairy beneath, **smooth-edged, prominently veined, abruptly pointed, ⅜–1" long;** stalks flattened, 1–1½" long; stipule scars encircling twigs; leaf scars horseshoe-shaped, 5–9-dotted; leaves yellow in autumn.

Flowers: Greenish-yellow, cupped, 2–3" long, odorless, bisexual; petals 6, erect, 1⅛–3⅛" long, ¾–1⅛" wide; sepals 3, petal-like, bending backward; stamens many, flattened; carpels pale yellow, spirally attached in a cone-like structure at the flower center; **flowers single at branch tips,** in April–May (as leaves expand).

Fruits: Leathery, fleshy pods (follicles), **shiny, dark red,** in erect, **cone-like clusters 2–3½" long;** seeds 1–2 per follicle, shiny, reddish-orange, ⅜–½" long; follicles open in late summer, seeds hang on white threads.

Habitat: Moist to wet, protected sites with deep, rich soils.

Origin: Native.

83

This small tree is occasionally planted for its attractive form, large leaves, unusual (though fetid) flowers and juicy fruits. Pawpaw thrives in rich, moist soils along rivers and at the edges of wetlands. It often forms dense colonies from suckers and is easily propagated from root cuttings.
• Native peoples once gathered the fleshy, edible fruits, but pawpaws are seldom eaten today. The flavor varies greatly from site to site, deteriorating gradually from south to north. It has been likened to that of bananas, pineapples, apples, custard, cream and even eau-de-cologne and turpentine. Pawpaws with orange flesh are said to be more flavorful than yellow-fleshed varieties. • Early settlers used the ripe pulp for making a yellow dye.
• The dark color and foul fragrance of the flowers suggest that flies are its chief pollinators. • Ripe pawpaw fruits can be hard to find, because many animals, including raccoons, opossums, squirrels, bears and wild turkeys, enjoy the sweet, juicy flesh.
• The generic name *Asimina* was taken from a Native name for pawpaw, *assimin*. The specific epithet *triloba* means "3-lobed" and refers to the flower parts, which are grouped in 3s.

Also Called: Common pawpaw, false banana, pawpaw custard-apple, tall pawpaw.

Size and Shape: Large shrubs or small trees 10–25' tall; crowns broad; spreading roots sprout to form colonies.

Trunks: Single, short, 2–8" in diameter; mature bark blotched, thin, with warty bumps; wood pale yellow, often red- or brown-streaked, lightweight, soft.

Branches: Straight, spreading; twigs rusty-hairy when young, slender, zigzagged; pith banded (in long-section); **buds reddish-hairy, lacking scales, flattened,** about ⅛" long; tip bud ¼–⅜" long.

Leaves: Alternate, simple, deciduous; **blades 4–12" long, hanging near branch tips,** green above, paler with reddish-brown veins beneath, foul-smelling when crushed, **widest toward tips, tapered to bases, with prominent veins looped to adjacent veins at their tips; stalks ¼–¾" long,** grooved; leaf scars crescent-shaped around a bud.

Flowers: Reddish-purple or maroon to pale greenish-yellow, fetid-smelling, 1⅛–1½" across, broadly bell-shaped, single or in small clusters, bisexual; petals 6 (3 large, 3 small), veiny; sepals 3; flowers in May–June (before or as leaves expand).

Fruits: Large **berries 1½–6" long,** yellowish at first, **dark brown with soft, yellow to orange flesh when ripe,** fragrant, cylindrical to pear-shaped, hanging along year-old twigs; **seeds bean-like,** dark brown, flattened, ½–1⅛" long, several in 1–2 rows; fruits mature in September–October.

Habitat: Moist woodlands and wooded slopes.

Origin: Native.

The light, brittle wood of sassafras has no commercial value, but the bark produces an orange dye, and the roots yield aromatic "oil of sassafras," which has been used as a fragrance in soaps and perfumes. • Sassafras bark was traditionally used to make a fragrant, invigorating tea and to flavor root beer. It was also added to some patent medicines. Sassafras roots were once believed to have great healing powers, but these claims proved false. **Caution:** Dried sassafras bark, available in health-food and gourmet stores, should be used with extreme caution, if at all. It contains safrole, a carcinogenic compound banned for use in foods in the U.S. and Canada.

• This moderately fast-growing tree can flower after only 10 years, with good seed crops every 2–3 years. Sassafras often forms dense colonies by sending up new shoots (suckers) from underground runners. Such vegetative reproduction, as well as seed dispersal (usually by birds), allows sassafras to quickly colonize disturbed habitats such as abandoned fields. • Wild turkeys, bobwhites, squirrels, black bears and foxes occasionally feed on the fruits of sassafras.

Also Called: White sassafras, red sassafras, cinnamon-wood, greenstick, mitten-tree.

Size and Shape: Large shrubs or small to medium trees 15–50' tall; crowns cylindrical, flat-topped; roots wide-spreading.

Trunks: Branched from near base, 8–24" in diameter, **zigzagged; bark fragrant, dark brown, with corky ridges;** wood fragrant, orange-brown to yellow, soft, light, coarse-grained, weak.

Branches: Crooked, wide-spreading with **upturned tips,** corky-ridged; twigs often glaucous or light green, brittle, often with **side-shoots longer than branch tips;** buds greenish, plump, several-scaled, ¼–½" long at twig tips (smaller below).

Leaves: Alternate, simple, deciduous, fragrant; blades bright green, **ovate or broadly 2- or 3-lobed** (all 3 shapes usually present), **3–8" long,** 2–4" wide; **leaves yellow to pink or red in autumn.**

Flowers: Greenish-yellow, about ¼" across, inconspicuous; unisexual with male and female flowers usually on separate trees; tepals 6; **flowers in loose, stalked clusters** at the base of new shoots, in April–May (with leaves).

Fruits: Dark blue, berry-like drupes, ⅜–½" across, each sitting in a bright red cup at the tip of a **club-shaped, red, 1⅜–1½" long stalk;** seeds single, in large, brown stones; drupes ripen September–October.

Habitat: Dry to moderately moist, open sites in woods, thickets and along roads.

Origin: Native.

85

A ll parts of spicebush, especially the bark and berries, have an agreeable spicy fragrance and flavor. During the Revolutionary War (1775–83), the fruits were dried and powdered as a substitute for allspice, which had previously been imported from England. Similarly, people in the blockaded South used spicebush leaves and twigs as a substitute for foreign teas during the Civil War (1861–65). In spring, the flowers added extra sweetness. • Pioneers used the aromatic oil in liniments for treating bruises, sore muscles, aching joints and neuralgia. In the 1800s, spicebush leaves and berries were sold as a stimulant and tonic for treating fevers, colds, coughs, indigestion and general aches and pains, as well as for expelling intestinal worms. Although there is little research to validate medicinal claims, bark extracts have been shown to inhibit *Candida albicans* (the yeast-like fungus that causes thrush and yeast infections). • The specific epithet *benzoin* refers to the plant's distinctive aroma, which is similar to the vanilla-like fragrance of benzoin tree (*Styrax benzoin*), an Asian plant that was the major source of benzoin. • This hardy native is an excellent ornamental, valued for its showy, early spring flowers, yellow autumn leaves and bright red "berries." • Caterpillars of the promethea moth (*Callosamia promethea*) and the green-clouded swallowtail (*Pterourus troilus*) feed on spicebush and sassafras (p. 85) leaves.

Also Called: Benzoin tree, wild-allspice, spicewood, fever-bush, snap-bush, Benjamin-bush • *Benzoin aestivale.*

Size and Shape: Tall, **aromatic shrubs** up to 15' tall; crowns round to flat-topped, open; roots shallow.

Trunks: Several, clumped, up to 3" in diameter; bark thin.

Branches: Numerous, arched; twigs slender, brittle, aromatic, green to olive brown, with pale, corky pores (lenticels); buds small, green, egg-shaped, placed one above another at joints, absent at branch tips; flower bud clusters are conspicuous in fall and winter.

Leaves: Alternate, simple, deciduous, variable in size, usually largest at branch tips; blades light green above, paler beneath, thin, hairless, with prominent veins, **ovate to elliptical, usually broadest above the middle,** 2–6" long, pointed, tapered to a wedge-shaped base, **smooth-edged;** stalks ¼–¾" long; leaves yellow in autumn.

Flowers: Honey yellow, fragrant, ¼–⅜" across, with **male and female flowers on separate trees;** tepals 6, soon shed; flowers numerous, on short stalks in **dense, ¾" wide clusters** at joints on previous year's twigs, in March–May (before leaves expand).

Fruits: Bright red, spicy-smelling, berry-like drupes, football-shaped, ¼–½" long; seeds single, in small stones; drupes **in small, compact clusters,** mature September–November.

Habitat: Rich, moist to wet woods.

Origin: Native.

A merican sycamore lives up to 250 years. This fast-growing tree is among the largest in the eastern deciduous forest. It can reach 65–80' in height by 20 years of age and may eventually exceed 115'. Trunks can reach 15' in diameter. • American sycamore wood has been used for cabinet making, furniture, boxes, interior trim and butchers' chopping blocks. Early French settlers hollowed out large sycamore trunks to make barges capable of carrying several tons of freight. • The small, stiffly hairy seeds are carried to new sites by wind and water. American sycamore is moderately shade-tolerant, but the seeds require light to germinate. • Seed-eating birds seldom feed on sycamore seeds, but some small rodents gather them. • American sycamore is sometimes planted as an ornamental shade tree, often outside its natural range. However, **London planetree (*P.* x *acerifolia***, probably a hybrid of *P. occidentalis* and *P. orientalis*) is more widely used in cities because it tolerates pollution and can grow with limited root space. London planetree is distinguished by its more deeply lobed leaves and by its paired flower and fruit clusters. It has not yet been found growing wild in Illinois.

Also Called: Buttonwood, buttonball-tree, American plane-tree.

Size and Shape: Trees 60–115' tall; crowns irregular, with **massive, crooked branches;** roots wide-spreading.

Trunks: Straight, 40–80" in diameter; **bark mottled,** reddish-brown, **jigsaw-like scales flaking off to expose pale inner bark;** wood light reddish-brown, hard, coarse-grained, weak.

Branches: Stout, spreading; twigs slender, zigzagged; buds shiny reddish-brown, ¼–⅜" **long,** 1-scaled, none at twig tips, covered by leaf stalk bases.

Leaves: Alternate, simple, deciduous; **blades 4–8" long, slightly wider and bright green above,** paler beneath, hairless (except lower veins), maple leaf–like, **shallowly 3–5-lobed,** coarsely and irregularly toothed; stipules prominent in spring, stipule scars encircling twigs; leaf scars narrow, encircling buds; **leaves orange to orange-brown in autumn.**

Flowers: Tiny, in dense heads; unisexual with **male and female flower clusters on separate**

branchlets of same tree; male flowers yellowish-green, in "balls" ¼–⅜" across, along 2nd-year twigs; female flowers dark red, in "balls" ⅜–½" across, near older twig tips; flowers in May (with leaves).

Fruits: Yellowish, seed-like achenes about ⅜" long, brownish-hairy, club-shaped, in **solitary "balls" ¾–1⅜" across, on slender stalks** 2¾–6" **long;** fruits mature by October and break apart slowly, some remaining through winter.

Habitat: Low woods in wet areas such as floodplains and lakeshores.

Origin: Native.

This slow-growing shrub is sometimes used in landscaping because of its showy, fragrant flowers and interesting, persistent fruits. Unlike most other trees and shrubs, witch-hazel blooms in autumn. • Witch-hazel oil, extracted from leaves, twigs and bark, is said to have astringent and sedative properties and to stop bleeding. This volatile oil has been used in liniments, medicines, eyewashes, aftershave lotions and salves for soothing insect bites, burns and poison ivy rashes. • Although the trunks are too small to provide lumber, evenly forked witch-hazel branches have been used as divining rods for locating underground water and minerals. • The name "witch-hazel," suggesting magical powers, probably originated with the divining powers attributed to the branches. The "hazel" in the name refers to the similarities between witch-hazel and the true hazels of the genus *Corylus* (p. 139). The name "snapping-hazel" alludes to the sound the capsules make when they shoot seeds up to 40' from the parent shrub. "Spotted-alder" and "striped-alder" indicate that the bark resembles that of alders (pp. 143–44).

Also Called: American witchhazel, snapping-hazel, spotted-alder, striped-alder, winterbloom • *H. macrophylla*.

Size and Shape: Shrubby trees or large, spreading shrubs 12–25' tall; crowns broad, rounded.

Trunks: Usually **2 or more,** crooked, 2–4" in diameter; bark light brown or grayish, often mottled, thin, with horizontal pores (lenticels); inner bark reddish-purple; wood light brown, hard, heavy.

Branches: Slender; twigs zigzagged; **buds flattened, stalked,** curved, with **dense reddish-** to yellowish-brown hairs, lacking scales, ⅜–½" long at twig tips (smaller below).

Leaves: Simple, alternate, deciduous; blades 2⅜–6" long, dark green above, paler beneath, hairless (except lower veins), with **asymmetrical bases, margins wavy-scalloped,** sometimes coarsely toothed, with **5–7 straight, parallel, ascending veins per side;** leaves yellow in autumn.

Flowers: Fragrant, small but showy, bisexual; **petals 4, bright yellow, twisted, ribbon-like,** ½–¾" **long;** sepals 4, orange-brown, hairy; **in flowers in 3s** along twigs, in **October–November** (as or after leaves fall).

Fruits: Short, thick, 2-beaked capsules ⅜–½" long, light brown and **woody when mature;** seeds 2 per capsule, black, shiny, ¼–⅜" long; capsules mature the following summer and shoot seeds from capsule tips; **empty capsules often persist** several years.

Habitat: Moist, shady woods with deep, rich soil to drier, more open woodlands.

Origin: Native.

Sweetgum is best known for its fragrant resin, which is called American storax, copal-balsam and copalm. This valuable commodity has been used for centuries in the manufacture of soaps, drugs and adhesives, as flavoring for soft drinks, tobacco, candy and chewing gum and as scent in perfumes. The resinous sap was traditionally collected each spring from cuts in the bark. The gum was applied directly or used in decoctions, ointments and salves to treat piles, itching, ringworm and chest ailments. The sap/gum (in spring), leaves (in summer) and bark (in winter) have been used in remedies for coughs and diarrhea. • Dried, sweet-flavored lumps of gum can be chewed for pleasure and are said to be superior to commercial chewing gum. • Sweetgum is commercially important as a source of hardwood in the southeastern U.S. The handsome wood, known as "satin walnut," takes an excellent finish and is used as a veneer for furniture and wall panels, as lumber and for making fur niture and containers. • Sweetgum is sometimes planted as a shade tree and is valued for its attractive, symmetrical shape and beautiful red to orange autumn leaves. • It is said that the Aztec emperor Montezuma served after-dinner cigarettes of tobacco flavored with sweetgum to the Spanish explorer Hernando Cortez.

Also Called: Red-gum.

Size and Shape: Trees 80–115' tall with **fragrant, resinous sap;** crowns small, usually pyramidal; roots shallow, spreading.

Trunks: Straight, long, 2–4' in diameter, often buttressed; bark gray-brown, deeply furrowed, with narrow, rounded ridges; wood dark reddish-brown, heavy, hard, not strong.

Branches: Slender, spreading; twigs green to reddish brown, hairless with age, usually developing **irregular, corky wings** in the 2nd year; buds shiny reddish-brown, broad-based, pointed, ¼–½" long at branch tips.

Leaves: Alternate, simple, deciduous; blades bright green, approximately **star-shaped, deeply cut into 5–7 triangular, slender-pointed lobes,** 4–8" wide**, finely sharp-toothed;** stalks equaling the blade; leaves brilliant orange to red or purplish in autumn.

Flowers: Tiny, green, lacking petals; unisexual with **male and female flowers on the same tree;** male flowers with many stamens, forming egg-shaped heads in erect, elongating, 2–4" clusters (racemes) at branch tips; female flowers numerous with 2 long styles ringed with sterile stamens, in 1–2 long-stalked, ½" heads near the base of male clusters; flowers in April–May (with the leaves).

Fruits: Light brown, 1–1½" in wide, round heads, aggregates of many capsules, **spiny with woody beaks (2 per capsule);** seeds 0–4 per capsule, ⁵⁄₁₆–½" long, flattened, narrowly wing-tipped; mature in September–November, persist through winter.

Habitat: Low, moist to wet woods.

Origin: Native.

89

Key to Genera in the Elm Family (Ulmaceae)

1a   Leaf blades with 3 main veins at the base; fruits berry-like drupes with thin flesh; branches with chambered pith . . . . ***Celtis*, hackberry** (key to species, see below)

1b   Leaf blades with many conspicuous, pinnate veins 2

2a   Fruits thin, winged samaras; leaves edged with sharp, usually double teeth
   . . . . ***Ulmus*, elm** (key to species, see below)

2b   Fruits unusual, nut-like drupes covered with finger-like projections; leaves edged with blunt, gland-tipped, single teeth. . . . . ***Planera*, planertree** (p. 96)

Key to the Hackberries (Genus *Celtis*)

1a   Leaves distinctly toothed to well below midblade; fruit stalks longer than adjacent leaf stalks; stones to 3/8" long, conspicuously pitted
   . . . . ***C. occidentalis*, common hackberry** (p. 97)

1b   Leaves smooth-edged or with a few scattered teeth above midblade; fruit stalks equal to or slightly shorter than adjacent leaf stalks; stones to 1/4" long, obscurely shallow-pitted. . . 2

2a   Leaves ovate, more than 1/2 as wide as long, tipped with a short, tapered point; style persisting on fruit . . . . ***C. tenuifolia*, dwarf hackberry** (p. 97)

2b   Leaves lance-shaped, less than 1/2 as wide as long, tipped with a slender, long-tapered point; style soon shed . . . . ***C. laevigata*, sugarberry** (p. 98)

Key to the Elms (Genus *Ulmus*)

1a   Flowers and fruits appearing in autumn, after the leaves; sepals separate
   . . . . ***U. serotina*, September elm** (p. 95)

1b   Flowers and fruits appearing in spring, before the leaves; sepals fused at the base to form a bell-shaped calyx 2

2a   Leaves small (3/4–23/4" long), single-toothed, with mostly symmetrical bases
   . . . . ***U. pumila*, Siberian elm** (p. 93)

2b   Leaves usually larger (often >23/4" long), double-toothed, with asymmetrical bases . . . 3

3a   Samaras fringed with hairs; leaves somewhat smooth on the upper surface, mostly with more than 15 pairs of veins 4

3b   Samaras not fringed with hairs; leaves very rough on the upper surface, mostly with 15 or fewer pairs of veins 6

4a   Flowers/fruits in tassel-like clusters; samara wings hairless (except for fringe along the edges) . . . . ***U. americana*, American elm** (p. 91)

4b   Flowers/fruits in elongated, branched clusters; samara wings hairy 5

5a   Mature leaves small (11/8–23/4" long); flower/fruit clusters short (3/8" long) with small (3/8") fruits. . . . . ***U. alata*, winged elm** (p. 95)

5b   Mature leaves larger (2–51/2" long); flower/fruit clusters 3/4–11/2" long with large (5/8–3/4") fruits. . . . . ***U. thomasii*, rock elm** (p. 94)

6a   Leaves mostly with 12 pairs of side veins; samaras hairless, 3/8–5/8" wide, with the notch at the tip extending almost to the seedcase . . . . ***U. procera*, English elm** (p. 92)

6b   Leaves mostly with 15 pairs of side veins; samaras either hairy or larger
   . . . . ***U. rubra*, slippery elm** (p. 92)

This graceful tree was common in parks and along roads and fence lines until Dutch elm disease decimated stands across eastern North America. This plague, caused by the fungi *Ophiostoma ulmi* and *O. novoulmi*, arrived in the North America around 1930 in infected logs. American Elm proved particularly susceptible, and by the 1950s, millions of elms had died. The fungal spores are carried from tree to tree by small beetles (*Scolytus scolytus* and *Hylurgopinus rufipes*). As the fungus grows, it blocks the flow of water in the trunk, killing the tree within a few months. Many methods have been tested to control Dutch elm disease, but most have proven either ineffective or too expensive and labor intensive. Attempts to breed disease-resistant trees have had consid-

erable success, and clones of these trees are available for landscaping. • Elm wood is tough and flexible and keeps well in water, so it has been used to make wharves, boat frames, wheel hubs and spokes, hockey sticks, tool handles, furniture and paneling. Because it is relatively odorless, the wood was used to make crates and barrels for cheeses, fruits and vegetables.

Also Called: White elm, gray elm, soft elm, swamp elm, water elm.

Size and Shape: Stately trees 65–100' tall; fan-, umbrella- or **vase-shaped;** crowns broadly rounded.

Trunks: Typically forked below crown and buttressed at base, 20–48" in diameter; bark grayish, with coarse, oblique ridges of corky, **alternating layers of thin, pale scales and thicker, dark scales;** wood pale yellowish-brown, hard, heavy, strong.

Branches: Gracefully arched, often weeping; twigs zigzagged, rarely corky-winged; **buds 6–9-scaled,** reddish-brown, slightly hairy, **lying flat in 2 rows,** absent at twig tips, but a side-bud near the tip may appear terminal (pseudoterminal bud).

Leaves: Alternate, simple, deciduous, **in 2 vertical rows; blades 4–6" long, thick,** usually **slightly rough above, oval,** abruptly pointed, with **rounded, asymmetrical bases;** veins 30–40, **prominent, straight,** ending in sharp teeth, **0–3 veins with forks;** leaves yellow in autumn.

Flowers: Small, bisexual; petals absent; sepals tiny, 6–9; anthers red; pistil single, tiny; flowers hanging in **tassel-like clusters** along year-old twigs in March–April (before leaves).

Fruits: Dry, oval, flat-winged nutlets (samaras) ¼–½" long, with a membranous wing around a seedcase, deeply notched at the tip, hairy along margins only, hanging on slender stalks in clusters; samaras drop in May (before leaves expand fully).

Habitat: Generally in moist bottomlands and protected slopes; also in disturbed, open sites such as pastures and roadsides.

Origin: Native.

91

Slippery elm is a moderately fast-growing species with a life span of about 200 years. Young trees usually start to flower at 15–20 years and produce good seed crops every 2–4 years. • Slippery elm wood is sometimes sold as "American elm" but is considered inferior. It has been used to make furniture, paneling, boxes and crates. • Some tribes used slippery elm bark to cover canoe shells when birch bark was unavailable. Early adventurers chewed the slippery inner bark to relieve thirst. The inner bark was also commonly used in traditional medicine. It was boiled, dried and then ground into a powder, which was used in teas for treating fevers, sore throats and various urinary-tract problems. Poultices of the fresh inner bark were sometimes applied to inflammations. • Slippery elm seeds provide food for finches and grouse, as well as for chipmunks, squirrels and other small rodents. White-tailed deer and rabbits sometimes browse the twigs. • This elm is also susceptible to Dutch elm disease, and some slippery elm trees die each year from infection. • The specific epithet *rubra* means "red" and describes the reddish-brown bark and buds.

Also Called: Red elm, budded elm, moose elm, slippery-barked elm, soft elm, sweet elm • *U. fulva.*

Size and Shape: Trees 50–80' tall; somewhat umbrella-shaped; crowns broad, flat-topped; roots wide-spreading.

Trunks: Straight, long, forked below the crown, 12–24" in diameter; bark reddish-brown, ¾–1" thick, with irregular ridges of **uniformly brown, corky layers; inner bark fragrant, slimy;** wood reddish-brown, hard, heavy.

Branches: Gradually spreading to arched; **twigs hairy, not corky,** often zigzagged; **buds dark brown, rusty-hairy, blunt,** about ¼" long, in 2 rows, absent at twig tips.

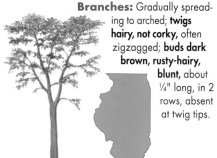

Leaves: Alternate, simple, deciduous; blades 4–8" long, **fragrant, thick,** dark green and **very rough above,** paler beneath, hairy on both sides, abruptly **long-pointed,** with sharp double teeth and **rounded, asymmetrical bases; veins prominent, straight, forked near** leaf edge; **leaf stalks ¼–⅜" long,** hairy; leaves yellow in autumn.

Flowers: Small, bisexual (usually); petals absent; sepals tiny, 5–9, fused in a bell-shaped calyx; anthers dark red, 5–9; pistil single with 2 red stigmas; short-stalked, in **dense, tassel-like clusters** on year-old twigs; flowers in March–April **(before leaves expand).**

Fruits: Dry, flat, green, winged nutlets (samaras) ⅜–½" long, with a membranous wing surrounding each seedcase, **rusty-hairy on seedcases only (not on wings), shallowly notched at tips,** in **tight clusters;** samaras drop in May (before leaves expand fully).

Habitat: Usually in moist, wooded sites; also in open, disturbed areas.

Origin: Native.

This fast-growing, moderately long-lived tree was introduced to North America from eastern Asia in the 1860s and now grows wild in most states and provinces across the continent. These hardy trees are capable of surviving extreme cold and long summer droughts, so they were often planted as windbreaks on the Great Plains. Siberian elm is also highly resistant to Dutch elm disease. On the negative side, these trees shed dead branches throughout the year, and their limbs snap easily under the weight of ice or heavy snow. Also, Siberian elms are highly susceptible to attacks from elm leaf beetles (*Pyrrhalta luteola*).

• This tree is readily identified by its small (1$\frac{1}{8}$–2$\frac{3}{4}$"), single-toothed, almost symmetrical leaves.

• Siberian elm is sometimes erroneously called Chinese elm, but that name correctly applies to another Asian species, *U. parvifolia*. The leaves of these 2 species are somewhat similar, but those of Chinese elm are almost evergreen and have more rounded teeth.

Also, Chinese elm produces flowers and fruits in autumn (rather than spring) and has relatively smooth (not furrowed), platy bark. Chinese elm is cultivated but not naturalized to Illinois. • Another introduced species, **English elm** (*U. procera*, also called *U. campestris*), shown in dark green (species overlap) on the map, has slender, pale brown, densely hairy twigs with very dark, round to ovoid buds and its rough textured, strongly asymmetrical leaves are 2$\frac{1}{4}$" to 3$\frac{1}{2}$" long. These trees lack the fragrant, slippery inner bark found in many native elms.

Also Called: Chinese elm (in error)
• *U. campestris*.

Size and Shape: Shrubby trees 35–80' tall; crowns irregular, domed; roots spreading.

Trunks: Short, 12–24" in diameter; **bark dark gray,** rough, deeply fissured between broad, interlacing ridges, **inner layers orange,** outer layers solid brown; wood hard, heavy.

Branches: Large, **wide-spreading,** often dead within the crown; **twigs brittle,** slender, green to gray, zigzagged; buds $\frac{1}{16}$–$\frac{1}{8}$" long, dark reddish-brown, with hairs along scale edges, in 2 rows, absent at twig tips.

Leaves: Alternate, simple, deciduous; blades lustrous dark green, **hairless** except on veins underneath, $\frac{3}{4}$–2$\frac{3}{4}$" **long,** elliptical, **nearly symmetrical,** edged with sharp, mostly **single teeth;** veins prominent, straight, about 10–12 per side, a few forked; **stalks about $\frac{1}{8}$" long;** leaves yellow in autumn.

Flowers: About $\frac{1}{8}$" wide on very short stalks, bisexual (mostly); petals absent; sepals tiny, fused in bell-shaped calyxes; stamens 4–5, purple; flowers in **compact tassel-like clusters** on year-old twigs, in March–April (before leaves expand).

Fruits: Round, greenish, **hairless, winged nutlets** (samaras), $\frac{3}{8}$–$\frac{1}{2}$" across, in dense, tassel-like clusters; nutlets with a broad, membranous wing **tipped with a deep, closed notch;** samaras drop in April–May (before leaves expand fully).

Habitat: Disturbed, open sites such as roadsides, fence lines and abandoned lots.

Origin: Introduced from Siberia and northern China.

Rock elm has the heaviest, toughest wood of any elm. In the 1800s, it was exported to England for use in shipbuilding. It was also used for automobile chassis and plows before steel became widely used. In North America, rock elm has been used for construction and in furniture, piano frames, tool handles and hockey sticks. Unfortunately, this strong, hard wood is no longer readily available. • This moderately fast-growing tree lives about 125 years, if not infected by Dutch elm disease. It begins to flower after 20–25 years and produces good seed crops every 2–3 years. Regeneration in the wild is slow. Seedlings can tolerate some shade, but they need full sunlight to grow quickly. Saplings may persevere for several decades in the forest understory, waiting to fill new openings in the canopy. • Rock elm seeds provide food for many birds, including pheasants, grouse and wood ducks. Beavers and muskrats sometimes eat the bark, and white-tailed deer along with squirrels, chipmunks and other small mammals feed on the twigs, buds and seeds. • This tree is very rare, and like most elms, is vulnerable to Dutch elm disease.

Also Called: Cork elm, winged elm
• *U. racemosa.*

Size and Shape: Rough, shaggy-looking trees 50–80' tall; crowns narrow, oblong, rounded; roots wide-spreading.

Trunks: Straight, undivided, 12–24" in diameter; bark shaggy, with interlacing, **corky ridges of alternating layers of thin, pale scales and thicker, dark scales;** wood light brown, fine-grained, hard, heavy, strong.

Branches: Short, almost horizontal, often drooping, gnarled and **corky-ridged;** twigs develop 2–4 corky, wing-like ridges in first year;

buds chestnut brown, sharp-pointed, pointing outward in 2 rows, about ¼" long, with fringed scales.

Leaves: Alternate, simple, deciduous; blades 2–5½" long, **thick, shiny, dark green above,** paler and somewhat hairy beneath, **abruptly pointed at tip, rounded and asymmetrical at the base;** veins about 40, **rarely forked,** ending in sharp, **incurved teeth; stalks about ¼" long;** leaves bright yellow in autumn.

Flowers: Reddish-green, small, bisexual (mostly); petals absent; sepals tiny, 7–8; flowers borne on year-old twigs, hang in **small clusters with slender central stalks,** in April–May **(before leaves expand).**

Fruits: Dry, flat, hairy, indistinctly winged nutlets (samaras) ⅜–¾" long, tapered to both ends, shallowly notched at the tip; samaras hang in elongated clusters, drop by May (before leaves expand fully).

Habitat: Usually in moist, rich forests.

Origin: Native.

This relatively inconspicuous elm is usually a minor component of the forest understory. It produces medium to heavy fruit crops every other year. The samaras provide limited quantities of food for many birds and rodents. • In the southern U.S., winged elm is sometimes planted as a shade tree along streets and boulevards. 'Lace Parasol' is a popular weeping cultivar. • Like most elms, winged elm is susceptible to attacks by Dutch elm disease, phloem necrosis virus and many insect defoliators, bark beetles, borers and sucking insects. Damage to this light-demanding tree is usually greatest in shaded sites. Similarly, reproduction can be prolific in forest openings but very sparse in shady understory sites. • The name "winged elm" refers to the broad, corky wings that develop on the vigorously growing twigs. • Another southern elm, **September elm (*U. serotina*)** has been reported to occur in Illinois. It is the only elm in the northeastern U.S. that flowers in the autumn. It has large, 2–4" long leaves edged with coarse, double teeth. The slender-stalked flowers are borne in elongating clusters (racemes). The distinctive fruits, fringed with long, silvery hairs (otherwise hairless), mature in October–November. September elm usually grows in rich woods along streams and on low hillsides.

Also Called: Wahoo.

Size and Shape: Lacy or somewhat drooping trees to 15–50' tall; crowns spreading, round-topped, fairly open.

Trunks: Short, usually straight, 1–1½' (occasionally 3¼') in diameter; bark rough, reddish-brown to gray, with flat, irregular ridges; wood light brown, hard, heavy, generally brittle.

Branches: Stout, spreading, often short; **twigs essentially hairless,** slender, reddish brown, usually developing 2 **opposite, thin plates (wings) of corky bark** in the 1st or 2nd season; **buds chestnut-brown, essentially hairless,** ⅛–¼" long, cone-shaped, sharp-pointed.

Leaves: Alternate, deciduous, simple; blades hairless to slightly rough-to-touch above, hairy beneath (at least on veins), **1⅛–2¾" long, uneven and slightly notched at the base, slender-pointed, coarsely double toothed;** veins ascending, often forked.

Flowers: Small, bisexual; petals absent; sepals 5–9; pistils single; **stamens usually 5,** with reddish pollen sacs; flowers on thread-like stalks in short (about ½" long) branched clusters (racemes), in February–March (before leaves expand fully).

Fruits: Dry, flat, elliptical, narrowly winged **nutlets (samaras),** ¼–⅜" **long, tipped with 2 slender teeth, white-hairy on the sides, fringed with dense, long hairs,** borne on short stalks in tassel-like clusters; **mature in spring.**

Habitat: Varied, including wooded slopes, bluffs, low woods and abandoned fields.

Origin: Native.

This interesting but rarely encountered tree is a native of the southeastern U.S. and just reaches the southern tip of Illinois, where it is endangered. The slow-growing planertree thrives in wet, swampy sites, which are common in many parts of the south. It also needs hot summers for good growth and fruit production. Able to thrive in shallow water and frequently flooded areas, planertree typically grows among other swamp-loving species such as bald-cypress, water oak and water tupelo. • The abundant, unusual fruits are an important winter food source for many species of waterfowl, especially ducks such as the mallard. Squirrels also eat the tiny nutlets. • The wood is relatively light, decays readily and has low fuel value, so these trees have little or no commercial value. Planertrees have occasionally been used for pulp. • *Planera* is a monotypic genus (with only one species) named in honor of Johann Jakob Planer (1743–89), a physician and professor of botany in Erfurt, Germany. • Planetree is very similar to its close relatives, the elms (*Ulmus* spp., pp. 91–95), and young trees can be difficult to distinguish. Mature, flowering/fruiting specimens are readily distinguished by their mainly unisexual flowers in early spring and by their unusual, soft-spiny fruits in summer.

Also called: Water-elm.

Size and Shape: Tall shrubs or trees 20–50' tall; crowns spreading, flat-topped; roots shallow.

Trunks: Short, 1–2' in diameter; **bark gray to light brown, about ¼" thick**, forming **large, longitudinal, shreddy scales;** wood light brown, soft, brittle, fine-grained.

Branches: Slender, spreading; twigs reddish-brown, with white pores (lenticels), slightly zigzagged; buds dark red-brown, almost goblet-shaped, ¼–½" [¹⁄₁₆??] long, with scales in 2 rows, absent at twig tips.

Leaves: Alternate, deciduous, simple; blades thick, dark green, paler and yellow-veined beneath, **slightly roughened** (usually on both surfaces), 1¾–3" long, rounded to notched and usually **asymmetrical at the base,** edged with **single, coarse, blunt, gland-tipped teeth; leaves in 2 vertical rows.**

Flowers: Tiny, unisexual (mainly), **male and female flowers on the same tree,** sometimes a few bisexual flowers; petals absent; calyx tiny, persistent; male flowers with 4–5 protruding stamens, 2–5 in tiny, stalkless, tassel-like clusters (umbels) on year-old twigs, **barely projecting** beyond bud scales; female flowers with 4–5 sterile stamens around a stalked ovary covered in bumps (tubercles) and bearing 2 downcurved styles, 2–3 in **tassel-like clusters** (umbels) in leaf axils; flowers in March–April (with leaves).

Fruits: Unusual, nut-like drupes, light brown, with **thick, leathery coats bristling with soft, finger-like projections,** ⅓–¼" long, slender-stalked; seeds single; mature 4–6 weeks after flowering.

Habitat: Swampy woods on floodplains.

Origin: Native.

This hardy, drought-resistant tree, with its broad crown and spreading branches, is used as a shade tree in landscaping in some areas. It is easily transplanted and readily sends up suckers after cutting or burning. • Common hackberry can live 150–200 years. The tiny, wind-pollinated flowers produce good crops of fruit most years. • The small, somewhat acidic "berries" are edible and are eaten by game birds and small mammals. • Hackberry wood has an attractive grain, but it is weak and has little commercial value. Settlers in Illinois used it to produce a medicine for treating jaundice. • Prior to 1974, **dwarf hackberry (C. tenuifolia,** also called Mississippi hackberry or *C. mississippiensis*), shown in dark green (species overlap) on the map, was commonly considered a variety of common hackberry. Dwarf hackberry is now distinguished by its smaller, brownish-orange fruit and smaller, broader, almost symmetrical leaves. Also, the leaves on its flowering shoots lack teeth. This small, shrubby tree (6–20' tall) grows in disturbed areas, where it is easily overlooked. In Illinois, the range of dwarf hackberry is limited to counties along the southern and eastern borders of the state, whereas common hackberry is found throughout.

Photo, bottom left: *C. tenuifolia*

Also Called: Northern hackberry, western hackberry, bastard-elm, nettle-tree, sugarberry, Georgia hackberry • *C. georgiana.*

Size and Shape: Small trees 15–65' (rarely to 110') tall; crowns broad, rounded.

Trunks: Short, forked, 8–24" in diameter; bark pale brown to silver gray, with **wart-like bumps** on irregular, **corky ridges;** wood brown, heavy, coarse-textured, weak.

Branches: Ascending to spreading, often with drooping tips; twigs slender, zigzagged, finely hairy; pith banded with cavities visible in long-section; **buds ⅛–¼" long,** 5–6-scaled, pointed, flattened, **in 2 rows** (absent at twig tips).

Leaves: Alternate, simple, deciduous; blades 2–5½" long, **bluish-green and usually rough above,** paler and hairy on **lacy network of veins beneath,** papery, **asymmetrical at bases,** tapered to tips, **15–40 coarse, sharp teeth per side;** leaves light yellow in autumn.

Flowers: Small, greenish; unisexual with male and female flowers on the same tree; petals absent; sepals 4–5; male flowers 4–5-stamened, clustered below new shoots; female flowers with 1 pistil, 1–3 in new leaf axils; flowers in April–May (as leaves expand).

Fruits: Dark reddish-purple, about ¼" long, dry, **berry-like drupes** hanging on slender stalks, wrinkled and prune-like with age; seeds single, in brown, pitted (dimpled) stones; drupes mature in September–October, often persisting through winter.

Habitat: Moist sites along rivers and streams; often associated with floodplains and limestone.

Origin: Native.

97

Sugarberry has limited value as a source of lumber, but this moderately fast-growing, drought-resistant tree is sometimes planted for shade along streets. Unfortunately, the branches are weak and often break as a result of stresses from wind, snow and ice. Sugarberry is fairly shade tolerant, but it grows best in sunnier sites, often shooting up to fill new openings in the forest. Trees rarely live for more than 125–150 years.
• Sugarberry typically starts to produce seed at about 15 years, but is most productive at 30–70 years of age. Trees regularly generate large crops of fruit that attract many birds, including robins, thrashers, cardinals, mockingbirds and sapsuckers. Occasionally, late frosts kill flowers and reduce fruit production. Mature seeds are widely distributed by both water and birds. • Sugarberry can be grown from seed, which germinates in early spring, or from cuttings. These thin-barked trees are easily injured by fire. Even light fires can kill young shoots and injure older trees, leaving them susceptible to fungal infections such as butt rot. Stumps of cut or burned trees sprout readily from the root collar, producing small clumps of young, fast-growing shoots.

Also Called: Southern hackberry, thick-leaved hackberry.

Size and Shape: Medium-sized trees 60–100' tall; crowns broadly rounded; roots spreading.

Trunks: Short, straight, 1½–2' in diameter; mature bark light gray, ¼–¾" thick, **covered with corky, wart-like bumps;** wood light yellow, soft, weak.

Branches: Stout, spreading to almost hanging; twigs slender, smooth, light green; buds dark brown, cone-shaped, with tiny scales.

Leaves: Alternate, simple, deciduous; blades yellowish-green above, paler beneath, ovate to lance-shaped, 1½–4¾" long, **often curved, broadest below midleaf,** slender-pointed, rounded to slightly notched and **asymmetrical at the base, smooth-edged** or sparingly toothed; stalks slender, ¼–½" long.

Flowers: Small, greenish; unisexual with male and female flowers on the same tree; petals absent; sepals 4–5; male flowers with 4–5 stamens, **clustered below new shoots;** female flowers with 1 pistil that is soon shed, usually **single in new leaf axils;** flowers in April–May (as leaves expand).

Fruits: Round, **yellow to orange, berry-like drupes,** ¼–⅜" long, ripen to dark purple, thin-skinned, hanging on slender, ⅛–¼" stalks that are equal to or shorter than the adjacent leaf stalk; seeds single within a stone; fruits mature in October–November, often persist until midwinter.

Habitat: Low, wet woods, often on floodplains.

Origin: Native.

This attractive, shade-intolerant tree thrives in a broad range of environments, often surviving stressful conditions. It has been widely planted as an ornamental and in windbreaks and hedgerows in eastern North America. • Once established, Osage-orange spreads readily from sprouting roots and can be difficult to eradicate. Cleaning up the heavy, fleshy fruits can be a messy chore each year. The juicy fruits resemble green oranges, but they are not edible. **Caution:** This tree's sap can cause skin reactions. • The tough, durable wood of the Osage-orange has little commercial value because the trunks are small. The wood does, however, make excellent fuel, and the Osage people used it for making bows. The roots and bark have been used to produce a yellow dye for coloring baskets, cloth and leather. The bark is also rich in tannins and has been used in tanning leather. Even the strong-smelling fruits have a use—they are recommended as a cockroach repellent. • Despite its sizable fruits, this tree is of little importance to wildlife. Squirrels and foxes may occasionally tear apart the pulpy balls to eat the seeds, but most animals avoid this messy snack.

Also Called: Hedge-apple, bodark, bow-wood.

Size and Shape: Small, **thorny trees** 15–40' tall, with **milky sap;** crowns irregular, rounded; roots wide-spreading, deep, with **peeling, orange bark.**

Trunks: Soon branched, 12–24" in diameter; bark orange-brown, irregularly ridged; **wood bright orange,** heavy, hard.

Branches: Stout, few, curved; twigs green to light orange-brown, zigzagged, slender, soon armed with **stout thorns; buds tiny,** brown, partly embedded in twigs, none at branch tips.

Leaves: Alternate, simple, deciduous; blades 2⅜–4¾" long, 2–2¾" wide, **thick, shiny, dark green above,** paler beneath, slender-pointed, **smooth-edged;** stalks slender, 1⅛–2⅜" long; leaves yellow in autumn.

Flowers: Tiny, without petals; **in dense, round clusters** at the tips of slender stalks; unisexual with male and female flowers on separate trees; male clusters 1–1½" across; female clusters ¾–1" across; flowers in May–June.

Fruits: Green, **4–5½" wide, dimpled, fleshy or pulpy aggregates** of many tiny fruits (achenes) containing bitter, milky juice; seeds small, flattened, embedded in flesh; fruits mature in September–October.

Habitat: Lowland sites with rich, deep soils to open, disturbed sites such as hedgerows and roadsides.

Origin: Introduced from south-central U.S.

The leaves of white mulberry are the main source of food for silkworms in eastern Asia. The milky juice is rich in rubber-like compounds said to add strength to the silk fibers spun by the worms. The silk industry has been especially important in China, and in that country, white mulberry has been cultivated for thousands of years. In order to accommodate the silkworms, the trees are repeatedly pruned back to the trunk (pollarded) to stimulate a dense head of leafy shoots. • Mulberry shrubs were first brought to North America along with silkworms, in an attempt to establish a western silk industry. This ambitious undertaking failed, but since then, these hardy trees have thrived and spread across eastern and southern North America. • White mulberry grows well in urban centers, and it is often used for landscaping. An attractive cultivar with drooping branches, 'Pendula,' is especially popular as an ornamental. • The Chinese and Japanese use white mulberry wood for decorative carving. In North America, this wood has also been used to make fences and boats. • White mulberry trees with dark red, purple or black (rather than white) fruits are sometimes called **Russian mulberry (*M. alba* var. *tartarica*** or *M. tartarica*). Russian mulberry grows in open, often disturbed sites scattered throughout Illinois.

Size and Shape: Small trees 15–50' tall, with **milky sap; crowns bushy,** spreading; roots wide-spreading.

Trunks: Short, 8–36" in diameter; mature bark pale grayish to yellowish-brown with **orange inner layers,** furrowed.

Branches: Stout, spreading; **twigs slender, light orange-brown;** buds plump, red-brown, about ⅛" long, in 2 rows along twigs.

Leaves: Alternate, simple, deciduous; blades light green, **lustrous, essentially hairless, coarsely toothed, unlobed to variously lobed,** 2–4" long, widest below the middle, curved to a broad, wedge-shaped tip; leaves yellow in autumn.

Flowers: Tiny, without petals, green; unisexual with male and female flowers in separate clusters on the same tree (usually) or on separate trees; male clusters loose and elongated; female clusters short, dense and cylindrical; flowers in May–June.

Fruits: White, reddish or purplish to blackish, rounded, **blackberry-like; clusters (multiple fruits)** ⅜–¾" **long,** composed of tiny, seed-like fruits (achenes) each surrounded by a small, juicy segment; fruits mature June–July.

Habitat: Open, upland sites, along streams, fences and railways and in woods.

Origin: Introduced from eastern Asia; grows wild in much of the eastern U.S.

R ed mulberry is found throughout Illinois, the only mulberry native to the state. Unfortunately, red mulberry frequently hybridizes with its European cousin, white mulberry (p. 100). This genetic alteration is probably the single greatest threat to the species. Hybrids are often difficult to identify. • Mulberry wood is very durable, so it has been used to make fence posts and barrels. • The sweet, juicy fruits are best fresh, though some people find them seedy, and can also be baked in pies and cakes. • **Caution:** Some people develop skin reactions from contact with mulberry leaves and branches. Green mulberry fruits cause stomach upset. • Many birds and small mammals such as raccoons and squirrels feed on mulberries and help to disperse the seeds. • This attractive, fast-growing species can be planted as an ornamental or fruit tree but requires sufficient space to accommodate its spreading branches. Female trees attract many birds and small mammals to parks and yards, but their abundant crops of fruit can stain lawns purple and may be messy to clean up. Sometimes mulberries are planted to lure birds away from other fruit. • Unlobed leaves are very similar to those of basswood (p. 233) but basswood has hairless, clearly asymmetrical blades.

Size and Shape: Small trees with **milky sap,** 15–35' tall, up to 60' in forests; crowns dense, broad and rounded.

Trunks: Short, 4–14" in diameter; **mature bark dark reddish-brown,** thin, with **long, flaky strips;** wood pale orange, soft, weak, light.

Branches: Spreading, stout; twigs green to gray-brown or reddish-brown; buds plump, about ¼" long, lustrous brown, in 2 rows along twigs, none at branch tips.

Leaves: Alternate, simple, deciduous; blades thin, **dull yellowish-green and sandpapery above, soft-hairy beneath, unlobed to broadly 2–5-lobed,** 2¾–5" long, abruptly tapered to a long-pointed tip, notched and **3-veined at the base,** coarsely sharp-toothed; leaves yellow in autumn.

Flowers: Tiny, green, without petals; unisexual with male and female flowers in separate clusters on separate trees, on the same tree or mixed in the same cluster (occasionally); male clusters loose, elongated, ¾–2" long; female clusters dense, short, about ¾" long; flowers in May–early June (before or with leaves).

Fruits: Red to dark purple or almost black, cylindrical, blackberry-like clusters (multiple fruits) ¾–1⅛" **long,** composed of tiny, seed-like fruits (achenes), each surrounded by a small, juicy segment; fruits mature in July.

Habitat: Moist, rich sites to open areas along fields.

Origin: Native.

Since its introduction to North America around 1750, paper-mulberry has become naturalized throughout much of the eastern U.S. The fleshy fruits are a favorite food of many birds and small mammals. • Humans have also used this plant for food. The leaves are edible, and the sweet, fleshy, red fruit can be eaten raw. • This attractive, fruit-producing shrub is widely planted as an ornamental in east Asia, Europe and eastern North America. • In China and Japan, paper-mulberry is commonly cultivated for its fibrous bark. For this purpose, it is grown as a bushy shrub, rarely more than 6–7' in height. Plants are cut back each year to stimulate the growth of vigorous young shoots. • The inner bark fibers are used for making paper and can also be woven into a fine cloth. This cloth was commonly used for clothing in southeast Asia at the time of Captain James Cook. • These hardy shrubs grow well on gravelly, nutrient-deficient soils, so they can help to stabilize soils in dry, poor sites. • *Broussonetia* is a small genus with only 4 species, native to eastern Asia. • This genus was named in honor of Pierre Broussonet (1761–1807), a botanist from Montpellier, France, who was French consul to Tenerife in the Canary Islands.

Also Called: *Papyrius papyrifera*.

Size and Shape: Tall shrubs of small trees to 50' tall, with **milky sap;** crowns broad, rounded, spreading; roots sending up numerous suckers from the tree base.

Trunks: Short, slender, usually clumped; **bark smooth,** gray, **mottled with age;** wood light-colored, soft.

Branches: Spreading; twigs soft, pithy, **densely silky-woolly;** buds with 3–2 outer scales.

Leaves: Alternate, opposite and whorled, simple, deciduous; blades firm, thin, often shaped like fig leaves, broadly ovate, **mostly unlobed** but **some 2–3 lobed with rounded notches,** 3–8" long, sharply toothed, **rough to touch above,** densely woolly beneath; stalks ⅜–3" long, silky-woolly (at least when young).

Flowers: Tiny, petals lacking; unisexual with **male and female flowers on separate trees;** calyx deeply cut, 4-lobed; male flowers with 4 stamens, forming slender, hanging, cylindrical clusters **(catkins)** 1½–3" **long;** female flowers with 1 long style, forming **dense, round heads** ⅜–¾" **across** on short hanging stalks; flowers in May–June.

Fruits: Orange to red spherical clusters (multiple fruits) ¾–1⅛" **across,** consisting mainly of enlarged, fleshy calyxes with protruding, orange achenes; mature in summer, fall in October.

Habitat: Open sites near homes, along roads and on farms.

Origin: Introduced from Asia.

Key to Genera in the Walnut Family (Juglandaceae)

1a   Leaflets usually 5–9, with the tip leaflet largest; branch pith uniform, lacking horizontal partitions (in long-section); fruit husks splitting into 4 parts
  . . . . **Carya, hickory** (key to species, see below)

1b   Leaflets usually at least 11, those near midleaf largest; branch pith with horizontal partitions (visible in long-section); fruit husks not splitting open
  . . . . **Juglans, walnut** (key to species, p. 104)

Carya laciniosa, shellbark hickory

Key to the Hickories (Genus *Carya*)

1a   Bud scales 2–6, paired, not overlapping; leaflets usually at least 9; fruit husks prominently keeled along the sutures 2

1b   Bud scales up to 12, overlapping; leaflets usually 5–7; fruit husks lacking prominent keels . . 4

2a   Nuts cylindrical and elongated; kernels sweet and edible; buds lacking yellow glands or scales, but sometimes with yellow hairs . . . . . . **C. illinoinensis, pecan** (p. 111)

2b   Nuts slightly flattened and as wide as long; kernels bitter and inedible 3

3a   Buds bright yellowish-orange with tiny, yellow, bran-like scales; fruit with wings extending halfway to the base; husks splitting halfway to the base; leaflets not usually sickle-shaped
  . . . .*C. cordiformis,* **bitternut hickory** (p. 112)

3b   Buds brown with yellow glands; fruits with wings extending to the base; husks splitting to the base; leaflets usually with strongly hooked tips, sickle-shaped
  . . . .*C. aquatica,* **water hickory** (p. 111)

4a Branch-tip buds $1/2$–1" long; fruits large (often >$1^3/8$" long), with $1/8$–$1/2$" thick husks soon splitting almost to the base to reveal a 4–6-sided nut 5

4b Branch-tip buds rarely more than $3/8$" long; fruits smaller (mostly <$1^3/8$") with thin (<$3/16$" thick) husks. 7

5a Leaflets 5 (rarely 7), fringed with hairs when young, essentially hairless beneath when mature, but the teeth often tipped with tiny tufts of hair; fruits $1^1/8$–2" across, single or paired . . . . *C. ovata*, **shagbark hickory** (p. 108)

5b Leaflets 7 or 9, with permanently hairy lower surfaces; fruits $5/8$–$2^3/4$", in small clusters . 6

6a Fruits $1^1/8$–$2^3/8$" across, strongly flattened, tapered to a wedge-shaped base . . . . *C. laciniosa*, **shellbark hickory** (p. 107)

6b Fruits $5/8$–$1^1/8$" across, round or only slightly flattened, with a rounded base . . . . *C. alba*, **mockernut hickory** (p. 107)

7a Buds with yellow scales. 8

7b Buds lacking yellow scales 9

8a Central stalk of leaf lacking reddish hairs; nuts white, with prominent angles . . . . *C. pallida*, **pale hickory** (p. 110)

8b Central stalk of leaf with reddish hairs (especially when young); nuts pale brown, scarcely angled. . . . . *C. texana*, **black hickory** (p. 110)

9a Leaf blades and stalks hairless or blades hairy beneath along the veins; leaflets 5 (rarely 7); twigs reddish-brown, hairless; mature bark close (not shaggy); fruit husks shiny, dark brown, sometimes slowly splitting open along 1–2 lines (if at all) . . . . *C. glabra*, **pignut hickory** (p. 109)

9b Leaves and twigs scurfy, with yellowish scales; leaflets usually 7; mature bark often shaggy, in small plates; fruit husks dull pale brown, promptly splitting in 4 . . . . *C. ovalis*, **red hickory** (p. 109)

Key to the Walnuts (Genus *Juglans*)

1a Leaf stalks, young twigs and fruits sticky-downy; fruits oblong-egg-shaped and somewhat pointed; twig pith chocolate brown. . . . . *J. cinerea*, **butternut** (p. 106)

1b Leaf stalks, young twigs and fruits finely short-hairy or slightly downy, but scarcely sticky; fruits almost spherical; twig pith tan to cream-colored. . . . . . . *J. nigra*, **black walnut** (p. 106)

Carya cordiformis, bitternut hickory

B utternuts are difficult to shell, and resins in the husks stain hands and clothing, but the sweet, oily kernels are delicious. They can be eaten like walnuts—either alone (plain, salted, hickory-smoked) or added to candies, cakes, pies and muffins. Some tribes boiled butternut kernels and skimmed off the oil to use like butter. The remaining kernels were dried and ground into a rich meal for adding to cornmeal mush. • The nut husks and root bark produce an orange or yellow dye. Butternut bark and nut husks were used (without a mordant) to dye uniforms for foot soldiers during the American Civil War (1861–65). The leaves, with an alum mordant, produce a brown to bronze dye. • The outer bark was once used in medicinal teas for treating toothaches and dysentery, and dried inner bark was taken to purge the system. • This fast-growing, relatively short-lived tree can survive about 80 years. The leaves, bark and nuts contain toxins that inhibit the growth of other plants nearby. • Butternut is disappearing rapidly, as trees succumb to a lethal blight introduced from Europe. Infected trees develop black, oozing cankers and soon die. In many parts of Illinois, it is already difficult to find butternut trees.

Also Called: White walnut, lemon walnut, oilnut.

Size and Shape: Trees 40–65' tall; crowns irregular, open, rounded; roots deep, spreading.

Trunks: Short, soon forked, 12–40" in diameter; mature bark rough with flat-topped, intersecting ridges; wood light brown to reddish-brown, light, soft, weak.

Branches: Few, stout, ascending; twigs orange-yellow, **rusty-hairy, sticky; pith dark brown, banded** with cavities (visible in long-section); buds hairy, mainly small, rounded and brownish, but **large (½–¾") and pale yellow at twig tips.**

Leaves: Alternate, deciduous, **12–30" long, aromatic,** sticky when young; compound, **pinnately divided into 11–17 leaflets** that are yellowish-green and rough above, paler and **thickly hairy beneath,** finely toothed, almost **stalkless,** 2–4¾" long, the **3 tip leaflets equal-sized,** gradually smaller downward; **leaf scars prominent,** with 3 vein scars, **downy-hairy across the flat top.**

Flowers: Tiny, green, without petals; unisexual with male and female flowers on the same tree; male flowers hang in catkins 2⅜–5½" long; female flowers about ¼" long, 1–7 in erect clusters (catkins); flowers in May (with leaves).

Fruits: **Lemon-shaped, green nuts,** 1 to few together, 1½–2⅜" long, with firm, sticky, hairy husks over hard, oblong, **irregularly jagged-ridged shells;** oily seed kernel inside shell has 2 irregular lobes (cotyledons); nuts mature in October and drop.

Habitat: Moist, rich woodlands; often with maples.

Origin: Native.

105

Black walnut is one of North America's most highly prized hardwoods. Standing trees have fetched $5000 at auction. The lustrous, rich chocolate brown wood has a beautiful grain, stains and polishes well, is easily worked and doesn't shrink or warp. It is used for rifle butts and stocks, high-quality furniture, veneers and boats. • Most of the original black walnut stands have been cut, but this valuable tree has been reintroduced to some regions through reforestation programs. These attractive, slow-growing nut trees are also planted as ornamentals. • The sweet, oily kernels can be used like domestic walnuts and butternuts. They are difficult to shell, and the husks stain hands and clothing, but cultivars with larger, thinner-walled nuts are being developed.

• Walnut husks are rich in tannins and toxins. Ground husks have provided insecticides, fish poison and black dye. • The toxin juglone is exuded from the roots and leached from decaying leaves, preventing other broad-leaved plants (including walnut seedlings) from growing nearby. • **English walnut (*J. regia*)**, introduced from Eurasia, is occasionally grown as an ornamental but does not grow wild in Illinois. It is readily distinguished by its leaves, with 5–9 hairless, smooth-edged leaflets, and by its large, easily shelled nuts—the commercially available walnut.

Also Called: American walnut, American black walnut, eastern black walnut.

Size and Shape: Trees 65–100' tall; crowns open, rounded; roots deep, spreading.

Trunks: Straight, 24–48" in diameter; mature bark almost black, with rounded, intersecting ridges; wood dark brown (heartwood) to almost white (sapwood), hard, heavy, strong, decay-resistant, straight-grained.

Branches: Few, large, ascending; twigs orange-brown, **faintly hairy, not sticky;** pith cream-colored, banded with cavities (visible in long-section);

buds small, pale gray-brown, slightly hairy, largest (¼–⅜") at twig tips.

Leaves: Alternate, deciduous, **8–24" long, aromatic;** compound, **pinnately divided into 13–23 leaflets** that are yellowish-green, smooth above, paler and **faintly hairy below,** finely toothed, short-stalked, 2–4" long, middle leaflets largest, **tip leaflet small or absent; leaf scars heart-shaped, not hairy;** leaves yellow in autumn.

Flowers: Green, tiny, without petals; unisexual with male and female flowers on the same tree; male flowers in hanging catkins 2–4¾" long; female flowers about ¹/₄" long, in erect clusters of 1–4; flowers in May (with leaves).

Fruits: Round, yellow-green to brown, aromatic nuts 1½–2⅜" across, with a hard, **irregularly smooth-ridged shell** in a firm, slightly hairy husk, hanging in clusters of 1–3; oily seed kernel inside shell has 2 irregular lobes (cotyledons); nuts mature in October and drop.

Habitat: Deep, well-drained, fertile lowlands.

Origin: Native.

This tree produces large nuts, with good crops every 1–3 years. The sweet, edible kernels are encased in thick, hard shells within thick, woody husks, so some effort is required to extract them. However, like pecans, they are delicious raw or in baked goods. • The thick, green husks were sometimes ground and used as a fish poison. • Shellbark hickory has tough, strong wood that makes excellent tool handles, ladders, baskets and fuel. • Foxes, black bears, deer, hares, rabbits, raccoons, muskrats, squirrels and chipmunks all seek out these nuts. Even ducks, wild turkeys and quail occasionally eat hickory nuts. The nuts are dispersed by animals and by flowing water. They can remain viable for several years. • **Mockernut hickory (*C. alba*,** also called *C. tomentosa*), shown in pink/dark green (species overlap) on the map, is an occasional resident of moist to dry woodlands throughout the southern ³/₄ of Illinois. Mockernut resembles shellbark hickory but has more densely woolly leaf stalks, dark brown twigs, smaller (¹/₂–1¹/₈"), more spherical nuts and tight, ridged (not shaggy) bark. • Hickories are highly variable, and identification can be difficult. Shellbark hickory also resembles shagbark hickory (p. 108), but shellbark hickory is a larger tree with larger leaves, buds, twigs and nuts.

Also Called: Big shellbark hickory, kingnut hickory, big shagbark hickory, bigleaf, bottom shellbark.

Size and Shape: Trees 50–80' tall; crowns narrow, open; taproot.

Trunks: Straight, 24–32" in diameter; **mature bark gray, in shaggy, 3–4' long strips;** wood dark brown, heavy, hard, elastic.

Branches: Short, spreading; **twigs stout, buff to pale orange-brown** (usually); **pith solid; buds dark brown, ³/₄–1¹/₈" long** at twig tips.

Leaves: Alternate, deciduous, 10–20" long, **aromatic;** compound, **pinnately divided into 7 (sometimes 9, rarely 5) leaflets** that are dark yellowish-green above, paler and **soft-hairy below,** finely toothed, edges hairless or with non-tufted hairs, **leaflets 5–8¹/₂" long, largest at leaf tips, much smaller downward;** leaf scars conspicuous, raised; leaves often drop leaflets before main stalk.

Flowers: Tiny, green, without petals; unisexual with male and female flowers on the same tree; male flowers yellow-green, in 4³/₄–8" long catkins that hang in 3s; female flowers about ¹/₈" long, in erect clusters of 2–5; flowers in May–early June (with leaves).

Fruits: Compressed, greenish-brown, aromatic **nuts 1¹/₂–2³/₄" long,** somewhat wedge-shaped at base, usually 1–2 hanging, with a thick, hard, **4-ridged shell** within a woody, ¹/₄–¹/₂" **thick husk that splits to the base along 4 lines;** seed kernel inside shell has 2 large, irregular lobes (cotyledons); nuts mature in October and drop.

Habitat: Rich, moist to wet sites in bottomlands.

Origin: Native.

Of all our native hickories, shagbark hickory has the best-quality wood and is the most important source of edible hickory nuts. The sweet, walnut-like kernels can be eaten alone or used in recipes. • Shagbark hickory nuts were a staple food for many tribes and remain the main hickory nut of commerce. Traditionally, the kernels were ground and boiled in water to produce a milky, oil-rich liquid that was used in cornbread and cornmeal mush. The sweet-tasting sap was boiled down to make syrup. Some isolated northern stands may have originated from nuts carried there by Native peoples. • The strong, resilient wood has been used to make wheel spokes, tool handles, plowing instruments and machine parts. It also makes excellent fuel. A cord produces almost as much heat as a ton of anthracite coal. Shagbark hickory wood is used for smoking meat (ham, bacon) and for producing high-quality charcoal. • The inner bark produces a yellow dye, which was patented in the 18th century, but more intense yellows were available, so there was limited demand. • The nuts are an important food source for squirrels. • One look at a mature tree, with its peeling sheets of rough bark, explains the common name.

Also Called: Upland hickory, scalybark hickory.

Size and Shape: Trees 60–70' tall; crowns somewhat open and narrow; taproot.

Trunks: Straight, 12–24" in diameter; **mature bark dark gray, shaggy,** with peeling plates 12–36" long; wood hard, heavy, fine-grained.

Branches: Short, stout, few; twigs stout, reddish-brown to grayish, shiny; pith solid; **buds greenish-brown, ½–¾" long at twig tips, upper (inner) scales hairy,** loosely overlapping, lower 2–4 scales paired, with abutting edges.

Leaves: Alternate, deciduous, 6–12" long, **aromatic;** compound, **pinnately divided into 5**

(occasionally 7) **leaflets** that are yellowish-green above, paler and **almost hairless beneath,** fine-toothed, **fringed with 2–3 white tufts per tooth** (especially when young), essentially stalkless, 3–7" long, **largest at leaf tip;** leaf scars conspicuous, raised; leaves golden yellow in autumn.

Flowers: Tiny, green, without petals; unisexual with male and female flowers on the same tree; male flowers in catkins 4–5" long, hanging in 3s; female flowers about ¼" long, in small, erect clusters of 2–5; flowers in May–early June (as leaves expand).

Fruits: Round, greenish- to dark reddish-brown, aromatic nuts, shorter than wide, ¾–1½" (rarely 2") long, with a hard, 4-angled shell within a thick, **woody husk that splits in 4 to the base;** seed kernel inside shell has 2 large, irregular lobes (cotyledons); nuts single or paired, mature in October and drop.

Habitat: Moderately dry uplands to rich, moist forests.

Origin: Native.

Pignut hickory is highly variable, and its relationship to **red hickory (*C. ovalis*,** also called *C. glabra* var. *odorata*), shown in pink/dark green (species overlap) on the map, is unclear. Some taxonomists do not consider red hickory a separate species and treat it as *C. glabra* var. *odorata*. Of those who recognize 2 species, some say the range of red hickory extends north into Canada and others consider it a more southern species found in the eastern U.S. Pignut hickory and red hickory are distinguished, respectively, on the basis of their twigs (smooth reddish-brown vs. yellowish-scurfy); leaflets (usually 5 vs. usually 7); bark (close and shallowly ridged vs. often shaggy with peeling plates); nut kernels (astringent vs. sweet); nut shells (slightly or not at all compressed and not angled vs. compressed and strongly angled above); and fruit husks (shiny, dark brown and splitting slowly or not at all vs. dull, warty, light brown and promptly splitting to the base). However, these features often intergrade, and characteristics of both "species" may be observed in a single tree. • The nutmeats are usually bitter and inedible and are best left to pigs and wild animals.

Also Called: Sweet pignut hickory, false shagbark hickory, black hickory, broom hickory, smoothbark hickory • *C. leiodermis*.

Size and Shape: Trees 50–65' tall; crowns narrow, irregular; taproot.

Trunks: Straight, 12–32" in diameter; young bark thin, gray, with pale **crisscross markings;** mature bark rough with **rounded ridges;** wood hard, heavy, strong.

Branches: Short, crooked; **twigs slender, shiny,** reddish-brown to gray, often long-ridged; **pith solid;** buds light brown or gray, ¼–½" **long at twig tips,** smaller below, upper scales hairy and overlapping, **lower 2–4 scales paired and soon shed.**

Leaves: Alternate, deciduous, 6–12" long, **aromatic;** compound, **pinnately divided into 5 (sometimes 7, rarely 9) leaflets** that are lustrous, dark yellow-green above, paler and hairless below (except on main veins), thick, **finely sharp-toothed, largest (3–6" long) at the tip,** much smaller below.

Flowers: Tiny, green, without petals; unisexual with male and female flowers on the same tree; male flowers in catkins 3–7" long, hanging in 3s; female flowers about ¼" long, in erect clusters of 2–5; flowers in May–June (as leaves expand).

Fruits: Pear-shaped, yellowish-brown to dark brown, **aromatic nuts** ½–1⅛" (rarely 1¾–2") long, with a hard, **thin, slightly flattened, smooth to 4-lobed shell** within a **thin, 4-ridged husk that** usually splits to the base along 4 lines; seed kernel inside shell has 2 large, irregular lobes (cotyledons); nuts hang in small clusters, mature in October and drop.

Habitat: Dry, open, well-drained upland forests.

Origin: Native.

Black hickory typically grows as scattered trees. Although it is not an important source of lumber, black hickory is sometimes cut for fuel. The nuts have sweet, edible kernels that are protected by a hard outer shell. This limits their availability to many animals, but some small mammals and larger birds such as jays feed on these nuts. • Black hickory reaches the northern limit of its natural range in Illinois, but it can be cultivated as far north as southern Canada. • This is the only hickory with tufts of rusty hairs on its twigs, buds and leaf stalks and on lower leaf surfaces. Most hairs are shed by the end of the growing season. Black hickory can be positively identified by its combination of slender ($<\frac{1}{4}$" wide), leaf-bearing twigs, 6 or more overlapping bud scales and 5–7 leaflets. The blocky bark of the older trees is also distinctive. • **Pale hickory (*C. pallida*)**, shown in dark green (species overlap) on the map, resembles black hickory and pignut hickory (p. 109), but is distinguished by the presence of yellowish scales and long, loose hairs on the stalks and midveins of its mature leaves. Its white, prominently angled, thin-shelled nuts are also distinctive. • Pale hickory is endangered in Illinois.

Also Called: Red hickory, Ozark hickory.

Size and Shape: Trees 25–50' tall; crowns narrow to spreading.

Trunks: Short, 1–2' wide; bark dark gray-brown to blackish; wood pale reddish-brown, hard.

Branches: Short, often crooked, spreading to drooping; twigs slender, rigid, smooth with age; buds yellowish, about ¼–½" long, tipped with white hair tuft, **resinous, rusty-hairy and yellow-brown scaly.**

Leaves: Alternate, deciduous, 8–12" long, compound, **pinnately divided into 7 leaflets** (sometimes 5); **leaflets largest at leaf tips,** shiny, dark green above, **paler, with dense, tufted, rusty hairs and tiny, reddish glands beneath when young,** edged with fine teeth and tufted hairs, 2½–5½" **long,** slender-pointed, bases tapered (tip leaflet) to unequal rounded (side leaflets).

Flowers: Tiny, green, without petals; unisexual with **male and female flowers on the same tree;** male flowers in ¼–½" long catkins hanging in 3s, on ⅓–½" stalks; female flowers pear-shaped, hairy, single or few at branch tips; flowers in April–May (with leaves).

Fruits: Round to broadly egg-shaped, pale brown **nuts resinous, aromatic, 1¼–1½" long,** with a hard, pale to reddish-brown shell that is **scarcely angled and only slightly compressed** (if at all); **outer husk ¹⁄₁₆–⅛" thick, splitting to the base along 4 indented lines** (sutures); seed kernel with 2 large, irregular lobes (cotyledons); nuts mature in October and drop.

Habitat: Dry, often rocky or sandy upland slopes.

Origin: Native.

This tallest of native hickories shades many southern streets. Mature trees can produce 500–1000
pounds of nuts each year. • The delicious kernels are
one of our most popular nuts, eaten alone or used to
make candy, flour, oil, syrup and baked goods such as
tarts, cookies and pecan pie. • Many cultivars have
been developed for hardiness and for the size, taste,
abundance and/or ease of shelling of their nuts. The
original pecan required a long, frost-free period, warm
summer temperatures and high humidity for the nuts
to grow and mature, but cultivars have been developed
for climatic conditions far outside the natural range.
More than 500 selections are now available, some with
nuts that are so thin-shelled they can be cracked by
hand. • The sweet, nutritious kernels provide valuable
food for waterfowl, game birds, deer, foxes and squirrels (a persistent pecan plantation pest). • Originally
named for Illinois, pecan is the state tree of Texas.
• Like pecan, **water-hickory (*C. aquatica*)**,
shown in dark green (species overlap) on the map,
has numerous (usually 9–11) leaflets, though the
tips of water hickory leaflets do not curve sharply to
one side. Unlike pecans, water-hickory nuts are bitter
and inedible, but they are still important to wildlife.
Water-hickory is also distinguished by its bark, which
separates into long scales.

Also Called: *C. pecan.*

Size and Shape: Trees to 100' tall; crowns
narrow-based, spreading to a rounded top.

Trunks: Straight, up to 5' in diameter; mature
bark thick, dark reddish-brown, with rough
ridges and scales; wood pale reddish-brown,
somewhat brittle.

Branches: Stout; twigs light brown and
hairy at first, smooth and reddish-brown with
elongated, orange pores by 2nd year; buds
yellowish-brown, hairy, with **4–6 large, abutting
scales,** flattened, pointed.

Leaves: Alternate, deciduous, pinnately
divided into **9–17 leaflets,** dark yellow-green
above, paler beneath, smooth to slightly hairy;
leaflets oblong-lance-shaped, usually conspicuously **sickle-shaped at the tip,** 3–8" long,
coarsely toothed; tip leaflet short-stalked; leaf
scars large, 3-lobed, elongated; leaves yellow
in fall.

Flowers: Tiny, hairy, greenish-yellow, without
petals; unisexual with male and female flowers
on the same tree; male flowers in 5–6" long
catkins that hang in 3s; female flowers in erect
spikes of 3–10; flowers in April–May.

Fruits: Dark brown, hairy, nuts 1⅛–2¼" long,
ellipsoidal to cylindrical, rounded and narrowly
winged at the base, pointed at the tip, with a
thick husk over a hard shell containing a sweet
kernel; **husk splits to the base along 4 lines**
(sutures); shell smooth, light to reddish-brown,
often with irregular black markings, sharp-
pointed, 1–1½" long; kernel with 2 large, **oily,**
irregular lobes (cotyledons); mature and drop in
October.

Habitat: Rich, wet woods along streams.

Origin: Native.

B itternut hickory is classified as a pecan hickory. "Pecan hickories" differ from "true hickories" in their distinctive buds (which lack overlapping scales), thin, 4-ridged fruit husks and larger number of leaflets. The sulfur yellow buds of bitternut hickory are easily identified year-round. • Bitternut hickory wood is brittle compared to that of other hickories, but amazingly shock resistant. It has been used in wooden wheels, tool handles, sporting goods, paneling and furniture. As fuel, it burns intensely, leaving little ash. Bitternut hickory is favored for smoking ham, bacon and other meats because it imparts a distinctive flavor. • Bitternut hickory kernels are relatively easy to extract from their thin husks and shells, but they are also extremely bitter. Even squirrels eat them only as a last resort. • The genus name *Carya* comes from the Greek *karuon*, an ancient name for a close relative, the walnut. Walnuts and hickories are distinguished, respectively, by the pith of their twigs (banded or chambered vs. solid), their fruit husks (remaining whole vs. splitting into 4) and their wood (light to dark brown vs. white to reddish-brown).

Also Called: Swamp hickory.

Size and Shape: Trees 50–80' tall; crowns short, broad, rounded; taproot.

Trunks: Straight, slender, 6–12" in diameter; young bark gray, smooth, with pale, vertical lines; mature bark with flat, shallow, grayish ridges (not shaggy); wood hard, heavy, close-grained.

Branches: Slender, ascending, stiff; twigs shiny, greenish- to grayish-brown and slender; **pith solid; buds sulfur yellow** to bright orange-yellow, with **2–4 large, abutting scales,** flattened and ⅜–¾" **long at twig tips,** smaller and 4-sided below.

Leaves: Alternate, deciduous, 6–12" long, aromatic; compound, **pinnately divided into 7–9 (usually 9, rarely 5 or 11) leaflets** that are shiny, dark green above, **paler, hairy and dotted with glands below, slightly curved,** toothed, 4–6" long, **uppermost largest;** leaves bright gold in autumn.

Flowers: Tiny, green, without petals; unisexual with male and female flowers on the same tree; male flowers in catkins 2¾–4" long, hanging in 3s from a slender stalk; female flowers hairy, about ⅛" long, erect, 1–5 in compact clusters; flowers in May–early June (as leaves expand).

Fruits: Round to broadly egg-shaped, greenish-brown, **aromatic nuts,** sharp-tipped, ¾–1⅜" long, with smooth, **thin shells** enclosed in **thin, yellow-felted, 4-ridged husks splitting in 4 to the middle; reddish-brown seed kernel** inside shell has 2 large, irregular lobes (cotyledons); nuts hang singly or in pairs, mature in October and drop.

Habitat: Moist, rich sites along streams to dry sites on higher slopes.

Origin: Native.

Key to Genera in the Beech Family (Fagaceae)

1a Fruit a single nut seated in a cup of firm, overlapping scales (acorn); leaves usually lobed, veins not extending beyond the lobe/tooth tips
. . . . ***Quercus*, oak** (key to species, see below)

1b Fruits with 1–4 (rarely 5) nuts enclosed in a prickly, bur-like covering that splits open along as many lines as there are nuts; leaves coarsely toothed; leaf veins various. **2**

2a Nuts sharply triangular, usually 2 in burs ³/₄–1¹/₈" wide; leaves oblong-ovate, shallowly toothed, with veins not extending beyond the teeth; bark smooth, pale gray
. . . . ***Fagus*, beech** (p. 116)

2b Nuts flattened on 1 or 2 sides, 2–4 in burs 2–3¹/₈" wide; leaves coarsely sharp-toothed, with veins extending beyond the tips of the teeth; bark rough, grayish-brown
. . . . ***Castanea*, chestnut** (p. 117)

Key to the Oaks (Genus *Quercus*)

1a Leaves smooth-edged, not lobed, bristle-tipped **2**
1b Leaves lobed or toothed, with or without a bristle tip **5**

2a Leaves widest in the upper ¹/₄, gradually tapered from near the tip to the base **3**
2b Leaves widest at or below the middle **4**

3a Leaves hairless, tapered to a wedge-shaped base . . . . . ***Q. nigra*, water oak** (p. 132)
3b Leaves minutely rusty-hairy beneath, tapered to a rounded to shallowly notched base
. . . . ***Q. marilandica*, blackjack oak** (p. 132)

4a Leaves 2–5" long, ¹/₂–1" wide, with surfaces hairless (or nearly so); acorn cap ⁵/₁₆–¹/₂" wide
. . . . ***Q. phellos*, willow oak** (p. 134)
4b Leaves 3–7" long, ³/₄–2" wide, with lower surfaces covered in star-shaped hairs; acorn cap at least ⁵/₈" wide . . . . ***Q. imbricaria*, shingle oak** (p. 133)

5a Leaves with sharp (rounded in water oak), bristle-tipped lobes; acorns maturing in the second year, woolly on the inner surface of the shell. **6**
5b Leaves with rounded to slightly pointed lobes or teeth, never bristle-tipped; acorns maturing in the first year, hairless on the inner surface of the shell **17**

Quercus macrocarpa, bur oak

6a   Mature leaves woolly, with star-shaped hairs beneath and often along the upper midvein; acorn cups downy on the inner surface and sometimes fringed. **7**

6b   Mature leaves essentially hairless (sometimes with tufts in vein axils); acorn cups hairless or with a few hairs around the scar, never fringed **10**

7a   Leaves widest in the upper 1/4, tipped with 3–5 broad lobes
    . . . . ***Q. marilandica*, blackjack oak** (p. 132)
7b   Leaves widest near the middle, edged with 5–11 (rarely 3) deeper, narrower lobes. **8**

8a   Lower leaf surfaces brown to reddish-brown, with relatively large, star-shaped hairs (discernible with a 10x lens); buds grayish, woolly, 1/4–1/2" long at branch tips
    . . . . ***Q. velutina*, black oak** (p. 126)
8b   Lower leaf surfaces grayish to yellowish, with tiny, star-shaped hairs (too small to see with a 10x lens); buds reddish-brown, essentially hairless, up to 1/4" long at branch tips **9**

9a   Leaves tipped with a long, slender lobe that often curves sharply to one side; buds at twig tips not angled; bark dark brown to blackish, with broad, scaly ridges
    . . . . ***Q. falcata*, southern red oak** (p. 131)
9b   Leaves tipped with a relatively wide, uncurved lobe; buds at twig tips angled; bark red-tinged and relatively smooth, like cherry bark   . . . . ***Q. pagoda*, cherry-bark oak** (p. 131)

10a   Leaves widest in the upper 1/4, gradually tapered from near the tip to the base. **11**
10b   Leaves widest at or below the middle. **12**

11a   Leaves hairless, tapered to a wedge-shaped base. . . . . .***Q. nigra*, water oak** (p. 132)
11b   Leaves minutely rusty-hairy beneath, tapered to a rounded or shallowly notched base
    . . . . ***Q. marilandica*, blackjack oak** (p. 132)

12a   Length of the largest leaf lobes (on leaves growing in full sun) equal to or slightly greater than the width of the middle part of the leaf (between opposing notches)
    . . . . ***Q. rubra*, northern red oak** (p. 127)
12b   Largest leaf lobes much (up to 3 times) longer than the width of the middle part of the leaf **13**

13a   Acorns large and round, 5/8–1 1/8" across. **14**
13b   Acorns relatively small, 3/8–3/4" across **15**

14a   Leaves usually with slender, long-tapered tips; bud scales fringed with hairs, often covered in fine, close hairs; acorn cups usually 5/8–3/4" wide
    . . . . ***Q. texana*, Texas red oak** (p. 129)
14b   Leaves not long-tapered at their tips; bud scales pale grayish-brown, hairless; acorn cups usually 3/4–1" wide . . . . ***Q. shumardii*, Shumard oak** (p. 129)

15a   Acorns round, 3/8–1/2" across, with saucer-like cups covering 1/4–1/3 of the nut
    . . . . ***Q. palustris*, pin oak** (p. 128)
15b   Acorns ellipsoid-cylindrical, 3/8–3/4" across, with deeper cups covering 1/3–1/2 of the nut
    . . . . **16**

16a   Leaf stalks >1/32" wide; acorns tipped with rings; acorn cups 5/8–3/4" wide
    . . . . ***Q. coccinea*, scarlet oak** (p. 130)
16b   Leaf stalks <1/32" wide; acorns lacking rings at their tips; acorn cups 3/8–5/8" wide
    . . . .***Q. ellipsoidalis*, northern pin oak** (p. 129)

17a Leaves coarsely toothed, with 3–14 teeth per side, indented less than ⅓ of the way to the midrib; lower leaf surfaces densely covered with whitish, star-shaped hairs **18**

17b Leaves with 1–5 distinct lobes per side, indented more than ⅓ of the way to the midrib; lower leaf surfaces various **22**

18a Acorns single or paired on long (¾–4") stalks; cup scales swollen, with pointed, recurved tips. . . . .*Q. bicolor*, **swamp white oak** (p. 122)

18b Acorn stalks absent or shorter than leaf stalks; cup scales only slightly swollen and lacking recurved tips. **19**

19a Hairs on lower leaf surfaces all erect and few-branched . . . . *Q. michauxii*, **swamp chestnut oak** (p. 123)

19b Hairs on lower leaf surfaces mostly short, spreading and star-shaped. **20**

20a Leaf teeth blunt and rounded; acorn cups ¾–1" wide; lower leaf surfaces sparsely hairy . . . . *Q. prinus*, **rock chestnut oak** (p. 123)

20b Leaf teeth tipped with a firm, projecting point (callus); acorn cups ½–⅝" wide; lower leaf surfaces woolly-hairy **21**

21a Leaves small (usually 1½–4" long) with 4–9 main veins per side; shrubby, rarely reaching the size of a small tree . . . .*Q. prinoides*, **dwarf chinquapin oak** (p. 125)

21b Leaves larger (about 4–7" long) with 8–15 main veins per side; tall shrub or medium-tall tree . . . . *Q. muehlenbergii*, **chinquapin oak** (p. 124)

22a Mature leaves essentially hairless beneath **23**

22b Mature leaves hairy beneath **24**

23a Lower leaf surfaces dull green; acorns ½–⅝" long . . . .*Q. nigra*, **water oak** (p. 132)

23b Lower leaf surfaces pale, with a whitish bloom; acorns ½–¾" long . . . . *Q. alba*, **white oak** (p. 118)

24a Leaves shallowly and irregularly lobed; acorns on long (¾–4") stalks; first-year twigs usually hairless . . . .*Q. bicolor*, **swamp white oak** (p. 122)

24b Leaves deeply notched below the middle and broadly lobed at the tip; acorns on shorter (<¾") stalks; first-year twigs hairy **25**

25a Leaves with 3–5 lobes, the upper 3 often forming a cross-like tip; acorns ⅜–⅝" wide . . . .*Q. stellata*, **post oak** (p. 119)

25b Leaves with 5–11 lobes, not cross-like at the tip; acorns ⅝–1⅛" wide. **26**

26a Acorn cups covering ½–¾ of the nut, edged with a distinctive fringe of hair-like scales . . . .*Q. macrocarpa*, **bur oak** (p. 121)

26b Acorn cups often covering almost all of the nut, never fringed . . . .*Q. lyrata*, **overcup oak** (p. 120)

Beech wood has been used for spindles, rungs, inexpensive furniture, handles, utensils, containers, flooring, plywood, railroad ties, barrels and casks. Because of its elastic qualities, it was once used to make all-wood clothespins. • Beech nuts are best after the first frosts. They make a tasty trail nibble but should be eaten in moderation because large amounts can cause intestinal inflammation. Dried, roasted and ground beech nuts make a traditional coffee substitute that can be mixed with coffee, milk or chocolate and sweetened with honey. Early settlers gathered beech nuts to extract the oil, which is similar to olive oil and was used as both food and lamp oil. • Beech nuts are eagerly sought by many birds and mammals, which then disperse the seeds. These fat-rich nuts are an important food for muskrats, squirrels, chipmunks, black bears and birds such as grouse, wood ducks and wild turkeys. • Beech bark disease, which is caused by fungus (three *Nectria* species), is killing many beech trees, especially those weakened by beech scale, an introduced, sucking insect (*Cryptococcus fagisuga*). Porcupines also kill beech trees by girdling the trunks.

Also Called: Red beech.

Size and Shape: Trees 60–80' tall; crowns rounded; roots wide-spreading.

Trunks: Often sinuous, 20–40" in diameter; **mature bark silvery gray, thin, smooth,** sometimes with dark markings; wood reddish-brown, heavy, hard, tough, but not durable.

Branches: Slender, smooth, crooked; twigs shiny, light olive-brown, slender, slightly zigzagged; buds reddish- to grayish-brown, **cigar-shaped, ⅜–1" long,** pointing outward, in 2 vertical rows.

Leaves: Alternate, simple, deciduous; blades 2–6" long, firm, dark bluish-green above, paler and lustrous below, leathery, narrowly oval, with **9–14 straight, parallel veins per side, each ending in a coarse tooth;** leaf scars small, semi-circular; leaves on lower branches or saplings **occasionally persisting into winter.**

Flowers: Tiny, yellowish-green, without petals; unisexual with male and female flowers on the same tree; male flowers clustered in dense, ¾–1" heads hanging on slender stalks; female flowers about ¼" long, erect, in compact clusters of 2–4; flowers in April–May (as leaves expand).

Fruits: Small **burs,** with **pairs of sharply 3-angled, ⅜–¾" long, smooth-shelled, reddish-brown nuts** enclosed in a prickly, greenish- to reddish-brown husk that splits in 2–4; seeds single kernels inside each nut; burs split open in late summer to autumn.

Habitat: Hardwood forests on moist slopes and in bottomlands.

Origin: Native.

The state's only native chestnut was once common in hardwood forests, but chestnut blight (*Endothia parasitica*), introduced from Asia in 1904, eliminated 99% of the chestnut trees in North America by 1937. The chestnut blight fungus spreads by wind-carried spores and causes uncontrolled bark growth. It commonly infects Eurasian chestnuts, but the New World species have almost no resistance. A few trees persist by sprouting from stumps, but shoots usually succumb to the blight before they reach 35' in height. Very few produce seed before dying. A less virulent strain of the fungus was introduced to compete with the deadly blight, but with limited success.

• American chestnut was an important commercial tree in the 19th century, valued for its durable wood and its large, sweet, edible nutmeats. • Settlers boiled the leaves to make a jelly for treating burns and sweaty feet. • A relatively blight-resistant horticultural species from Korea and China, **Chinese chestnut** (**C. mollissima**, also called *C. bungeana* and *C. formosana*), shown in pink on the map, occasionally grows wild in Illinois. It resembles American chestnut, but its leaves are woolly-hairy beneath.

Also Called: Sweet chestnut.

Size and Shape: Trees 10–35' (up to 80' before the blight) tall, from sprouting stumps; taproot.

Trunks: Straight, up to 6" (up to 40" before the blight) in diameter; young bark dark brown, smooth; mature bark with low, broad, flat-topped ridges; wood reddish-brown, straight-grained, hard, resistant to decay.

Branches: Stout; twigs shiny reddish-brown, stout; **pith star-shaped** in cross-section; buds greenish-brown, hairless, egg-shaped, about ¼" long, 2–3-scaled.

Leaves: Alternate, simple, deciduous; blades yellowish-green, smooth, **narrowly oblong, 6–10" long; veins straight, parallel, 15–20 per side, ending in coarse, bristle-tipped teeth;** stalks short, finely hairy.

Flowers: Tiny, creamy white, fragrant; unisexual with male and female flowers on the same tree; male flowers in stiff, 4¾–8" long, **semi-erect catkins; female flowers about ⅛" long,** 1–3 at the base of smaller (2⅜–5⅛" long), mainly male catkins near branch tips; flowers in June–July (immediately after leaves expand).

Fruits: Large burs **(chestnuts)** 2–2¾" across, with 1–3 (rarely 4–5), brownish, pointed, smooth-shelled nuts enclosed in a husk; husk greenish- to reddish-brown, bristling with stiff, needle-like spines**, splits in 4,** with single kernels inside nuts; chestnuts mature in autumn, drop after first frost.

Habitat: Woods on rocky, well-drained sites.

Origin: Native.

W hite oak, one of our most important hardwoods, is the state tree of Illinois. The strong, durable wood is amazingly elastic. Before the widespread use of steel, oak was the mainstay of shipbuilding and was also used in automobile and airplane frames and in plows. White oak wood is still used for cabinets, floors, paneling, veneer, plywood, support timbers, caskets, pianos and organs. Oak wood is famous for its use in watertight barrels, which give aged whiskey and wine a special color and flavor. • Boiled bark tea was once used for treating diarrhea, intestinal inflammation and bleeding gums. Such medicinal uses are not advised, because the concentrated tannins may be **toxic** and **carcinogenic.** • White oak acorns were an important source of food for many tribes. The edible, somewhat sweet kernels can be eaten raw, but traditionally they were usually dried, ground into meal and made into cakes or used to thicken soups. Acorns were also roasted in coals or boiled, then peeled and eaten as a vegetable or snack, often with suet. • Dark-roasted, ground kernels are said to make an excellent, caffeine-free coffee substitute. Acorn flour adds an interesting flavor to breads, muffins and cakes. • **Bebb oak (*Q. x bebbiana*)** is a common hybrid of white oak and bur oak (p. 121). Its leaves resemble those of white oak, but with bur oak's shallower sinuses appearing on the upper half.

Also Called: Northern white oak, stave oak.

Size and Shape: Trees 50–80' tall; crowns broad, full; taproot plus deep spreading roots.

Trunks: Short, straight, 24–48" in diameter; **mature bark pale gray,** often red-tinged, variable, coarsely flaky or with low, flat ridges; wood light brown, hard, heavy, water-impermeable, decay-resistant.

Branches: Wide-spreading, gnarled with age; twigs greenish and woolly to reddish and finally **smooth** and ash gray; **pith 5-pointed** in cross-section; buds reddish-brown, about ⅛" long,

with **broad, hairless scales;** buds at twig tips clustered, side-buds spreading.

Leaves: Alternate, simple, deciduous; blades 4–8" long, bright green above, paler beneath, firm, **hairless when mature, deeply pinnately lobed; lobes rounded, 5–9;** leaves brownish- to reddish-purple in autumn, a few may persist in winter.

Flowers: Tiny, without petals; unisexual, with male and female flowers separate on same tree; male flowers yellowish, numerous, in hanging, 2–3" long catkins; female flowers reddish, about ⅛" long, usually 2–4 in a cluster; flowers in April–May (as leaves expand).

Fruits: Elongated nuts **(acorns)** ½–¾" long, single or paired, with leathery shells; tips rounded with a small, abrupt point, **lower ¼ seated in a cup of overlapping, knobby scales, not fringed;** seeds single, **white kernels;** acorns remain in cup, mature in first autumn.

Habitat: Rich, moderately to well-drained sites in upland woods.

Origin: Native.

Post oak has been labeled the ultimate drought-resistant tree. Stunted, 400-year-old specimens can persist on dry, rocky, south-facing slopes, eking nutrients from hot, thin soils. This amazing tree can also survive and grow in flatland soils that are saturated with water in spring and brick-hard by midsummer. Despite this, the wide-spreading roots are very sensitive to disturbance and to excessive artificial flooding. When prairie fires are controlled, post oak can spread rapidly into former grass-lands by sprouting. In the southern plains, mixed with blackjack oak and hickories, post oak forms western extensions of the eastern deciduous forest. Post oak is an early-successional species, intoler-ant of competition and shade. On richer sites, it is usually quickly overtopped by other oaks, but on exposed slopes it may be dominant, because it is the only tree that can survive such extreme conditions.
• Trees begin to produce acorns at 20–30 years of age, with good crops every 2–4 years. Large trees in the canopy and subcanopy are most productive. These sweet acorns are an important food for white-tail deer, turkeys, raccoons and squirrels. • The wood, usually sold as "white oak," is used for mak-ing furniture and interior finishes and for burning as fuel. • Post oak is best grown from acorns, which germinate readily and grow in almost any soil.

Size and Shape: Trees 33–66' tall, often gnarled; crowns broad; roots extensive and spreading.

Trunks: Straight to crooked, 1–2' in diameter; bark reddish-brown to dark gray, thick, with rounded, scaly ridges lacking loose plates; wood hard, fine-grained, durable.

Branches: Few, stout, spreading; twigs hairy and reddish-brown at first, gray and hairless with age, **pith 5–pointed** in cross-section; buds dark chestnut brown, hairy, round to pear-shaped, ⅛–¼" long, with overlapping scales.

Leaves: Alternate, deciduous, simple; **blades lustrous and dark green above, thick,** leathery, **3–8" long, often deeply cut into 3–5 broad, rounded to slightly notched lobes,** variable, **usu-ally roughly cross-shaped;** leaves brown to burnt orange in late fall–early winter.

Flowers: Tiny, hairy, yellowish-green, without petals; unisexual with male and female flowers separate on the same tree; male flowers in hanging, 3–4" long catkins; female flowers in clusters of 1–4 in leaf axils; flowers in April–May (with leaves).

Fruits: Elongated nuts **(acorns)** ½–¾" long, with reddish-brown, leathery shells, tips rounded with a small, abrupt point, **lower ⅓–½ seated in a rounded to pear-shaped cup** of thin, flat overlap-ping scales; seeds single, **white kernels;** acorns essentially stalkless, remain in cup to mature and drop in September–November of first autumn.

Habitat: Dry bluffs to seasonally flooded flatlands.

Origin: Native.

Once these slow-growing trees begin to flower at 25–30 years of age, they are easily identified by their distinctive acorns, in which ⅔ to almost all of the nut is covered by a deep cup of overlapping scales. When the acorns are absent, distinguishing characteristics include hairless first-year twigs or twigs with a few hairs over a clearly visible cuticle and leaves usually more than 2" wide, widest above the middle but with round to slightly pointed (but not bristle-tipped) lobes from top to bottom. • Mature trees produce large crops of acorns every 3–4 years and much smaller crops in intervening years. The sweet, edible acorns provide valuable food for white-tailed deer, turkeys, squirrels and other small rodents. • The strong, heavy wood is usually cut and sold as "white oak." • Like most oaks, this species often hybridizes with close relatives, including swamp white oak (p. 122) and post oak (p. 119). • Overcup oak is extremely flood tolerant and can thrive in areas that may remain flooded for the entire growing season. Water also helps disperse its acorns, which can float for long periods using their large, thick cups. In the southern U.S., below USDA Zone 5, this shade-tolerant tree gradually replaces swamp white oak as a dominant species in swamps and bottomlands.

Also Called: Swamp white oak.

Size and Shape: Trees 30–65' tall; crowns broad, rounded.

Trunks: Tall and straight to short and crooked, 24–40" in diameter; bark reddish- to grayish-brown, ½–1" thick with thin, squarish plates; wood dark brown, hard, durable.

Branches: Stout, spreading, crooked; twigs becoming hairless and reddish- to grayish-brown with age, **pith 5-pointed** in cross-section; buds light-brown, rounded, ¹⁄₁₆–⅛" long, with overlapping scales.

Leaves: Alternate, deciduous, simple; **blades smooth dark green above, paler and densely soft-hairy beneath** (sometimes hairless with age), with erect, few-branched hairs and (often) spreading, star-shaped hairs, 6–10" long, with **5–9 rounded lobes, some cut over halfway to the midvein,** tapered to a narrow base; dull gold to crimson in both early spring and fall.

Flowers: Tiny, yellowish-green, without petals; unisexual with male and female flowers separate on the same tree; male flowers hanging in 4–6" long catkins; female flowers in few-flowered clusters in leaf axils; flowers in April–May.

Fruits: Round to broad-based, light brown, leathery-shelled nuts **(acorns),** ½–1" long, tipped with a small, abrupt point, **½ to completely immersed** in a cup of thick, pointed, overlapping scales; seeds single, **white kernels;** acorns remain in cup, shed in the first September–October.

Habitat: Swampy lowland and bottomland woods.

Origin: Native.

Bur oak is one of North America's most common and widespread white oaks. With its thick bark and deep roots, it is fire and drought resistant enough to grow in grasslands, but it can also tolerate periodic flooding and thrive in seasonally wet lowlands. • Bur oak wood, acorns, bark and leaves are similar to those of white oak (p. 118) and have been used in the same ways, with the same limitations. • This attractive tree is often planted in parks, gardens and boulevards as a shade-giving ornamental. It tolerates air pollution in urban centers, but its deep taproot can make it difficult to transplant. • Oaks are generally divided into 2 main groups: 1) White oaks, which have smooth-edged to blunt-toothed or round-lobed leaves that lack bristle tips, sweet, edible acorns that ripen in one season, acorn shells with smooth inner surfaces and scaly bark (the white oaks in this guide are on pp. 118–25); and red and black oaks, which have smooth-edged, sharp-toothed or sharp-lobed leaves that have bristle-tipped points, bitter acorns that ripen in 2 years, acorn shells with hairy inner surfaces and non-scaly bark (the red and black oaks in this guide are on pp. 126–34).

Also Called: Mossycup oak, blue oak, mossy oak, over-cup oak, scrubby oak.

Size and Shape: Trees 40–80' tall; crowns broad, full; taproot deep.

Trunks: Straight, 24–48" in diameter, often with small branches from dormant buds; mature bark gray, often reddish-tinged, with thick, irregular, scaly ridges; wood hard, heavy, water-impermeable, decay-resistant.

Branches: Spreading to ascending; twigs thick, woolly-hairy, **often corky-ridged; pith 5-pointed** in cross-section; **buds hairy,** about ⅛" long, **flat-lying,** broad-scaled with a few **loose, slender basal scales.**

Leaves: Alternate, simple, deciduous; blades shiny and dark green above, paler and white-hairy beneath, firm, 4–10" long, **deeply pinnately lobed; lobes rounded,** with 2–4 (sometimes 6–8) small lobes below a broad, coarse-toothed upper lobe; some leaves may persist in winter.

Flowers: Tiny, without petals; unisexual with male and female flowers on the same tree; male flowers yellowish-green, hairy, in hanging catkins 4–6" long; female flowers reddish, hairy, about ⅛" across, in clusters of 1–5; flowers in May–June (as leaves expand).

Fruits: Round nuts **(acorns)** ½–1⅛" long, usually single; tips rounded with a small, abrupt point, **the lower ½–¾ or more in a conspicuously fringed cup of overlapping, knobbly, pointed scales;** seeds single, **white kernels;** acorns remain in cup, mature in first autumn.

Habitat: From savannas to rich bottomlands.

Origin: Native.

This tree can live 300 years or more, but its shallow roots and relatively thin, scaly bark make it susceptible to fire damage. Swamp white oak usually begins to flower at about 25–30 years of age, and it produces large acorn crops every 3–5 years. • Swamp white oak wood is similar to and is sometimes sold as "white oak," but the swamp type is knottier and of poorer quality. Still, it has been used in barrels, furniture, cabinets, interior finishing, veneers and construction. • The sweet, edible acorns can be used like those of white oak for food. • With a magnifier, you may be able to see the star-like shapes of some hairs on the velvety undersides of the leaves. The specific epithet *bicolor* means "two-colored" and refers to the contrasting shiny, green upper and fuzzy, white lower leaf surfaces. The genus name *Quercus* means "tree above all others" and was the traditional Latin name for oak. It may have been derived from the Celtic *quer cuez*, meaning "fine tree." • This oak often crosses with bur oak (p. 121) to produce hybrids (**Q. x schuettei**) with intermediate characteristics.

Also Called: Blue oak, swamp oak.

Size and Shape: Trees 40–65' tall; crowns broad, irregular and rounded, **untidy below;** roots shallow.

Trunks: Straight, 24–40" in diameter; young bark reddish-brown, scaly, peeling; mature bark grayish-brown, flat-ridged; wood light brown, hard, heavy, close-grained, water-impermeable, decay-resistant.

Branches: Ascending to spreading, with **crooked, hanging branchlets** on lower branches; twigs stout; **pith 5-pointed** in cross-section; buds reddish-brown, hairy, about ⅛" long, tip bud in a cluster.

Leaves: Alternate, simple, deciduous; blades 4¾–8" long, **shiny and dark green above, pale and white-woolly beneath,** firm, widest above the middle, **shallowly pinnately lobed** to coarsely wavy-toothed, with 4–6 main veins per side, each ending in a rounded lobe or tooth; leaves yellowish-brown to orange in autumn, some may persist.

Flowers: Tiny, without petals; unisexual with male and female flowers on the same tree; male flowers yellowish-green, hairy, in hanging catkins 2¾–4" long; female flowers hairy, reddish, about ⅛" across, in stalked clusters of 1–5; flowers in Aprl–May (as leaves expand).

Fruits: Round nuts **(acorns)** with leathery shells, ¾–1⅛" long, **1–2 on stalks ¾–4" long;** tips rounded with a small point, ¼–½ of the base in a cup of thick, overlapping scales with outcurved tips; seeds single, white kernels; acorns mature in first autumn.

Habitat: Rich, wet sites on shores and floodplains and in swamps.

Origin: Native.

These large, edible acorns are eagerly sought by many animals, including whitetail deer, turkeys, black bears, squirrels, and chipmunks. Cattle also enjoy this sweet treat, hence the name "cow oak." Consequently, regeneration from seed can be sparse. Late spring frosts sometimes cause complete crop failure. Trees begin producing acorns after about 25 years, but optimum production begins at about 40 years of age, with heavy crops every 3–5 years. The acorns are spread mainly by hoarding animals such as squirrels. • The tough, durable wood is used in flooring and veneers. • Swamp chestnut oak prefers relatively open, seasonally flooded sites with deep, rich soils. The striking contrast of whitish bark and scarlet autumn leaves is a beautiful combination. • **Rock chestnut oak** (*Q. prinus*, also called *Q. montana* or simply chestnut oak), shown in pink/dark green (species overlap) on the map, is a similar tree, sometimes included in swamp chestnut oak. It is distinguished by the erect, few-branched hairs (vs. short, star-shaped hairs) on its lower leaf surfaces and by the often rounded (vs. pointed) teeth along its leaf edges. Also, the scales of its acorn cups are free (vs. fused) near the cup base and are usually fringed (vs. smooth) near the cup rim. In Illinois, rock chestnut oak is a rare tree of rocky sites.

Also Called: Basket oak, cow oak.

Size and Shape: Medium-sized to large trees 60–115' tall; crowns narrow, rounded, compact.

Trunks: Long, straight, 2–3' in diameter; mature bark light gray to whitish, thick, with narrow, flaky ridges; wood light brown, hard, dense.

Branches: Stout, ascending; twigs green to reddish-brown; pith 5-pointed in cross-section; buds red, hairy, egg-shaped, pointed, ¼" long, covered with thin, pale-edged scales.

Leaves: Alternate, deciduous, simple; blades shiny, dark green, grayish soft-hairy beneath with erect, few-branched hairs, 4–8½" long, ovate, broadest above midleaf, pointed, edged with 10–15 pairs of coarse, pointed to blunt, often gland-tipped teeth (shallow lobes); leaves deep scarlet in autumn.

Flowers: Tiny, without petals; unisexual with male and female flowers separate on the same tree; male flowers hanging in slender, 4–6" long catkins; female flowers in small, short clusters of 1–3 in leaf axils; flowers in April–May (as leaves expand).

Fruits: Bright brown, broad-based nuts (acorns) 1–1½" long, ¾–1⅜" wide, with leathery shells, rounded with a relatively long, abrupt point at the tip, lower ⅓ of the nut seated in a ¾–1½" wide, bowl-shaped cup of thick, hairy, free (not fused), wedge-shaped scales; seeds single, white kernels; acorns remain in cup, mature and fall in September–October of the first autumn.

Habitat: Low woods and swamps.

Origin: Native.

Chinquapin oak wood is sometimes sold as "white oak." Although strong and durable, it has little commercial value, largely because of limited supply. It has been used for construction, railway ties, split-rail fences and fuel. • The sweet, edible acorns are milder than those of most other oaks. They can be eaten fresh from the tree or prepared like white oak acorns. • This tree is sometimes planted as an ornamental. • **Rock chestnut oak** (*Q. prinus*, p. 123) is sometimes confused with chinquapin oak but can be distinguished by its sparsely hairy lower leaf surfaces, rounded (not bristle-tipped) leaf teeth and larger acorn cups (¾–1" wide). • The name "chinquapin" is a Native word for the American chestnut tree (p. 117). The yellowish-green young leaves of chinquapin oak and this tree's similarity to chestnut oak have given rise to another common name, "yellow chestnut oak."

Also Called: Chinkapin oak, yellow oak, yellow chestnut oak, rock oak.

Size and Shape: Trees 40–50' tall (to 80' in forests); crowns narrow, rounded.

Trunks: Straight, 12–24" in diameter, often enlarged at the base; **mature bark pale grayish, thin-scaled, flaky;** wood brown, hard, heavy, close-grained, decay-resistant.

Branches: Short; twigs green to grayish-brown or orange-brown, stiff, slender; **pith 5-pointed** in cross-section; buds pale reddish-brown, hairless, ⅛–¼" long, buds at twig tips clustered.

Leaves: Alternate, simple, deciduous; **blades 4–7" long,** widest above the middle, glossy, yellowish-green to deep green above, paler and densely hairy with star-shaped hairs beneath, firm, with **8–15 straight, parallel veins per side** ending in large, pointed (sometimes slightly rounded), **minutely bristle-tipped teeth;** some leaves may persist in winter.

Flowers: Tiny, without petals; unisexual with male and female flowers on the same tree; male flowers hairy, yellow, in hanging catkins 2¾–4" long; female flowers silver-woolly, reddish, in compact clusters of 1–5; flowers in April–May (as leaves expand).

Fruits: Slightly elongated, leathery-shelled nuts **(acorns)** ½–¾" long, single or paired; tips rounded with a small, abrupt, white-downy point, **lower ⅓–½ in a cup of silvery-hairy, overlapping, slightly thickened scales;** seeds single white kernels; acorns mature in first autumn.

Habitat: Dry to moist woodlands.

Origin: Native.

Dwarf chinquapin oak is well named. It is a true dwarf tree, capable of producing acorns when it is scarcely 10' tall. It bears large crops of sweet, edible acorns annually or every other year. • This sun-loving shrub often produces colonies on exposed hillsides by sending up suckers from widely spreading roots. When an old stem dies, its roots may remain alive and sprout a ring of vigorous shoots around the base of the dead trunk. • Like most oaks, dwarf chinquapin oak produces hard, dense, high-quality wood, but its trunks are too small to be of any commercial value. • Dwarf chinquapin oak is like a smaller, shrubbier version of chinquapin oak (p. 124). It also differs from its larger cousin in its smaller leaves (mostly 1½–4" long vs. 4–7" long), with fewer (4–9 vs. 10–15) veins and teeth per side. These 2 species often hybridize, making identification even more difficult. • Dwarf chinquapin oak, chinquapin oak, swamp chestnut oak (p. 123) and swamp white oak (p. 122) are sometimes classified as "chestnut oaks." Trees in this group have toothed to shallowly lobed leaves, unlike the deeply lobed leaves usually associated with oaks.

Also Called: Dwarf chinkapin oak, dwarf chestnut oak.

Size and Shape: Small trees (occasionally) or spreading shrubs (usually), **3–15' tall;** crowns scruffy, rounded; roots deep, spreading.

Trunks: Short, crooked, usually leaning and clumped, 3–5" in diameter; **mature bark pale brown, thin-scaled, flaky;** wood hard, heavy, close-grained, decay-resistant.

Branches: Spreading; twigs reddish-brown to pale gray, smooth, slender, brittle; **pith 5-pointed** in cross-section; buds light brown, about ⅛" long, buds at twig tips clustered.

Leaves: Alternate, simple, deciduous; **blades 1½–4¾"** (rarely to 6") long, widest above the middle, shiny, bright yellowish-green above, densely hairy with white, star-shaped hairs beneath, firm, with **3–9 (usually 6) straight, parallel veins per side ending in large teeth that vary** from long and pointed to shallow and blunt; some leaves may persist in winter.

Flowers: Tiny, without petals; unisexual with male and female flowers on the same tree; male flowers yellow, hairy, in hanging catkins 1–2¾" long; female flowers yellowish-red, stalkless, 1–2 per cluster; flowers in April–May (as leaves expand).

Fruits: Slightly elongated, **chestnut brown,** leathery-shelled nuts **(acorns)** ⅜–¾" **long,** single or paired; tips rounded with a small, abrupt point, lower ⅓–½ in a **downy-lined cup** of hairy, overlapping, slightly thickened scales; seeds single, **white kernels;** acorns mature in first autumn.

Habitat: Dry, open, usually calcareous sites.

Origin: Native.

The thick, tannin-rich inner bark of black oak was sometimes used for tanning leather. It contains the yellow pigment quercitron, which became a popular dye in Europe and was sold commercially until the late 1940s. • White-tailed deer, small mammals, wild turkeys, jays and grouse all eat the bitter acorns and help to disperse the seeds. • This highly variable oak hybridizes with northern red oak (p. 127) and northern pin oak (p. 129), further complicating identification. Generally, black oak is distinguished from other species with bristle-pointed leaves (the red and black oaks) by its woolly, 4-angled buds (vs. shiny, egg-shaped buds), the star-shaped hairs on the undersides of its leaves (vs. hairless leaves), the loose (vs. compact) scales of its fringed (vs. non-fringed) acorn cups and its bright yellow-orange (vs. usually reddish) inner bark. • The species name *velutina* means "like velvet," a reference to the silvery-woolly buds and hairy leaves. • Like many black or red oaks, this species is susceptible to oak wilt. This long-lived, shade-intolerant tree is considered a good indicator of sites with dry to very dry conditions. • Black oak often hybridizes with blackjack oak (p. 132) to produce **Bush oak (*Q.* x *bushii*).**

Also Called: Yellow-barked oak, yellow oak, quercitron oak.

Size and Shape: Trees 50–80' tall; crowns open, irregular; roots deep (taproot), spreading.

Trunks: Straight, 12–48" in diameter; **mature bark dark grayish-brown to blackish,** deeply cracked into rectangles; **inner bark yellow to yellowish-orange;** wood light brown, hard, heavy.

Branches: Horizontal to ascending, with irregular branchlets; **twigs stout, stiff, dark reddish-brown, becoming hairless; pith 5-pointed** in cross-section; **buds gray- to white-woolly, 4-angled,** pointed, ¼–⅜" long.

Leaves: Alternate, simple, deciduous; blades 4–8" long, **glossy, dark green above, dull yellowish-brown beneath,** with **star-shaped hairs on veins and in vein axils,** deeply pinnately lobed; **lobes 5–7, parallel-sided,** perpendicular to main axis; teeth few, coarse, bristle-tipped; **notches U-shaped.**

Flowers: Tiny, without petals; unisexual with male and female flowers on the same tree; male flowers hairy, in hanging catkins 4–6" long; female flowers reddish, about ¼" long, in small clusters; flowers in April–May (as leaves expand).

Fruits: **Round,** reddish-brown, leathery-shelled nuts **(acorns)** ½–¾" **long,** single or paired, **lower ⅓–½ in a dull brown, slightly fringed cup of thin, loose, overlapping scales;** tips with a small, abrupt point; seeds single, yellow kernels; acorns mature in second autumn; both large (2nd-year) and small (1st-year) acorns usually present.

Habitat: Dry, well-drained sites in upland forests.

Origin: Native.

126

Northern red oak is an attractive shade tree that transplants readily, grows quickly and resists most pests and disease. It is, however, occasionally susceptible to oak wilt. Introduced to Europe in 1724, it now grows wild in European forests. • Northern red oak wood is prized for its durability and beautiful grain, but it is susceptible to decay under moist conditions because it is "ring porous." If you dip a piece in soapy water, remove it and blow on one end, bubbles will form at the other end. Northern red oak has been used to make furniture, interior trim, hardwood floors and veneers. It makes excellent barrels, but they can be used for storing only dry goods. • The bitter acorns can be eaten in small quantities only. Eating raw acorns has poisoned cattle. Some Native tribes soaked the acorn kernels in flowing water for several days to draw out the **toxic** tannins. Alternatively, the kernels were buried over winter or were boiled in water with wood ash (lye) to improve their edibility. • Small mammals such as raccoons and squirrels, as well as white-tailed deer, black bears, wild turkeys and blue jays, eat the acorns. Deer also browse on the young twigs in winter.

Also Called: Red oak, gray oak • *Q. borealis*.

Size and Shape: Trees 65–100' tall; crowns broad, round; roots deep (taproot), spreading.

Trunks: Straight, 12–40" in diameter; young bark smooth, slate gray; mature bark with long, low, pale gray ridges, **eventually checkered; inner bark pinkish-red;** wood pinkish to reddish-brown, hard, heavy, coarse-grained.

Branches: Stout, spreading; **twigs stout, reddish-brown and hairless; pith 5-pointed** in cross-section; **buds shiny reddish-brown,** mostly hairless, pointed, about ¼" long.

Leaves: Alternate, simple, deciduous; **blades firm, 4–9" long, deeply pinnately lobed** to shallowly lobed on lower branches or simply toothed on young trees, dull, dark yellowish-green above, paler beneath, vein axils often hairy-tufted; **lobes 5–11, roughly triangular;** teeth few, coarse, **tipped with bristles;** notches rounded, V-shaped; leaves red in autumn.

Flowers: Tiny, without petals; unisexual with male and female flowers on the same tree; male flowers hairy, yellowish-green, in hanging catkins 4–5" long; female flowers hairy, bright green, about ⅛" long, usually single or paired; flowers in April–May (as leaves expand).

Fruits: Round, reddish-brown, leathery-shelled nuts **(acorns)** ½–1⅛" **long,** single or paired, **lower** ¼ (rarely ⅓) **in a saucer-shaped cup of thin, hairless, reddish-brown scales;** tips rounded with a small, abrupt point; seeds single, yellowish kernels; **acorns mature in second autumn;** both large (2nd-year) and small (1st-year) acorns generally present.

Habitat: Well-drained, upland forests.

Origin: Native.

This attractive, symmetrical tree provides checkered shade in many parks and gardens. Pin oak is shallow-rooted and easily transplanted, and it is capable of tolerating urban conditions in areas well outside its natural range. • This fast-growing tree is among the first oaks to bloom each spring. It can live 100–200 years. • Because of taxonomic confusion, trees sold as pin oak may be northern pin oak (p. 129) or scarlet oak (p. 130). • The knotty, poor-quality wood is coarse-grained and ring-porous, with a distinct ring of large pores laid down each spring. Pin oak wood is sometimes sold as "red oak" for construction, fence posts and firewood. • White-tailed deer, small mammals, wild turkeys and waterfowl eat the bitter acorns. • This species is susceptible to oak wilt and chlorosis. • The common name "pin oak" could refer to the stiff, persistent, "pin-like" branchlets that often project from the trunks and lower branches of larger trees. It has also been attributed to the tiny dots or "pin-knots" that speckle pin oak lumber. These tiny knots are created by the abundant, persistent side-branches.

Also Called: Swamp oak, Spanish oak, water oak.

Size and Shape: Trees 35–65' tall; crowns compact, cylindrical to pyramidal; roots shallow.

Trunks: Straight, 12–24" in diameter; mature bark grayish-brown, **smooth or with small, inconspicuous ridges; inner bark reddish;** wood light brown, hard, heavy.

Branches: Slightly drooping (lower) to ascending (upper) with many short, spur-like side-branches; dead branches often persist; twigs reddish-brown, slender, soon becoming hairless; **pith 5-pointed** in cross-section; buds light chestnut brown, about ⅛" long, essentially hairless.

Leaves: Alternate, simple, deciduous, often persisting until early spring; blades 2¾–6" long, **shiny, dark green above,** paler beneath, with hair tufts in main vein axils, **deeply pinnately lobed; lobes 5–7,** each 3 times as long as the width between opposite notches, **wide-spreading, the upper sides perpendicular to the midvein;** teeth few, coarse, each with **bristle at tip;** notches widely U-shaped; stalks slender; leaves bright red in autumn.

Flowers: Tiny, without petals; unisexual with male and female flowers on the same tree; male flowers yellowish, numerous, in hanging, hairy catkins 2–4" long; female flowers woolly, reddish, about ⅛" long, in clusters of 1–4 on short, hairy stalks; flowers in May (as leaves expand).

Fruits: Round, leathery-shelled nuts **(acorns)** ⅜–½" **long,** 1–3 together, **lower ¼ in a finely hairy, reddish-brown, saucer-shaped cup** of thin, pointed scales; tips rounded with a small, abrupt point; seeds single, yellow to pale brown kernels; acorns mature and separate from cup in second autumn.

Habitat: Low, wet sites.

Origin: Native.

Northern pin oak resembles pin oak (p. 128) but prefers upland sites, rather than low, wet habitats. Also, it has slightly elongated acorns with deep cups, rather than round acorns with saucer-shaped cups. This species often hybridizes with black oak (p. 126) and could be confused with that species, but northern pin oak has smaller leaves, pale yellow (not bright yellow) inner bark and persistent "pin-like" branchlets on its trunks plus larger branches (both absent on black oak).
• A similar species, **Shumard oak (*Q. shumardii*)**, shown in pink on the map, grows in southern, rather than northern, Illinois. Shumard oak can be confused with black oak and northern red oak (p. 127), and was once considered a hybrid of those species. It is

identified by its more deeply indented leaves and its preference for moist, clayey soils (rather than sandy sites). It is a large (65–130' tall) tree with large (4–8"), 7–11 lobed leaves and large ($^1/_2$–$1^1/_8$"), round acorns with tam-shaped cups over $^1/_4$–$^1/_3$ of the nut. • **Texas red oak (*Q. texana*,** also called Nuttall's oak, *Q. nutalli*), shown in dark green (species overlap) on the map, is another close relative. It is distinguished by its finely hairy (vs. hairless) buds, its slender, tapered leaf tips and its narrower ($^5/_8$" vs. $^3/_4$" wide), deeper, pointed (vs. shallow, rounded) acorn cups that cover $^1/_3$–$^1/_2$ of the nut. This southern species is endangered in Illinois.

Also Called: Hill's oak, jack oak, upland pin oak.

Size and Shape: Trees 50–65' tall; crowns narrow, cylindrical, rounded; taproot.

Trunks: Straight, 12–24" in diameter, with many stubby branches; mature bark dark grayish-brown, with **shallow, narrow ridges; inner bark light yellow;** wood pale reddish-brown, hard, heavy.

Branches: Stout, spreading to ascending; twigs bright reddish-brown and hairy at first, soon grayish-brown and hairless; **pith 5-pointed** in cross-section; buds shiny, reddish-brown, $^1/_8$–$^1/_4$" long.

Leaves: Alternate, simple, deciduous, often persisting until early spring; **blades 3–5" long, shiny, bright green above,** paler with hairy-tufted vein axils beneath, **deeply pinnately lobed; lobes 5–7,** each 3 times as long as the width between opposite notches, **wide-spreading, upper lobes perpendicular to the midvein;** teeth few, **bristle-tipped;** notches widely U-shaped; stalks slender, hairless; leaves bright red in autumn.

Flowers: Tiny, without petals; unisexual with male and female flowers on the same tree; male flowers hairy, in hanging catkins 1–2¾" long; female flowers red, hairy, about $^1/_8$" long, in compact clusters of 1–3; flowers in April–May (as leaves expand).

Fruits: Ellipsoidal to almost round, light brown, leathery-shelled nuts **(acorns)** ½–¾" long, single or paired, **lower $^1/_3$–½ in cup of finely hairy, light brown, thin scales;** tips abruptly small-pointed; seeds single yellow kernels; acorns mature in second autumn.

Habitat: Well-drained, upland woods.

Origin: Native.

With its rapid growth, broad, open crown and bright red autumn leaves, scarlet oak is a popular ornamental tree. It is often cultivated as a hardy shade tree in parks and gardens. • Scarlet oak is closely related to northern pin oak (p. 129), and some taxonomists feel that both belong in a single species complex, grading from scarlet oak in the south to northern pin oak in the north. Scarlet oak is distinguished by its white (vs. yellow) nut kernels, hairy-tipped (vs. hairless) buds and clear trunks (lacking persistent branch stubs almost to the ground). Hybridization with other species such as black oak (p. 126) and northern red oak (p. 127) further confuses the picture, along with a similar north–south species gradation between black oak and northern red oak. • Large, round galls called "oak apples" appear on the leaves of some oaks. These growths are caused by a substance that certain insects such as wasps release when they lay eggs in the leaves. The substance causes cells to undergo unusually rapid growth, and the leaf lays down more and more tissue around the egg. Inside the galls, the eggs hatch, and the young larvae find themselves surrounded by protective layers of nutritious leaf cells. Most larvae spend this entire stage inside the gall, then pupate to emerge as adult insects.

Also Called: Red oak, black oak.

Size and Shape: Trees 50–65' tall; crowns open, broad; taproot.

Trunks: Straight, 12–24" in diameter; **bark dark grayish-brown, thin, smooth to scaly; inner bark reddish;** wood light reddish-brown, hard, heavy.

Branches: Slender; twigs hairy and green at first, soon hairless and light brown; **pith 5-pointed** in cross-section; buds dark reddish-brown, about ¼" long, hairy near the tips.

Leaves: Alternate, simple, deciduous; **blades 3–6" long and almost as wide, firm, green, shiny above,** paler beneath, **deeply pinnately lobed; lobes 5–9,** wide-spreading; teeth few, coarse, each with **bristle at tip;** notches widely U-shaped; stalks slender; leaves scarlet in autumn.

Flowers: Tiny, reddish, hairy, without petals; unisexual with male and female flowers on the same tree; male flowers with yellow anthers, in hanging, 2¾–4" catkins; female flowers woolly, bright red, about ⅛" long, in clusters of 1–4 on short, hairy stalks; flowers in April–May (as leaves expand).

Fruits: Round, pale reddish-brown, leathery-shelled nuts (acorns) ½–¾" long, usually with concentric rings around a small, abrupt point, **lower ½ in a finely hairy, reddish-brown to orange cup** of pointed scales; seeds single, whitish kernels; acorns mature and separate from cup late in second autumn.

Habitat: Dry, well-drained sites in upland woods.

Origin: Native.

This graceful, moderately fast-growing, fairly long-lived (100–150 years) tree is one of the most common oaks in upland forests and along urban streets in the southeastern U.S. Southern red oak is a major component of 2 southern forest types (Virginia pine–southern red oak; shortleaf pine–oak) and is also common in several other pine-hardwood forests. • Squirrels are especially important for spreading seed by "planting" the bitter acorns in caches. • The wood is not considered prime timber, but it has been used in general construction, for making crates and furniture and for burning as fuel. In open stands, profuse branching along the trunk further reduces the quality of the wood. • Based on the highly variable leaves, botanists have described several varieties and forms. • **Cherry-bark oak (*Q. pagoda*,** also called *Q. pagodifolia*), shown in dark green (species overlap) on the map, is sometimes considered a variety of southern red oak (*Q. falcata* var. *pagodifolia*). It is a larger tree (up to 130' tall) with a straighter, clearer (more branch-free) trunk and smooth, narrow-ridged, red-tinged bark, similar to that of wild black cherry (p. 174). The leaf lobes are more regular and more wide-spreading than those of southern red oak, and the tip lobe is relatively short and broad and never curves. Cherry-bark oak grows in rich lowlands in southernmost Illinois.

Also Called: Spanish oak, water oak
• *Q. triloba*.

Size and Shape: Trees 65–80' tall; crowns high, round (forests) to broad, open (clearings).

Trunks: Long and straight in forests, 2–3' in diameter; mature bark dark brown to almost black, with broad scaly ridges; wood pale reddish brown, coarse, hard.

Branches: Large; twigs stout, orange-hairy at first, soon dark gray and nearly hairless; **pith 5-pointed** (in cross-section); buds reddish, hairy, with overlapping scales, not strongly angled.

Leaves: Alternate, deciduous, simple; blades **shiny and dark green above, grayish-green and woolly beneath,** 4¾–9" long, widest above mid-leaf, mostly with 3–7 slender-tapered, **bristle-tipped lobes that often curve sharply to one side** (falcate); uppermost lobe often elongated; **some leaves shallowly 3-lobed** at the tip; leaves crimson to drab in autumn.

Flowers: Tiny, hairy, without petals; unisexual with male and female flowers separate on the same tree; male flowers hang in slender, 3–5" catkins; female flowers single or paired in leaf axils; flowers in April–May.

Fruits: Round, **orange-brown nuts (acorns),** about ½" long, with leathery shells, tipped with a relatively long, abrupt point (old style), **lower ⅓ seated in a shallow, top-shaped cup** of blunt, hairy, red-brown, flat scales; seeds single **yellow kernels;** acorns single or paired, drop in second September–October; large (2nd-year) and small (1st-year) acorns usually present.

Habitat: Dry woods, usually in uplands.

Origin: Native.

Blackjack oak is a pioneer species that invades newly exposed, barren ground, especially after fires. On richer sites, it is quickly outcompeted by other trees, so blackjack usually grows in inhospitable areas such as rocky bluffs and sand flats. Its presence is sometimes used as an indicator of thin, poor-quality soils. • Although blackjack oak is too small to be of commercial value, it provides important habitat for wildlife, including squirrels, turkeys and deer. The scrubby trees create cover in otherwise barren areas and provide food in the form of nutritious acorns. • On good soil, cultivated blackjack oaks can grow into attractive, symmetrical trees, but at a very slow rate. The dense, twiggy crowns can provide good windbreaks and visual barriers. In exposed sites, blackjack is recommended as a trouble-free, colorful tree capable of withstanding both heat and drought. • A more southern tree, **water oak (*Q. nigra*)**, shown in dark green (species overlap) on the map, has recently been reported in Illinois. Water oak resembles blackjack oak, but its leaf blades are usually narrower (about ½ as wide and as long) with tapered, wedge-shaped bases and hairless undersides. Water oak grows in mixed stands along streams and on floodplains. Its leaves are highly variable, and sometimes remain fresh on the tree until January.

Size and Shape: Small, scrubby trees, 30–60' tall; crowns compact to open; taproot deep.

Trunks: Usually to 1' in diameter; mature bark nearly black, irregularly checked; wood dark brown, hard, strong.

Branches: Short, often twisted or slightly drooping; twigs numerous, stout, hairy and reddish-brown when young; **pith 5-pointed** in cross-section; buds at leaf bases, egg-shaped, rusty-hairy.

Leaves: Alternate, deciduous, simple; blades firm, leathery, shiny and dark green above, with rusty, **flat-lying** (rarely soft, star-shaped and woolly) **hairs beneath,** 3–6" (rarely 12") long and **almost as wide, resembling a webbed bird's foot, highly variable,** sometimes without lobes, **rounded to slightly notched at the base;** leaves crimson or orange in autumn, often persist into winter.

Flowers: Tiny, without petals; unisexual with male and female flowers separate on the same tree; male flowers in slender, 2–5" long catkins; female flowers single or paired; flowers in April–May (with leaves).

Fruits: Round, leathery-shelled nuts **(acorns)** ⅜–⅝" long, tipped with a small, abrupt point, **lower ⅓–½ seated in a top-shaped cup** of large, silky-hairy scales; rows of smaller scales form a **thickened rim;** seeds single, **white kernels;** acorns single or paired, **mature in second** October–November; large (2nd-year) and small (1st-year) acorns usually present.

Habitat: Relatively dry, open sites in upland woods and on bluff tops.

Origin: Native.

This attractive, relatively fast-growing oak is sometimes planted as an ornamental. It is rarely grown in Europe, but in North America it has been planted as a shade tree and also in hedges and windbreaks. Unlike most oaks, shingle oak often holds its dry, brown leaves in winter. • Shingle oak was known to pioneers for its heavy, straight-grained wood, which could be split into thin sheets and used as clapboard, shakes and shingles. This gave rise to the common name "shingle oak" and the scientific name *imbricaria*, "overlapping." Today, shingle oak is occasionally cut in mixed stands and marketed as "red oak." • The bitter acorns are eaten by deer, squirrels, wild turkeys and waterfowl such as mallards and wood ducks. • Bristle-tipped leaves reflect the link between shingle oak and the red and black oaks (pp. 126–34). Shingle oak hybridizes with several of these species, producing offspring that have leaves edged with small lobes or bristles. Two of the most common hybrids are **Q. x *runcinata*** (offspring of shingle oak and northern red oak, p. 127) and **Q. x *leana*** (offspring of shingle oak and black oak, p. 126). Hybrids with scarlet oak (p. 130) are much rarer.

Also Called: Jack oak, northern laurel oak.

Size and Shape: Symmetrical trees 35–65' tall; young crowns pyramidal, rounded with age.

Trunks: Straight, 12–32" wide; **bark light grayish-brown,** with low, broad, scaly ridges; wood light reddish-brown, coarse-grained, decay resistant.

Branches: Tough, wide-spreading; twigs slender, dark green to brown, soon lustrous and smooth; **pith 5-pointed** in cross-section; buds shiny, light brown, about ⅛" long, pointing outward, clustered at branch tips.

Leaves: Alternate, simple, deciduous; blades yellow at first, **lustrous, dark green and hairless with raised veins above,** paler and **soft-hairy beneath,** leathery, **smooth- or slightly wavy-edged, 5–7" long, bristle-tipped** (or with a spine scar); leaves yellow, tan or red-brown in autumn.

Flowers: Tiny, yellowish, without petals; unisexual with male and female flowers on the same tree; male flowers in slender, woolly-hairy, hanging catkins 2–2¾" long; female flowers usually 1–2 on slender, woolly stalks in axils of expanding leaves; flowers in May–June (with leaves).

Fruits: Nuts **(acorns)** with dark brown, often striped, leathery shells, ½–¾" long, tips rounded with a small point, the **lower ⅓–½ seated in a cup about ¼" deep** of hairy, reddish-brown scales; seeds single, white, very bitter kernels; **acorns single or paired on stout, ⅜" long stalks,** remain in cup, **mature in second year.**

Habitat: Floodplains, swamp forests, dry, upland woods, roadsides and edges of clearings.

Origin: Native.

This large southern tree is probably the most common and best known of the "no-lobers." The fast-growing, long-lived willow oak is widely planted as an ornamental shade tree along streets and in gardens in the South. It is easily grown from seed, but its acorns have a dormancy period and need to be stratified or left in the ground over winter to germinate. Unlike most oaks, willow oak is readily transplanted. This species is one of the hardiest narrow-leaved oaks and can be grown successfully as far north as Michigan and southern Ontario, well beyond its natural range. • The unusual, willow-like leaves may suggest that it is a hybrid between a willow and an oak, but willow oak is not even distantly related to the willow family, so a natural hybrid is all but unthinkable. • Trees begin to produce acorns at about 20 years of age, and a mature tree can produce almost 2 bushels of acorns every year. Although these nutritious nuts are too bitter for the human palate, they are an important food for squirrels, whitetail deer, turkeys and ducks, as well as an occasional food for quail and various songbirds. Because willow oak acorns are smaller than those of most oaks, more animals are able to eat them. • Willow oak stands support large-scale lumber operations in the southern U.S. The strong, heavy wood is sold as "red oak" and is used for making railings, stairways and furniture.

Size and Shape: Trees 65–100' tall; crowns dense and rounded to cone-shaped.

Trunks: Straight, 2–4' in diameter; bark light reddish-brown to nearly black, ½–¾" thick, slightly roughened with irregular scaly plates; wood reddish-brown, fine-grained, ring porous.

Branches: Spreading; twigs slender, reddish-brown, dark reddish- or grayish-brown by the 2nd year; buds chestnut-brown, egg-shaped, pointed, with pale-edged, overlapping scales.

Leaves: Alternate, deciduous, simple; blades shiny and green above, dull, paler and essentially hairless beneath, **shaped like willow leaves, 2–5" long,** ½–1" wide, tapered at both ends, **bristle-tipped,** smooth- or wavy-edged (not lobed); leaves green late into fall, some turn rich yellow in November.

Flowers: Tiny, without petals; unisexual with male and female flowers separate on the same tree; male flowers in slender, 2–3" long catkins; female flowers in few-flowered clusters in leaf axils; flowers in April–May (just before leaves).

Fruits: Round, greenish to yellowish brown nuts with leathery shells **(acorns),** ⁵⁄₁₆–⅝" long, tipped with a small, abrupt, curved point (style), **lower ¼ seated in a ⁵⁄₁₆–½" wide, saucer-shaped cup** of hairy, dark red, overlapping scales; seeds single, **yellow kernels;** acorns single or paired, mature in the second August–October; both large (2nd-year) and small (1st-year) acorns usually present.

Habitat: Swampy woods and streambanks.

Origin: Native.

Key to Genera in the Birch Family (Betulaceae)

1a   Female catkins tiny (about $1/8$" long), egg-shaped, with distinctive reddish stigmas protruding from the tips; fruits large ($3/8$–$1/2$"), hard-shelled nuts within a $1/2$–$2\,3/4$" long, flask-shaped sac of enlarged involucral bracts. . . . .***Corylus*, hazelnut** (p. 139)

1b   Female catkins larger ($1/4$–$3/4$" long), oblong to cylindrical; fruits small ($1/8$–$3/8$") nutlets protected by scales or inflated bladders, borne in hanging, $1\,1/8$–6" long clusters (catkins) **2**

2a   Nutlets in persistent, woody, cone-like catkins; pith 3-sided in cross-section . . . .
. . . .***Alnus*, alder** (key to species, see below)

2b   Nutlets not borne in woody "cones"; pith round or oval in cross-section **3**

3a   Twigs and leaves often gland-dotted; nutlets tiny, winged, numerous, protected by small, 3-lobed scales in compact, elongating catkins
. . . .***Betula*, birch** (key to species, p. 136)

3b   Twigs and leaves not gland-dotted; nutlets wingless **4**

4a   Bark smooth, pale or bluish-gray, over muscle-like ridges; leaf veins not forked; nutlets borne at the base of leafy, 2–3-lobed bracts in loose, elongated catkins
. . . . ***Carpinus*, blue-beech** (p. 138)

4b   Bark shaggy, light brown, with rough, lengthwise strips; leaf veins forked; nutlets enclosed in inflated bladders in compact catkins. . . . . ***Ostrya*, hop-hornbeam** (p. 137)

Key to the Alders (Genus *Alnus*)

1a   Seed catkins $5/8$–$1\,1/8$" long, very sticky, in clusters of 2–5; leaves widest at or above midleaf, usually with 5–6 veins per side, blunt or notched at the tip
. . . . ***A. glutinosa*, European alder** (p. 144)

1b   Seed catkins $1/2$–$5/8$" long, not sticky, in clusters of 3–10; leaves widest below midleaf, usually with 9–12 veins per side, pointed at the tip **2**

2a   Leaves coarsely double-toothed, rounded at the base
. . . . ***A. incana* ssp. *rugosa*, speckled alder** (p. 143)

2b   Leaves finely single-toothed . . . .***A. serrulata*, brookside alder** (p. 143)

Carpinus caroliniana, blue-beech   *Ostrya virginiana,* hop-hornbeam

Key to the Birches (Genus *Betula*)

1a   Mature bark yellowish-gray to reddish- or blackish-brown; leaves usually with 8 or more pairs of prominent side-veins. **2**

1b   Mature bark whitish; leaves with 7 or fewer pairs of prominent side-veins **3**

2a   Twigs and bark with the smell and flavor of wintergreen; leaves with 8–12 veins per side . . . .*B. alleghaniensis*, **yellow birch** (p. 140)

2b   Twigs and bark not smelling or tasting of wintergreen; leaves with 6–10 veins per side . . . . *B. nigra*, **river birch** (p. 140)

3a   Leaves broadly triangular, with a squared base and long, slender-pointed tip . . . . *B. populifolia*, **gray birch** (p. 142)

3b   Leaves not as above **4**

4a   Branches slender and drooping; mature bark peeling in long strands; leaves hairless beneath; introduced tree, escaped from cultivation . . . . *B. pendula*, **European white birch** (p. 142)

4b   Branches ascending; mature bark peeling in sheets; leaves hairy beneath (at least in vein axils when young) **5**

5a   Leaves 1¹⁄₈–2" long (on fertile shoots), edged with relatively few coarse teeth (about 14 per side); a Eurasian escape occasionally found growing in wet habitats . . . . *B. pubescens*, **downy birch** (p. 142)

5b   Leaves 2–4" long, edged with many fine teeth (30+ per side); a widespread native tree, growing in a wide range of habitats . . . . . . *B. papyrifera*, **paper birch** (p. 141)

Betula papyrifera, paper birch   *B. pendula*, European white birch

This slow-growing tree is too small to be of any commercial importance, but it produces extremely dense, hard, resilient wood. Hop-hornbeam wood makes excellent tool handles, mallets and sleigh runners. Although it is also a very good fuel, it is almost impossible to split. The trunks have been used occasionally to make fence posts. • This attractive tall shrub or small tree, with its unusual fruit clusters, is cultivated as an ornamental in European parks and gardens. • The inconspicuous spring flowers are wind-pollinated. • White-tailed deer browse on hop-hornbeam twigs. The seeds, buds and catkins provide food for squirrels, grouse and various songbirds. • The genus name *Ostrya* is derived from the Greek *ostrua* or *ostuoes*, the name for a tree with very hard wood. The specific epithet *virginiana* means "of Virginia." The frequent name "ironwood" refers to the hard wood, but this name has also been applied to blue-beech (p. 138) and to various other trees in other parts of the world. The fruit clusters resemble those of hops, hence the common name "hop-hornbeam."

Also Called: Eastern hop-hornbeam, ironwood, American hop-hornbeam, leverwood, deerwood, rough-barked ironwood.

Size and Shape: Trees 25–50 [74'] tall; crowns wide-spreading, rounded to cone-shaped; taproot.

Trunks: Straight, 6–12" [37"] in diameter; mature bark grayish-brown, thin, moderately corky, **shaggy, with narrow, peeling strips** loose at both ends; wood light brown, fine-grained, very hard, tough, heavy.

Branches: Long, slender; twigs pale green, finely hairy, becoming dark reddish-brown and hairless; buds greenish-brown, slightly hairy, about 1/8" long, **pointing outward.**

Leaves: Alternate, simple, deciduous; 2⅜–5" long, arranged **in 2 rows,** largest at twig tips; blades dark **yellowish-green,** soft, **sharply double-toothed,** tapered to a sharp point, with **straight veins forked near leaf edges;** leaves dull yellow in autumn, often persistent in winter.

Flowers: Tiny, greenish, without petals; unisexual with male and female flowers on the same tree; male flowers in dense, cylindrical, hanging catkins ½–2" long; female flowers 4–10 in loose, elongated catkins about ¼" long; flowers in April–May (as leaves expand).

Fruits: Hop-like, **in hanging, 1⅛–2⅜" long clusters of greenish to brownish, flattened-ovoid, ⅜–¾" long, papery, inflated sacs,** each sac containing a ¼" long nutlet; seeds single, inside **flattened nutlets about ¼" long;** fruits mature in September, drop in winter.

Habitat: Shady, well-drained sites in upland woodlands, almost always with white oak.

Origin: Native.

This small, short-lived tree is not very important commercially, but it has exceptionally dense, strong wood. Blue-beech wood is so hard that it is used to make levers, hammer handles and wedges for wood-splitting. It does not split or crack, so pioneers used it for making bowls and plates. Despite its toughness, however, blue-beech wood rots quickly when left in contact with soil. • This attractive, shade-tolerant species, with its scarlet to golden fall leaves, makes an excellent ornamental. Unfortunately, it is seldom used in landscaping. • Because of its smooth, blue-gray bark, musclewood is often confused with the true beeches of the genus *Fagus* (e.g., American beech, p. 116). Beech trees have very smooth trunks without muscle-like ridges, and their leaves are not double-toothed. • Birds and small rodents such as squirrels eat the buds, flower clusters and seeds, but browsing mammals seldom touch the twigs. In some regions, selective browsing has created understories almost entirely of blue-beech and other unpalatable species, severely limiting the replacement of overstory trees. *Carpinus* comes from the Celtic *car*, "wood," and *pen* or *pin*, "head," referring to the use of the wood in yokes.

Also Called: American hornbeam, musclewood, ironwood, muscle-beech, smooth-barked ironwood, water-beech.

Size and Shape: Small trees 10–35' [40'] tall; crowns low, flat-topped, bushy; roots shallow.

Trunks: Usually short and crooked, 4–12" [13"] in diameter, single or clumped, with **muscle-like ridges; mature bark slate gray, thin, smooth, tight;** wood heavy, hard, strong.

Branches: Few, short, irregular, slender, zigzagged, forming **flat sprays;** twigs greenish and hairy to reddish-brown or gray and hairless;

buds about ⅛" long, reddish-brown with pale scale edges, **pressed against the twig in 2 rows,** absent at twig tips.

Leaves: Alternate, simple, deciduous, arranged **in 2 rows,** largest at twig tips; **blades 2–4" long, hairless and bluish-green above,** yellowish-green beneath, firm, **sharply double-toothed,** tapered to a sharp point, with **straight veins only slightly forked** (if at all); leaves red to golden in autumn.

Flowers: Tiny, greenish, without petals; unisexual with male and female flowers on the same tree; male flowers in dense, cylindrical, hanging catkins 1–1½" long; female flowers hairy, in loose catkins ⅜–¾" long; flowers in April–May (as leaves expand).

Fruits: Ribbed nutlets ¼–⅜" long, single in axils of green, 3-lobed, ¾–1⅛" long, leaf-like bracts that hang in clusters 4–6" long; seeds 1 per nutlet; nutlets mature in midsummer, some may persist into winter.

Habitat: Rich, moist woods, often near water.

Origin: Native.

The delicious edible nuts of this tree have a flavor similar to European hazelnut or filbert (*C.
avellana*). Some Native tribes preferred young
hazelnuts (in the milk stage) to harder, oilier
mature nuts. Hazelnuts were eaten raw or prepared
in a number of ways, including roasted in ovens
(to reduce bitterness), cooked in cakes and desserts, ground to make nut butter and nut flour and
dried for winter use. Crushed nuts mixed with bear
fat, berries and meat provided tasty, high-calorie
cakes or sausages—an early version of today's
high-energy bars. • The male catkins of American
hazelnut often develop a distinctive kink, caused
by insect attacks. • **Beaked hazelnut (*C. cornuta*,** also called *C. rostrata*), shown in dark
green (species overlap) on the map, is a similar,
slightly smaller (3–10' tall) shrub, identified by
its smooth (hairless, without glands) leaf stalks
and twigs and by the bristly, flask-shaped covering
of fused bracts encasing each nut. Its nuts are also
edible and were widely used by Native peoples.
However, the bristly hairs on the husks act like
tiny, irritating splinters in fingertips. Some people
buried the nuts in wet mud for 10 days to rot away
the prickles. Better yet, caches of husked nuts can
sometimes be found in squirrels' nests.

Photo, bottom right: *C. cornuta*

Also Called: Hazelnut.

Size and Shape: Tall, bushy shrubs 10–13'
tall; crowns irregular; roots spreading, often
suckering to form thickets.

Trunks: Usually clumped, 23" in diameter;
bark smooth, gray.

Branches: Alternate; twigs slender, brown,
glandular-hairy; buds small, brown, round, with
several finely hairy scales, absent at twig tips.

Leaves: Alternate, simple, deciduous; blades
leathery, dark green and hairless above, paler
and soft-hairy beneath, oval to round, 1½–6"
long, abruptly slender-pointed, rounded to
notched at the base, **finely double-toothed,**
straight veined, folded lengthwise in bud; **stalks
soft-hairy, with gland-tipped bristles.**

Flowers: Tiny, without petals or sepals;
unisexual with **male and female flowers on
the same shrub;** male flowers 4-stamened, in
slender, hanging catkins 1½–3" long, borne **on
short, woody stalks** from side-buds on previous year's twigs; female flowers fewer, **in tiny,**
bud-like clusters about ⅛" long, tipped with 2 tiny
red threads (stigmas), borne at the tips of leafy
shoots; flowers develop in autumn and mature in
March–April (**before leaves**).

Fruits: Hard-shelled nuts, light brown, ⅜–⅝"
long, slightly flattened, surrounded by 2 hairy,
broad, ¾–1¼" **long, leaf-like bracts with deeply
cut edges** (involucre); seeds 1 per nut; nuts
single or in clusters of 2–4 (rarely 6) in August–
September.

Habitat: Relatively open sites in dry to moist
woodlands and thickets.

Origin: Native.

Yellow birch is an important source of hardwood lumber. The hard, golden to reddish-brown wood can be stained and buffed to a high polish. It has been used to make furniture, hardwood floors, doors, paneling, veneer, plywood, tool handles, snowshoe frames, sledges and railway ties. In the 1700s, yellow birch was preferred over oak for building submerged parts of ships. • The aromatic twigs and leaves make excellent tea. Trees can also be tapped in spring, and the sap can be boiled down to make syrup or fermented to make beer. • Never tear bark from living trees, as this can scar or even kill the tree. • Yellow birch is endangered in Illinois. • Occasionally, it hybridizes with the shrubby bog birch (*B. pumila*) to produce the even rarer **purpus birch (B. x purpusii)**, found only in Lake County, a shrubby tree distinguished by its relatively small leaves (veins 7 or fewer per side), gray, non-peeling bark and relatively large (at least 0.4" thick) fruiting catkins. • A similar, relatively widespread species, **river birch (B. nigra)**, shown in pink/dark green (species overlap) on the map, has tattered, pinkish bark and leaves with fewer veins and pale lower surfaces. Also, its twigs have no wintergreen flavor. True to its name, river birch grows along streams and on floodplains.

Also Called: Swamp birch, curly birch, gold birch, hard birch, red birch, tall birch • *B. lutea.*

Size and Shape: Trees 50–80' tall; crowns broad, rounded; roots shallow, wide-spreading.

Trunks: Straight, 24–40" in diameter; **young bark shiny reddish-brown,** with prominent, **horizontal pores** (lenticels); **mature bark yellowish to bronze, tightly curling in papery shreds,** not peeling easily, eventually platy; wood hard, often wavy-grained.

Branches: Large, spreading to drooping; twigs with a **moderate wintergreen fragrance** and flavor, slender, shiny, with **dwarf shoots** near the base; buds brown, mostly hairy,

flat-lying, about ¼" long, 5–7-scaled at twig tips, 3-scaled below, absent at twig tips; **scales 2-toned.**

Leaves: Alternate, simple, deciduous; blades 2½–4½" long, deep yellowish-green above, paler beneath, with **8–12 straight veins per side, each ending in a large tooth with 2–3 smaller intervening teeth;** stalks short, grooved; leaves yellow in autumn.

Flowers: Tiny, without petals; unisexual with male and female flowers on the same tree; male flowers purplish yellow, in hanging catkins 2–4" long; female flowers greenish, in erect, cone-like catkins ½–¾" long; flowers form by autumn, mature in April–June (before leaves expand).

Fruits: Small, flat, **2-winged nutlets** (samaras) in the axils of **3-lobed, hairy scales** about ¼" long, borne in **erect, cone-like catkins ¾–1½" long;** seeds 1 per nutlet; nutlets mature in autumn, gradually drop over winter.

Habitat: Rich, moist, often boggy woods.

Origin: Native.

Paper birch is a northern tree that inhabits forests and wetlands across North America, north to the edge of the tundra. The widespread species reaches its southern limit in Illinois. • This sun-loving colonizer is more common and widespread now than it was 200 years ago, because cutting and burning have created many suitable sites. • Native peoples used the tough, pliable bark of paper birch to make birch-bark canoes, sewing (with spruce roots) sheets of bark over white-cedar frames. Fir or pine resin was used for waterproofing. Birch bark also covered wigwams and provided material for baskets, cups and message paper. Strips of bark with lenticels were used as "sunglasses" to prevent snow blindness. • In spring, trees were tapped for their sap. The sap was used as a sweet drink, boiled down to make syrup or fermented to make birch beer. • When several layers of outer bark are removed, the exposed inner bark soon blackens and dies. Exposure of large sections can kill the tree. • Young paper birches resemble yellow birch (p. 140) but lack the distinctive wintergreen fragrance or flavor.

Also Called: White birch, canoe birch, silver birch, spoolwood.

Size and Shape: Trees 50–65' tall; crowns somewhat conical.

Trunks: Often leaning and clumped, 12–24" in diameter; young bark dark reddish, **thin, smooth,** with **horizontal pores** (lenticels); **mature bark white, peeling in large sheets,** eventually furrowed and almost black on lower trunk; inner bark orange; wood moderately hard, pale reddish-brown, odorless.

Branches: Ascending to spreading, long and slender, with occasional short, spur-like side-branches; **twigs slender,** dark reddish-brown, **with scattered, warty resin glands; buds resinous,** about ¼" long, **with 3 brown-tipped, greenish scales,** absent at twig tips.

Leaves: Alternate on long shoots, in 3s on short spurs, simple, deciduous; blades 2–3" long, dull green above, paler beneath, with **5–9 straight veins per side ending in large teeth with 3–5 smaller intervening teeth,** ovate, **widest below the middle,** slender-pointed; leaves yellow in autumn.

Flowers: Tiny, without petals; unisexual with male and female flowers on the same tree; male flowers brownish, in clusters of 1–3 hanging catkins 2¾–4" long; female flowers greenish, in erect catkins ⅜–1½" long; flowers form by autumn, mature next April–June (before leaves expand).

Fruits: Small, flat, broadly **2-winged nutlets** (samaras), about ¹⁄₁₆" long, **in axils of 3-lobed, usually hairy scales** within **hanging catkins 1⅛–2" long;** seeds 1 per nutlet; nutlets mature in September–October, disintegrate over winter.

Habitat: A wide variety of substrates, from wooded ravines to dune ridges.

Origin: Native.

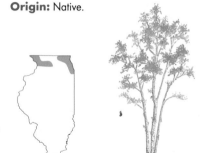

141

In Europe, this fast-growing, sun-loving tree has been used as a nurse tree to protect young plantations of hardwood trees such as beech. • Many cultivars of this small, graceful tree have been developed, including 'Laciniata' and 'Dalecarlica,' with deeply cut leaves on delicate, weeping branches. • The durable wood of European white birch has been used for making skis, clogs and spindles and as a source of cellulose and firewood. • The leaves were used traditionally to make medicinal teas for treating urinary tract infections and kidney stones. The resin glands are sometimes used in hair lotions. • European white birch is often confused with the endangered native tree **gray birch (*B. populifolia*)**, shown in pink/dark green (species overlap) on the map. Gray birch has leaves with longer, more slender points and more numerous teeth (18–47 vs. 9–28 per side). Also, gray birch has single or paired male catkins, densely hairy catkin scales and non-peeling bark. • Another European introduction, **downy birch (*B. pubescens,*** sometimes included in *B. alba*) may escape to grow wild on well-drained sites. This European counterpart of paper birch is distinguished by its resinous buds, small leaves (1⅛–2" long on fertile shoots), small female catkins (½–1⅛" long) and more stiffly erect branches. It is highly prone to bronze birch borer (*Agrilus anxius*), which may limit landscape trees to less than 20 years.

Also Called: European birch, weeping birch, European weeping birch, silver birch • *B. verrucosa*.

Size and Shape: Trees 30–50' tall; crowns open, broad to egg-shaped; roots shallow, weak.

Trunks: Usually clumped, to 12" in diameter; young bark thin, smooth, with horizontal pores (lenticels); mature bark bright chalky white, peeling in long strands, eventually blackened and furrowed near the trunk base; wood yellowish-white, moderately hard.

Branches: Spreading, with drooping tips; twigs reddish-tinged, spindly, hairless, dotted with tiny resin glands; buds 3-scaled.

Leaves: Alternate, simple, deciduous; blades 1⅛–2¾" long, hairless, with 5–9 straight veins per side ending in large teeth with smaller intervening teeth, triangular to broadly oval, slender-pointed; stalks long, slender; leaves yellow in autumn, persist 3–4 weeks longer than leaves of native birches.

Flowers: Tiny, without petals; unisexual with male and female flowers on the same tree; male flowers in clusters of 2–4 hanging catkins 1½–3½" long; female flowers in stout catkins ⅜–1⅛" long; flowers form by autumn, mature the following spring (before leaves expand).

Fruits: Small, flat, 2-winged nutlets (samaras) in axils of sparsely hairy, 3-lobed scales within hanging catkins ¾–1½" long; seeds 1 per nutlet; nutlets mature in autumn, drop over winter.

Habitat: Open, sandy woods.

Origin: Introduced from Eurasia.

S peckled alder is too small to be of economic importance, but it does play an important ecological role in shading and stabilizing streambanks and enriching soil. This fast-growing, short-lived pioneer species readily invades land exposed by fire or clear-cutting. Speckled alder cannot tolerate shade, so other trees and shrubs soon replace it. • Native peoples and settlers extracted a dark dye from the bark for tanning and staining hides. The bark was also boiled to make medicinal teas for treating rheumatism, and it was applied to wounds as a poultice for reducing bleeding and swelling. Alder bark has astringent properties and contains salicin, a compound similar to aspirin. • This tree produces some of the earliest flowers each spring, which are eagerly sought by bees. • **Brookside alder** (*A. serrulata*, also called common alder, smooth alder and tag alder), shown in pink on the map, is similar to speckled alder, but its leaves have green (not whitened) lower surfaces. True to its name, brookside alder grows along rocky streams in southern (not northern) Illinois.

Also Called: Gray alder, hoary alder, red alder, river alder, rough alder • *A. rugosa*.

Size and Shape: Shrubs or small trees 5–25' tall; crowns open, broad, irregular; roots shallow.

Trunks: Usually clumped, crooked, 1⅛–4" in diameter; bark dark reddish-brown, **smooth,** with conspicuous **pale orange, horizontal pores** (lenticels); inner bark reddish; wood reddish-brown, light, soft.

Branches: Spreading, twisted; twigs zigzagged, hairy; **pith 3-sided** in cross-section; buds reddish-brown, **stalked, blunt-tipped, with 2–3 equal (not overlapping) scales,** absent at twig tips.

Leaves: Alternate, simple, deciduous; blades 2–4" long, **dull dark green above, paler green to hoary beneath,** thick, with **6–12 conspicuous, straight veins per side,** broadly ovate, **edges undulating, with sharp double teeth, never sticky;** leaves green in autumn.

Flowers: Tiny, without petals; unisexual with male and female flowers on the same tree; male flowers brownish, in stalked, hanging clusters of 2–4" long catkins; female flowers in clusters of 2–5 **short-stalked, cone-like catkins;** catkins form in autumn, persist over winter, mature in March–June **(before leaves expand).**

Fruits: Small, flat, **narrowly 2-winged nutlets** (samaras) in axils of 5-lobed, **woody scales in hanging, ⅜–⅝" long cones that persist year-round;** seeds 1 per nutlet; nutlets drop in late summer to autumn.

Habitat: Moist thickets on shores and in lowlands.

Origin: Native.

Black alder is an aggressive weed, displacing native trees and shrubs along streams and in wetlands. It was introduced to North America for producing charcoal, a key ingredient in gunpowder. In Scotland, this species was known as "Scottish mahogany" and was used to make fine furniture. Elsewhere, it was made into clogs, cart and spinning wheels, bowls, spoons, wooden heels and cigar boxes. Wood buried in bogs developed the color, but not the hardness, of ebony. Because of its ability to withstand rot in wet conditions, black alder was widely used in pumps, troughs, sluices and pilings. • Europeans traditionally used the bark for dying, tanning and dressing leather and for making fishing nets. The bark was also boiled to make a wash for treating inflammation, especially around the throat. In the Alps, peasants applied bags of heated alder leaves as a cure for rheumatism. • In eastern North America, black alder has been widely planted as an ornamental shade tree and as a companion tree for improving soil nitrogen in conifer plantations. • This fast-growing tree readily sends up suckers, especially when the parent plant is cut back.

Also Called: European alder, European black alder.

Size and Shape: Trees 30–50' tall; crowns rounded.

Trunks: Single or clumped, relatively straight, 8–12" in diameter; **young bark thin, smooth,** with large, pale, **horizontal pores** (lenticels); inner bark reddish; mature bark dark brown, becoming rough; wood reddish-brown, light, soft.

Branches: Spreading; **twigs often sticky,** somewhat hairy; **pith 3-sided** in cross-section; **buds** stalked, blunt-tipped, with 2–3 equal scales.

Leaves: Alternate, simple, deciduous; blades 1½–3" long, smooth and dark green above, paler and finely hairy beneath, with **5–6 prominent, straight veins per side,** broadly ovate to almost round, widest above the middle, **blunt-tipped to notched,** coarsely **double-toothed, sticky when young;** leaves green to brown in late autumn.

Flowers: Tiny, without petals; unisexual with male and female flowers on the same tree; male flowers in stalked clusters of hanging catkins 2–4" long; female flowers in small clusters of **short-stalked, cone-like catkins ¾–1" long;** catkins form by autumn, mature in March–May (before leaves expand).

Fruits: Small, flat, **narrowly 2-winged nutlets,** in axils of 5-lobed, **woody scales in sticky, ⅝–1⅛" long cones that persist year round;** seeds 1 per nutlet; nutlets drop in late summer–autumn.

Habitat: Floodplains and streambanks.

Origin: Introduced from Europe.

Key to Genera in the Willow Family (Salicaceae)

1a Buds with a single scale; leaves typically lance-shaped to linear, more than 3 times as long as wide . . . . ***Salix*, willow** (key to species, see below)
1b Buds covered by several overlapping scales; leaves ovate to round or triangular, less than 3 times as long as wide . . . . ***Populus*, poplar** (key to species, p. 148)

Key to the Willows (Genus *Salix*)

1a Twigs and leaves conspicuously contorted . . ***S. matsudana*, twisted willow** (p. 166)
1b Twigs and leaves relatively straight, not conspicuously contorted. **2**

2a Leaves opposite to sub-opposite, purplish . . . ***S. purpurea*, purple-osier willow** (p. 163)
2b Leaves alternate, not purplish **3**

3a Leaf stalks with glands just below the blade **4**
3b Leaf stalks lacking glands near the blade **12**

4a Leaves linear to narrowly lance-shaped, more than 5 times as long as wide, widest below the middle. **5**
4b Leaves lance-shaped to ovate-oblong, up to 4 times as long as wide, often widest at or above the middle. **9**

5a Stipules (small leafy bracts at leaf stalk base) well developed and persistent, especially on young shoots **6**
5b Stipules absent or slender, soon shed. **7**

6a Leaves green above and beneath (sometimes faintly whitish beneath), with tips often sharply curved to one side. ***S. nigra*, black willow** (p. 155)
6b Leaves green above, strongly whitish beneath, with tips not sharply curved to one side . . . . ***S. caroliniana*, Carolina willow** (p. 157)

7a Branches slender, "weeping," with long, hanging tips; seed catkins often 1–1⅛" long . . . . ***S. babylonica* hybrids, weeping willows** (p. 156)
7b Branches stouter, sometimes hanging but not long-drooping; seed catkins usually more than 1½" long. **8**

Salix alba, white willow S. *nigra*, black willow

145

8a Mature leaves essentially hairless, glossy and dark green above; branchlets brittle-based, easily broken. . . . .*S. fragilis*, **crack willow** (p. 161)

8b Mature leaves silvery-silky, dull green above; branchlets not brittle-based
. . . .*S. alba*, **white willow** (p. 156)

9a Leaves whitish beneath with a conspicuous dull, waxy bloom **10**
9b Leaves green above and below, without a notable waxy bloom **11**

10a Flowers and fruits produced in late summer–autumn; young leaves hairless; mature leaves leathery, edged with gland-tipped teeth . . . .*S. serissima*, **autumn willow** (p. 157)
10b Flowers and fruits produced in spring–early summer; young leaves sparsely hairy; mature leaves thin, edged with fine, sharp teeth . . . .
. . . .*S. amygdaloides*, **peachleaf willow** (p. 164)

11a Leaves usually 3–6 times as long as wide, with a long, slender point, pale green and shiny beneath; twigs and young leaves not fragrant when crushed
. . . .*S. lucida*, **shining willow** (p. 157)
11b Leaves about 1½–3 times as long as wide, more abruptly pointed, only slightly paler beneath; twigs and young leaves aromatic with fragrant resin
. . . .*S. pentandra*, **laurel willow** (p. 158)

12a Leaves smooth-edged or with irregular, rounded teeth **13**
12b Leaves with distinct, regular teeth **14**

13a Capsules on visible slender stalks that are at least twice as long as the pale, yellowish scales, borne in loose catkins, appearing with the leaves; branchlets widely spreading; leaves dull green with raised veins beneath (especially when young)
. . . .*S. bebbiana*, **Bebb's willow** (p. 166)
13b Capsules on short stalks that are obscured by dark brown scales, forming dense catkins, appearing before the leaves; branchlets not wide-spreading; leaves shiny and green above, relatively smooth beneath . . . .*S. discolor*, **pussy willow** (p. 165)

14a Mature leaves mostly 1½–3 times as long as wide, abruptly sharp-pointed **15**
14b Mature leaves narrower, mostly 4–8 times as long as wide **16**

Salix pentandra, laurel willow

S. discolor, pussy willow

15a Leaves lance-shaped to ovate, $1^1/2$–$3^1/2$" long, $^5/8$–$1^3/4$" wide; leaf edges with blunt, gland-tipped teeth; catkins with hairless capsules
. . . . ***S. myricoides*, blueleaf willow** (p. 162)
15b Leaves broadly ovate to almost round, 2–5" long, 1–3" wide; leaf edges blunt-toothed and irregularly rolled under; catkins with densely gray-hairy capsules
. . . . ***S. caprea*, goat willow** (p. 165)

16a Branches slender, "weeping," with long, hanging tips; seed catkins often 1–$1^1/8$" long
. . . . ***S. babylonica* hybrids, weeping willows** (p. 156)
16b Branches stouter, sometimes hanging but not long-drooping; seed catkins usually more than $1^1/2$" long **17**

17a Mature leaves hairless or with just a few hairs on the veins beneath **18**
17b Mature leaves hairy, at least on the lower surface **24**

18a Leaves very narrow and linear, 2–6" long, $^1/8$–$^1/2$" wide, edged with widely spaced teeth; tall colonial shrubs, often forming thickets on floodplains
. . . . ***S. exigua*, sandbar willow** (p. 159)
18b Leaves wider relative to their length, usually lance-shaped, edges wavy or closely toothed; tree/shrub form various **19**

19a Leaves on young and non-flowering shoots lacking stipules (small leafy bracts at leaf stalk base) or young leaves soon shedding their stipules **20**
19b Leaves on young and non-flowering shoots with noticeable, persistent stipules **23**

20a Leaves narrowly egg-shaped, tapered to a long, slender tip; buds pointed
. . . . ***S. amygdaloides*, peachleaf willow** (p. 164)
20b Leaves narrower, lance-shaped to linear, tipped with a sharp to slightly tapered point; buds rounded **21**

21a Branches hanging, "weeping"; leaves linear, finely sharp-toothed, with hairy stalks
. . . . ***S. babylonica* hybrids, weeping willows** (p. 156)
21b Branches not "weeping"; leaves lance-shaped, sharp-toothed, with hairless stalks. . . . **22**

22a Leaf stalks mostly $^1/8$–$^1/4$" long; leaf blades finely toothed, usually with a few hairs on the veins beneath . . . . ***S. petiolaris*, slender willow** (p. 160)
22b Leaf stalks mostly >$^1/4$" long, sometimes with glands near the blade; leaf blades coarsely toothed, completely hairless . . . . ***S. fragilis*, crack willow** (p. 161)

23a Leaves green above and beneath . . . . ***S. nigra*, black willow** (p. 155)
23b Leaves green above, pale with a whitish bloom (glaucous) beneath
. . . . ***S. eriocephala*, heartleaf willow** (p. 162)

24a Leaves woolly, edges smooth, wavy or irregularly blunt-toothed, often down-rolled; young branches with distinctive, lengthwise ridges just under the bark
. . . . ***S. cinerea*, large gray willow** (p. 165)
24b Leaves silky-hairy to hairless, edged with fine, gland-tipped teeth; twig wood lacking distinct ridges **25**

25a Leaves rounded at the base; catkin stalks absent or $^1/8$–$^3/8$" long; catkin scales pale yellowish, soon shed . . . . ***S. eriocephala*, heartleaf willow** (p. 162)
25b Leaves tapered to a wedge-shaped base; catkin stalks $^3/8$–$1^1/2$" long; catkin scales dark brown to blackish, persistent in fruit. . . . . ***S. alba*, white willow** (p. 156)

Key to the Poplars (Genus *Populus*)

1a Mature leaves white- or grayish-woolly beneath, edged with 3–5 blunt, palmate lobes and/or a few irregular teeth; leaf stalks nearly round, flattened only near the blade
. . . . ***P. alba*, white poplar** (p. 149)

1b Mature leaves neither woolly beneath nor lobed, edged with regular teeth; leaf stalks round or variously flattened **2**

2a Leaf stalks round, often channeled above, usually shorter than the blade; leaf blades ovate, clearly longer than wide **3**

2b Leaf stalks flattened (at least near the blade), usually equaling or longer than the blade; leaf blades triangular to heart-shaped or rounded, about as long as wide; buds with or without fragrant resin **4**

3a Leaf blades ovate, rounded or squared at the base; buds sticky with fragrant resin
. . . . ***P. balsamifera*, balsam poplar** (p. 152)

3b Leaf blades heart-shaped, notched at the base; buds not sticky resinous
. . . .***P. heterophylla*, swamp cottonwood** (p. 154)

4a Leaves more or less triangular or 4-sided, edged with a definite translucent border created by callus-tipped teeth; buds sticky with fragrant resin; bark rough. **5**

4b Leaves more or less round, without a translucent border, teeth blunt-tipped; buds neither sticky nor fragrant; bark smooth (rough near the trunk base with age). **6**

5a Leaves triangular, usually with 2–5 glands at the base of the blade, edged with coarse teeth (up to $1/16$–$3/16$"); capsules splitting into 3–4 parts; a native, open-crowned tree
. . . . ***P. deltoides*, cottonwood** (p. 153)

5b Leaves typically diamond-shaped (sometimes squared at the base), rarely glandular at the base, edged with fine teeth (up to $1/32$–$1/16$"); capsules splitting in half; an introduced, usually columnar tree. . . . . ***P. nigra*, European black poplar** (p. 153)

6a Leaves edged with 20–30 fine ($<1/32$"), regular teeth, blades shorter than their stalks, essentially hairless . . . . ***P. tremuloides*, quaking aspen** (p. 151)

6b Leaves edged with 7–15 coarse (up to $1/16$–$1/4$"), wavy teeth, blades shorter than their stalks, conspicuously woolly beneath when young
. . . . ***P. grandidentata*, large-toothed aspen** (p. 150)

Populus tremuloides, quaking aspen

W hite poplar was among the first trees introduced to North America. It can withstand salt spray and was often used for shelters near the ocean. • Although still widely planted as an ornamental, this fast-growing tree may cause problems. The spreading roots raise sidewalks and clog sewers, and abundant suckers shoot up in undesirable places. White poplar can also be an aggressive weed, displacing native plants from natural environments such as dunes. • North American poplars can divided into 4 main taxonomic groups, called sections: 1) Leucoides, represented by swamp cottonwood (p. 154); 2) Taca-mahaca or balsam poplars, represented by balsam poplar (p. 152) and balm-of-Gilead (p. 152); 3) Aigeiros or cottonwoods, represented by cotton-wood (p. 153); 4) Leuce or aspen poplars, represented by quaking aspen (p. 151), large-toothed aspen (p. 150) and the introduced white poplar. Confusingly, some of the Tacamahaca are called cottonwoods, a name usually applied to the Aigeiros. • **Gray poplar** (*P. x canescens*), shown in dark green (species overlap) on the map, occasionally grows wild in Illi-nois. This introduced hybrid of white poplar and Eur-asian aspen (*P. tremula*) is sometimes considered a true species. Gray poplar is dis-tinguished by it coarsely toothed (rather than lobed) leaves which become almost hairless with age. • Vigorous shoots of white poplar may be mistaken for those of a maple, but the poplar is distinguished by its woolly (not smooth), alternate (not opposite) leaves.

Also Called: Silver poplar, silver-leaved pop-lar, European white poplar.

Size and Shape: Large trees 50–80' tall; crowns broad, rounded; roots deep, forming colonies by suckers.

Trunks: Often forked, 24–48" in diameter; young bark smooth, greenish- to grayish-white with dark, diamond-shaped pores (lenticels); mature bark darker, black and deeply furrowed near the base; wood pale reddish-yellow, light, soft.

Branches: Large, spreading, crooked; twigs white-woolly; **pith 5-pointed** in cross-section; buds densely white-hairy, ⅛–¼" long, pointed, 5-7-scaled, **lowest scale directly above the leaf scar.**

Leaves: Alternate, simple, deciduous; blades 2–4¾" long, dark green above, **densely white-woolly beneath, broadly ovate and wavy-edged to round and palmately 3–5-lobed (maple leaf–like),** irregularly coarse-toothed; stalks flattened, woolly; leaf scars 3-sided, with 3 vein scars.

Flowers: Tiny, without petals; unisexual with male and female flowers on **separate trees** (only female trees known in the western Great Lakes region), borne in hanging catkins 1½–3" long; flowers in April–May (**before leaves expand**).

Fruits: Tiny, pointed capsules in hanging catkins 4–6" long; seeds ¹⁄₁₆–⅛" long, tipped with a **tuft of silky, white hairs; capsules mature in May–June** (with leaves).

Habitat: Fields, fence lines and other disturbed sites.

Origin: Introduced from Eurasia.

149

Large-toothed aspen and quaking aspen (p. 151) are both important for revegetating recently cut or burned land, holding soil in place and protecting other, slower-growing species of plants. These fast-growing, shade-intolerant pioneer trees typically live 75–100 years. Mature trees (greater than 20 years old) produce abundant seed every 4–5 years. The catkins mature 4–6 weeks after flowering. Although aspen seeds live only a few days, they are very numerous and sprout quickly on bare ground. These species will not grow from cuttings, but once a few trees are established, they will send up suckers from their roots. • This tree's wood is similar to the wood of quaking aspen and has become a major source of pulp. • In spring, the whitish-downy twigs and buds make large-toothed aspen stand out among the other trees. • A similar tree occasionally found in low woods in north-central Illinois, **Barnes' poplar (*P. x smithii*)** is believed to be a hybrid of large-toothed aspen and trembling aspen. Barnes' poplar leaves have 12–25 teeth (averaging 20) compared to averages of 10 in large-toothed aspen, and 31 in quaking aspen. Other intermediate characteristics include hairy buds, similar to those of large-toothed aspen and short (⅛–¼") leaf stalks, similar to those of quaking aspen.

Also Called: Bigtooth aspen, big-toothed aspen, big-tooth poplar, large-tooth poplar.

Size and Shape: Trees 50–65' [132'] tall; crowns short, rounded; roots very wide-spreading.

Trunks: Straight, 12–24" [33"] in diameter, self-pruning; young bark smooth, olive to yellow-gray with diamond-shaped marks about ⅜" wide; mature bark dark gray, furrowed near trunk base; wood pale, soft, straight-grained.

Branches: Coarse, spreading to ascending; twigs relatively stout, greenish- to brownish-gray, downy to almost hairless, with orange pores (lenticels); pith 5-pointed in cross-section; buds dusty brown, grayish-downy, not resinous, not fragrant, ¼–⅜" long, 5–7-scaled, lowest scale above the leaf scar, tips pointing outward.

Leaves: Alternate, simple, deciduous; blades grayish-hairy at first, soon hairless, dark green above, paler beneath, 2–5" long, ovate to almost round, usually short-pointed, with 6–15 coarse, uneven, blunt teeth per side; stalks flattened, usually shorter than blades; leaves yellow in autumn.

Flowers: Tiny, without petals; unisexual with male and female flowers in hanging catkins on separate trees; catkins with hairy bracts, slender, 1⅛–3" long; flowers in April (before leaves expand).

Fruits: Downy, pointed, ¼" long capsules, numerous, in hanging catkins 3–6" long; seeds 1/16–⅛" long, tipped with a tuft of silky, white hairs; capsules mature in May–June (as leaves expand).

Habitat: Well-drained, often disturbed woodlands.

Origin: Native.

Quaking aspen usually reproduces vegetatively. It sends up suckers from spreading roots, producing groups of genetically identical trees (clones) that can include thousands of trees covering areas up to 200 acres. Some clones are believed to have originated from trees that colonized land exposed by retreating Pleistocene glaciers 9500–11,000 years ago, making the clones among the oldest and largest living organisms on earth.
• Freshly cut aspen is too heavy to float, so it must be transported by land. Aspen wood is an important source of fiber for chipboard, oriented strand board and paper. The wood is also used for excelsior, matchsticks, chopsticks, crates and fences. • About 500 species of plants and animals use aspen. The bark and twigs are a preferred food of deer, moose, beaver and snowshoe hare. Many birds feed on the buds and catkins. • Many parasites infect aspens. Heart-rot fungus (*Fomes ignarius populinus*) produces hollow trunks used by cavity nesters such as flying squirrels, woodpeckers, wood ducks and owls. • The flat-stalked leaves flutter in every breeze, hence a number of Native names meaning "woman's tongue" or "noisy tree."

Also Called: Trembling aspen, aspen poplar, golden aspen, popple, small-toothed aspen.

Size and Shape: Trees 40–80' [109'] tall; crowns short, rounded; roots shallow, wide-spreading.

Trunks: Straight or crooked, 10–24" [39"] in diameter, self-pruning; young bark smooth, **pale greenish-gray to almost white,** with dark, diamond-shaped marks, often whitish-powdery; mature bark dark gray and furrowed near trunk base; wood pale, light, soft, straight-grained.

Branches: Slender, spreading to ascending; twigs slender, shiny, dark green to brownish-gray, with orange pores (lenticels); **pith 5-pointed** in cross-section; **buds shiny, reddish-brown,** slightly resinous, not gummy, not fragrant, about ¼" long, 6–7-scaled, **lowest scale above the leaf scar.**

Leaves: Alternate, simple, deciduous; blades dark green above, paler beneath, **broadly ovate to almost kidney-shaped,** short-pointed, 1⅛–2¾"

long, with **20–30 fine, uneven, blunt teeth per side; stalks flattened,** slender, usually **longer than the blades;** leaves yellow in autumn.

Flowers: Tiny, without petals; unisexual with male and female flowers in **slender, hanging catkins** 1½–3" long, **on separate trees;** flowers develop in March–April **(before leaves expand).**

Fruits: Hairless, pointed, about ¼" long capsules, numerous, in hanging catkins up to 4" long; seeds ⅟₁₆–⅛" long, tipped with a **tuft of silky, white hairs;** capsules split open in **May–June** (as leaves expand).

Habitat: Low, moist sites in woods and marshes.

Origin: Native.

151

Balsam poplar is often planted as a windbreak. This fast-growing pioneer tree usually lives about 70 years. It reproduces primarily by sending up sprouts from roots and stumps. Detached branches can also take root. • Balsalm poplar wood resembles that of aspen and is used in similar ways. It has a pleasant odor when burned, but logs are often "punky" with fungus. Wet balsam poplar is hard to split, but frozen logs (10°F or colder) split easily. • The bud resin was used traditionally in cough medicines and in antiseptic ointments for stopping bleeding. Balsam poplar buds have similar properties to balm-of-Gilead buds, which are sold in health food stores. • Balsam poplar hybridizes with several other poplars, including eastern cottonwood (p. 153). This cross yields the **balm-of-Gilead (*P. x jackii*,** also called *P. x gileadensis*). A single female clone of this hybrid has been widely cultivated for medicinal and horticultural uses. Balm-of-Gilead does not grow wild in Illinois. • The name balm-of-Gilead is also applied to a subspecies of balsam poplar with heart-shaped leaves (*P. balsamifera* ssp *balsamifera*, previously called *P. candicans*). This subspecies is also believed to have originated from a single female clone. • Grouse and songbirds eat the aromatic buds, and bees incorporate the sticky resin into spring honeycombs.

Also Called: Hackmatack, tacamahac, balm poplar, liard, balsam, rough-barked poplar • *P. tacamahacca.*

Size and Shape: Trees 50–80' tall; crowns narrow, irregular; roots shallow, spreading.

Trunks: Straight, 12–24" in diameter, self-pruning; **young bark smooth, greenish-brown,** usually with dark markings; mature bark dark gray, furrowed; wood pale, light, soft.

Branches: Few, ascending; twigs orange-brown, gray with age, stout, with large, orange pores (lenticels); **pith 5-pointed** in cross-section; **buds shiny, orange-brown,** sticky, with a fragrant resin, pointed, ½–1" long, 5-scaled, lowest scale above the leaf scar.

Leaves: Alternate, simple, deciduous; blades firm, glossy, dark green above, silvery green to yellowish-green beneath (often brown-stained), oval, tapered to a point, 2⅜–6" long, edged with blunt teeth and with 2 warty glands at the base; stalks 1⅛–1½" long, round (not flattened); leaves yellow in autumn.

Flowers: Tiny, without petals; unisexual with male and female flowers in slender, **hanging catkins on separate trees;** male catkins 2¾–4" long; female catkins 4–5" long; flowers in April–May **(before leaves expand).**

Fruits: Numerous, egg-shaped capsules about ¼" long, in hanging catkins 4–6" long; seeds brown, ¹⁄₁₆" long, numerous, tipped with a **tuft of silky, white hairs; capsules split open in May–June** (as leaves expand).

Habitat: Moist lowlands and sandy sites.

Origin: Native.

Eastern cottonwood (*P. deltoides* ssp. *deltoides*) is found from the Atlantic Coast inland to Iowa and Texas, whereas the **plains cottonwood** (*P. deltoides* ssp. *monilifera*) ranges west across the Great Plains to British Columbia, Wyoming and New Mexico. Plains cottonwood has minutely hairy (vs. hairless) buds, pale yellow (vs. reddish-brown) twigs and leaves with 10–30 (vs. 40–50) teeth and 1–2 (vs. 3–5) basal glands. • This amazingly fast-growing tree can reach 150' in height in 30 years. Unfortunately, it is not suitable for city landscaping. Moisture-seeking roots often raise sidewalks and clog drainage pipes, brittle branches litter the ground, and cottony masses of wind-borne seeds clog window screens. • Hybrids between cottonwood and the distinctly columnar **Lombardy poplar** (*P. nigra* 'Italica,'* also called European black poplar), shown in dark green (species overlap) on the map, are widely cultivated. One male hybrid called **Carolina poplar** (*P.* x *canadensis*), is grown in plantations for wood and bark fiber and as a fast-growing, seed-free shade tree. The protein-rich leaves of hybrid poplars are fed to chickens, sheep and cattle. The leaf concentrate contains as much protein as meat but is faster and cheaper to produce. Eventually, poplars could provide food for both humans and livestock.

Also Called: Necklace poplar, big cottonwood, common cottonwood, liard.

Size and Shape: Trees 65–100' tall; crowns broad (open-grown) to narrow (in forests); roots usually shallow, spreading, not suckering.

Trunks: Sometimes massive, 24–60" in diameter; young bark smooth, yellowish-gray; mature bark dark gray, furrowed; wood light, soft, fine-grained.

Branches: Typically ascending at 45°; **twigs stout, vertically ridged below buds,** with sparse, linear pores (lenticels); **pith 5-pointed** in cross-section; **buds shiny,** yellowish-brown, fragrant, **resinous,** pointed, ½–¾" long, 5–7-scaled, **3-sided at twig tips, pointing outward below.**

Leaves: Alternate, simple, deciduous; blades firm, shiny and green above, paler beneath, **rounded-triangular,** 2–4¾" long, **warty glands** at the base of the blade; leaf edges with **callus-tipped teeth; stalks slender, flat,** 2–3" long; leaf scars 3-lobed, with fringed upper edges; leaves yellow in autumn.

Flowers: Tiny, without petals; unisexual with male and female flowers in **slender, hanging catkins on separate trees;** male catkins reddish, 2–4" long; female catkins 6–8" long; flowers in April–May **(before leaves expand).**

Fruits: Egg-shaped, pointed capsules ¼–½" long, in loose, hanging catkins 6–10" long; seeds ¹⁄₁₆–⅛" long, tipped with **silky, white hairs; capsules split into 3–4 in late May–June** (as leaves expand).

Habitat: Moist sites near streams.

Origin: Native.

153

This attractive, fast-growing poplar is sometimes planted as a shade tree. • Short-lived swamp-cottonwood produces seed at about 10 years of age and heavy crops each subsequent year. Fluffy parachutes carry the tiny seeds by wind and help seeds float on water to new sites. Like most poplars, swamp cottonwood has tiny seeds with limited food reserves and short lives. Seed must land on wet, exposed mineral soil soon after it has been released in order to germinate. • The straight trunks free of branches for over half their length make swamp cottonwood a desirable timber tree, though it is now too scarce to be of economic importance in Illinois. Also, the wood is soft and light (about half as dense as oak), and therefore has been used in expendable articles such as crates, boxes and excelsior. • Despite its common name, swamp cottonwood is not a true cottonwood. Cottonwoods belong to the Section *Aigeiros*, but swamp cottonwood is a member of the Section Leucoides. This smaller group is distinguished by its elevated stigmas and elongated styles (vs. low, stalkless stigmas), few stamens (12–20 vs. 20–80) and dry (vs. sticky, resinous) buds.

Also Called: Swamp poplar, black cottonwood, downy poplar, balm-of-Gilead.

Size and Shape: Trees 65–100' tall; crowns narrow, open, irregular; roots wide-spreading.

Trunks: Straight, 24–36" in diameter; young bark woolly-hairy, lightly furrowed; mature bark dull brown, furrowed or shaggy, with long, narrow plates peeling from both ends; wood pale, light, soft, straight-grained.

Branches: Short, spreading; twigs stout, **white-woolly at first,** becoming shiny, dark brown to gray, with large pores (lenticels); pith orange, 5-pointed in cross-section; buds reddish-brown, **more or less hairy,** about ¼" long, **scarcely if at all sticky.**

Leaves: Alternate, deciduous, simple; **blades white-woolly when young,** dark green above, paler beneath, **hairy on veins and lower blade, broadly ovate, 4–8" long, blunt-tipped or only slightly pointed, notched to rounded at the base,** edged with fine, blunt, incurved teeth; **stalks round** or slightly flattened near the tip, hairless, 2⅜–3½" long.

Flowers: Tiny, without petals; unisexual with **male and female flowers on separate trees,** borne on ⅛–¼" **long stalks in hanging catkins** in the axils of **fringed bracts; stamens 12–20;** stigmas on elongated styles; flowers in April–May **(before leaves).**

Fruits: Reddish-brown, egg-shaped **capsules ¼–½" long, on stalks ⅜–½" long,** in loose catkins 1–2⅜" long; seeds tiny, reddish-brown, tipped with a **tuft of silky, white hairs;** capsules split into 2–3 parts in spring **(with leaves).**

Habitat: Wet woods, swamps and shores.

Origin: Native.

This common tree is North America's largest native willow. It is our only tree willow with leaves that are fairly uniformly green on both surfaces and with conspicuous stipules on fast-growing shoots in late summer. • Black willow has little commercial value, but it has been used locally for construction timbers and fuel and for making wicker baskets and furniture. During the American Revolution, the wood of black willow (and of other willows) was made into fine charcoal, which was used to make gunpowder. • The brittle-based branches of black willow are easily broken by wind, and on moist ground, they often take root and grow into new trees. This form of vegetative reproduction is especially effective along rivers and streams, where flowing water can carry branches great distances and establish colonies in new locations. Black willow cuttings can be embedded in riverbanks to control erosion. • The tiny, fluffy seeds disperse in wind and water, and they grow readily on moist, sunny sites. However, they must germinate within 24 hours of falling or die. • The species name *nigra* means "black" and refers to the striking black bark of mature trees.

Also Called: Swamp willow.

Size and Shape: Trees or tall shrubs 35–65' tall; crowns broad, irregular; roots dense, spreading.

Trunks: Often leaning and forked into 2–4 trunks, 12–40" in diameter; mature bark dark brown to blackish, flaky to stringy, deeply furrowed; wood light, soft, fine-grained.

Branches: Spreading, stout; twigs pale yellowish-brown to reddish- or purplish-brown, ridged lengthwise below leaf scars, **tough and flexible but brittle-based; buds 1-scaled,** sharp-pointed, flat-lying, about ⅛" long.

Leaves: Alternate, simple, deciduous; **blades uniformly green above and below,** thin, **2–6" long,** typically **tapered to an abruptly curved (scythe-like) tip,** rounded to wedge-shaped at the base, **fine-toothed;** stalks ⅛–⅜" long, hairy, usually with glands near the blade; **stipules large, persistent,** fine-toothed; leaves yellow in autumn.

Flowers: Tiny, without petals, in axils of **pale yellow, hairy, deciduous bracts;** unisexual with male and female flowers in catkins on separate trees; male flowers with 3–7 (usually 6) stamens; catkins ¾–2" long, **on leafy shoots ⅜–1⅛" long;** flowers in April–May **(as leaves expand).**

Fruits: **Light brown, hairless capsules about ⅛" long,** in loose, hanging catkins ¾–3" long; seeds tiny, green, silky-hairy; capsules split open in June–July.

Habitat: Moist to wet habitats along streams, on floodplains and in wetlands.

Origin: Native.

155

The silver gray leaves of this attractive shade tree often sweep the ground. White willow is the most common willow in Europe and one of the most frequently planted in North America. Unfortunately, it is plagued by many diseases and insects. Also, its fallen leaves and branches often litter the ground, and its rapidly spreading roots can clog drains. • White willow wood does not split, so it has been used to make clogs, carvings and balls and mallets for croquet and cricket. • White willow trees are often pollarded to produce tufts of straight shoots suitable for weaving. • Large willows with pendulous branches are called weeping willows. The true **weeping willow (*S. babylonica*)** shown in pink/dark green (species overlap) on the map, is not hardy in the northern U.S., but hybrids of *S. babylonica* and *S. alba* (**weeping willow, *S.* x *sepulcralis***) and of *S. babylonica* and *S. fragilis* (**Wisconsin weeping willow, *S.* x *pendulina***) occasionally grow wild here. Also, *S. alba* frequently crosses with crack willow (*S. fragilis*, p. 161) to produce **hybrid crack willow (*S.* x *rubens*)**. This hybrid is probably more common than either parent. • A popular cultivar of *S. alba*, **golden weeping willow (*S. alba* var. *vitellina* 'Pendula')**, has flexible, hairless, yellow twigs and leaves with hairless upper surfaces.

Also Called: Golden willow, common willow, European white willow, French willow.

Size and Shape: Trees or shrubs 50–80' tall; crowns broad; roots deep, spreading.

Trunks: Straight, 24–48" in diameter; mature bark light brown to dark gray, corky, furrowed; wood light, even, resilient.

Branches: Stout, ascending; **twigs greenish-brown to yellow, slender, flexible but brittle-based, often hanging; buds 1-scaled,** hairy, flattened.

Leaves: Alternate, simple, deciduous; blades bright to grayish-green above, whitish with a waxy bloom beneath, **silky-hairy (especially when young), lance-shaped,** tapered at both ends, 1½–7" long, with **fine, gland-tipped teeth;** stalks hairy, often glandular near the blade; stipules small, soon shed; leaves yellow in autumn.

Flowers: Tiny, without petals, in axils of **small, greenish-yellow, hairy bracts** that are soon shed; unisexual with male and female flowers in catkins on separate trees; male flowers with 2 (sometimes 3) stamens; **catkins erect,** 1⅛–2" long, **on shoots ⅜–1½" long, with 2–4 small leaves;** flowers April–June (**as leaves expand**).

Fruits: Hairless, ⅛–¼" long, **essentially stalk-less capsules** in stalked catkins 1½–2⅜" long; seeds tiny, green, tipped with a tuft of silky hairs; capsules split open in May–June.

Habitat: Open, moist to wet sites, often in disturbed areas.

Origin: Introduced from Europe and central Asia.

This attractive native willow is sometimes planted as an ornamental. • Many animals, such as moose, deer, squirrels, rabbits and porcupines, feed on the leaves, buds, catkins and bark of shining willow. • The leaves of shining willow resemble those of peachleaf willow (p. 164), **autumn willow (*S. serissima*)**, shown in dark green (species overlap) on the map, and **Carolina willow (*S. caroliniana*, also called *S. wardii*)**, shown in dark pink on the map. However, peachleaf willow has less glossy leaves with prominent, pale midveins, and the leaves of autumn willow and Carolina willow are usually white-waxy beneath. Also, autumn willow blooms later (in June) and has hairless leaves and twigs, while Carolina willow has somewhat hairy leaves and twigs and narrowly oblong, lance-shaped leaf blades. • Yet another similar species, laurel willow (p. 158), is distinguished by its relatively short-pointed leaves, yellow-green (vs. green to brownish) female flowers and consistently 5-stamened male flowers. • In Illinois, willows are the only alternate-leaved woody plants with flat-lying buds each covered by a single scale. American sycamore (p. 87) also has single bud scales, but its buds stick out from the twigs. • A hairy variety of shining willow, ***S. lucida* var. *intonsa***, is sometimes encountered. It is distinguished by the persistent reddish hairs on its leaves and twigs.

Also Called: Yellow willow.

Size and Shape: Small trees or tall shrubs 10–20' tall; crowns broad.

Trunks: Short, small, rarely to 8" in diameter; young bark smooth; mature bark brown, irregularly furrowed; wood light, soft.

Branches: Upright; twigs shiny yellowish- to chestnut brown, rusty-hairy at first, soon hairless, slender; buds 1-scaled, pale brown, flat-lying.

Leaves: Alternate, simple, deciduous; blades reddish and rusty-hairy when young, shiny, dark green and hairless when mature, shiny but paler beneath, lance-shaped, slender-pointed, 1½–6" long, with rounded or wedge-shaped bases, edged with fine, gland-tipped teeth; stalks ¼–½" long, glandular near the blade; stipules glandular-toothed, semicircular, sometimes absent.

Flowers: Tiny, without petals, in the axils of small, yellowish, thinly hairy bracts (shed before capsules ripen); unisexual with male and female flowers in catkins on separate trees; male flowers with 3–6 stamens; catkins erect, ½–2" long, on leafy shoots ⅜–1" long; flowers in May (as leaves expand).

Fruits: Pale brown, hairless capsules about ¼" long, on stalks ¹⁄₁₆" long, in catkins ½–2" long and ⅜–½" wide; seeds tiny, silky-hairy; capsules split in half in June–July.

Habitat: Wet, often sandy sites along streams and in ditches and various wetlands.

Origin: Native.

157

Laurel willow was introduced to North America as a hardy small ornamental tree whose fragrant leaves were sometimes used to flavor food. It is still cultivated and is especially popular in regions with acidic soils, though it does well in a broad pH range. Laurel willow now grows wild in most of the northern U.S. and southern Canada. • Willows have been cultivated since at least the time of ancient Greece and Rome. Many species are highly valued in landscaping and are easily propagated from cuttings. • The epithet *pentandra* comes from the Greek *penta*, "five," and *andron*, "male," and refers to the 5-stamened male flowers. • This species could be confused with shining willow (p. 157), but the leaves of shining willow have long, slender, tapered tips, whereas those of laurel willow are relatively short-pointed. • Laurel willow is also very similar to **autumn willow (*S. serissima*)**, a native shrub that can reach 13' in height. However, the leaves of autumn willow have whitish lower surfaces with a thin, waxy bloom and the tiny bracts of the catkins are hairy from base to tip, whereas those of laurel willow have hairless tips.

Also Called: Bayleaf willow.

Size and Shape: Small trees or tall shrubs up to 25' tall; crowns broad.

Trunks: Usually clumped, often leaning; mature bark gray-brown; wood light, soft.

Branches: Upright to spreading; twigs shiny reddish-brown, slender; **buds 1-scaled, yellow,** flat-lying.

Leaves: Alternate, simple, deciduous; **blades shiny and dark green above** with yellow midveins, green or slightly paler beneath, hairless, **fragrant, ovate,** with pointed tips and rounded to wedge-shaped bases, 1½–4" long, edged with gland-tipped teeth; stalks with glands near the blade; stipules small, glandular.

Flowers: Tiny, without petals; unisexual with male and female flowers in catkins on separate trees; male flowers with 4–9 (usually 5) stamens; catkins 1⅛–2⅜" long, on **short, leafy shoots** in the axils of **deciduous, pale yellow, hairy bracts with hairless tips,** flowers in May (**as or slightly after leaves expand**).

Fruits: Hairless, yellow-green capsules about ¼" long, on stalks ¹⁄₁₆" long in catkins 1⅜–2¾" long; seeds tiny, green, silky-hairy; capsules split open in June–July.

Habitat: Wet sites such as riverbanks, dunes and low fields.

Origin: Introduced from Eurasia.

158

This fast-growing pioneer species spreads quickly over newly exposed sandbars and alluvial flats by sending up shoots from its extensive shallow roots. In this way, it forms dense thickets that stabilize the soil and prepare the way for later species such as alders, poplars and other willows. • Sandbar willows are relatively small, and their wood is light and soft, so these shrubs have little economic value. Some tribes, however, used the flexible twigs and bark of sandbar willow to make rope, string and baskets. Bark fibers were woven together to make bags, blankets and clothing. Finely shredded inner bark provided absorbent padding for diapers and sanitary napkins. The wood was often used to smoke fish, meat and animal skins and was also used to make snowshoes and bows. The tips of willow twigs were sometimes chewed to separate the fibers and then used as toothbrushes. • The species

name *exigua*, "meager," refers to the extremely narrow leaves. The earlier name, *interior*, referred to sandbar willow's mainly interior (rather than coastal) distribution. • This species varies greatly over its broad North American range, which extends from Alaska to Mexico. It can be considered either a single species with many varying forms or a complex of numerous, difficult-to-distinguish species.

Also Called: Basket willow, coyote willow, narrowleaf willow, slenderleaf willow, pink-barked willow • *S. exigua* ssp. *interior, S. interior.*

Size and Shape: Tall shrubs 5–25' tall; crowns rounded; roots shallow, spreading, often suckering to form **extensive colonies**.

Trunks: Numerous, 2–6" in diameter; bark thin, smooth, with raised pores (lenticels), furrowed with age; wood soft, straight-grained, tough, odorless.

Branches: Slender, erect; twigs yellowish- to reddish-brown, hairless with age, slender, flexible; **buds 1-scaled,** flattened, absent at twig tips.

Leaves: Alternate, simple, deciduous; blades deep yellowish-green, paler beneath, lacking a waxy bloom, **linear, 2–6" long, tapered at both ends,** edged with **irregular, widely spaced, gland-tipped teeth** (rarely toothless); stalks ⅛–¼" long; stipules tiny, soon shed; leaf scars V-shaped, with 3 vein scars; leaves yellow in autumn.

Flowers: Tiny; **unisexual** with male and female flowers in catkins on separate trees, in axils of small, **pale yellowish bracts** that are **soon shed;** male flowers with 2 stamens; **catkins on leafy branches** 1⅛–4" long; flowers in April–May **(after leaves)** and sometimes again in midsummer.

Fruits: Slender, **lance-shaped capsules** about ¼" long, silky-hairy at first, often hairless with age, short-stalked, in **nodding catkins ¾–2⅜" long;** seeds tiny, tipped with a tuft of silky, white hairs; capsules mature in summer.

Habitat: Sandy streambanks and floodplains.

Origin: Native.

This common willow is sometimes browsed so heavily by deer that it never reaches over 3' in height. • The bitter-tasting inner bark of most willows contains salicin, a compound similar to acetylsalicylic acid (ASA). Willow-bark extracts have been used for centuries to relieve pain and combat fevers. • Willow flowers provide nectar and pollen for bees each spring. • Slender willow can provide a low-quality fuel. The branchlets were sometimes used to make baskets, hence the alternate name "basket willow." • Willow leaves and twigs are often deformed by large, round blisters or pimple-like growths. These are galls created by flies, wasps, aphids and other insect parasites. Each insect produces a particular type of gall on a specific part of the plant. When females deposit their eggs in the leaf or twig, the tree responds by producing a tumor-like growth. When the eggs hatch, the insect larvae grow and develop inside the gall, fed and protected by its tissues, until they finally emerge as adults. Occasionally, galls are caused by fungi. The cone-like galls at the tips of willow twigs are created by the willow pine-cone gall midge (*Rhabdophaga stobiloides*). • Slender willows with more or less permanently hairy leaves have sometimes been called *S.* x *subsericea*, but these shrubs are now included in *S. petiolaris*.

Also Called: Petioled willow, meadow willow, basket willow, stalked willow • *S. gracilis*.

Size and Shape: Low to medium shrubs 3–23' tall; crowns broad; roots shallow.

Trunks: Clumped, 2–4" wide; young bark grayish-green to chestnut brown, smooth; mature bark dark brown, scaly; wood light, soft.

Branches: Upright; twigs yellowish-green to olive-brown and hairy when young, hairless and nearly black with age, long, slender; buds **1-scaled,** pressed to twigs.

Leaves: Alternate, simple, deciduous, **pointing upward, often overlapping;** blades reddish and hairy when young, **shiny, green and usually hairless when mature,** paler with a **whitish bloom beneath, thin, linear-lance-shaped, pointed at both ends,** 1½–4¾" long, **finely glandular-toothed** (at least above the middle); stalks yellowish, ⅛–⅜" long; **stipules absent.**

Flowers: Tiny, without petals or sepals; **unisexual with male and female flowers in catkins on separate trees,** in axils of hairy bracts; male flowers 2-stamened, in catkins ⅜–1⅛" long; **catkins loosely flowered, on short, leafy shoots, often forming long series along branches,** flowers in April–June **(with leaves).**

Fruits: Silky-hairy, slender-beaked capsules ⅛–¼" **long, on hairy stalks about** ⅛" **long,** in catkins ½–1½" long; seeds tiny, silky-hairy; capsules split open in late May–June.

Habitat: Marshy ground on shores and in low prairies, marshes, bogs and rich woods.

Origin: Native.

Crack willow is one of the largest willows in the world, but it is not economically important. It is sometimes cut for firewood, and in colonial times, it was imported for making high-quality charcoal to use in cannon powder. In Scotland, the attractive wood has been used in boat finishing. • Branch fragments often litter the ground after windy weather and soon root in moist soil. Streams carry twigs to new locations, helping to spread the species. The specific epithet *fragilis* means "brittle" or "fragile" and refers to this species' brittle, easily broken branches. • Crack willow is widely planted as an ornamental shade tree. It commonly escapes to grow wild, but pure specimens are rare. Hybrids between crack willow and white willow (p. 156), called hybrid crack willow (p. 156), are much more common and display characteristics of both parents. • Crack willow branches and twigs spread at an angle of 60–90°, whereas those of white willow spread at 30–45°. • Crack willow is commonly confused with black willow (p. 155). Black willow leaves have green (not whitish) lower surfaces, finely (not coarsely) toothed edges and large, persistent stipules.

Also Called: Brittle willow, snap willow.

Size and Shape: Trees 50–100' tall; crowns open, spreading; **roots reddish,** often conspicuous on eroded shores.

Trunks: Up to 6' in diameter; mature bark dull, dark gray, deeply furrowed, narrow-ridged; wood soft, reddish, tough, fine-grained.

Branches: Long, ascending to spreading; **twigs yellowish, greenish or dark reddish-brown, shiny, slender, stiff, brittle-based; buds reddish-brown, 1-scaled,** gummy, flat-lying, ⅛–¼" long.

Leaves: Alternate, simple, deciduous; blades green above, paler with a whitish bloom beneath, lance-shaped, 2¾–8" long (larger on rapidly growing shoots), tapered at both ends, **edged with coarse (10–17 per inch), irregular, gland-tipped teeth;** stalks usually with prominent glands near the blade; stipules tiny or absent.

Flowers: Tiny, without petals, in the axils of

small, pale yellow to yellowish-green, hairy bracts (soon shed); unisexual with male and female flowers in catkins on separate trees; male flowers with 2 (sometimes 3–4) stamens; **hanging catkins ¾–2⅜" long, on leafy shoots ⅜–2" long;** flowers in April–May **(as leaves expand).**

Fruits: Hairless, lance-shaped capsules ⅛–¼" **long,** in catkins 2–3" long; seeds tiny, silky-hairy; capsules split open in May–July.

Habitat: Wet sites in woodlands, pastures, streambanks, lakeshores and roadsides.

Origin: Introduced from Europe and Asia Minor.

161

Heartleaf willow typically has silvery galls caused by small insects. In the past, these galls were steeped to make a medicinal tea for stimulating urination and relieving fluid retention. • Willows are easily recognized as a group, but individual species are often difficult to identify. For one thing, many trees may not have all the features necessary to make a positive identification. In cases where fruit characteristics are important for identification, immature trees and male trees are especially troublesome. Also, the leaves can vary greatly with age and habitat. For example, leaves on young, vigorous shoots may be much larger and hairier or less regularly toothed than those on mature trees. To further complicate matters, willows often hybridize, producing offspring with intermediate characteristics. • **Blueleaf willow** (*S. myricoides*, also called bayberry willow, *S.* x *myricoides* and *S. glaucophylloides*), shown in pink/dark green (species overlap) on the map, is another tall, native willow with hairless capsules in the axils of dark brown to blackish scales. Blueleaf willow is usually a shrub, but occasionally it reaches the size of a small tree (15' tall). Its leaves are reddish-tinged when young, heavily white-waxy beneath when mature and usually black when dried. Blueleaf willow grows on sandy or calcareous shores of ponds and marshes.

Also Called: Broadleaf willow, diamond willow, Missouri willow, erect willow, yellow willow • *S. rigida* [misapplied], *S. cordata*.

Size and Shape: Shrubby trees or tall shrubs 5–15' tall; crowns spreading.

Trunks: Clumped, 3–6" in diameter; mature bark thin, gray to black, scaly; wood light, soft.

Branches: Upright; **twigs yellowish-green and downy when young, reddish-brown and hairless with age; buds 1-scaled,** reddish-brown, flat-lying.

Leaves: Alternate, simple, deciduous; **blades reddish and white-hairy when young, hairless and dark purplish-green above when mature,** silvery-whitish beneath with reddish hairs along some veins, stiff, oblong-lance-shaped, **rounded to notched at the base,** 2–6" long, **finely glandular-toothed;** stipules glandular-toothed, ¼–¾" long, persistent; leaves deep red and veiny in autumn.

Flowers: Tiny, without petals, in axils of dark brown, crinkly-hairy bracts ¹⁄₁₆" long; unisexual with male and female flowers in catkins on separate trees; male flowers 2-stamened, in catkins ⅜–1⅛" long; **catkins on leafy shoots up to ⅜" long** (usually), often in long series along twigs, flowers in April **(as or slightly before leaves expand).**

Fruits: Brown **(reddish when young),** hairless or hairy, **lance-shaped capsules about ¼" long, on stalks ¹⁄₁₆" long** (stalks longer than bracts); **capsules crowded, spreading, in catkins ¾–3" long;** seeds tiny, silky-hairy; capsules split open in summer.

Habitat: Streambanks, floodplains, shores, ditches and swamps.

Origin: Native.

The mostly opposite leaves of this species are unique among our willows. • Purple-osier willow is widely planted and has escaped cultivation across much of eastern North America. It is hardy as far north as southern Lake Superior. • Most willows grow readily from cuttings, and thousands of offspring can be propagated from an individual tree. This property is particularly useful in the production of cultivars from single trees that have desirable attributes. Some willows have been perpetuated for centuries in this way, each genetically identical to the original parent tree. • This attractive willow has been cultivated since ancient times as a source of withes for making baskets. Its striking purplish shoots can be woven with branches from other willows to produce contrasting patterns and trims. Many willows produce strong, slender, flexible withes ideal for weaving. • Willow bark has been used for years to relieve pain, inflammation and fever. It contains salicin, from which acetylsalicylic acid (ASA) was derived. Both of these compounds are named after the genus *Salix*. • The generic name *Salix* is derived from the Celtic words *sal*, "near," and *lis*, "water," in reference to the usual habitat of most willows.

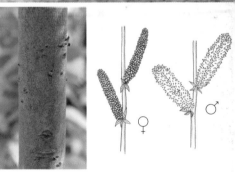

Also Called: Purple willow.

Size and Shape: Shrubs or shrubby trees up to 20' tall; crowns spreading.

Trunks: Clumped; young bark smooth; wood light, soft, odorless.

Branches: Upright to ascending, 3–4" in diameter; twigs yellowish-green to **dark purple,** hairless, slender, flexible; **buds essentially opposite, 1-scaled, purplish,** small, flat-lying, ¼–½" **long** on sprouts.

Leaves: Essentially **opposite** (at least near twig tips), simple, deciduous; **blades dull green and often purplish above** with **prominent pale midveins,** paler with a **whitish bloom beneath,** essentially hairless, lance-shaped, usually **widest above the middle,** ¾–2⅜" long, smooth-edged or with fine gland-tipped teeth near the tip; stalks ¹⁄₁₆–⅛" long.

Flowers: Tiny, without petals; unisexual with male and female flowers in catkins on separate trees, in axils of small, hairy, blackish bracts (sometimes pale-centered and/or becoming hairless); male flowers 2-stamened, with filaments (and sometimes anthers) fused; **catkins** ¾–1⅛" **long, often paired,** on short, leafy shoots or stalkless; flowers in spring **(before leaves expand).**

Fruits: **Densely short-hairy, egg-shaped, plump, stalkless capsules** ⅛" **long, in catkins** ¾–1⅛" **long;** seeds tiny, silky-hairy; capsules split open in summer.

Habitat: Low, wet sites, often near streams and pools.

Origin: Introduced from Eurasia.

163

Like most willows, peachleaf willow has little commercial value. Because of its drooping branch tips, it is sometimes popular for landscaping. It is rarely cut for timber but is sometimes used for firewood or as a source of charcoal. The tannin-rich bark produces a pale brown dye.
• The dense, tenacious roots of peachleaf willow have saved many streambanks from erosion.
• Willows provide food and shelter for many birds and mammals. Deer and moose browse on the leaves and twigs, while squirrels and rabbits eat the tender shoots and bark. The early-blooming flowers can be an important source of spring nectar for bees. • The specific epithet *amygdaloides* comes from the Greek *amugdalos*, "almond," and *öides*, "resembling," in reference to the almond-shaped leaves of this species.
• Peachleaf willow could be confused with black willow (p. 155), but black willow has smaller, narrower leaves with curved tips and pale green (not waxy-whitish) lower surfaces. Also, black willow has brittle-based branches, hairy young leaves and large, persistent stipules. • Peachleaf willow and shining willow (p. 157) have similar leaves, but the lower surfaces of shining willow leaves are shiny, pale green.

Also Called: Peach willow.

Size and Shape: Trees or tall shrubs 15–65' tall; crowns narrow, irregular to rounded.

Trunks: Often leaning, in clumps of 2–4, up to 12–16" in diameter; young bark reddish or yellowish, smooth; mature bark grayish-brown, with flat, shaggy, interlacing ridges; wood light, soft, fine-grained.

Branches: Ascending, often nodding at the tips; twigs yellowish- to reddish-brown with lighter pores (lenticels), **slender, flexible; buds shiny, brown, sharp-pointed, 1-scaled,** flat-lying, ⅛" long.

Leaves: Alternate, simple, deciduous; **blades reddish and sparsely hairy when young, dark green to yellowish-green and hairless when mature, whitish with a waxy bloom beneath,** thin, with a **prominent midvein, lance-shaped, slender-pointed,** unevenly rounded at the base, 2–6" long, **fine-toothed;** stalks usually lack glands; stipules usually absent.

Flowers: Tiny, without petals; in the axils of deciduous, **pale yellow, hairy bracts;** unisexual with male and female flowers on separate trees, in catkins on leafy shoots; male flowers with 3–7 (typically 5) stamens, in catkins 1⅛–2⅜" long; flowers in April–May **(as leaves expand).**

Fruits: Reddish or yellowish, hairless, short-beaked, lance-shaped capsules about ¼" long, in loose catkins 1½–3½" long; seeds tiny, tipped with a tuft of silky hairs; capsules split open in June–July.

Habitat: Moist, open sites on floodplains and shores.

Origin: Native.

Pussy willow is sometimes planted as a hardy, fast-growing ornamental shrub. • Willow catkins provide important food for bees and other insects in early spring. Pollen and nectar in the catkins attract insects, which in turn pollinate hundreds of the tiny willow flowers. • Pussy willow can be confused with **goat willow (*S. caprea*,** also called florist's willow),

shown in dark green (species overlap) on the map, a widely planted European species that occasionally grows wild. Goat willow has smaller (¹/₄"), densely gray-hairy capsules and broader, sometimes almost round, leaves. • An occasional European escape, **large gray willow (*S. cinerea*,** also called gray willow or pussy willow), found only in DuPage County, is similar to goat willow but has narrower, woollier leaf blades that taper to both ends. The branches have distinctive, long, prominent ridges on their wood, but the bark must be stripped away before they can be seen. • Fuzzy, immature willow catkins have been likened to the soft paws or toes of a cat, hence the name "pussy willow." Catkin-bearing branches from all 3 of these willows are gathered each spring for use in bouquets. Male pussy willows should not be collected, because they may shed their pollen in the house. If bud-bearing twigs are brought indoors in late winter and set in water, they can be "forced" to produce pussy willows early. In the wild, pussy willow catkins are the first to appear each spring.

Also Called: Tall pussy willow, glaucous willow, pussy feet.

Size and Shape: Trees or tall shrubs **6–25' tall;** crowns rounded; roots shallow.

Trunks: Few, clumped, 4–8" in diameter; mature bark gray-brown, furrowed; wood light, soft.

Branches: Upright, rather stout; twigs dark reddish-brown with pale pores (lenticels), shiny, sometimes with a waxy bloom, becoming hairless; buds 1-scaled, reddish-purple, ¹/₄–³/₈" long, flat-lying.

Leaves: Alternate, simple, deciduous; **highly variable, blades reddish-hairy at first, becoming green and hairless above** with hairless (or persistently few-haired) **undersides coated in a waxy bloom,** oblong to elliptical, 1¹/₈–4" long, wedge-shaped at the base, **smooth-edged to irregularly toothed or almost wavy-edged** (especially above midleaf); stalks green, ¹/₄–¹/₂" long; stipules large on vigorous shoots.

Flowers: Tiny, without petals, in axils of dark brown, white-hairy, ¹/₁₆–¹/₈" long bracts; unisexual with male and female flowers in catkins on separate trees; male flowers 2-stamened, in ³/₄–1¹/₂" long catkins; **catkins densely hairy,** on short, leafy shoots or stalkless; flowers in March–May **(before leaves expand).**

Fruits: Minutely gray-hairy capsules ¹/₄–¹/₂" long, long-beaked, with styles <¹/₁₆" long, hanging in dense catkins 2–3¹/₂" long; seeds tiny, tipped with a tuft of silky hairs; capsules split open in late May–June.

Habitat: Low, boggy sites.

Origin: Native.

165

A pioneer species, Bebb willow is often among the first woody plants to appear after a fire. It can live about 20 years. Like many willows, it is an important source of food and shelter for a wide range of birds and mammals. • The wood of Bebb willow has been used for baseball bats and wickerwork. It was also once used to make charcoal for gunpowder. • Diamond-shaped patches on some branches are caused by fungal infections, which produce attractive reddish-orange to brown patterns in the pale wood. Peeled and sanded, such "diamond willow" branches are used to make walking sticks, lamp-posts, furniture and rustic plaques and clock faces. • The specific epithet *bebbiana* honors American botanist Michael Schuck Bebb (1833–95). • Bebb willow has extremely variable leaves and twigs. Raised, netted veins on the undersides of young leaves help to identify this species. • An unusual introduced willow, **corkscrew willow (S. matsudanda 'Tortuosa,'** or twisted willow) is a cultivated variety of Peking willow. Though rare in its native China, corkscrew willow is widely planted as an ornamental and now grows wild in several states. Corkscrew willow is easily recognized by its curiously contorted and curled leaves and twigs.

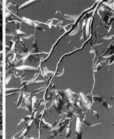

Photo, bottom right: *S. matsudana*

Also Called: Beaked willow, long-beak willow, diamond willow, gray willow, Bebb's willow.

Size and Shape: Trees or tall shrubs 10–25' tall; crowns broad, rounded.

Trunks: Clumped, 2⅜–6" in diameter; young bark reddish-brown to gray; mature bark grayish-brown, furrowed; wood light, soft, tough.

Branches: Upright to spreading; twigs reddish-purple to orange-brown with pale pores (lenticels), eventually hairless; **buds 1-scaled,** shiny, brown, blunt, flat-lying.

Leaves: Alternate, simple, deciduous; blades silky-hairy and sometimes reddish when young, **dull green above when mature, whitish with a waxy bloom, hairy and prominently net-veined beneath,** often widest above midleaf, ¾–3" long, smooth- to wavy-edged, may be irregularly glandular-toothed toward the base; stipules tiny, soon shed, larger and persistent on vigorous shoots.

Flowers: Tiny, without petals; unisexual with male and female flowers in catkins on separate trees; male flowers 2-stamened, in catkins ⅜–1⅛" long; catkins in the axils of **yellowish or straw-colored** (often reddish-tipped), **sparsely hairy, ¹⁄₁₆–⅛" long bracts** on leafy, ¼–¾" long shoots, in May **(as leaves expand).**

Fruits: Finely gray-hairy, long-beaked, about ¼" capsules on ⅛" stalks in loose catkins, ¾–2¾" **long;** seeds tiny, tipped with a tuft of silky hairs; capsules split open in June–July.

Habitat: Low-lying, boggy sites.

Origin: Native.

Key to Genera in the Rose Family (Rosaceae)

1a Leaves compound, divided into leaflets
. . . . **Sorbus, mountain-ash** (key to species, p. 171)
1b Leaves simple, not divided into leaflets. **2**

2a Fruits fleshy drupes . . . . . . **Prunus, cherry, plum, peach** (key to species, p. 168)
2b Fruits fleshy pomes (apple-like) **3**

3a Branches usually thorny; fruits containing 1–5 bony, seed-like stones
. . . . **Crataegus, hawthorn** (discussion and key to species, pp. 172–173)
3b Branches lacking thorns; fruits otherwise **4**

4a Pith 5-pointed in cross-section; fruits dark reddish-purple to blackish, berry-like, usually
10-seeded, borne in elongated clusters
. . . . **Amelanchier, serviceberry** (key to species, p. 171)
4b Pith round in cross-section; fruits green or yellow to reddish, apple-like, containing 2–5
papery or leathery compartments that are easily opened to expose the seeds, borne singly or
in small, rounded clusters **5**

5a Leaves smooth-edged; fruits fuzzy, yellow, pear shaped, 2¼–4" wide; twigs black;
flowers 1½–2¾" across . . . . **Cydonia, quince** (p. 185)
5b Leaves toothed and sometimes lobed; fruits smooth-skinned, variously colored and shaped;
twigs and flowers varied **6**

6a Young leaves folded in bud, expanding from lengthwise pleats; branches often thorny; mostly
native species . . . . **Malus, crabapple** (key to species, p. 170)
6b Young leaves expanding from rolled edges; branches not thorny; introduced fruit trees . . **7**

7a Young leaves with up-rolled edges gradually revealing the upper leaf surface; twigs hairless;
fruits broad-based, with many grit cells in the flesh . . . . **Pyrus, pear** (p. 184)
7b Young leaves with down-rolled edges gradually revealing the lower surface; fruits round,
lacking grit cells . . . . **Malus, apple, crabapple** (key to species, p. 170)

Pyrus communis, common pear

167

Key to the Cherries, Plums, and Peaches (Genus *Prunus*)

1a   Branches usually with rough thorns, not tipped with buds; leaves edged with prominent, outward-pointing teeth; fruits large, slightly oblong drupes (plums) **2**

1b   Branches lacking thorns, tipped with buds; leaves edged with very fine, oblique teeth; fruits smaller, round drupes (cherries) **7**

2a   Leaf teeth sharp, not gland-tipped; sepals without glands **3**

2b   Leaf teeth rounded, some tipped with glands; sepals usually with glands. **4**

3a   Leaf stalks usually with glands near the blade; leaf blades broadly rounded at the base; sepals hairy on the outer side; never forming thickets
. . . . *P. mexicana*, **bigtree plum** (p. 180)

3b   Leaf stalks usually lacking glands; leaf blades squared to tapered to a wedge-shaped base; sepals hairless on the outer side; often forming thickets
. . . . *P. americana*, **American plum** (p. 180)

4a   Leaves 1¹⁄₈–2¹⁄₄" long, usually folded lengthwise; sepals lacking glands along edges
. . . . *P. angustifolia*, **Chickasaw plum** (p. 181)

4b   Leaves usually 2–5" long, not folded lengthwise; sepals edged with gland-tipped teeth . . **5**

5a   Leaves broadly oval, less than twice as long as wide; petals about ¹⁄₂" long; buds blackish
. . . . *P. nigra*, **Canada plum** (p. 183)

5b   Leaves ovate to lance-shaped or elliptical, more than twice as long as wide; petals about ¹⁄₄" long; buds reddish-brown. **6**

6a   Flowers expanding before the leaves; leaf teeth low, blunt, with a gland near the base
. . . . *P. munsoniana*, **Munson plum** (p. 182)

6b   Flowers appearing when the leaves are half-grown; leaf teeth triangular, with a gland at the forward-pointed tip . . . . *P. hortulana*, **wildgoose plum** (p. 182)

7a   Flowers and fruits in elongated clusters **8**

7b   Flowers and fruits in small, rounded, usually tassel-like clusters **10**

8a   Flowers with elliptical, ¹⁄₄–³⁄₈" long petals, borne on long (³⁄₈–⁵⁄₈") stalks; fruits ¹⁄₄–³⁄₈" across, with a sculpted stone, inedible; introduced species
. . . . *P. padus*, **European bird cherry** (p. 175)

8b   Flowers with rounded, <³⁄₁₆" long petals, borne on short (³⁄₁₆–⁵⁄₁₆") stalks; fruits ⁵⁄₁₆–³⁄₈" across, with a smooth stone, edible; native species. **9**

9a   Leaves leathery, edged with incurved teeth, brownish-hairy beneath along the midrib; sepals pointed, usually longer than wide, smooth-edged or with inconspicuous, irregular, gland-tipped teeth, persisting at the base of the fruit
. . . . *P. serotina*, **wild black cherry** (p. 174)

9b   Leaves thinner (not leathery), edged with straight teeth, hairless beneath; sepals blunt, usually wider than long, conspicuously glandular-toothed, soon shed
. . . . *P. virginiana*, **chokecherry** (p. 175)

10a   Flowers and fruits stalkless, usually single or paired. **11**

10b   Flowers and fruits distinctly stalked **13**

11a   Leaves woolly beneath, oval to egg-shaped, widest at or above the middle, less than 2³⁄₄" long; fruit a slightly hairy cherry . . . . *P. tomentosa*, **Manchu cherry** (p. 177)

11b   Leaves hairless beneath, round to oblong-lance-shaped, 2–6" long; ovary and fruit velvety or woolly **12**

12a   Fruit a peach, up to 4" across, with a deeply pitted stone; leaves lance-shaped to oblong-lance-shaped, 3–6" long; flowers pink, 1–1$\frac{1}{2}$" across . . . ***P. persica*, peach** (p. 177)

12b   Fruit an apricot, <2" across, with a smooth stone; leaves round to broadly ovate, 2–4" long; flowers pink, $\frac{3}{4}$–1$\frac{1}{8}$" across. . . . . ***P. armeniaca*, apricot** (p. 177)

13a   Flowers rarely >$\frac{5}{8}$" across, petals $\frac{3}{16}$–$\frac{1}{4}$" long; fruits <$\frac{5}{8}$" in diameter **14**

13b   Flowers $\frac{3}{4}$–1$\frac{1}{8}$" across, petals $\frac{3}{8}$–$\frac{5}{8}$" long; fruits $\frac{5}{8}$–1" in diameter. **15**

14a   Flower and fruit clusters tassel-like, naked at the base (without leafy bracts); petals hairy beneath; cherries bright red; leaf blades usually more than twice as long as wide
. . . . ***P. pensylvanica*, pin cherry** (p. 176)

14b   Flower and fruit clusters with a short, branched central stalk, leafy-bracted at the base; petals hairless; cherries nearly black; leaf blades less than 1.5 times as long as wide
. . . . ***P. mahaleb*, Mahaleb cherry** (p. 177)

15a   Leaves soft and rather droopy, somewhat hairy beneath; calyx lobes smooth-edged, constricted below the base; mature leaves hairy beneath on the midvein, with glands on the stalk just below the 2$\frac{3}{8}$–4$\frac{3}{4}$" long blade; fruit sweet. . . . .***P. avium*, sweet cherry** (p. 178)

15b   Leaves firm, ascending, hairless; calyx lobes glandular-toothed, not constricted below the base; mature leaves hairless, with glands on the edge of the 1$\frac{1}{2}$–3$\frac{1}{2}$" long blade (not on the stalk), fruit sour . . . . ***P. cerasus*, sour cherry** (p. 179)

Prunus persica, peach

169

Key the Apples and Crabapples (Genus *Malus*)

1a Flowers brightly rose-colored (fading to white) with red or pink anthers; leaves pleated lengthwise in bud, sharply toothed and often more or less lobed when mature, soon hairless;
branches usually thorny; mostly native species **2**

1b Flowers whitish or pinkish with yellow anthers; leaves rolled lengthwise in bud, never lobed;
branches not thorny; introduced species **5**

2a Calyx soon shed, absent on fruit; styles 3–4; fruit <$^1/_2$" across; introduced species, escaped
from cultivation. . . . .*M. sieboldii*, **Japanese crabapple** (p. 187)

2b Calyx persistent, present at tip of fruit; styles 5; fruit $^5/_8$–1$^3/_8$" across; native species **3**

3a Flower base, fruit and fruit/flower stalk woolly-hairy; leaves always hairy beneath
. . . . **M. ioënsis, prairie crabapple** (p. 189)

3b Flower base, fruit and fruit/flower stalk hairless or sparsely silky-hairy; leaves usually
hairless **4**

4a Leaves ovate to broadly lance-shaped, 1–2 times as long as wide, tips abruptly or gradually
tapered to a point . . . .**M. coronaria, wild crabapple** (p. 186)

4b Leaves lance-shaped to elliptical, 2$^1/_2$–3 times as long as wide, tips blunt to rounded
. . . . **M. angustifolia, narrow-leaved crabapple** (p. 186)

5a Leaves blunt-toothed, rounded or notched at the base, more or less woolly beneath; leaf stalks,
young twigs and calyx lobes woolly; apples 2$^3/_8$–4$^3/_4$" in diameter
. . . .**M. pumila, common apple** (p. 188)

5b Leaves sharp-toothed, wedge-shaped at the base, nearly hairless beneath; leaf stalks, young
twigs and calyx lobes various; crabapples <1" in diameter **6**

6a Sepals hairless, tapered to a long, slender point; fruit <$^1/_2$" across
. . . .**M. baccata, Siberian crabapple** (p. 187)

6b Sepals hairless or woolly, pointed but not gradually tapered to a slender point; fruit $^5/_8$–1"
across . . . .**M. prunifolia, pearleaf crabapple** (p. 187)

Malus ioënsis, prairie crabapple

Key to the Mountain-ashes (Genus *Sorbus*)

1a Twigs, leaf stalks and flower stalks densely white-woolly (at least at flowering time); leaves usually permanently hairy beneath; winter buds with silky, white hairs, not sticky
. . . . *S. aucuparia*, **European mountain-ash** (p. 191)

1b Twigs, leaves and flower stalks essentially hairless (sometimes with a few sparse hairs); winter buds hairless, gummy **2**

2a Leaflets usually 3–5 times as long as wide, tapered to a long, slender point, broadest below the middle; fruits $^3/_{16}$–$^1/_4$" in diameter
. . . . *S. americana*, **American mountain-ash** (p. 190)

2b Leaflets usually 2–3 times as long as wide, more abruptly pointed, broadest near the middle; fruits $^5/_{16}$–$^1/_2$" in diameter . . . . *S. decora*, **showy mountain-ash** (p. 190)

Key to the Serviceberries (Genus *Amelanchier*)

1a Leaves densely white-woolly beneath when young, somewhat silky-hairy on lower surfaces and stalks when mature, unfolding after the flowers have appeared; fruits dry and flavorless, on stalks up to $^1/_2$" long . . . . *A. arborea*, **downy serviceberry** (p. 202)

1b Leaves red- or purple-tinged when young, essentially hairless, unfolding as the flowers appear; fruits juicy and sweet, on stalks up to 1–1$^1/_2$" long **2**

2a Flower/fruit base hairless . . . . *A. laevis*, **smooth serviceberry** (p. 203)
2b Flower/fruit base woolly-hairy . . . .*A. interior*, **inland serviceberry** (p. 203)

Sorbus americana, American mountain-ash   *S. acuparia*, European mountain-ash

Hawthorns (Genus *Crataegus*)

When it comes to taxonomic problems, few groups are thornier than the hawthorns. The shrubs and small trees in this large, complex group have been classified and reclassified over the years. The number of named species in North America has ranged from a few dozen in the 1800s to over 1200 by 1925.

Much of the confusion with hawthorns stems from their tendency to hybridize, producing offspring with intermediate characteristics, and from their ability to produce seed without fertilization (apomixis). Some species are relatively static and clearly defined, while others are highly variable and difficult to delineate. Also, many species are very similar to one another and can only be distinguished when specimens are of excellent quality. In many cases, both fruit and flower characteristics are needed to correctly identify a species. Trees with neither flowers nor fruits usually cannot be identified to species, even by experts.

The following suggestions may help you identify hawthorns:

- Whenever possible, examine both flowers and fruits from the same tree (never from two trees that just look the same).
- When trees are in flower, look for last year's fruits on the ground.
- Anther color is based on fresh flowers with unopened anthers.
- Stamen, style and sepal characteristics can often be determined by carefully examining remnants on the tips of fresh fruits. The number of styles is usually the same as the number of nutlets (unless some ovaries failed to mature).
- Leaves of flowering branches can differ from leaves on vegetative shoots, and both may need to be considered in combination with several other factors. The "lobes" of hawthorn leaves are very shallow compared to other groups (e.g., oaks, pp. 118–134) and sometimes approach coarse double teeth.

Because of the identification difficulties associated with hawthorns and the large number of taxa found in the state, not all species are discussed in detail in this guide. Instead, 22 of the most widely recognized species are described, representing 13 series. A series is a set of very closely allied species. The Illinois series can be distinguished using the following key, based on the work of Phipps and Muniyamma (1980).

Key to the Series of Illinois Hawthorns (Genus *Crataegus*)

1a   Leaves mostly deeply lobed, with main veins extending to both the lobe notches and the lobe tips. **2**
1b   Leaves toothed or shallowly lobed, with main veins extending to lobe or tooth tips only **4**

2a   Flowers with 1 style and fruits containing 1 stone (rarely 2–3); anthers red
         . . . . **Series Oxyacanthae (*C. monogyna*, oneseed hawthorn,** p. 192)
2b   Flowers with 3–5 styles and fruits containing 3–5 stones; anthers pale yellow **3**

3a   Leaf tips sharp- to slender-pointed; leaves usually $1^{1}/_{8}$–$1^{3}/_{4}$" wide and notched at the base; fruits usually smooth-tipped (without persistent sepals)
       . . . . . .**Series Cordatae (*C. phaenopyrum*, Washington hawthorn,** p. 200)
3b   Leaf tips blunt to somewhat pointed; leaves usually $5/_{8}$–$1^{3}/_{8}$" wide and wedge-shaped to rounded at the base; fruits usually tipped with persistent sepals
      . . . . . **Series Microcarpae (*C. spathulata*, three-lobed hawthorn,** p. 196)

4a   Leaves 1–3 times as long as wide, narrowly wedge-shaped at the base, finely toothed and sometimes also shallowly lobed; thorns long and slender **5**
4b   Combination of leaves and thorns not as above **6**

5a Leaves glossy, dark green, finely toothed and only slightly lobed; flower clusters lacking dense hairs; fruits with 2–3 styles and stones
. . . .**Series Crus-galli (*C. crus-galli*, cockspur hawthorn,** p. 193)

5b Leaves dull to slightly glossy, regularly shallow-lobed; flower clusters with dense, short hairs; fruits with 3–5 styles and stones
. . . . **Series Punctatae (*C. punctata*, dotted hawthorn,** p. 194)

6a Leaves relatively small (<1½" long), about as wide as long (triangular, circular) or diamond-shaped, usually with distinct lobes, rarely broadest above midleaf and scarcely lobed; leaf stalks often with a few glands; flowers <⅝" across; thorns 1⅕–3⅛" long, thin when long; ripe fruits typically dull red, round and ⁵/₁₆–⅜" across
. . . **Series Rotundifoliae (*C. chrysocarpa*, fireberry hawthorn; *C. dodgei*, Dodge hawthorn; *C. margarettiae*, Margaret's hawthorn,** p. 196)

6b Leaves either clearly longer than wide, or if broad, then >2" long when mature. **7**

7a Mature fruits round, about ⁵/₁₆–½" across, pink to mauve or crimson, coated with a waxy, white bloom; green and ripe fruits often present; persistent sepals at the fruit tip strongly elevated . . . . **Series Pruinosae (*C. pruinosa*, frosted hawthorn,** p. 198)

7b Mature fruits red, without a waxy, white bloom, or large (>⅝") fruits occasionally with a bloom; persistent sepals only slightly elevated (if at all). **8**

8a Mature fruits at least ⅜" long, round to ellipsoidal; mature leaf blades broad (>2" long). . . . **9**

8b Mature fruits generally <⅜" long; mature leaf blades generally <2" long **11**

9a Flowers large (⅞–1⅛" across); fruits large (>⅝"), with a whitish, waxy bloom
. . . .**Series Dilatatae (*C. coccinioides*, Kansas hawthorn,** p. 199)

9b Flowers smaller; fruits without a waxy bloom **10**

10a Mature leaves firm, with stout stalks and hairy lower leaf surfaces; anthers whitish, on relatively short stalks (filaments); thorns relatively slender
. . . . **Series Molles (*C. mollis*, downy hawthorn,** p. 199)

10b Mature leaves relatively thin, with slender stalks and essentially hairless lower leaf surfaces; anthers pink to red, on relatively large stalks (filaments); thorns relatively stout
. . . .**Series Coccineae (*C. pedicellata*, scarlet hawthorn; *C. holmesiana*, Holmes' hawthorn,** p. 198)

11a Fruit stones with cavities on the lower side; leaves hairy beneath; thorns stout or absent; young growth with conspicuous coral red buds; flowers clusters densely hairy; fruits glossy, scarlet, often succulent . . . . . **Series Macracanthae (*C. succulenta*, fleshy hawthorn; *C. calpodendron*, pear hawthorn,** p. 201)

11b Plants without the above combination of characteristics **12**

12a Flower clusters clearly bracted when flowers mature; sepals edges with glandular teeth; leaves elliptical; thorns often long and slender
. . . .**Series Intricatae (Copenhagen hawthorn, *C. intricata*; *C. neobushii*, newbush hawthorn,** p. 200)

12b Flower clusters with few noticeable bracts when flowers mature; sepals usually smooth-edged; leaves elliptical to triangular-egg-shaped; thorns stout, of various lengths, sometimes absent. **13**

13a Leaves of flowering shoots rounded to notched at the base; mature leaves with woolly tufts in vein axils beneath. . . . .*C. viridis*, green hawthorn, p. 195

13b Leaves of flowering shoots tapered to a wedge-shaped base; mature leaves essentially hairless beneath . . . .**Series Tenuifoliae (*C. flabellata*, fanleaf hawthorn; *C. macrosperma*, bigfruit hawthorn,** p. 197)

Wild black cherry wood is easily worked and polishes beautifully. It is considered equal in quality to black walnut, with a rich, red color similar to mahogany. Black cherry was once very popular in furniture and in frames for engravings and etchings. It has also been used in cabinets, paneling, veneers, interior trim, musical instruments and tool handles. Because of its early popularity of use, this tree is now scarce in much of its range. • In 1629, wild black cherry became one of the first trees introduced to English horticulture from North America. • Wild black cherry fruits can be eaten raw or used in jelly, syrup, wine, juice and pies. • The leaves and inner bark were once used in tonics, sedatives and cough syrups. **Caution:** All parts of this tree except the cherry flesh contain hydrocyanic acid. Wilted leaves have poisoned cattle, and children have died from chewing on twigs. • The cherries provide food for many game birds, songbirds and small mammals. Chipmunks and deer mice cache the pits, which are poisonous to human beings. White-tailed deer eat the fresh green leaves in spring but may be poisoned by wilted leaves in autumn.

Also Called: Black chokecherry, rum cherry, cabinet cherry, timber cherry, wine cherry.

Size and Shape: Trees or tall shrubs 50–80' tall; crowns spreading, rounded; taprooted to spreading.

Trunks: Straight (in forests) to twisted (open-grown), 12–32" in diameter; young bark dark reddish-brown to almost black, smooth, with conspicuous horizontal pores (lenticels); **mature bark rough with outcurved, squared scales,** reddish-brown beneath; wood reddish-brown, fine-grained, hard.

Branches: Few, arched with drooping tips;

twigs slender (some side-shoots short and stubby), reddish-brown, smelly when broken; **buds chestnut brown,** often greenish-tinged, ⅛–¼" long, pointing outward slightly.

Leaves: Alternate, simple, deciduous; **blades thick, waxy and dark green above,** paler beneath with **fine, white (eventually rusty) hairs on both sides of the lower midvein,** 2–6" long, widest near midleaf and tapered to both ends, edged with **fine, incurved teeth;** stalks usually with **2 red glands near the blade.**

Flowers: White, cupped, on ¼" long stalks, bisexual; petals 5; sepals 5; flowers hang in narrow, elongated, 4–6" long clusters (racemes) at the tips of short, new, leafy shoots in May (as leaves expand fully).

Fruits: Reddish to blackish cherries (drupes) with dark purple flesh, juicy, about ⅜" across, with **persistent sepals at the base;** seeds single, within a ¼" stone; cherries hang in elongated clusters of 6–12, ripen August–September.

Habitat: Open, well-drained woodlands.

Origin: Native.

Chokecherry fruits are edible raw, but even fully ripe fruits can be rather astringent. Green chokecherries cause severe puckering and even choking, hence the common name. Usually, chokecherries are cooked and used to prepare syrups, sauces, preserves, wines and jellies, especially when mixed with pectin-rich apples. • **Caution:** All parts of this tree except the cherry flesh contain poisonous hydrocyanic acid, which gives the bark and leaves an unpleasant, bitter-almond smell when crushed. Although the cherry stones contain this toxin, Native peoples have been eating chokecherries, stones and all, for centuries. Sun-dried cakes of pulverized chokecherries were an important food in some cultures. Drying and/or cooking may reduce toxicity. • Chokecherry grows prolifically from sprouting stumps and root suckers. This fast-growing, light-loving, short-lived tree quickly invades logged land, abandoned farms and exposed streambanks, stabilizing soil and reducing erosion. • **European bird cherry (*P. padus*)**, shown in dark green (species overlap) on the map, is a small, introduced tree similar to chokecherry but is distinguished by petals larger (¼–⅜") and longer than the stamens, longer (⅓") flower stalks and smaller (¼") inedible fruits with sculpted stones. This exotic Eurasian tree rarely escapes from cultivation in Illinois.

Also Called: Eastern chokecherry, common chokecherry, chuckley-plum, sloetree.

Size and Shape: Small trees or tall shrubs 10–35' tall; crowns rounded or irregular; roots spreading, **often forming thickets** from suckers.

Trunks: Often twisted and/or inclined, 2–6" in diameter; **bark dark gray-brown, smooth or finely scaly,** with prominent lenticels when young; wood light brown, fine-grained, hard, heavy.

Branches: Slender, ascending; twigs smooth, reddish- to grayish-brown, **strong-smelling** when crushed; buds ⅛" long (¼–½" at branch tips), with **dark brown, pale-edged scales.**

Leaves: Alternate, simple, deciduous; blades deep green above, paler beneath, thin, hairless, usually **widest at or above midleaf, abruptly sharp-pointed,** 1½–4¾" long, edged with small, **slender, sharp teeth;** stalks with 1 to several **glands near the blade.**

Flowers: White, saucer-shaped, about ⅜" across, bisexual; petals 5, round; sepals 5; flowers on stalks about ¼" long, in **cylindrical, 2–6" long clusters** of 10–25, **hanging from the tips of short, new, leafy shoots,** in May **(before leaves expand fully).**

Fruits: Shiny, **deep red or black cherries** (drupes), rarely yellowish, ¼–⅜" across, with tiny, persistent sepals at the base; seeds single, within a stone; cherries hang in **elongated clusters,** ripen July–September.

Habitat: Open woodlands and thickets.

Origin: Native.

Pin cherry can live about 40 years, and once mature, it usually produces abundant fruit each year. The stones remain viable for decades on the ground, waiting for the proper conditions (fluctuating temperatures and light exposure) to trigger germination. • These little cherries are edible but sour. Mashed and strained, they make excellent jellies and cold drinks. • **Caution:** The leaves, bark and stones are toxic. • Pin cherry wood is seldom used, except as firewood. • This attractive shrub is sometimes planted as an ornamental, but it spreads quickly via suckers from underground runners. Because of this tendency, pin cherry is sometimes planted to stabilize soil. After fire, this shrub grows rapidly, reducing erosion and improving conditions for the establishment of other species. It soon disappears under a forest canopy. • The clusters of small, round, shiny fruits have been likened to clusters of glass-headed pins stuck into a pincushion, hence the name "pin cherry." • The heavy, succulent fruits depend on animals (mainly birds) for dispersal and propagation. The alternate name "bird cherry" refers to the popularity of the fruits among songbirds.

Also Called: Bird cherry, fire cherry, wild red cherry, hay cherry, pigeon cherry.

Size and Shape: Small trees or tall shrubs 15–35' tall; crowns narrow, rounded; roots spreading, forming colonies from suckers.

Trunks: Straight, 6–10" in diameter; **mature bark shiny, reddish-brown,** smooth, peeling in thin horizontal strips, with conspicuous, **orange-powdered, horizontal pores** (lenticels); wood light brown, soft, porous.

Branches: Slender, ascending when young, horizontal with age; twigs reddish, slender, sour-smelling when bruised or broken; **buds** 1/16–1/8" **long,** rounded, **several clustered at twig tips.**

Leaves: Alternate, simple, deciduous; blades shiny green, hairless, thin, **lance-shaped, slender-pointed,** rounded at the base, 1½–6" long, edged with **tiny, uneven, incurved teeth;** stalks with **glands near the blade;** leaves bright red to purplish-red in autumn.

Flowers: White, 3/8–½" across, bisexual; petals 5, round, about ¼" long, **hairy at the base;** sepals 5; flowers on 3/8–¾" long stalks, in tassel-like clusters (umbels) of 2–7, in April (as leaves expand).

Fruits: Bright red cherries (drupes), about ¼" **in diameter,** hanging on slender stalks in **small, flat-topped clusters;** seeds single, within a round stone; cherries ripen July–September.

Habitat: Open woodlands or disturbed sites, often in sandy soil.

Origin: Native.

The peach has been cultivated since ancient times for its sweet, juicy fruits. Many varieties have been developed, including the freestone peach, favored for its thick fruits with flesh that separates readily from the stone. Clingstone peach fruits do not separate readily, but the firmer flesh makes excellent preserves. • Some peaches are planted for their flowers, and various cultivars have single or double corollas in colors ranging from red to white. • Wild peach trees occasionally spring up from discarded pits near roads, trails and rivers. • Many *Prunus* species have been brought purposely to North America, and some occasionally escape from cultivation. **Apricot (*P. armeniaca*)**, found in Champaign County, is a rare European escape, distinguished from peach by its smaller, white to pink-tinged flowers, smaller fruits, smooth stones and broader (sometimes almost round) leaves. **Mahaleb cherry** or perfumed cherry (*P. mahaleb*), shown in pink/dark green (species overlap) on the map, is a European ornamental, cultivated for its prolific, fragrant flowers and dark red, aromatic wood. Mahaleb cherry resembles pin cherry (p. 176) but has relatively broad leaves, hairless petals and deep red to black fruits. **Manchu cherry** or Nanking cherry (*P. tomentosa*), found in DuPage County, is a small, spreading tree or tall shrub with stalkless flowers and fruits and finely sharp-toothed leaves. Unlike peach, it has woolly lower leaf surfaces. This Asian species rarely grows wild in Illinois.

Size and Shape: Small, spreading trees up to 35' tall; crowns broad and rounded.

Trunks: Short, often crooked, up to 12" in diameter, usually marked with horizontal streaks; bark dark reddish-brown, smooth at first, rough with age.

Branches: Spreading; twigs dark reddish-brown to green, smooth, long, slender, with short spur-shoots.

Leaves: Alternate, simple, deciduous; blades shiny green, paler beneath, **3–6" long, lance-shaped**, slender-pointed, rounded to wedge-shaped at the base, finely saw-toothed, often **with sides upcurved from the midvein;** stalks short, with small glands near the blade.

Flowers: Pink, 1–1⅜" **across**, bisexual; petals 5, rounded; sepals 5; **flowers single** (sometimes paired), in April–May **(before leaves expand)**.

Fruits: Velvety, yellowish to pink peaches (drupes), round, slightly grooved, up to 4" across and soft-fleshed in cultivation, **2–3" across** and firmer in the wild; seeds single, within a somewhat flattened, **deeply sculpted stone;** peaches single on **very short stalks,** mature in summer.

Habitat: Open, often disturbed sites on roadsides, in thickets and near abandoned homes.

Origin: Introduced from Eurasia.

Sweet cherry has large, luscious fruits—the common, commercially available cherries. This popular *Prunus* species has been cultivated in North America for over a century, and many varieties are grown in orchards across the continent. The cherries are larger and sweeter and keep longer than those of most other species and are delicious fresh from the tree. • The strong, hard wood takes a polish well. In Europe, it has been used in interior finishing and for making furniture, musical instruments and small household items. • Unlike many other cherries, sweet cherry does not produce suckers. • Sweet cherry is one of the most widely cultivated domestic cherries and occasionally escapes and grows wild. Next to humans, birds are its most important dispersal agent. Many birds, including grouse, thrashers, robins and cedar waxwings, enjoy eating the cherries. When ripe fruits hang on the trees, farmers face a never-ending battle with persistent winged bandits. At other times of the year, white-tailed deer and rabbits can damage trees by eating the leaves and twigs. • The epithet *avium*, from the Latin *avis*, "bird," refers to the popularity of the fruits among birds. • 'Bing cherry' is the most widely grown cultivar of sweet cherry. It was developed in 1875 by Ah Bing, a Chinese nursery worker in Oregon.

Also Called: Mazzard cherry, gean, Bing cherry.

Size and Shape: Trees up to 35' tall; crowns cylindrical to pyramidal.

Trunks: Tall, reaching 24–36" in diameter in the wild, shorter and smaller in orchards; **bark reddish-brown, smooth, with conspicuous horizontal pores** (lenticels), sometimes peeling; wood yellowish-red, strong.

Branches: Stout, spreading; twigs reddish-brown under a grayish film, smooth; buds shiny, brown, **some clustered at tips of short spur-shoots.**

Leaves: Alternate, simple, deciduous; blades dull dark green above, paler and **hairy on veins beneath, 2⅜–4¾" long,** widest above midleaf, pointed, with sharp, gland-tipped, double teeth; **stalks ¾–1½" long, with 2 glands near blade.**

Flowers: White, ¾–1⅛" across, bisexual; petals 5; **sepals 5, hairless; flowers in tassel-like clusters** (umbels) of 1–5 on leafy spur-shoots, in April–May (before or as leaves expand).

Fruits: Dark red to almost black (sometimes yellow), fleshy cherries (drupes), **round to heart-shaped, ½–1" across,** hanging on slender, ¾–1⅛" long stalks, in small, flat-topped clusters on spur-shoots; seeds single, within round stones; cherries ripen June–July.

Habitat: Open, often disturbed sites.

Origin: Introduced from Asia Minor.

Sour cherry is widely grown in orchards across North America. Some double-flowered cultivars are grown as ornamentals, but usually this species is cultivated for its fruit. The tart, juicy cherries can be sweetened and baked in pies and cakes, mashed and boiled to make jams and jellies or canned in syrup. • Sour cherry can reproduce vegetatively by sending up numerous shoots (suckers) from underground runners. It often escapes cultivation and spreads to new regions via seeds. Birds often swallow the hard, protective stones and deposit them, undigested, in new sites. • Game birds, songbirds, raccoons and foxes all eat the cherries, and rabbits and white-tailed deer browse on the leaves and twigs. • The specific epithet *cerasus* is a Greek word meaning "cherry tree." It is also the name of the town, Cerasus of Pontus, in the region where this cherry originated. • Sour cherry could be confused with sweet cherry (p. 178), but sweet cherry leaves have hairs on the undersides of the veins and glands on the stalks just below the blades. Also, sweet cherry fruits are larger, sweeter and usually more deeply colored.

Also Called: Pie cherry, mazzard cherry, morello cherry.

Size and Shape: Small trees up to 35' tall; crowns usually broadly rounded; roots shallow, spreading.

Trunks: Short, soon branched; bark grayish.

Branches: Stout; twigs with stubby spur-shoots; buds shiny, reddish-brown, **some clustered at the tips of short spur-shoots,** pointing outward.

Leaves: Alternate, simple, deciduous; **blades dark green, lustrous, hairless beneath** (when mature), firm, elliptical to ovate, widest above the middle, 1½–3½" **long, tipped with a blunt point,** edged with **double or single, rounded teeth** and with a **gland on the blade near the stalk;** stalks usually less than ¾" long, lacking glands.

Flowers: White, ¾–1⅛" across, bisexual; petals 5; **sepals 5, hairless;** flowers in small, flat-topped clusters of 2–5 at tips of leafy spur-shoots, in April–May (before or as leaves expand).

Fruits: Bright red cherries (drupes), juicy, round, ⅜–¾" **across,** in small, flat-topped clusters at the tips of leafy spur-shoots; seeds single, within a round stone; cherries ripen July.

Habitat: Open, often disturbed sites.

Origin: Introduced directly from southern Europe, but probably from Asia Minor originally.

This small, attractive tree grows quickly but doesn't live long. It has been cultivated in orchards, parks and gardens across North America for its beautiful, fragrant flowers and edible fruits. Hundreds of large-flowered cultivars have been developed. • The fruits have tough, sour outer skins, but their sweet, juicy flesh is delicious, making excellent jams, jellies, preserves and pies. • American plum wood is hard and attractive but is not commercially valuable because of the tree's small size. • **Caution:** All parts of this tree except the flesh and skin of the plums contain toxic hydrocyanic acid. • **Bigtree plum** (*P. mexicana*, also called Mexican plum), shown in dark green (species overlap) on the map, is found mainly in the midwestern and south-central U.S., but its range extends north into Illinois, where it grows in woods and at the base of cherty cliffs. Bigtree plum resembles American plum, but is distinguished by its hairy sepals, hairy leaf stalks with 2 or more glands near the blade, broadly rounded leaf blade bases and relatively large (1–1¼") fruits. Also, bigtree plum does not form colonies from suckers.

Also Called: Wild plum, brown plum, red plum, yellow plum.

Size and Shape: Trees or tall shrubs 20–35' tall; crowns broad; roots spreading, with suckers often forming thickets.

Trunks: Short, 5–8" in diameter; young bark smooth, with horizontal pores (lenticels); mature bark reddish- to gray-brown or nearly black, rough with plates; wood reddish-brown, hard, strong.

Branches: Spreading, somewhat thorny with **spine-like, dwarf twigs;** twigs reddish- to grayish-brown, with a **bitter-almond flavor;** buds grayish, ⅛–⅜" long, with 2-colored, chestnut to grayish-brown scales.

Leaves: Alternate, simple, deciduous; blades dark green above, paler beneath, lance-shaped to oval, **narrowed at the base,** 1½–4½" long, **edged with fine, sharp, slender-pointed teeth** often tipped with a callus or bristle (not a gland); stalks usually lacking glands near the blade.

Flowers: White, ½–1" across, saucer-shaped, **very fragrant,** on stalks ⅜–1" long, bisexual; petals 5, ⅜–½" long; flowers in flat-topped clusters of 2–4, in late April–May **(before or as leaves expand).**

Fruits: Yellow to red plums (drupes) with a thin, waxy bloom, ¾–1⅛" long, yellow-fleshed; seeds single, within a flattened stone; **plums single or 2–4 together,** mature August–September.

Habitat: Moist, well-drained soils in thickets and woodlands.

Origin: Native.

Chickasaw plum is an attractive, finely textured ornamental, with narrow leaves similar to those of an olive (*Olea europea*). • This fast-growing, short-lived plum grows throughout the southeastern and south-central states, reaching the northern edge of its range in Illinois. In the northern half of the state it is uncommon, and has probably spread there from planted trees. • Because of its ability to tolerate poor, dry soil and to form thickets from spreading suckers, Chickasaw plum is sometimes used to control erosion on exposed or unstable slopes. • Chickasaw plums provide food for many animals, including whitetail deer, bears, raccoons, squirrels and a variety of birds. More importantly, the dense, thorny branches create protective cover for numerous birds and small mammals. • In

the southern U.S., wild Chickasaw plums are sometimes gathered and sold at markets. The juicy flesh can be rather acidic or soft and sweet, and is usually used to make jellies and preserves. In North Carolina, the Lumbee people reportedly used Chickasaw plums to relieve fevers and cure dandruff. • **Bigtree plum** (p. 180, described under American plum) could be mistaken for Chickasaw plum, but bigtree plum has leaves with sharp, glandless teeth and its flowers (⅝" across) and fruits (1–1¼" across) are larger.

Also Called: Mountain cherry.

Size and Shape: Tall shrubs or small trees to 16' (occasionally to 25') tall; roots spreading, sending up suckers; thicket-forming.

Trunks: Rarely over 8" in diameter; mature bark dark reddish-brown, thin, with long scales and shallow furrows; wood reddish-brown, soft, weak.

Branches: Slender, spreading, numerous, somewhat thorny; twigs slender, shiny and bright red at first, dull reddish-brown with age.

Leaves: Alternate, deciduous, simple, folded in bud; blades thin, **trough-shaped,** lustrous bright green above, paler and dull beneath, hairless when mature, **lance-shaped to narrowly elliptical,** 1⅛–3⅛" **long,** pointed, edged with fine, blunt, gland-tipped teeth (4–7 teeth per ⅛"); stalks ⅜–½" long, with **2 red glands near the base of the blade.**

Flowers: White or cream-colored, saucer-shaped, ¼–⅜" **across,** bisexual; petals 5, broadest near the rounded tip, abruptly narrowed to a short, slender base (claw); **sepals 5,** hairy on the inner side, **lacking glands,** forming a bell-shaped calyx; stalks 1–3" long; flowers in **flat-topped clusters (umbels) of 2–4** on year-old twigs, in April–May **(before leaves).**

Fruits: Bright red to yellow plums (drupes), shiny (no whitish bloom), **about ½" across,** juicy; seeds single, inside **egg-shaped,** ⅜–½" **long stones** slightly grooved on 1 side; plums ripen in June–August.

Habitat: In thickets, usually on well-drained soil.

Origin: Native.

Wildgoose plum is often considered a natural hybrid of Chickasaw plum (p. 181) and American plum (p. 180). Native populations are relatively rare, typically growing on moist sites along streams. However, wildgoose plum is widely cultivated, and planted trees often spread to roadsides and other disturbed areas. Populations in the northern ⅓ of Illinois probably have spread from cultivation. • Wildgoose plum is the parent of many cultivars, including 'Miner' and 'Wayland.' The plums are sweet, but the flesh tends to cling to the stone. • A man in Tennessee shot a wild goose and discovered a plum stone in its crop. The seed was planted or thrown away with the bird's remains, and one of the first known trees of this species grew from the spot, hence "wildgoose plum." • Another thicket-forming species, **Munson plum** (*P. munsoniana,* also called Munson wildgoose plum), shown in pink/dark green (species overlap) on the map, can be confused with wildgoose plum. Munson plum is most easily distinguished in early spring, when its flowers open before the leaves have expanded. A close examination of its relatively small (2–4" long), narrow, elliptical to lance-shaped, yellowish-green leaves reveals shallow, almost rounded (rather than triangular) teeth with a gland near the base (rather than at the tip).

Photo, bottom: *P. munsoniana*

Also Called: Hortulan plum.

Size and Shape: Small trees or shrubs to 33' tall; crowns rounded; roots spreading, suckering, sometimes forms thickets.

Trunks: Short, nearly 1' in diameter; mature bark grayish-brown, thin.

Branches: Spreading, rigid, **without spines;** twigs reddish-brown.

Leaves: Alternate, deciduous, simple, peach-like; **blades dark green above,** sparsely hairy to hairless beneath, ovate to oblong-lance-shaped, 4–6" long, tapered to a slender point, broadest below midleaf, rounded or notched at the base, edged with **fine, ascending, gland-tipped, triangular teeth;** stalks slender, about 1" long, usually with 2 glands near the blade.

Flowers: White, saucer-shaped, ½–⅝" across, bisexual; petals 5; sepals 5, edged with gland-tipped teeth, hairy on the inner surface, hairless on the outside; stalks hairless, ⁵⁄₁₆–⅝" long; flowers in flat-topped clusters (umbels) along year-old twigs, in March–April or May **(with or after leaves).**

Fruits: Deep red to yellowish-red plums (drupes) with little or no whitish bloom, short egg-shaped to almost round, ¾–1⅛" **across,** thin-skinned, juicy-fleshed; seeds single, within a **thick-walled, rounded stone;** plums ripen in August–early October.

Habitat: Open sites in bottomlands, often along streams and roads.

Origin: Native.

Canada plum is often planted as an ornamental for its beautiful, fragrant spring blossoms and its attractive, edible fruit. The cultivar 'Princess Kay' has showy double flowers. • The skins of the plums are usually tough and astringent, and the flesh also can be very sour, especially when it is still firm. After the first frosts, Canada plums become soft and juicy. They can be eaten fresh, stewed to make jelly or jam, puréed to make juice or baked in pies. • **Caution:** Children have died from eating too many plums without removing the stones. As with other plums, all parts of this tree except the skin and flesh of the fruits contain the toxin hydrocyanic acid. • Canada plum seems to prefer basic soils, but it is not restricted to calcareous regions. • White-tailed deer, black bears, foxes, bobcats, raccoons, muskrats, squirrels, small rodents and large birds all feed on the succulent fruits. • Plum trees often harbor an aphid that is deadly to potatoes, so gardeners should avoid planting plums and potatoes together. • The specific epithet *nigra* means "black" and refers to the dark, almost black bark of the branches.

Also Called: Red plum, black plum, wild plum, horse plum.

Size and Shape: Straggly trees or tall shrubs 20–35' tall; crowns irregular, flat-topped; roots shallow, spreading, usually forming thickets from suckers.

Trunks: Short, crooked, 5–10" in diameter, often clumped; young bark dark reddish-brown to blackish with gray horizontal pores (lenticels), soon splitting and curling; mature bark gray-brown, rough with thick, outcurved scales; wood reddish-brown, heavy, hard, fine-grained.

Branches: Upright, crooked, somewhat thorny, with **spine-like dwarf twigs;** twigs green to dark reddish-brown, **bitter-almond flavored;** buds reddish- to grayish-brown, hairless, ⅛–⅜" long, flat-lying, absent at twig tips.

Leaves: Alternate, simple, deciduous; **blades dull dark green above,** paler beneath, with prominent veins, broadly oval, 2¼–5½" long, abruptly slender-pointed, thin, with **rounded, mostly gland-tipped, double teeth;** stalks stout, with 1–2 large, dark glands near the blade.

Flowers: White, turning pinkish, saucer-shaped, ½–1⅛" **across,** fragrant, bisexual; petals 5; sepals 5; flowers on reddish, ⅜–¾" long stalks, in flat-topped clusters of 2–5 on year-old twigs, in May (**before or as leaves expand**).

Fruits: Red, scarlet or yellow plums (drupes) **without a waxy bloom,** ¾–1⅛" **long,** thick-skinned, yellow-fleshed; seeds single, within flattened stones ¾–1" long; plums single or 2–4-clustered, ripen August–September.

Habitat: Moist, open woodlands, often along rivers and streams.

Origin: Native.

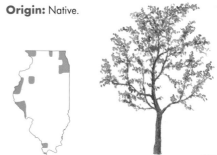

For centuries, people have used and propagated pears. Today, cultivars of the original Eurasian species are grown in many parts of North America. Usually, the trees are heavily pruned to improve fruit production and make harvesting easier, so they rarely reach their full height. • The hard, fine-grained wood has been used to make drawing instruments, rulers, tool handles, carvings and wood engravings. • This long-lived, slow-growing tree produces fruit each year, but heavy crops are often followed by a year with low production. • Like their domestic counterparts, wild-growing pear trees have edible fruits, but they are usually smaller (less than 2¼" long), inconspicuous, drier and grittier. • **Chinese pear (*P. pyrifolia*)**, found in Union County, resembles common pear, but its leaves have sharp teeth, and its pears are almost spherical. **Ornamental pear (*P. calleryana*,** also called Callery pear or Bradford pear), found in DuPage County, is distinguished by its heart-shaped leaves and smaller (up to ¾" across) flowers, with 2–3 (not 5) styles. Both of these rare escapes originated in China.

Size and Shape: Trees or shrubs to 30' tall; crowns round to cylindrical; roots spreading.

Trunks: Straight, up to 12" in diameter; mature bark dark brown to blackish, with small, squared scales; wood reddish-brown, fine-grained.

Branches: Short, stout, ascending, often with **spine-like spur-shoots;** twigs reddish- to olive brown, with yellow pores (lenticels); buds chestnut brown to grayish, hairy.

Leaves: Alternate, simple, deciduous; **blades thick, leathery, hairless** (when mature), **shiny and dark green above,** paler beneath, sharp-pointed, rounded at the base, 1–3" long, edged with fine blunt teeth, **twisted in bud; stalks often equal to or longer than blade;** leaves yellow in autumn.

Flowers: Showy, fragrant, pink fading to white, about ¾–1⅜" wide, bisexual; sepals 5, hairy; **anthers 20–30, purple;** flowers in flat-topped clusters on spur-shoots in early spring (as leaves expand).

Fruits: Fleshy pomes **(pears)** with gritty stone cells in the pulp, firm at first, juicy when ripe, **widest toward the tip and bearing old sepals, tapered to the base** (stalk), ¾–4½" long; seeds in leathery chambers in a core; pears hang near branch tips when ripe in autumn.

Habitat: Fields, fence lines, disturbed sites and woodland edges.

Origin: Introduced from Eurasia.

This Central Asian tree was introduced to Europe many centuries ago and was present in Britain by 1275. Today, it is naturalized in many parts of Europe and North America. • The small fruits have a wonderful, mouth-watering fragrance (heavy and overpowering to some) but are usually hard, acidic and unpalatable raw. The flesh softens and becomes less astringent after a few weeks in storage. Quinces are used mainly for flavoring cooked apple and pear dishes and for making jams, jellies, ices and candy. They can also be stewed, baked, made into fruit butter or used to flavor meat dishes and casseroles. • The seeds, soaked in water, produce large amounts of mucilage, which has been used medicinally to soothe irritations of the eyes, mucous membranes and skin.

• Pliny reported that quince could ward off the influence of the "evil eye." References to quince are common in Greek mythology, where it was a symbol of love and happiness, a token of love given to Venus by Paris. Greek statues, wall paintings and mosaics usually show quince in the paws of a bear. • The genus *Cydonia* is distinguished from *Pyrus* by its many-celled flower buds, in which the petals are twisted together and ovules are arranged horizontally rather than vertically. This last characteristic is easiest to see in the fruit. • The genus was named after Cydon in Crete, the source of a popular variety.

Also Called: Chinese quince • *Pyrus cydonia*.

Size and Shape: Thornless, crooked trees or tall shrubs 12–20' tall; crowns rounded, with a 10–15' spread.

Trunks: Small; young bark glossy, dark-brown with many russet pores (lenticels); wood hard, dense and brittle.

Branches: Coarse, numerous, **gnarled, wide-spreading** to horizontal; twigs russet, sometimes with a whitish bloom, **covered with thick, white felt at first,** hairless with age; buds dun-colored, conical, scales edged with rusty, felt-like hairs.

Leaves: Alternate, deciduous, simple; **blades dark green above, densely gray-woolly beneath** (especially when young), clearly veined, oval or elliptical, 2–4" long, 1½–2¼" wide, smooth edged to gently serrated; leaves rich yellow in autumn.

Flowers: Pale pink or white, cupped, **about 2" across,** perfect, self-fertile; petals 5, broad; sepals 5; stamens 20; pistils 5; **flowers single,** on ⅛–¼" long stalks from short twigs, in May–June (after leaves expand).

Fruits: Green or orange to pale yellow, pear-shaped pomes (sometimes almost spherical), **fragrant,** usually covered with a thick, yellow-green felt at first, smooth with a greasy film when mature, 3–4" long, hard, always with gritty cells; **seeds 2–8 in each of 5 compartments,** glossy, ⅛" long, **poisonous;** mature in late autumn.

Origin: Introduced from Asia.

This slow-growing, short-lived tree is sometimes cultivated for its showy flowers, spicy fragrance and dense growth form. In 1897, this beautiful blossom was declared the official state flower of Michigan. • Although it produces only small fruit, wild crabapple is very hardy, so the trunks are used as stock for grafting more productive but less hardy apple varieties. • Crabapple wood has been used to make tool handles, spear and harpoon shafts and even some of the working parts in gristmills. Interesting patterns and colors in the wood are exploited in carvings and furniture. • Wild crabapples are edible but sour, so usually they are cooked and sweetened to reduce their tartness. The small apples are rich in pectin and make excellent jelly. They often are mixed with fruits low in pectin to improve jelling and also give a special scent to preserves. • **Narrow-leaved crabapple** (*M. angustifolia*, also called southern crabapple or *Pyrus angustifolia*), shown in dark green (species overlap) on the map, is a southern species that reaches the northern edge of its range in Illinois. It resembles wild crabapple but is distinguished by its smaller, narrower (2½–3 times as long as wide), oblong to lance-shaped, relatively blunt-tipped leaves and by its more southern distribution.

Also Called: Sweet crabapple, American crabapple, garland-tree • *M. glabrata, P. coronaria.*

Size and Shape: Small trees or tall shrubs 15–25' tall; crowns broad, irregular; roots spreading, often forming thickets from suckers.

Trunks: Short, crooked to straight, 6–12" in diameter; mature bark gray to reddish-brown, scaly; wood hard, strong, flexible, fine-grained.

Branches: Spreading, crooked, with many **thorn-like spur-shoots;** twigs red-brown with flaky grayish skin, grayish-woolly at first; **buds bright red, hairy,** about ⅛" long (⅛–¼" at twig tips), flat-lying.

Leaves: Alternate, simple, deciduous; blades shiny and bright green above, paler beneath, woolly at first, **hairless when mature,** ovate to long-triangular, 1⅛–4" long, rounded or notched at the base, **coarsely toothed at the tip to almost lobed at the base, folded lengthwise in bud;** stalks slender, often with 2 glands near the middle.

Flowers: Showy, delicate, fragrant, pink fading to white, ¾–2" across, bisexual; **sepals hairless on the outer surface,** woolly inside; **anthers pinkish,** 10–20; flowers in **clusters of 2–6 on leafy dwarf shoots,** in April–May **(after leaves expand).**

Fruits: Green to yellowish-green, **waxy pomes (apples),** ¾–1½" **across,** fragrant; remaining hard; crabapples mature by September–October, may persist through winter.

Habitat: In the understory of deciduous woodlands and along roads and fences.

Origin: Native.

Many cultivars of this species and other domestic crabapples have been developed. These small trees are widely planted as ornamentals for their spectacular, lightly fragrant flowers, attractive fruit and dense branches. The flowers may be single or double (with extra petals) and may have red, purple, pink or white petals. The abundant fruits often remain on the tree well into winter, providing food for birds. Types with different leaf colors, ranging from green to bronze to deep wine red, are also available for landscaping. Most have a broad crown, but weeping and columnar forms have also been developed. • **Pearleaf crabapple** (*M. prunifolia*, also called *Pyrus prunifolia* and Chinese crabapple), shown in pink/dark green (species overlap) on the map, resembles Siberian crabapple, but has hairy twigs, woolly, lance-shaped sepals and slightly larger (⅝–1" wide) fruits tipped with persistent sepals. This attractive ornamental has been introduced from Asia and now grows wild in disturbed woods. • A rare Asian escape, **Japanese crabapple** (*M. sieboldii*, also called *P. sieboldii* or Toringo crabapple), found throughout the state, produces showy, pink or rose-tinged flowers in April–May. Its tiny, ³⁄₁₆–⁵⁄₁₆" wide fruits are smooth-tipped (without persistent sepals) and the leaves of its long shoots often have 3 (rarely 5) lobes. *M. sieboldii* includes *M. floribunda*, *M. sargentii* and *M.* x *zumi*.

Also Called: Flowering crabapple • *P. baccata*.

Size and Shape: Small, wide trees 20–50' tall; crowns broadly domed.

Trunks: Short; wood hard, reddish-brown.

Branches: Spreading; **twigs hairless.**

Leaves: Alternate, simple, deciduous; **blades lustrous green above,** paler beneath, **hairless** when mature, 1¼–4" long, ovate to ovate-oblong, tipped with a slender point, rounded to wedge-shaped at the base, finely toothed; stalks hairless; leaf scars with 3 vein scars; leaves yellow in autumn.

Flowers: White, 1–1⅜" across, bisexual; petals oblong to ovate, widest above the middle, relatively narrow and widely spaced; **sepals long, slender, tapered, hairless when mature,** soon shed; **anthers yellow;** ovary single; **flowers in showy, few-flowered flat-topped clusters** (corymbs), **in April–May** (as leaves expand).

Fruits: Yellow or red pomes (apples), spherical, ½–¾" **long, without persistent sepals at the tip,** hairless when young; crabapples hang on long, slender stalks, mature in autumn and persist in winter.

Habitat: Fields, thickets and clearings.

Origin: Introduced from Siberia and northern China.

The common apple, first cultivated in Greece, is probably the most popular fruit in North America. By 1000 AD, at least 30 varieties had been developed. Since then, thousands of cultivars have been developed from the common apple and from Siberian crabapple (p. 187). Apple trees are usually propagated by grafting cuttings, because trees grown from seed often produce inferior fruit. Some varieties are hardy as far north as the Canadian prairies and the Alaskan coast. • Apples are commonly eaten raw, but they are also delicious baked, stewed or cooked in pies, cakes, muffins and puddings. Apples are rich in pectin, so they are often mixed with other fruits in jams, jellies and preserves. • **Caution:** The small seeds are toxic and can prove fatal in large quantities. The almond-like fragrance is produced by cyanide-like toxins. • Most wild apple trees probably originate from cores discarded by people. • Apple wood is solid and fine-grained. It has been used to make furniture, bowls, tools and carvings. It also makes excellent firewood, and its sawdust is used for smoking meat. • The taxonomy of the common apple is confusing. Most of the scientific synonyms listed below are currently used in some floras. *M. sylvestris* now usually refers to European crabapple.

Also Called: Wild apple, paradise apple • *M. sylvestris, M. domestica, M. communis, Pyrus pumila, P. malus.*

Size and Shape: Small, widely spreading trees, up to 50' tall; crowns low, broadly domed.

Trunks: Short; mature bark dark brownish-gray with flaky plates; wood red-brown, hard.

Branches: Spreading, crooked, with stubby (not thorn-like) spur-shoots; twigs and buds hairy.

Leaves: Alternate, simple, deciduous; blades dark green above, **lightly to densely hairy beneath, untwisting from bud,** elliptical to ovate, 1½–4" long, abruptly pointed, rounded at the base, edged with **fine, sharp teeth;** stalks hairy; leaves yellow in autumn.

Flowers: Showy, pink fading to white, 1⅛" across, bisexual; **sepals hairy on the outside; anthers yellow,** numerous; **flowers in small clusters** on spur-shoots, in spring (after leaves expand).

Fruits: Large, 2¼–4½" in diameter, green, yellow or red, juicy pomes **(apples),** indented at both ends, tipped with a cluster of tiny, **persistent sepals;** seeds dark brown, shiny, in small, leathery chambers in a core; apples mature and drop in autumn.

Habitat: Along roadsides, in clearings and near the edges of woods.

Origin: Introduced from Eurasia.

Prairie crabapple is one of the most beautiful and useful trees of the U.S. savannah and can live for more than 100 years. • This handsome, slow-growing tree has relatively few serious enemies, with the exception of fire. Evolution in areas exposed to frequent prairie fires encouraged the development of a cloning species capable of sprouting from roots after the crown had been burned. These clonal thickets provide productive, almost impenetrable wildlife habitat, with dense cover and ample food. Prairie crabapples are an important food for game birds, songbirds and rodents such as squirrels. Whitetail deer eat the fruit, twigs and leaves. • Prairie crabapple is sometimes cultivated as an ornamental. The double-flowered cultivar 'Bechtel' is especially popular in parks and gardens. • Prairie crabapple fruits look tasty, but they are usually too hard, tart and seedy for eating raw. They do, however, make lovely, deep red jelly, with a rich apple flavor and fragrance. • The spring combination of red buds and pale-pink to white flowers has been likened to a peppermint stick. Bud production for next year's blooms begins in early summer, so pruning should be done in spring, soon after the trees finish flowering.

Also Called: Iowa crabapple, western crabapple • *Pyrus ioensis.*

Size and Shape: Tall shrubs or small trees 20–30' tall; crowns open, rounded; roots spreading, suckering.

Trunks: To 18" wide; bark silvery reddish-brown, scaly, with vertical ridges; wood heavy.

Branches: Stout, spreading, intricately branched; twigs slender, densely white-woolly at first, smooth and dark gray to reddish-brown with age, some **short side-shoots forming sharp spines;** buds reddish-brown, hairy, egg-shaped, with overlapping scales.

Leaves: Alternate, deciduous, simple, **folded in bud;** blades firm, **shiny and dark green above, paler and white-woolly beneath,** broadly elliptical or ovate, 2–4⅛" long (much larger on young shoots), usually blunt-tipped and tapered to a wedge-shaped base, **coarsely blunt toothed, usually with small, shallow lobes;** stalks stout, hairy; young leaves red; senescing leaves orange-red in fall.

Flowers: Pink to white, fragrant, 1⅛–2" across, bisexual; petals with broad, rounded tips; sepals 5, in **densely woolly, bell-shaped calyxes;** anthers numerous, pink or salmon-colored; ovary single with **5 styles;** stalks silky-hairy, 1–1⅜" long; flowers in **showy, 3–7-flowered clusters on short side-shoots, in May** (as leaves expand).

Fruits: Yellowish-green pomes (apples), dull, waxy, depressed at both ends, ¾–1½" **long, tipped with tiny persistent sepals,** hanging on woolly stalks; crabapples mature in autumn.

Habitat: Woods and thickets.

Origin: Native.

189

American mountain-ash is a relatively slow-growing, short-lived tree that is sometimes cultivated for its attractive flowers, fruits and leaves. The moderately light, close-grained, weak wood has no commercial value. • The fruits (fresh or dried) contain iron and vitamin C. They are also acidic and rich in tannins, however, and should be eaten in moderation. Fruits gathered after the first frost are bittersweet and can be made into jelly, jam, marmalade or juice. Mountain-ash "berries" can also be used to make wine and to flavor liqueurs. Some tribes dried the fruits and ground them into meal. • The fruits have mild laxative, diuretic, astringent and digestive effects, so they were sometimes eaten with hard-to-digest foods. The Algonquian peoples prepared a mild stimulant by boiling American mountain-ash twigs, new white spruce twigs, wintergreen leaves and elderberry flowers. • Grouse, cedar waxwings, grosbeaks, thrushes, squirrels and bears feed on the plentiful fruits. • American mountain-ash can be confused with the rare species **showy mountain-ash (*S. decora*,** also called *Pyrus decora*, northern mountain-ash, northern-ash dogberry and showy northern-ash), shown in pink on the map. Showy mountain-ash is distinguished by slightly wider, blue-green leaflets, larger (⅜") fruits with a grayish bloom and larger (about ⅛" wide) flowers, which appear about a week later than those of American mountain-ash.

Also Called: American rowan-tree, dogberry, catberry, pigberry, service-tree • *P. americana.*

Size and Shape: Trees or shrubs 12–35' tall; crowns open, **narrow, rounded.**

Trunks: Short, 4–10" in diameter; young bark pale gray with horizontal pores (lenticels), smooth; mature bark reddish-brown, slightly scaly; wood pale, soft, fine-grained, weak.

Branches: Spreading, slender; twigs dark reddish- to grayish-brown, **soon hairless; buds dark, shiny, gummy, essentially hairless,** ⅜–½" long with narrow, curved tips.

Leaves: Alternate, deciduous, **positioned on edge and arching;** compound, **pinnately divided into 9–17 leaflets;** leaflets dull yellowish-green, paler beneath, thin, lance-shaped to narrowly oblong, 2–2¾" (rarely 4") long, **3–5 times as long as wide, taper-pointed, finely sharp-toothed, short-stalked,** roughly paired; leaflets often drop before main stalk (rachis); leaves clear yellow in autumn.

Flowers: White, less than ¼" across, bisexual; petals 5, widest above middle; sepals 5, fused in bell-shaped calyxes; stamens 15–20, anthers yellow; flowers on hairless stalks in **showy, many-branched, flat-topped or rounded, 2–8" wide clusters** (corymbs), in May–July (after leaves expand).

Fruits: Bright orange-red, berry-like pomes (like tiny apples), with thin flesh, about ¼" **across in branched, flat-topped clusters;** seeds shiny, chestnut brown, 1–2 per fruit; mature in September–October, **may persist through winter.**

Habitat: Moist, rocky forests.

Origin: Native.

This fast-growing ornamental is widely planted in gardens and parks and along streets. • The wood of European mountain-ash is relatively hard. It has been used for tool handles, spinning wheels and other wooden products. • Birds frequently carry mountain-ash seeds to new sites, and the trees can become invasive pests in natural habitats near our towns and cities. • In Scandinavia, the bitter-tasting fruits were used, fresh or dried, to flavor sauces and game (especially fowl). The vitamin C–rich "berries" can be used to make delicious jellies. They have also been used in herbal remedies for diarrhea, hemorrhoids, scurvy and other ailments. • Scottish Highlanders planted this tree beside their homes for protection from witchcraft. • *Sorbus* was the classical Latin name for European mountain-ashes. The specific epithet *aucuparia* means "I catch birds" and refers to the bird-attracting fruits. European bird catchers often planted this tree to lure prey. The alternative common name "rowan-tree" comes from an old Scandinavian word meaning "red," in reference to the brilliant red fruits. • European mountain-ash is distinguished from native mountain-ash species by its hairier young twigs, downy-white, non-sticky buds and smaller, hairier leaves.

Also Called: Rowan-tree, dogberry • *Pyrus aucuparia.*

Size and Shape: Trees or tall shrubs 15–50′ tall; crowns open, rounded.

Trunks: Short, slender, up to about 20″ in diameter; **young bark shiny, gray-brown with elongated, horizontal pores** (lenticels), thin, smooth; mature bark scaly; wood pale brown, fine-grained, hard.

Branches: Coarse, spreading; twigs grayish, shiny, **hairy when young;** buds dark purple, **white-woolly,** ⅜–½″ long, **not gummy.**

Leaves: Alternate, deciduous; compound, **pinnately divided into 9–17 sub-opposite leaflets** on a central stalk (rachis); leaflets green above, **whitish and hairy beneath, short-pointed** or blunt, **coarsely sharp-toothed** (except near the base), 1⅛–2″ long; leaflets often drop before the main stalk.

Flowers: White, tiny, bisexual; petals 5, round, ³⁄₁₆″ long; sepals 5, tiny; stamens 15–20, anthers yellow; flowers numerous, on **hairy** stalks in erect, flat-topped, 4–6″ wide, many-branched clusters (corymbs), in May–July (after leaves expand).

Fruits: Orange-yellow to scarlet, berry-like **pomes** (like tiny apples), fleshy, ⅜–½″ across, hang in round-topped clusters; seeds 1–2, shiny, dark brown, about ¹⁄₄″ long; pomes mature in September, **may persist through winter.**

Habitat: Moist sites in wet woods, bogs and swamps.

Origin: Introduced from Europe.

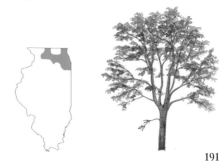

This attractive small tree was introduced to North America for its showy flowers. It is one of the most common trees in Great Britain, where countless miles of oneseed hawthorn were planted in the 17th and 18th centuries to produce tough, thorny, livestock-proof hedges. • Hawthorn species are notoriously difficult to tell apart, but oneseed hawthorn is quite distinctive. It is the only species in Illinois with leaves cut more than halfway to the midvein and the only one with single styles and single nutlets. However, oneseed hawthorn occasionally hybridizes with dotted hawthorn (p. 194), producing offspring with intermediate characteristics. • Another introduced species that rarely grows wild in Illinois is **inkberry hawthorn (*C. multiflora*)**, shown in dark green (species overlap) on the map, This ornamental is not important for its flowers, but the edible fruit has been used in jams, jellies and marmalade. Inkberry hawthorn has been found growing wild around Chicago. • *Crataegus* was the traditional Latin name for hawthorn, derived from the Greek word *kratos*, "strength," in reference to the strong, hard wood. The specific epithet *monogyna* means "with a single pistil or gynoecium" and refers to the single-seeded fruits.

Also Called: English hawthorn, maythorn.

Size and Shape: Trees or shrubs up to 25–35' tall; crowns broadly domed.

Trunks: Crooked, sometimes clumped, up to 12" in diameter; mature bark dark gray to brownish, slightly scaly; wood heavy, hard.

Branches: Numerous, crooked, spreading; twigs lustrous; **thorns shiny, gray, straight, ⅜–¾" long, in leaf axils and at the tips of 1⅛–3" branchlets; buds round,** dark brown, often 2–3 together (1 producing a thorn).

Leaves: Alternate, simple, deciduous; blades dark green, paler beneath, firm, triangular to broadly ovate, ½–2" long, **cut over halfway to the midvein into 3–7 lobes tipped with sharp, irregular teeth;** leaves often persist into late autumn.

Flowers: Rose-colored (cultivars dark red to white), unpleasant-smelling, ⅜–½" across, bisexual; petals 5; sepals 5, bases fused in a tube; **flowers in branched, flat-topped clusters** (corymbs), on dwarf shoots in May.

Fruits: Bright red haws (pomes, like small apples), thin-fleshed, rounded to ellipsoidal, about ¼" wide, tipped with sepals and **1 protruding style;** seeds within **bony nutlets, 1 per fruit;** hips mature in September–October, **often persist through winter.**

Habitat: Open, often disturbed sites in clearings and open woodlands and along roadsides and fence lines, especially on calcium-rich soils.

Origin: Introduced from Europe and western Asia.

This highly variable species has been variously classified over the years because of its extreme variability, and most botanists now take a broad view of the species. • Cockspur hawthorn is a fast-growing, short-lived tree that readily invades cleared land, but because it requires high light levels, it is soon shaded out when other trees become established. • The specific epithet *crus-galli* comes from the Latin *crus*, "shin or leg," and *gallus*, "cock," alluding to the sharp thorns that resembles a rooster's spurs. • The leaves described below are typical of flowering or fruiting shoots and are usually more than twice as long as wide. Leaves on vegetative shoots can be very different. They are often elliptical to oblong and widest near the middle. Also, leaves on vegetative shoots may be somewhat lobed and can grow to twice the size of those on flowering shoots, reaching 2–3½" in length and 1⅛–3" in width. Such variability between vegetative and flowering branches is common in hawthorns. In some cases, the range of variation on a single tree or within a single population exceeds that often found between species. The larger leaves on short (flowering) shoots are usually the most useful for identifying hawthorns to species.

Also Called: Cockspur thorn • *C. acanthocolonensis, C. arduennae, C. attenuata, C. bushii, C. fontanesiana, C. pachyphylla, C. pyracanthoides, C. tenax* and over 20 other names.

Size and Shape: Trees or tall shrubs 20–25' tall; crowns broadly domed or depressed.

Trunks: Sometimes clumped; mature bark gray-brown, slightly scaly; wood heavy, hard.

Branches: Numerous, crooked, **stiff, wide-spreading, horizontal;** twigs hairless; **thorns many, ¾–2¾" long,** straight or slightly curved; **buds rounded,** dark brown, often 2–3 together (1 producing a thorn).

Leaves: Alternate, simple, deciduous; **blades glossy and dark green above,** dull and paler below, **leathery, ovate, widest above middle, with broad tips and wedge-shaped bases,** 1⅛–2" long, sharp-toothed (at least above the middle), **mostly unlobed;** stalks ⅛–½" long.

Flowers: White, unpleasant-smelling, ⅜–½" wide, bisexual; petals 5, soon shed; sepals 5, slender, bases fused; anthers about 10, white, pale yellow or pink; flowers many, in **loose, hairless, flat-topped clusters** (corymbs) on dwarf shoots, in May.

Fruits: **Green to dull red haws** (pomes, like small apples), **often dark-dotted,** rather hard, with thin, dry flesh, **short egg-shaped to almost round, often 5-sided, about ⅜" wide,** tipped with sepals and protruding styles; **seeds in bony nutlets, 1–2 (sometimes 3) per fruit;** hips mature in September–October, **often persist through winter.**

Habitat: Open, often disturbed sites in thickets and woodlands.

Origin: Native.

This abundant native species is one of our more easily recognized hawthorns. The numerous horizontal branches and pale gray branchlets of dotted hawthorn make it conspicuous in winter. In autumn, the leathery, dull, broad-tipped leaves and pale-dotted, red to yellow haws identify this species. The leaves are always longer than wide, though they can vary greatly on the same tree. Leaves on vegetative shoots are often more lobed and much wider-tipped than those on flowering shoots. Sometimes the leaves on vegetative shoots are almost fan-shaped and have notched (rather than pointed or blunt) tips. • Many hawthorns are planted as ornamentals for their showy flowers, and the attractive clusters of fruit can add color to the winter landscape. When planted as a hedge, hawthorns can provide an impassable barrier of dense, thorny branches. However, these fast-growing trees can also become pests when they invade open areas such as pastures and parks. The long, sharp thorns are seldom appreciated along paths and fence lines and can be especially hazardous when unwanted trees must be removed. • The specific epithet *punctata*, "dotted," refers to the pale dots that speckle the haws of this species.

Also Called: Whitehaw • *C. collina, C. mortonensis, C. sucida, C. verruculosa.*

Size and Shape: Trees or shrubs to 25–35' tall, often in thickets; crowns open, broad.

Trunks: Mostly single, **with branched thorns;** mature bark brownish-gray, fissured; wood hard.

Branches: Stiff, stout, wide-spreading, with **short, 3–9-leaved side-shoots;** twigs lustrous, hairless; **thorns slender, ¾–3" long, straight, slightly curved or branched; buds rounded,** often 2–3 together (1 producing a thorn).

Leaves: Alternate, simple, deciduous; **blades dull green with impressed veins above,** paler and **slightly hairy beneath, firm,** elliptic-oblong to ovate, ¾–3" long, **widest and sharply single- or double-toothed above midleaf, often unlobed,** bases tapered.

Flowers: White, unpleasant-smelling, ⅜–¾" across, bisexual; petals 5, soon shed; sepals 5, densely gray-hairy, slender, with fused bases; anthers about 20, pink, red or yellow; flowers many, in **loose, flat-topped clusters** (corymbs) on dwarf shoots, in May–June.

Fruits: Dull red or orange-red, sometimes yellow (var. *aurea*), **pale-dotted haws** (pomes, like small apples), pear-shaped to **spherical, ⅜–½" wide,** tipped with sepals and protruding styles, mellow-fleshed to scarcely succulent; seeds within bony nutlets, 3–5 per fruit; hips mature in September–October, **often persist through winter.**

Habitat: Open woods, thickets and pastures.

Origin: Native.

This beautiful little tree is widely cultivated for its year-round appeal as an
ornamental. In spring, it produces showy,
white flowers, followed by a dense, shady
canopy of leaves. In autumn, the leaves
turn golden and provide a striking contrast
to the showy, red fruits. In winter, the
attractive fruits and unusual bark continue
to add interest to the landscape. The cultivar 'Winter King' is noted for its consistently large, showy fruit. • This fast-growing tree usually grows at a rate of 12–18
inches per year. Even young trees produce
showy flowers and fruits. Specimens grown
from seed may not produce true-to-type
stock, so green hawthorn is usually propagated by budding onto seedling under-

stock. Because of its small size, green hawthorn can be planted in
gardens where space is limited. It is used as a hedge or screen and
is also grown as a single specimen or in clumps. Green hawthorn
can tolerate a wide range of conditions, including urban pollution
and poor soils, but it prefers sites with well-drained loamy soils
and full sun. Unlike most hawthorns, it is relatively free of pests
and diseases such as scab and rust. • The species name, *viridis*,
"green," refers to the silvery green twigs.

Also Called: *C. dawsoniana, C. durifolia,
C. lanceolata, C. mitis, C. pechiana, C. schneckii.*

Size and Shape: Trees or shrubs to 20–35'
tall and wide, often in thickets; crowns broad,
rounded.

Trunks: Mostly single; **mature bark with
beige-gray outer layers peeling** or flaking away
to expose the **copper-cinnamon inner bark;**
wood hard.

Branches: Silvery gray, with **few or no
thorns;** twigs silvery green.

Leaves: Alternate, simple, deciduous; **blades
thin,** variable, glossy, green, **obscurely veined
above,** paler with persistent **woolly tufts in vein
axils beneath,** lacking glands, toothed (often
almost to the base) and lobed (leaves on flowering shoots lacking lobes), **broadest at or above
midleaf, tapered to a wedge-shaped base,**
¾–2½" long, ½–1¼" wide; **veins running to tips
of teeth or lobes;** autumn leaves gold, tinged
with red or purple.

Flowers: White, ½–¾" across, bisexual, with
an unpleasant odor; petals 5; sepals 5, usually
shed; anthers about 20, pink, red or yellow; flowers numerous, on slender, hairless stalks in repeatedly branched, **flat-topped clusters** (cymes) on
dwarf side-shoots, in mid-May.

Fruits: Bright red or orange-red, rarely yellow,
pale-dotted haws (pomes, like small apples),
mealy, ¼–½" **thick;** seeds within bony, **smooth
nutlets,** 3–5 per fruit; hips mature in September–
October, **often abundant and persistent in winter.**

Habitat: Low woods.

Origin: Native.

195

The round, red haws of fireberry hawthorn are usually fleshy and mellow when ripe. • The species name *chrysocarpa*, from the Greek *chryso*, "golden," and *karpos*, "fruit," is not very appropriate, because the fruits are usually red. • Fireberry hawthorn is one of 3 Illinois species in Series Rotundifoliae, including **Dodge hawthorn** (*C. dodgei* or *C. flavida*), found in McDonough County, and **Margaret's hawthorn** (*C. margarettiae*, sometimes misspelled *C. margaretta*), shown in pink on the map. All these hawthorns are shrubby and typically have small, round leaves with delicate, glandular stalks. They also have numerous, slender thorns, spherical fruits and clusters of a few small flowers that appear early in the year. Fireberry hawthorn is distinguished by the conspicuous, spreading lobes of its leaves. Some taxonomists include *C. margarettiae* in *C. chrysocarpa*. • The Series Microcarpae is represented in Illinois by a single species, **three-lobed hawthorn** (*C. spathulata*, also called little-hip hawthorn). Three-lobed hawthorn is identified by its small (⅛–¼"), round, red fruits and its small (³⁄₁₆–1³⁄₁₆" long by ¼–⅝" wide), thin leaves with veins ending at the bases of the teeth (rather than at the tooth tips). Three-lobed hawthorn is rare in Illinois, but it has been found growing in wet woods in Pulaski County.

Also Called: Round-leaved hawthorn
• *C. aboriginum, C. brunetiana, C. faxonii, C. rotundifolia.*

Size and Shape: Trees or shrubs to 20' tall, often forming thickets; crowns broad.

Trunks: Crooked, sometimes clumped; mature bark scaly; wood heavy, hard.

Branches: Numerous, stout, usually thorny; twigs lustrous, smooth; **thorns shiny black, slender,** straight or slightly curved, ¾–3" long; **buds round,** often 2–3 together (1 producing a thorn).

Leaves: Alternate, simple, deciduous; **blades usually dull yellowish-green,** often with slightly impressed veins above, soon becoming hairless, firm, ¾–3½" long, **usually about as wide as long,** pointed to round-tipped, **edged to below midleaf with gland-tipped teeth and 7–13 shallow lobes; stalks slender, often with tiny glands** near the blade.

Flowers: White, unpleasant-smelling, ⅜–½" across, bisexual; petals 5, soon shed; sepals 5, edged with glands, fused at the base; anthers white or pale yellow; flowers in flat-topped, branched clusters (corymbs) on dwarf shoots, in May.

Fruits: Hairy, deep red (rarely yellow) haws (pomes, like small apples), tipped with tiny sepals and protruding styles, **round, about ⅜" wide;** seeds within bony nutlets, 3–4 per fruit; fruits mature in August–October, **often persist through winter.**

Habitat: Open, well-drained sites on woodlands, thickets, and pastures.

Origin: Native.

Fanleaf hawthorn belongs to Series Tenuifoliae but forms a link with Series Rotundifoliae through its affinities with fireberry hawthorn (p. 196). These 2 species occupy the same geographical region, and fanleaf hawthorn may have contributed genes to fireberry hawthorn. • It is easy to determine if a tree is a hawthorn, but it is much more difficult, and sometimes impossible, to identify the species. *Crataegus* is a large, complex genus with over 1000 "species" described from North America alone. However, many of these taxa are hybrids or poorly defined varieties. • It has been suggested that the evolutionary diversification of North American species began when hawthorns invaded areas cleared for agriculture by Native peoples. These clearings opened new habitats where hawthorn species could spread and intermix. • Another widespread member of Series Tenuifoliae, **bigfruit hawthorn (*C. macrosperma*,** including *C. blothra, C. cyanophylla, C. depilis, C. eganii, C. ferrissii, C., hillii, C. sextilis, C. taetrica*), shown in dark green (species overlap) on the map, is distinguished by its early spring flowering. Many taxonomists include *C. macrosperma* and *C. flabellata* in the same species.

Photo, bottom: *C. macrosperma*

Also Called: New England hawthorn
• *C. densiflora, C. grayana.*

Size and Shape: Trees or shrubs 15–20' tall, often in thickets; crowns broad.

Trunks: Crooked, clumped; mature bark scaly; wood heavy, hard.

Branches: Numerous, stout; twigs lustrous, hairless, slender; **thorns numerous, slender, straight or slightly curved, 2–2⅜"** (sometimes 1⅛–4") **long; buds rounded,** often 2–3 together (1 producing a thorn).

Leaves: Alternate, simple, deciduous, **often bent backward;** blades hairless when mature, ovate to diamond-shaped or triangular (often nearly round on vegetative shoots), 1⅛–2" (sometimes to 3") long, tapered to a point, wedge-shaped or squared at the base, **edged with 7–13 pointed, sharply toothed lobes** (often with tips curved out or back).

Flowers: White, unpleasant-smelling, ½–¾" across, bisexual; petals 5, soon shed; sepals 5, **slender, smooth-edged,** bases fused; anthers 10–20, pink; flowers numerous, in loose, **flat-topped clusters** (corymbs) on dwarf shoots, in May.

Fruits: Crimson, thick-fleshed, juicy haws (pomes, like small apples), tipped with sepals and protruding styles, oblong to round, ⅜–½" across, sometimes slightly angled; seeds within bony nutlets, 3–5 per fruit; fruits mature in September–October, **often persist in winter.**

Habitat: Thickets in open, often calcareous sites.
Origin: Native.

Polyploidy (having 3 or more sets of chromosomes) and apomixis (producing seed without fertilization) have contributed to the expansion of the genus *Crataegus* and to a good deal of taxonomic inconsistency. Through apomixis, even sterile hybrids can produce large groups of genetically identical plants with relatively stable characteristics, and these groups may eventually be described as species. In the long term, this lack of genetic diversity could become a weakness, but meanwhile, it allows one plant to produce hundreds or even millions of identical offspring. • Scarlet hawthorn belongs to Series Coccineae. Confusingly, the species for which the group was named, *C. coccinea*, is no longer recognized. Instead, has been variously reclassified among other species, including scarlet hawthorn and fireberry hawthorn (p. 196). • The most widespread member of Series Coccineae in Illinois is **Holmes' hawthorn** (***C. holmesiana***, also called *C. amicta*), shown in pink/dark green (species overlap) on the map, identified by its rough, broadly ovate leaves, hairless flower stalks and large (½–⅝") fruits. • Members of another series, Pruinosae, have pinkish to purplish or crimson, waxy-coated fruits tipped with prominent, elevated sepals. The series' type species, **frosted hawthorn** (***C. pruinosa***, or waxyfruit hawthorn, *C. conjuncta*, *C. gattingeri* and *C. platycarpa*), is identified by its leaves (>2" long, hairless, widest above midleaf), anthers (20, white or pink) and sepals (smooth-edged).

Photo, bottom: *C. pruinosa*

Also Called: *C. albicans*, *C. assurgens*, *C. aulica*, *C. ellwangeriana*, *C. elongata*, *C. paucispina*, *C. robesoniana*, *C. trachyphylla*, *C. subrotundifolia*.

Size and Shape: Trees or shrubs to 35' tall, highly variable; **crowns usually compact** and conical.

Trunks: Crooked, sometimes clumped; mature bark scaly; wood heavy, hard.

Branches: Numerous, slender, spreading; twigs lustrous, hairless with age; **thorns smooth, shiny, stout, usually slightly curved,** ¾–2⅜" long; **buds rounded,** dark brown, often 2–3 together (1 producing a thorn).

Leaves: Alternate, simple, deciduous; blades dark green and hairless above, **often rough-hairy beneath** (especially when young), **with veins ending at tooth tips,** ovate to almost round, **widest below midleaf,** 2⅜–3½" long, broad-based, edged with sharp, double teeth and 7–11 shallow lobes.

Flowers: White, with a sweet but unpleasant smell, ½–¾" across, bisexual; petals 5, soon shed; sepals 5, **glandular-toothed;** anthers 10–20; flowers numerous, in branched, **slender-stalked, flat-topped clusters** (corymbs) on dwarf shoots, in May.

Fruits: Bright red, thick-fleshed, often juicy haws (pomes, like small apples), tipped with tiny persistent sepals and protruding styles, **spherical,** ⅜–½" across; seeds within bony nutlets, 3–5 per fruit; fruits mature in autumn, **often persist through winter.**

Habitat: Open, often disturbed sites in thickets and moist woods.

Origin: Native.

Many parts of hawthorn trees have been used in medicine. Dried leaves or flowers have been administered in capsules, teas and tinctures for treating heart and circulatory problems. Studies have shown that hawthorn dilates blood vessels, thereby improving circulation, increasing oxygen supply to the heart and stabilizing blood pressure. Hawthorn may also strengthen the heart by making it pump harder. Extracts have been used to treat moderate congestive heart failure, heart arrhythmia and mild angina, but more often, hawthorn is recommended for preventing future heart problems. Some studies suggest that hawthorn may be effective in controlling or even lowering cholesterol, triglyceride and blood sugar levels. High doses also slow the central nervous system, and extracts have been used as a sedative for treating insomnia.
• Downy hawthorn is the only member of Series Molle in Illinois. • Series Dilatatae is represented by a single species, **Kansas hawthorn (*C. coccini-oides**, also called scarlet hawthorn), shown in dark green (species overlap) on the map. Kansas hawthorn is identified by its broad-based leaves with hairless upper surfaces and crisped edges (at maturity). It also has round, ½–1⅟₁₆" wide fruits and its large (1" wide) flowers have 20 stamens. Kansas hawthorn flowers in May in thickets and rocky woods of southern Illinois.

Also Called: Red haw • *C. altrix, C. declivatis, C. lanigera, C. nupera, C. pachyphylla, C. ridgwayi, C. sera, C. valens, C. venosa, C. verna.*

Size and Shape: Trees or shrubs up to 25–35' tall, often forming thickets; crowns broad.

Trunks: Crooked; mature bark brownish-gray, slightly scaly; wood heavy, hard.

Branches: Numerous, slender, spreading; twigs reddish-brown and silky-hairy when young, smooth and gray with age; **thorns few, reddish-brown, straight, slender, ¾–2⅜" long; buds rounded,** often 2–3 together (1 producing a thorn).

Leaves: Alternate, simple, deciduous; **blades densely short-hairy above and woolly beneath when young,** dark green and hairless above and slightly hairy beneath when mature, **widest at or below midleaf, 1½–3" long and almost as wide, sharply double-toothed or with 9–11 sharp-toothed lobes.**

Flowers: White, unpleasant-smelling, ¾–1" across, bisexual; petals 5, soon shed; sepals 5, **woolly, glandular-toothed,** fused at the base; **anthers 20, white or pale yellow;** flowers in **showy, hairy-branched, flat-topped clusters** (corymbs) on dwarf shoots, in May.

Fruits: Bright red haws (pomes, like small apples), usually thick-fleshed and mellow, **hairy** (at least near the ends), tipped with sepals and protruding styles, **round,** ⅜–½" across; seeds in bony nutlets, usually 5 per fruit; fruits mature in autumn, **often persist through winter.**

Habitat: Moist, open woods.

Origin: Native.

199

One of the showiest hawthorns for ornamental planting originated in Washington, DC, and was originally planted in hedges. With its large, white flowers, shady canopy, bright orange to scarlet leaves and bright red persistent, Washington hawthorn has been widely planted in parks and gardens across North America and Europe. • This moderately hardy species is also one of the least susceptible to fire blight. Washington hawthorn is the only member of Series Cordatae in Illinois. • Another small series, Intricatae, is represented in Illinois by **Copenhagen hawthorn** (*C. intricata* including *C. bealii, C. diversifolia, C. foetida, C. meticulosa, C. rubella* and *C. wheeleri*), shown in pink/dark green (species overlap) on the map, and **newbush hawthorn** (*C. neobushii*, sometimes included in *C. intricata*), shown in dark pink on the map. This unusually thorny group is noted for its bright red, rather dry fruits, which are tipped with glandular-toothed sepals. • Hawthorn trunks are usually small, but the hard, strong wood has been used for carving and lathe work and for making toothpicks, awls, pins and fishhooks. • Most people find the sweet-fetid scent of hawthorn flowers unpleasant. Many insects, however, find it delightful and are tempted to feed on the pollen and nectar, cross-pollinating the flowers in the process.

Also Called: Washington-thorn, red-haw, Virginia hedge thorn, Virginia heart-leaved thorn • *C. cordata.*

Size and Shape: Small trees or tall shrubs 25–30' tall; crowns regular, oval to rounded, 20–30' across.

Trunks: Short, to 12" in diameter; bark thin, smooth, light brown, scaly with age.

Branches: Upright, with numerous, slender thorns 1⅛–2" long; twigs shiny, brown.

Leaves: Alternate, simple, deciduous; blades glossy and dark green above, paler beneath, essentially hairless, ovate to **broadly triangular in outline, often 3–5 lobed, pointed, ¾–2⅜" long and almost as wide, lobed and coarsely, irregularly toothed;** lobes 1–4 per side, largest at the base, much smaller upward, **cut less than halfway to the midrib; veins ending at lobe tips and lobe bases;** stalks ⅜–2" long, lacking glands; leaves bright orange to scarlet in autumn.

Flowers: White, ⅜–½" across, bisexual; petals 5; sepals 5, short-triangular; **stamens about 20,** with pale yellow anthers; styles usually 5 (sometimes 3); **flowers numerous** in broad, hairless, multiple-branched clusters (cymes), in May–June.

Fruits: Tiny, **shiny, bright scarlet pomes** (haws) with thin, dry pulp, about ¼" across, usually **shedding sepals from tips and leaving nutlet tips clearly exposed** (almost exserted); seeds usually 5, 1 per nutlet; fruits mature in October–November, often persist until spring.

Habitat: Open woods and thickets.

Origin: Native in the southeastern U.S.

The haws of fleshy hawthorn are succulent and juicy when ripe, but sometimes they remain hard and dry until late in the season. All hawthorn haws are edible, but flavor and fleshiness can vary greatly with the species, habitat and time of year. Although haws are rich in pectin, they are often very seedy, so they are usually combined with other fruit to make jams, jellies and compotes. Some tribes mixed the flesh of haws with dried meat to make pemmican. • Fleshy hawthorn belongs to Series Macracanthae. According to ITIS (2003) and Voss (1985), the species for which this group is named, *C. macracantha,* is now included in *C. succulenta* as var. *macracantha.* • Another species in the Macracanthae, **pear hawthorn** (***C. calpodendron,*** also called urn-shaped hawthorn, *C. champanii, C. fontanosiana, C. hispidula, C. mollicula, C. structilis, C. tomentosa*), shown in pink/dark green (species overlap) on the map, is very similar to fleshy hawthorn but has woolly- to silky-hairy young twigs and larger (2–3½" long by 1½–3" wide), more prominently hairy, dull yellowish-green leaves. Pear hawthorn is also smaller (at most 10–13' tall) with small (¼–⅜" long), shiny, orange-red, pear-shaped haws and few, if any, thorns. The name *calpodendron,* "urn-tree," refers to the shape of the fruit.

Also Called: Succulent hawthorn • *C. corporea, C. gaultii, C. gemmosa, C. illinoensis, C. laxiflora, C. leucantha, C. longispina, C. macracantha, C. vegeta.*

Size and Shape: Trees or shrubs up to 20–25' tall; crowns broadly domed.

Trunks: Crooked, clumped; mature bark scaly; wood heavy, hard.

Branches: Numerous, spreading; **twigs dark, lustrous, hairless** (or slightly hairy when young); **thorns glossy, blackish, strong,** 1⅛–1¾" (sometimes to 3") long; **buds rounded,** often 2–3 together (1 producing a thorn).

Leaves: Alternate, simple, deciduous; **blades lustrous and dark green with impressed veins above,** paler and **finely hairy (at least on veins) beneath,** firm, broadly elliptical to ovate or diamond-shaped, 1⅛–2⅜" (sometimes to 3") long, **finely sharp-toothed, shallowly 9–11-lobed above midleaf; stalks** usually glandless, grooved **and winged** near the blade.

Flowers: White, unpleasant-smelling, ⅜–¾" across, bisexual; petals 5, soon shed; **sepals 5, glandular-toothed,** bases fused, tips bent backward or shed; anthers 10–20, white, pale yellow or pink; flowers in branched, **flat-topped clusters** (corymbs) on dwarf shoots, in May.

Fruits: **Glossy, bright red haws** (pomes, like small apples), tipped with persistent sepals and protruding styles, **round, ¼–½" across;** seeds within bony nutlets, **2–3 per fruit;** hips mature in September–October, **often persist through winter.**

Habitat: Dry to moist woods and thickets.

Origin: Native.

201

The fruits of downy serviceberry are rather dry and flavorless, but Native peoples used them to make a pudding, said to be almost as good as plum pudding. • "Serviceberry" is a variation of an earlier name, "sarvissberry," from "sarviss," a transformation of *Sorbus* (mountain-ash), and long-time natives to eastern woodlands pronounce the common name that way. "Downy" refers to the silvery-hairy young leaves of this species. The inclusion of "shad" in some common names alludes to the shad fish migration, which coincides with the blooming of this shrub. • It is easy to identify the genus *Amelanchier*, but identifying the species is much more difficult and sometimes impossible. Taxonomic problems stem from a combination of hybridization, polyploidy (the production of 3 or more sets of chromosomes) and apomixis (the production of seed without fertilization). Serviceberries often produce fertile triploid offspring (plants with 3 sets of chromosomes). Most serviceberries hybridize freely and produce relatively fertile intermediate offspring. Even the most distinctive species can blend together in a continuous series of shrubs with intergrading characteristics. • Smooth serviceberry (p. 203) is sometimes included in this species.

Also Called: Downy juneberry, Allegheny serviceberry, apple shadbush, common serviceberry, shadblow.

Size and Shape: Small trees or shrubs to 35' tall; crowns irregular, narrow.

Trunks: Usually **clumped,** 4–12" in diameter; **bark bluish-gray, thin, smooth,** slightly fissured with age; wood heavy, hard, reddish-brown.

Branches: Slender; twigs greenish to purplish when young, ridged lengthwise below leaf scars; **buds slender, twisted, pointed, ¼–½" long,** approximately 5-scaled.

Leaves: Alternate, simple, deciduous; **blades densely whitish-woolly beneath and folded when young,** dark green and hairless above when mature, paler beneath with a **few hairs on the veins,** oval, thin, 2–4" long, sharp-tipped, with **about 25 regular, sharp teeth and fewer than 12 prominent veins per side; stalks finely hairy,** slender, ¾–1⅛" long.

Flowers: White, bisexual; petals 5, strap-like, ⅜–½" long; sepals 5, in bell-shaped calyxes; flowers on silky-hairy stalks in axils of slender, reddish, silky-hairy bracts, forming **showy, branched clusters** (racemes) at branch tips, in March–May **(as leaves expand).**

Fruits: Dark reddish-purple, berry-like but dry pomes (like tiny apples), ¼–½" across; tipped with persistent sepals; **lowermost stalks about ½" long;** seeds hard, 5–10 per pome; pomes ripen and drop in June–August.

Habitat: Dry woodlands, slopes and buffs.

Origin: Native.

Serviceberries seldom grow large enough to produce wood of commercial importance, but their hard, heavy trunks have been used to make tool handles, walking sticks and other small articles. • The sweet, juicy fruits are edible and rich in iron and copper. They can be eaten fresh from the tree, served with milk and sugar, added to pancakes, muffins and pies or made into jellies, jams and preserves. Native peoples dried the small pomes like raisins or mashed and dried them in cakes. Often the dried fruits were mixed with meat and fat to form pemmican, a lightweight, high-energy food that could support winter travelers for long periods if the diet was supplemented with vitamin C (usually in the form of rose hips or spruce tea) to prevent scurvy. • The twigs have a faint bitter-almond taste. • This hardy, attractive shrub, with its showy flower clusters and edible, bird-attracting fruits, is often planted in gardens and parks. • A rare Illinois shrub, **roundleaf serviceberry (*A. sanguinea*)**, shown in dark green (species overlap) on the map, is distinguished by the long (>1 cm) stalks and wool-covered tips of its fruits. Also, the leaves of this tall, bushy shrub have relative few teeth (less than twice as many teeth as veins).

Also Called: Smooth juneberry, Allegheny serviceberry • *Amelchier arborea* var. *laevis*.

Size and Shape: Trees or shrubs 6–35' tall; crowns irregular, narrow.

Trunks: Often clumped; **bark thin, smooth, gray,** with dark, vertical lines; wood heavy, hard.

Branches: Slender; twigs purplish, hairless, ridged lengthwise below leaf scars; **buds narrowly egg-shaped, pointed, ¼–½" long, twisted,** approximately 5-scaled.

Leaves: Alternate, simple, deciduous; **blades coppery red, hairless and folded when young,** dark green when mature, paler beneath, essentially hairless, thin, oval to elliptical, 1⅛–3" long, abruptly pointed, **with about 25 sharp teeth and 10 or fewer veins per side; stalks hairless,** slender, ⅜–1⅛" long.

Flowers: White, bisexual; petals 5, strap-like, ⅜–¾" long; sepals 5, in a bell-shaped calyx, about ⅛" long, bent backward; **flowers on** hairless, ⅜–1⅛" **long stalks** in axils of slender, ephemeral bracts, forming **showy, elongated, drooping clusters** (racemes), in March–June **(when leaves are at least half grown).**

Fruits: Dark reddish-purple to black, berry-like, **fleshy, juicy pomes** (like tiny apples), ¼–⅜" wide, tipped with sepals; **lowermost stalks 2–4" long;** seeds hard, 5–10 per pome; pomes ripen and drop in July–August.

Habitat: Woodlands, usually on well-drained sites.

Origin: Native.

This species is larger than true buckthorns (genus *Rhamnus*) in North America. On richer sites, it can reach 70–80' in height, with trunks almost 3' in diameter. Old trees on severe sites are often twisted and picturesque. Woolly southern-buckthorn is an excellent example of a tough native tree. It can thrive on barren, rocky bluffs, exposed to heat and drought. This hardy tree can even tolerate road salt. • Buckthorns generally have little economic importance and limited value for wildlife. The soft, weak wood is seldom used. The olive-like fruits are said to be edible when ripe, but there is little evidence that they were used by people. The fruits are eaten by birds such as quail and turkey. Deer also feed on the fruits and occasionally browse the leaves. The wood and bark do produce a clear gum called "chicle," which has been used in chewing gum. • Woolly southern-buckthorn is sometimes planted as an ornamental. • In the northern part of its range, leaves persist well into winter, and in the south, trees can be sub-evergreen. Trees can be propagated from seed, but the seeds must be scarified before they are planted in fall. • The Illinois trees described here are var. *oblongifolia*.

Also Called: Woolly-buckthorn, gum bully, gum bumelia • *Bumelia lanuginosa.*

Size and Shape: Tall shrubs or trees, 20–60' tall, with **milky sap;** crowns narrow, rounded.

Trunks: Straight, 1–2' in diameter; mature bark reddish brown to dark gray-brown, with narrow ridges, deep fissures and thick scales; wood light yellow-brown, heavy, close-grained.

Branches: Short, thick, **usually with either short spines or stout, erect, slightly curved spines;** twigs slender, **rusty silky-woolly at first,** red-brown to ash-gray and hairless with age; buds

rusty-scaled, broadest toward the blunt tip, about ⅛" long.

Leaves: Alternate, deciduous, simple; blades shiny and dark green above, **rusty silky-woolly beneath,** usually widest toward the **rounded tip,** wedge-shaped at the base, 1–4" long, smooth-edged, clustered near branch tips; stalks reddish-brown, **sparsely hairy; leaves shed in winter.**

Flowers: White, ⅛" long, bisexual, with 5 unequal, **woolly calyx lobes,** 5 corolla lobes alternating with 5 petal appendages, 5 fertile stamens and 5 sterile, petal-like stamens (staminodes); **stalks slender, woolly, ⅛" long,** longer than adjacent leaf stalks; flowers in upper leaf axils in **tassel-like clusters** (cymose umbels) of about 10–20, in June–July.

Fruits: Fleshy, **shiny, black berries, ⁵⁄₁₆–⅝" long, oblong to round,** on slender stalks in clusters of 2–3; seeds single, shiny, ¼–⅜" long; mature in late September.

Habitat: Dry, often rocky woods.

Origin: Native.

Southern-buckthorns are recognized by their slender, thorny twigs, sticky, milky juice, continuous pith, smooth-edged leaves and tiny buds embedded in the bark with thorns on either side. The absence of several characteristics also helps to identify these trees. They lack stipules and stipule scars, fragrant leaves and twig-tip buds. • Smooth southern-buckthorn is uncommon throughout its range and is easily overlooked because it usually grows scattered through stands

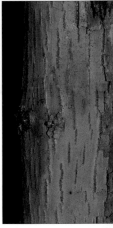

of other broad-leaved trees. This moisture-loving tree of river flats and moist slopes is less tough than its hardy cousin woolly southern-buckthorn (p. 204). Smooth southern-buckthorn is readily distinguished by its hairless (smooth) twigs, leaves and flower and fruit stalks. It is a semi-evergreen tree that usually keeps some leaves over winter; but after severe winters in northern parts of its range, very few leaves persist until spring • The ripe fruits are said to be edible raw, but are rarely used. The wood is of no commercial value. Although it is quite heavy, it breaks easily. The scientific name *Sideroxylon* was derived from the Greek *sidêros*, "iron," and *xylon*, "wood," and refers to the weight of the wood, not its strength. • An earlier scientific name, *Bumelia*, was taken from the Greek *bous*, "ox" and *melia*, "ash tree."

Also called: Gum bully, gum bumelia, southern buckthorn • *Bumelia lycioides*.

Size and Shape: Tall shrubs or small trees 30–40' tall, with **milky sap;** crowns open.

Trunks: Short, to 7" in diameter; bark reddish-brown to gray, thin, smooth or thin-scaled; wood yellowish-brown, very hard.

Branches: Stout, flexible, slightly thorny, usually with **short, stout spines;** twigs short, thick, reddish brown, **woolly at first,** smooth with age, tough, flexible; buds dark brown, <¹⁄₁₆" long.

Leaves: Alternate, deciduous, simple; blades firm, bright green and **hairless above, paler and essentially hairless beneath** (though often silky at first), prominently net-veined, elliptical to lance-shaped, usually widest toward the **pointed (rarely blunt) tip,** wedge-shaped at the base, 1½–6" **long,** smooth-edged, often clustered near branch tips; stalks reddish-brown; **leaves shed gradually in fall–winter.**

Flowers: White, ¹⁄₁₆" long, bisexual, with 5 unequal, **blunt, hairless calyx lobes,** 5 corolla lobes alternating with 5 petal appendages, 5 stamens and 5 petal-like sterile stamens (staminodes); **stalks essentially hairless, 1½–4" long,** about equal to adjacent leaf stalks; flowers in upper leaf axils in dense, **tassel-like clusters** (cymose umbels) of 10–60, in June–August.

Fruits: Fleshy, **black berries,** ⁵⁄₁₆–³⁄₄" long, egg-shaped and broad-tipped to almost round, on hairless stalks; seeds single, round, ¼–³⁄₈" long; mature in autumn.

Habitat: Moist woods, riverbanks and rocky cliffs.

Origin: Native.

The genus *Oxydendrum* is monotypic (with a single species), native to the eastern U.S. and naturalized in Illinois. • Sourwood trees are sometimes planted as ornamentals in the eastern and northwestern U.S. and west-central Europe for its narrow shape and graceful inflorescences. Young trees begin to flower when they are only 6½–10' tall. • The fragrant, bell-shaped flowers attract thousands of bees, which then produce highly prized sourwood honey. Sourwood trees have few natural enemies, but deer browse on the leaves and twigs. • Although the wood is quite heavy, it is of little commercial importance. Because of its attractive grain, it is sometimes used for making paneling and tool handles. • The slightly acidic leaves and bark are sometimes eaten as a trail nibble or salad ingredient, but sourwood was used most often as medicine. Leaves or bark were chewed or brewed into medicinal teas for treating upset stomachs, ulcers, diarrhea and bladder problems. Sourwood tea was also recommended as a cooling drink for relieving fevers.

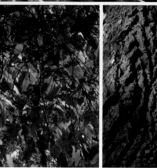

Size and Shape: Slender trees 20–60' tall, sometimes shrubby in cultivation; crowns pyramidal to oblong.

Trunks: Straight, 1–2' in diameter, short in open sites, long in forests; bark gray with a reddish tinge, thick, with broad, scaly ridges; wood reddish-brown, hard.

Branches: Slender, spreading; twigs leaf-green in shade, red in sunny sites, angular, zigzagged, hairless; buds dark red, partly embedded in bark, tiny, growing to 1" long, absent at branch tips.

Leaves: Alternate, deciduous, simple; **blades hairless**, shiny and dark green above, paler beneath, finely net-veined, 4–7" long, slender-pointed, wedge-shaped at base, smooth-edged to **finely sharp-toothed; brilliant crimson to purple-red in early autumn.**

Flowers: Creamy-white, urn-shaped, numerous, tipped with 5 small, back-curled lobes, **about** ¼" long, bisexual; sepals 5, persistent; petals 5, fused, finely white-hairy; anthers 10, linear, tipped with a long tube; stalks hairy, curved, with 2 tiny bracts (bracteoles) near the middle; **flowers along 1 side of 4–7 elongating arms in widely branched, 6–8" long clusters** (panicles), in **June–July** (long after leaves).

Fruits: Pale yellow, 5-sided, egg-shaped capsules tipped with a persistent style, ¼–½" **long,** woody, finely hairy, splitting lengthwise into 5; seeds pale brown, pointed; capsules hanging in 12" long clusters, mature in September (as leaves turn scarlet), often persist for over a year.

Habitat: Well-drained, wooded areas.

Origin: Introduced from the southeastern U.S.

The genus *Vaccinium* is a large one with over 400 species (including blueberries and cranberries), but farkleberry is the only species that reaches tree size. This hardy, slow-growing shrub can thrive under extreme condition on exposed, rocky bluffs, but it takes decades to reach tree size. Tenacious, older specimens often take on the twisted appearance of a bonsai. • Farkleberry can be grown from seeds sown on sandy-peaty soil in spring. However, its use as a horticultural subject is limited by its slow growth. • The black, mealy berries have been described as "of good flavor," "scarcely edible" and "inedible." Unlike their cousins the blueberries and huckleberries, farkleberries are not usually eaten by humans. However, they do provide food for many animals, including mammals such as foxes, raccoons and opossums, as well as a variety of game birds and songbirds. White-tail deer browse on twigs, young leaves and fruits.
• Farkleberry wood is quite heavy, but the trunks are too small to be of commercial value. The wood has been used to make small articles such as tool handles. • Farkleberry is the most astringent *Vaccinium* species. Its berries, leaves and root-bark have been used to make medicines for treating diarrhea, dysentery and other intestinal problems. Farkleberry tea was also recommended as a remedy for soothing sore mouths and throats and inflamed eyes (ophthalmia). Strong decoctions have also been used to tan leather.

Also Called: Sparkleberry, tree huckleberry • *Batodendron arboreum.*

Size and Shape: Tall shrubs or small, slender trees 10–30' tall; crowns irregular.

Trunks: Up to about 1' in diameter; mature bark attractive, flaky, peeling in large scales; wood reddish-brown, hard, tough.

Branches: Crooked, widely spreading; twigs slender, <⅛" **wide in first year**, smooth or slightly hairy; buds absent at branch tips.

Leaves: Alternate, simple, deciduous; **blades evergreen or almost evergreen, firm,** leathery, shiny and dark green above, paler, **prominently net-veined,** dull and sometimes **finely hairy beneath,** variable, usually broadest above midleaf, ⅝–2¾" long, smooth-edged or with tiny, gland-tipped teeth, blunt or abruptly sharp-pointed, tapered to the base; **red when shed during winter.**

Flowers: White, bell-shaped to broadly urn-shaped, <¼" long, tipped with 5 shallow lobes, bisexual; style projecting from flower mouth; **stamens 10, within the flower; anthers tipped with 2 slender tubules and 2 bristle-like appendages** (spurs); flowers nodding, single or in slender, **leafy-bracted, elongating clusters** (racemes) in the axils of leaves of the previous year, in May–June.

Fruits: Shiny, black berries, ³⁄₁₆–⁵⁄₁₆" across, with scanty, slightly sweet, mealy pulp; seeds small, 8–10; mature in September–October, often remain on branches through winter.

Habitat: Well-drained sites on sandstone cliffs.

Origin: Native.

207

This attractive ornamental originated in tropical parts of India and China. In its native range, the leaves and flowers are sometimes used for food • Rose-of-Sharon was introduced to European gardens around 1600. Today it remains a traditional favorite, said to bring an air of yesteryear to the garden. Usually it is grown as a bushy shrub or is trimmed into a hedge, but it can also be pruned as a small tree. • Rose-of-Sharon prefers rich, moist, well-drained soil and full sun. It responds well to shaping. Young plants are pinched to encourage bushy growth, and branch tips are pruned in early spring to encourage larger flowers. Older shrubs can develop unsightly "legs," so low, bushy perennials are often planted around the base to hide bare stems. • Rose-of-Sharon is highly valued for its late, showy flowers. Many cultivars have been developed with different flower colors, including 'Aphrodite' (rose pink with a red center), 'Blue Bird' (blue with a red center), 'Diana' (white), 'Helene' (white with a red or pink center) and 'Woodbridge' (pink with a deep pink center). • Many cultivars are sterile, but traditional varieties can be prolific seed producers. These are capable of spreading rapidly to sites outside the garden as an exotic weed.

Also Called: Althaea, shrubby althaea.

Size and Shape: Tall, bushy shrubs, rarely small trees, 10–20' tall; crowns pyramidal to rounded.

Trunks: Clumped, sometimes pruned to a single-stemmed tree, short; bark thin, fairly smooth, with brown and gray striping.

Branches: Numerous, erect; twigs hairy when young, brown with raised leaf scars; buds tiny.

Leaves: Alternate, deciduous, simple; blades dull green, ovate in outline, but **usually 3-lobed,**

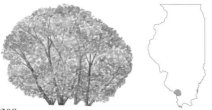

1½–4¾" long, **coarsely toothed,** hairless or with few star-shaped hairs; main veins radiating from the base; stalks ¼–½" long; shed early.

Flowers: White, pink, red, violet or blue, often with a crimson center, **broadly trumpet-shaped,** 2¼–4" across, with slender, green bracts at the base, bisexual; **petals 5, broad, 1½–2⅜" long,** spreading; sepals with dense, star-shaped hairs; **stamens fused into a tube with anthers along the sides and 5 elongated style branches projecting from the tip;** flowers single in upper leaf axils in July–September.

Fruits: Dry **capsules,** ½–¾" long, egg-shaped, pointed, hairy, **splitting lengthwise along 5 lines;** seeds dark, flattened, about ¼" long, fringed with hairs; mature in late summer–fall, persist in winter.

Habitat: Open, disturbed sites.

Origin: Introduced from eastern Asia.

These slow-growing trees are sometimes planted as ornamentals for their attractive, bell-shaped flowers and delicious, orange fruits. Female trees begin producing fruit around 10 years of age, with optimum production at 25–50 years. • In some regions, large numbers of persimmons are gathered from wild trees. Firm, underripe fruits are very bitter and astringent, but wrinkled, mushy persimmons gathered after the first frost are sweet and delicious. These gooey, sugary, vitamin-rich fruits are eaten fresh or used to make jelly, jam, pudding and nut bread. They were also popular with moonshiners for making persimmon beer, wine and brandy. • Roasted persimmon seeds can be ground as a coffee substitute and the dried leaves make a delicious, full-bodied tea rich in vitamin C. • The fruits and bark have been used to make medicinal teas for healing mouth sores, athlete's foot and thrush and for stopping bleeding and diarrhea. The tea was also taken as a tonic for patients suffering from colds and fevers. Ripe fruits were used to clean infected wounds, but this also caused "exquisite pain." • Persimmon wood has limited commercial value because of the tree's small size. However, it polishes well and has been used to make tool handles, shuttles, golf clubs, billiard cues and turned wooden wares.

Size and Shape: Tall shrubs or trees 15–65' tall; crowns broad, rounded; roots spreading.

Trunks: Short, usually straight, 5–18" in diameter (rarely larger); mature bark grayish-brown to nearly black, with **distinctive square, scaly blocks and deep furrows;** wood dark brown, very hard, strong, heavy.

Branches: Stout, spreading; twigs slender, smooth; **buds dark reddish-brown,** broad-based, with **2 overlapping scales,** absent at branch tips.

Leaves: Alternate, deciduous, simple; **blades lustrous and dark green above,** pale beneath, essentially hairless, **leathery with age, smooth-edged, 2–6" long,** slender-pointed; stalks stout, usually hairy; leaf scars with 1 elongated vein scar; leaves often shed early.

Flowers: Greenish-yellow to cream, **urn-shaped** to tubular, tipped with 4 spreading lobes; unisexual with **male and female flowers on separate trees** (a few bisexual flowers sometimes present); male flowers ⅜–½" long, with 18 anthers; female flowers ⅝–¾" long, with 1 pistil and 8 sterile stamens (usually); female flowers solitary, male flowers 1–3, in leaf axils on branchlets, in May–June (with leaves).

Fruits: juicy, **pale orange berries, often with a purplish cast,** ¾–2⅜" across, with 4 enlarged, persistent sepals at the base; **seeds 6, reddish-brown, flattened,** ½–¾" long; mature in September–November.

Habitat: Dry woods, fields, roadsides, fencerows and clearings.

Origin: Native.

This attractive, fast-growing tree has been cultivated as an ornamental since the 1800s and is widely planted in both the U.S. and Europe. Trees live about 100 years and begin to flower profusely at a young age, producing showy clusters of nodding, bell-shaped flowers each spring. The variety *vestita* is valued for its beautiful, pale pink flowers. In autumn, the unusual brownish fruits and yellow leaves add an interesting touch to parks and gardens. • Mountain silverbell grows well in full sun to light shade and thrives on rich, well-drained, acid to neutral soil. It can be propagated by seed or by layering. • Silverbell wood has little value. When a tree does reach saw-lumber size, it can be used for lumber, paneling and cabinets. • The acidic fruits are sometimes chewed for their refreshing quality and have been suggested as a possible candidate for pickling. • Mountain silverbell is a southern species that barely reaches southern Illinois and Ohio. However, it is often cultivated well north of its natural range and occasionally escapes to sheltered sites. • The name *Halesia* honors the English physiologist Stephen Hales (1677–1761). • This small genus, with 3 species in the eastern U.S. and one in China, demonstrates a link between woody plants in North America and northeastern Asia.

Also Called: Carolina silverbell, silverbell tree, silver-bell tree, snowdrop-tree, opossumwood, calico-wood • *H. monticola* (misapplied).

Size and Shape: Medium trees about 35–80' tall; crowns rounded.

Trunks: Usually clumped, straight, 4–12" in diameter; bark reddish-brown, thin, with broad, scaly ridges, shed in large plates; wood light brown, soft, fine-grained.

Branches: Stout, upcurved; twigs with dense, **star-shaped hairs** when young, smooth and dark green to grayish-brown with age; **pith chambered;** buds pinkish to dark red, hairy, pointed, about ⅛" long.

Leaves: Alternate, deciduous, **simple; blades downy with white, star-shaped hairs when young,** deep yellow-green and hairless above with age, paler and hairy beneath, papery, oblong to elliptical, 3–7" long, often broadest above the middle, finely saw-toothed; stalks hair-like, ⅜–1⅛" long; leaves yellow in autumn.

Flowers: White (rarely pinkish), **bell-shaped, ½–1⅛" across, bisexual; petals 4,** broad, fused, ½–1" long; sepals about ¼" long, fused in a cone with 4 spreading lobes; **stamens 8–16,** with **filaments fused into a tube;** flowers hang on slender, ⅜–¾" long stalks, **in small, umbrella-shaped clusters** (umbels) of 2–5 on year-old wood, in April–May.

Fruits: Dry, dark brown, **pod-like berries with 4 conspicuous, lengthwise wings,** oblong, 1–2" long, with a long, slender tip; seeds 4; fruits mature in autumn, **persist into winter.**

Habitat: Moist woods, often near streams.

Origin: Introduced from the southeastern U.S.

This attractive ornamental shrub has been cultivated since 1794 for its fragrant, bell-shaped flowers and contrasting dark green leaves. Snowbells prefer sunny to partly shady locations with moist, well-drained, lime-free, loamy soil. Although bigleaf snowbell takes time to establish, this small, graceful tree or shrub is worth waiting for. They grow well nestled among and protected by other plants and are capable of thriving under intense root competition. • Bigleaf snowbell is often propagated by layering or grafting. It often produces abundant seed, but complex dormancy

demands special treatment for successful germination. Once established, the trees are relatively pest- and disease-free. • Snowbells have unusual "superposed" buds (one above the other on the stem) that lack protective outer scales. In bigleaf snowbell, there is a definite space between the upper 2 buds, and the top bud is thumb-shaped. • **American snowbell** (*S. americanus*, also called storax and *S. americanum*), shown in dark green (species overlap) on the map, is a smaller species, rarely more than 10–13' tall. It has narrower, essentially hairless leaves and smaller flowers with ½" long corolla lobes and glandular-scurfy sepals. In Illinois, American snowbell is found only rarely, in swampy southern woods.

Also Called: Large-leaved storax, spring orange. • *S. grandifolium, S. grandifolia.*

Size and Shape: Tall shrubs or rarely small trees, 10–40' tall; crowns rounded; roots often suckering to form colonies.

Trunks: Tall, straight, 4–9½" in diameter; bark dark reddish-brown to dark gray, ⅜–½" thick, smooth.

Branches: Short, spreading; **twigs slender, scurfy, with star-shaped hairs,** yellowish, chestnut brown to gray with age, slightly zigzagged; buds pointed, ¹⁄₁₆–⅛" long, naked, in 2s and 3s above leaf scars.

Leaves: Alternate, simple, deciduous, **hairless and dark green above, paler to grayish with dense star-shaped hairs beneath** (at least when young), widest at or above midleaf, **2–8" long,** pointed, tapered to the base, smooth edged or with a few fine teeth; stalks hairy, ¼–½" long.

Flowers: White, fragrant, bell-shaped, about 1" across, bisexual; petals 5, spreading, pointed, fused at the base, finely yellow-hairy outside

(sometimes also within), vertically twisted in bud; **calyx 5-lobed, <¼" long, with gray, star-shaped hairs;** stamens 10; **flowers 5–20, in leafy-bracted, unbranched clusters** (racemes) to 5" long, at tips of short side-branches, in May.

Fruits: Dry, round, drupes with dense, short hairs, ¼–½" long; outer shell splitting irregularly in 3–4; stones 1–2, large, dark orange-brown; mature in late summer–autumn.

Habitat: Moist to wet, well-drained sites along wooded stream.

Origin: Native.

This rare tree was uncommon in 1796, when it was discovered by the French botanist Michaux, and has remained so to the present day. Its natural range appears to be shrinking, but cultivated trees still thrive well beyond the reach of wild populations, north into USDA Zone 3 in Canada. • A handsome, slow-growing, moderately long-lived tree, yellow-wood is planted as an ornamental in the eastern U.S. and Europe. Mature trees produce spectacular displays of delicate flowers in some years, but flowers are not always produced, especially in Europe. Popular cultivars include 'Rosea' or 'Perkins Pink' (with pink flowers) and 'Sweet Shade' (with relatively large, white flower clusters). The fall leaves are also very attractive, contrasting nicely with the silvery bark. The smooth, thin bark is easily marked and cut, so like beeches, these trees are sometimes defaced by unthinking visitors who carve initials and signs in the bark. • The name *Cladrastis* means "brittle branch." Yellow-wood trees are susceptible to storm damage and subsequent infections by fungus and other disease organisms. Broken limbs create problems in ornamental trees, but weak branches can be eliminated to some extent with corrective pruning when trees are young. • The durable wood takes a beautiful finish and is a favorite material for making gunstocks. The bright yellow wood yields a yellow dye.

Also Called: Kentucky yellow-wood • *C. lutea.*

Size and Shape: Trees 30–50' tall; crowns vase-like in forests, wide-spreading in open sites, with rounded tops.

Trunks: Straight, to 2' in diameter; **bark silvery gray, smooth,** thin, sometimes with cracks showing the lighter-colored inner bark; wood bright yellow when first cut, hard, medium weight.

Branches: Stout, spreading; **twigs slender, hairless, brittle,** zigzagged; **buds tiny, without protective scales,** hidden under leaf bases and later ringed by leaf scars.

Leaves: Alternate, deciduous, 8–12" long, **pinnately divided into 5–11 alternate leaflets;** leaflets yellowish-green, nearly hairless, broadly elliptical to ovate, 2–5" long and about half as wide, blunt-pointed; stalks hollow at the base; leaves clear, bright yellow to warm gold-orange in autumn.

Flowers: White, pea-like, fragrant, about 1" long, bisexual; calyx short, narrowly bell-shaped, 5-toothed; petals 5 (a round banner, 2 oblong wings and 2 forming a keel); **stamens 10, separate;** pistil hairy; stalks slender, hairy, ½–¾" long; **flowers numerous, in loose, hanging, 8–14" long, branched clusters** (panicles) at branch tips, in May.

Fruits: Dry, thin, hairless, **flattened pods (legumes), 3–4" long,** $5/16$–½" wide, short-stalked, papery; seeds brown, 4–6, slightly flattened; mature in August–September and persist into winter.

Habitat: Rich, well-drained sites on wooded slopes.

Origin: Native.

Black locust was introduced to Europe from North America in the early 1600s and is now naturalized across the continent. • Like most members of the pea family, this tree has root nodules containing nitrogen-fixing bacteria. Black locust has been used to reforest waste areas (e.g., mine spoils) where few other trees could survive. Its root suckers produce dense colonies that help prevent erosion. The strong root networks have even been used to support dikes. • Cattle and humans have been poisoned by the toxic inner bark and leaves. Some tribes used the poisonous wood in arrows. Although the seeds are toxic to humans, many animals eat them with impunity. • The decay-resistant wood of black locust was once used for railway ties, fence posts, stakes and pilings and was exported to England for shipbuilding. Although it can be used as firewood, black locust wood tends to flare and throw sparks. • **Clammy locust (*R. viscosa*)**, shown in dark green (species overlap) on the map, is an ornamental from the southern U.S. that occasionally escapes from cultivation in Illinois. Unlike black locust, it has pink, odorless flowers and sticky twigs, leaf stalks and pods.

Also Called: False acacia, common locust, white locust, yellow locust.

Size and Shape: Trees 30–50' tall; crowns open, irregular; roots wide-creeping, suckering.

Trunks: Irregular, 12–24" in diameter; mature bark dark brown, deeply furrowed, scaly; **inner bark yellow;** wood yellowish-green, hard, heavy.

Branches: Brittle, short; **twigs spiny,** reddish-brown, slender, **zigzagged; spines paired at each bud or leaf base/scar,** about ⅜" long, largest on vigorous shoots; buds tiny, clustered (usually 3–4), embedded under leaf stalk bases.

Leaves: Alternate, deciduous, 8–14" long; compound, **pinnately divided into 7–21 leaflets (with a terminal leaflet)** in pairs along a 8–12" long stalk; leaflets dull green, oval, ¾–2" long; leaf scars 3-cornered, with 3 vein scars.

Flowers: White with a yellow blotch on the upper petals, fragrant, pea-like, ½–1" long, bisexual; **flowers hang in loose, showy, 4–6"** long clusters near shoot tips, in May–June (about 1 month after leaves expand).

Fruits: Reddish-brown to black, flattened, thin-walled, hairless pods (legumes), **2¾–4" long,** clustered; **seeds dark, pea-like, hard,** about ⅛" long, 4–8 per pod; pods persist through winter.

Habitat: Thickets and woodlands, often in disturbed areas.

Origin: Native in extreme southeastern Illinois; introduced and commonly naturalized elsewhere.

With its showy, pink flowers in early spring, followed by a broad, shady canopy in summer, redbud is a lovely ornamental that is generally hardy throughout Illinois. These small, well-formed trees are especially attractive when planted beside evergreens. Eastern redbud grows rapidly under good conditions and begins to flower at about 5 years of age. Once mature, it blooms prior to leafing almost every year, and in cool weather, the spring flower display can continue for 3 weeks. • Eastern redbud reaches its northern limit in Illinois and southern Michigan, though its natural range is difficult to determine because this beautiful tree has been so widely planted and frequently escapes cultivation. • On hot summer days, the broad leaves may curl and almost fold in half. This helps to reduce water loss and can also lower leaf temperature by reducing the surface exposed to sunlight. • Boiled in water, eastern redbud twigs produce a yellow dye. • The generic name *Cercis* comes from the Greek *kerkis*, "shuttlecock," which was thought to describe the shape of the pods. • Until recently, *Cercis* was considered a member of the pea family (Fabaceae or Leguminosae). Some taxonomists now place it in the cassia family (Caesalpiniaceae).

Also Called: Judas-tree, redbud.

Size and Shape: Small trees 12–25' tall; crowns low, spreading, flat or rounded.

Trunks: Short, straight, 4–12" in diameter; young bark grayish, smooth; mature bark scaly, reddish-brown; wood dark brown, hard, weak.

Branches: Stout, horizontal to ascending; twigs grayish to reddish-brown, slender, zigzagged, with 3 lengthwise ridges from each leaf scar; leaf buds dark reddish-brown, about ⅛" long, 5–6-scaled, sometimes with a tiny secondary bud at the base; **flower buds larger, rounded, clustered, stalked.**

Leaves: Alternate, simple, deciduous; **blades glossy and dark green above,** paler beneath, **broadly heart-shaped,** thin, 2¾–4¾" long, with **5–9 prominent veins radiating from the stalk; stalks swollen near the blade;** leaves warm yellow in autumn.

Flowers: Deep to pale pink, pea-like, showy, **about ⅜" long,** bisexual; anthers 10, with filaments at the middle, splitting lengthwise; flowers on ⅜" long stalks in **abundant, 4–8-flowered, tassel-like clusters along branches** (not on new twigs) and **sometimes on trunks,** in April–May (before leaves expand).

Fruits: Reddish-brown, flat, thin pods (legumes), tapered at both ends, 2–4" long, hanging in small clusters; seeds 10–12 per pod, shiny, brown, flattened, about ¼" across; pods mature in autumn and persist into winter.

Habitat: Moist, fertile sites in forests and along streams.

Origin: Native.

Although honey-locust grows wild in southern regions, it has also been widely planted and occasionally escapes cultivation, so its native range is unclear. • Honey-locust pods have been used to make beer. They contain a sweetish substance that tastes like a mixture of castor oil and honey, hence the "honey" in the common name. • The hard, heavy wood is easily polished but fairly brittle. It has been used for fence posts, furniture and occasionally lumber. The long, hard thorns were sometimes made into nails and pins. • The sweet flowers attract many bees. White-tailed deer, rabbits, squirrels and quail eat the seeds and the sweet pulp of the pods. Cattle also eat the seeds, pods and tender young plants. • Gardeners often prune young trees to form protective thorny hedges. Honey-locust is also considered an excellent lawn tree because the delicate foliage casts light shade, though it tends to send persistent suckers up from roots. Cuttings from male-flowered branches grow into trees with pollen flowers only, so they do not produce fruit. • Cultivars of a thornless form, **thornless honey-locust (*G. triacanthos* f. *inermis*)**, boast straight trunks and spreading canopies and are common in plantings along city streets.

Also Called: Thorny-locust, sweet-locust, tree-thorned acacia.

Size and Shape: Trees 50–80' tall; crowns broad, open; roots deep, spreading.

Trunks: Usually short, 24–40" in diameter, with **long (up to 12"), branched thorns;** young bark brownish, smooth, with horizontal pores (lenticels); mature bark dark gray, furrowed, scaly-ridged; wood reddish-brown, hard, heavy, resistant to decay.

Branches: With reddish, smooth, forked thorns; twigs of 2 types: long, greenish- to reddish-brown, **zigzagged shoots and very short, leaf- and flower-bearing shoots; buds small, 3 or more one above the other,** absent at twig tips.

Leaves: Alternate, deciduous, **6–12" long;** compound, **once or twice pinnately divided,** with 18–30 leaflets, but **no tip leaflet;** twice-compound leaves have 4–7 pairs of branches on the main stalk (rachis); leaflets dark green above, paler beneath, oblong to lance-shaped, ¾–2" long; leaves yellow in autumn.

Flowers: Greenish-white, about ¼" across; petals 5; unisexual (occasionally some bisexual) with male and female flowers on the same tree; male flowers in dense, 2¾–3½" long clusters (racemes); female flowers few, in loose, 2¾–3½" long clusters; flowers in May–June.

Fruits: Brownish, **leathery, flattened, spirally twisted pods (legumes),** 6–18" long; seeds bean-like, hard, about ¾" apart in pods, embedded in sweet pulp; pods mature by autumn, drop over winter without opening.

Habitat: Woods in moist, rich lowlands.

Origin: Native.

In some parts of the southern U.S., this handsome tree forms forests on rich floodplains that are subject to frequent flooding. • Water-locust resembles honey-locust (p. 215), and these 2 species can be difficult to distinguish without fruits. Water-locust is a smaller tree with relatively short, slender (though extremely numerous) thorns. It is most easily identified by its miniature seedpods (rarely over 4" long), single seed and lack of pulpy lining found in honey-locust pods. Water-locust also differs in its choice of habitat, preferring swamps and other frequently flooded sites, to the rich forests where honey-locust usually grows. • Although water-locust wood is very durable and heavy, it has almost no commercial value. It has occasionally been used for cabinet-making and interior finishing, but primarily provides fence posts and fuel. • Water-locusts could be used to create a formidable hedge. This thorny tree is a valuable species for planting in wet situations. It is sometimes used for stabilizing banks and marshes.

Size and Shape: Trees 50–65' tall; crowns broad, open, often flat-topped; roots deep, spreading.

Trunks: Usually **short**, 1–2' wide, **with long thorns;** young bark smooth, with **conspicuous pores** (lenticels); mature bark dark gray to almost black, thin, vertically ridged; wood reddish-brown, hard, heavy, strong, resists decay.

Branches: Stout, crooked, thorny, rough with corky pores (lenticels); **thorns shiny, dark red, smooth, mostly unbranched,** to 4" long; twigs of 2 types: long, shiny, zigzagged, with a few thorns, and short leaf- and flower-bearing side-shoots; buds small, 3 or more one above the other.

Leaves: Alternate, deciduous, **6–12" long,** compound, **once or twice pinnately divided,** with 6–24 branches or leaflets (no tip leaflet); **leaflets thick, shiny, dark green,** ½–1" long, rounded or notched at the tip, smooth-edged or obscurely blunt-toothed; leaves usually paired on knobby side-branches, yellow in autumn.

Flowers: Greenish-white, about ¼" across; unisexual (or some bisexual) with male and female flowers on same tree; male flowers in dense, 4–6" long clusters (racemes); female flowers few, in loose, 2–4" long clusters (racemes); flowers in May–June (after leaves).

Fruits: Dry, shiny brown, flattened pods (legumes), **hairless, elliptical to ovate, 1–3½" long;** seeds 1–2 (rarely 3), **shiny, orange-brown,** bean-like, about ½" across; pods long-stalked, mature in September–December, drop over winter without opening.

Habitat: Frequently flooded swamps.

Origin: Native.

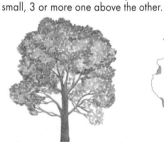

At up to a yard in length, the leaves of Kentucky coffee-tree are by far the largest of any native tree in the state. It is easy to mistake leaf branches or leaflets for individual leaves. • Kentucky coffee-tree is often used in landscaping well beyond its natural range because it transplants easily and can tolerate urban conditions, though it prefers fertile, well-drained soil. • Wild animals rarely eat the bitter seeds, and cattle can become sick from drinking water contaminated with the leaves or fruits. • **Caution:** The raw seeds are **poisonous,** but roasting may destroy the toxins. Some tribes reportedly ate the roasted seeds like nuts, and early settlers are said to have used ground roasted seeds as a coffee substitute. Hence the common names coffeenut and coffee-tree. Others report that such names refer more to the coffee-like appearance of the "beans" than to historical uses. Given the bitterness and potential toxicity of these seeds, their use as a food is not recommended. • Kentucky coffee-tree is too uncommon to have commercial value, but the moderately heavy, decay-resistant wood has been used in cabinets, fence posts, railroad ties and general construction.

Also Called: Coffeenut.

Size and Shape: Trees 50–80' tall; crowns narrow.

Trunks: Straight, 16–36" in diameter; mature bark dark gray, hard, with thin ridges of outcurled scale edges; wood reddish-brown, hard.

Branches: Stout, widely spaced; **twigs coarse, knobbly,** grayish-brown, with orange pores (lenticels); **buds dark brown,** silky-hairy, ¼–⅜" long, **in groups of 2–3 above leaf scars,** absent at twig tips.

Leaves: Alternate, early-deciduous; compound, **twice pinnately divided, with 3–7 pairs of branches (no terminal branches or tip leaflets) on a sturdy, 12–36" long central stalk** (rachis) that is easily mistaken for a slender twig; leaflets bluish-green, ovate, 1½–2⅜" long, pointed, short-stalked, seldom opposite, usually about 70; leaf scars large, heart-shaped.

Flowers: Greenish-white, soft-hairy, ½–¾" across, 5-petaled; unisexual, usually with male and female flowers on separate trees; anthers 10, with filaments at the middle, splitting lengthwise; flowers in open, **many-branched, 2⅜–4" (male) and 8–12" (female) long clusters** (panicles), in May–June (as or after leaves expand).

Fruits: Dark reddish-brown pods (legumes), **leathery, becoming woody, flattened but thick, 4–10" long,** hanging on stout stalks; seeds 4–7, dark brown, hard, slightly flattened, ⅜–¾" across, embedded in sticky pulp; pods mature in autumn, **persist through winter.**

Habitat: Moist woods with deep, rich soil, often on floodplains.

Origin: Native.

This popular, fast-growing ornamental is widely planted in North America and Europe. The club-like branches and large leaves add a dramatic touch—likened to the lush look of a palm, but without the need for a winter in Florida. • Many birds feed on the black "berries," and despite the array of formidable prickles, whitetail deer browse on the twigs. • An introduced aralia, **Japanese angelica-tree (*A. elata*, also called Japanese aralia**), shown in pink on the map, is sometimes misidentified as Hercules-club. Although both species are cultivated, *A. elata* is hardier and grows wild farther north. Japanese angelica-tree is distinguished by its stalkless (vs. short-stalked), regularly toothed (vs. remotely toothed) leaflets, its spreading leaf veins (which run to the tooth tips, rather than joining below the leaf edge) and its very broad (vs. elongated) flower clusters. Tender shoots and young leaves of Japanese angelica-tree are eaten as a springtime vegetable in East Asia. In Japan, this tasty treat, battered and fried tempura-style, is considered as delicacy. • **Caution:** The fruits of Hercules-club are said to be **poisonous**. • The root, bark and berries of Hercules-club have been used for medicine only occasionally, but in Asia, Japanese angelica-tree is considered a valuable medicinal plant as a stimulating tonic for relieving physical and mental fatigue and depression.

Also Called: Devil's-walkingstick.

Size and Shape: Prickly trees or tall shrubs, 10–30' tall; crowns flat-topped; roots shallow, often sending up shoots to form thickets.

Trunks: Long, 4–5" (rarely 12") in diameter; inner bark yellow; bark straw-colored to dark brown, ridged, armed with orange prickles; wood yellow to brown, soft, light, fine-grained.

Branches: Prickly, stout, club-like, few, upright to spreading; **twigs prickly, massive** with a large pith; buds cone-shaped at twig tips, smaller and flat-lying below, few-scaled.

Leaves: Alternate, deciduous, crowded near twig tips, **20–60" long,** 20–40" wide, **twice pinnately divided** into numerous paired branches and leaflets on a prickly main stalk; leaflets dark green, hairless, **sharply toothed, essentially stalkless,** ovate, about 1–4" long, often prickly beneath; **stalks with broad, sheathing bases;** leaf scars numerous, conspicuous, **narrowly crescent-shaped** with a **row of about 20 dots** (vein scars), almost encircling twigs; leaves yellow in autumn.

Flowers: Tiny, creamy white, bisexual; petals 5; stamens 5; **flowers in small, round groups (umbels) within larger, many branched clusters** (panicles) at branch tips, in July–August.

Fruits: Fleshy, dark purple to black, egg-shaped, 5-ribbed, **berry-like drupes,** about ¼" long; seed solitary, enclosed in a flattened nutlet; drupes mature in early fall.

Habitat: Prefers rich, moist, wooded slopes.

Origin: Native.

Key to Genera in the Cashew Family (Anacardiaceae)

1a   Leaves with a single blade (simple) . . . . ***Cotinus***, smoketree (p. 223)

1b   Leaves pinnately divided into 7–31 leaflets (compound) **2**

2a   Leaflets smooth-edged, containing allergenic oils that cause severe skin reactions; fruits smooth, whitish to yellowish berries in loose aclusters . . . .
. . . . ***Toxicodendron,*** poison sumac (p. 222)

2b   Leaflets toothed, not highly allergenic; fruits fuzzy, red berries in dense, pyramidal clusters
. . . . ***Rhus,*** sumac (see below)

Key to the Sumacs (Genus *Rhus*)

1a   Main axis of the leaf (rachis) winged; twigs hairless
. . . . ***R. copallina,*** winged sumac (p. 221)

1b   Main axis of the leaf not winged; twigs velvety or hairless **2**

2a   Leaf stalks hairy; twigs velvety-hairy . . . . ***R. typhina,*** staghorn sumac (p. 220)

2b   Leaf stalks and twigs hairless . . . . ***R. glabra,*** smooth sumac (p. 220)

Cotinus coggygria, European smoketree

With its striking form, showy fruit clusters and brilliant autumn foliage, staghorn sumac is sometimes planted as an ornamental. However, its spreading, suckering roots can be troublesome. • The wood is sometimes used for decorative finishing and novelty items. • The tannin-rich fruit, bark and leaves were used to tan hides. The leaves and fruits were also boiled to make black ink, and the dried leaves were an ingredient in smoking mixtures. The milky sap has been used as a treatment for warts. • The juicy fruits can be eaten as a trail nibble or gathered in larger quantities to make jelly. They should not be consumed in large quantities, because they contain tannic acid. • The fuzzy, widely spreading branches look like velvet-covered deer antlers, hence the name "staghorn." • Staghorn sumac can be confused with **smooth sumac (*R. glabra*)** shown in pink/dark green (species overlap) on the map, but smooth sumac has hairless leaves and twigs. These 2 species often cross-pollinate to produce **pulvinate sumac (*R.* x *pulvinata*).** • Oldtimers often pronounce sumac "shoe-mack."

Photo, bottom right: *R. glabra*

Also Called: Velvet sumac, sumac vinegar-tree • *R. hirta.*

Size and Shape: Shrubs or small trees up to 35' tall; crowns flat-topped; roots shallow, spreading, usually **forming thickets** from suckers.

Trunks: Short, forked, 2–4" in diameter; young bark dark yellowish-brown, thin, with prominent pores (lenticels); mature bark scaly; wood orange-green, soft, brittle.

Branches: Few, wide-spreading; **twigs dark velvety-hairy, stout,** exuding **milky juice** when broken; **pith yellowish-brown, large;** buds densely hairy, without scales, about ¼" across, absent at branch tips.

Leaves: Alternate, deciduous; compound, **pinnately divided into 11–31 leaflets; central stalks reddish, hairy,** 8–20" long; leaflets dark green above, paler and finely hairy beneath, lance-shaped, 2–5" long, slender-pointed, sharp-toothed, stalkless; leaf scars almost encircle buds; leaves scarlet, orange or purplish in autumn.

Flowers: Yellowish-green, tiny; usually unisexual with male and female flowers on separate trees; petals 5; **stamens 5;** flowers in **dense, erect, 5–10" long, cone-shaped clusters** (panicles) at branch tips, in June–July (after leaves expand).

Fruits: Reddish, fuzzy drupes ⅛–¼" long, **in dense, erect, cone-shaped clusters** at branch tips; seeds 1 per fruit, in small stones; fruits mature in July–August, **persist through winter.**

Habitat: Open woodlands and disturbed areas, often on dry, coarse-grained soil.

Origin: Native.

This attractive, hardy shrub, with its showy flowers and fruits, glossy summer foliage and scarlet autumn leaves, is a lovely but uncommon ornamental shrub. • This fast-growing, short-lived tree thrives on sunny sites and can also tolerate heavy, alkaline soils. In the wild, it grows vigorously after fires, often spreading rapidly to form thickets from suckers. • The tart, red fruits can be nibbled as a trail snack or gathered to make a lemonade-like drink. • Winged sumac can attract many different animals. Grouse, quail, wild turkeys, pheasants and numerous songbirds eat the fruit; deer and rabbits browse on the twigs and eat the bark. • The sour red "berries" were sometimes chewed to prevent bedwetting and to heal mouth sores. The root tea is astringent and was also used to treat dysentery. • Winged sumac was an important source of copal resin. This transparent, slightly brownish substance was dissolved in turpentine and other solvents, producing a clear, highly valued varnish known as "copal varnish." The specific epithet *copallina* means "with copal gum." • Winged sumac is easily identified by its winged leaf stalks and watery (rather than milky) sap. Its common name refers to the distinctive winged main axis of the leaves.

Also Called: Shining sumac, dwarf sumac, black sumac, upland sumac, smooth sumac • *R. copallinum.*

Size and Shape: Small trees or shrubs, to 25' tall; crowns open, rounded; roots shallow, suckering.

Trunks: Short, up to 4" in diameter; bark light brown or gray, scaly; wood light brown, soft.

Branches: Stout, often ridged and warty with age; twigs stout, greenish-brown to purplish-gray, **finely reddish-hairy,** soon hairless; **pith yellowish-brown, large;** buds densely hairy, without scales, round, about ⅛" across, absent at branch tips.

Leaves: Alternate, **deciduous,** 6–16" long; compound, **pinnately divided into 7–21 leaflets; leaflets glossy, dark green and hairless above,** paler, dull and finely hairy beneath, 1⅛–4" long, **stalkless, usually smooth-edged; central stalks with a wing,** narrowed at each leaflet; leaf scars horseshoe-shaped around buds; leaves red to dark reddish-purple in autumn.

Flowers: Greenish-yellow, ⅛" wide, 5-parted; unisexual with male and female flowers on separate plants; flowers in **erect, cone-shaped clusters (panicles) up to 6" long** at branch tips, in July–September (after leaves expand).

Fruits: Dark red, berry-like drupes covered in sticky, red, glandular hairs, about ⅛" long; **in dense, erect to nodding, cone-shaped clusters;** seeds single, in small stones; fruits mature in late August–September, persist into winter.

Habitat: Open, well-drained sites in woods and fields.

Origin: Native.

221

It is very important to recognize poison-sumac, because most people develop severe skin reactions from contact with it. Those who have gathered sprays of the beautiful, white fruits and dark, glossy leaves for decorations have paid dearly for their mistake. **Caution:** If you touch this plant, wash your hands thoroughly with soap and warm water to remove the allergenic oil. Never use oil-based salves or liniments on your skin, because they can dissolve and spread the toxin. • The allergenic oil in all parts of this shrubby tree can be picked up directly from the plant or indirectly from contaminated pets, clothing or other items. Smoke from burning plants also carries the oil and can cause severe reactions of skin, eyes and mucous membranes in the nose, mouth and throat. • Game birds and many songbirds eat the "berries" with impunity and disperse the seeds. • Poison-sumac is distinguished from true sumacs (pp. 220–21), mountain-ashes (pp. 190–91) and elderberries (p. 279) by its smooth-edged (not toothed) leaves. Ash trees (pp. 262–66) and **common prickly-ash (*Zanthoxylum americanum*,** also spelled *xanthoxylum*) shrubs may have toothless leaves, but ash leaves are opposite (not alternate), and common prickly-ash has thorny branches. • Poison-sumac's persistent fruits facilitate year-round identification.

Also Called: Swamp-sumac, poison-dogwood, poison-elderberry, poison-elder, poison-oak • *Rhus vernix.*

Size and Shape: Tall shrubs or small trees 10–25' tall; crowns small, rounded.

Trunks: Slender, often branched from bases, 2⅜–3" in diameter; bark gray, smooth, thin; wood moderately soft, weak.

Branches: Moderately stout, spreading; twigs slender, drooping, dark green and hairy to mottled brownish-yellow and hairless, dotted with pores (lenticels); damaged twigs exude milky sap; buds purplish-brown, hairy, several-scaled, conical, ⅜–¾" long at branch tips, smaller below.

Leaves: Alternate, deciduous; compound, pinnately divided into 7–13 leaflets, often crowded in umbrella-like clusters at branch tips; central stalks 6–12" long, not winged; leaflets lustrous, dark green, whitened beneath, essentially hairless, oblong to elliptical or ovate, 2–4" long, short-stalked, pointed, smooth-edged (sometimes wavy); leaf scars shield-shaped.

Flowers: Yellowish-green, tiny; unisexual with male and female flowers on separate plants; petals 5; stamens 5; flowers in elongated, nodding, branched clusters (raceme-like panicles) up to 8" long, from leaf axils, in May–July (after leaves expand).

Fruits: Glossy, whitish, pearl-like drupes, dry, ⅛–¼" across, in loose, arching to hanging clusters; seeds single, within stones; drupes mature in August–September, persist through winter.

Habitat: Swampy ground around bogs and marshes.

Origin: Native.

European smoketree is often planted as an ornamental for its unusual feathery flower and fruit clusters and its beautiful fall foliage. Some popular cultivars have bright purple leaves throughout the growing season. • The name "smoketree" refers to the tree's airy plumes of tiny flowers and feathery fruit clusters. They get their hazy appearance from an abundance of long, fluffy, green to pinkish hairs on the flower and fruit stalks. • European smoketree was introduced to America in the mid-1600s. The unusual looking, relatively pest-free shrubs and small trees are recommended for specimen planting, as shrubby borders and as backdrops for other plants. The hardy, drought-tolerant shrubs grow best in full sun. Smoketrees can thrive under a wide range of conditions, including well-drained to wet, acidic to alkaline substrates with sandy, loamy or clay-rich soils. • Although European smoketree occasionally escapes cultivation to grow wild, it is not considered a threat to native vegetation. • The roots and branches have been used to make an orange-yellow dye, but the color doesn't persist. • The genus *Cotinus* contains only 2 species. **American smoketree (*C. obovatus*),** a native of the southern U. S., has large (4") broad leaves that are rounded and hairy (at least when young). Although its range extends north to Kentucky and Missouri, American smoketree has not yet been discovered growing wild in Illinois.

Also called: Common smoke-tree, Asian smokebush, cloud tree, mist tree, Jupiter's beard • *Rhus cotinus*.

Size and Shape: Long shrubs10–15' tall, with gummy, strong-smelling sap; crowns broad, rounded, bushy, to 12' across.

Trunks: Clumped, up to 8" in diameter; bark thin, gray to black; **wood yellow, fragrant** with strong-smelling, juicy sap.

Branches: Spreading, drooping at tips with age; twigs exude fragrant sap when broken; buds reddish-brown, 1/16" long, with several overlapping scales.

Leaves: Alternate, deciduous, simple, with an **orange-peel-like fragrance; blades light green** (purple in some cultivars), broadly elliptical, 1½–3¾" long, tapered to a **wedge-shaped base, hairless, smooth-edged;** stalks slender, >1" long; leaf scars broadly triangular with 3 dots (vein scars); **leaves yellow to red or purple in autumn,** highly variable.

Flowers: Cream-colored to pink; unisexual (occasionally bisexual) with **male and female** flowers on separate trees; mostly **sterile,** bearing numerous, **conspicuous, fluffy hairs that turn several shades of grayish-pink;** petals 5; flowers in airy, elongating, 6–8" long clusters (panicles), in May–June.

Fruits: Brown, dry, oval but irregularly shaped drupes about 1/8" long, on slender, fuzzy stalks with several reddish, hair-like branches at the base; seeds single; fruits in large, fluffy clusters, mature in August.

Habitat: Disturbed areas.

Origin: Introduced from Eurasia, where it ranges from southern Europe to the Himalayas.

This eastern holly approaches the western limits of its range in Illinois. Although winterberry rarely reaches tree size, it is often planted as an ornamental for its thick, green foliage and conspicuous, bright red berries. The attractive berries on winter branches are sometimes used in Christmas decorations.
• **Caution:** Winterberries are **toxic** and can cause nausea, vomiting and diarrhea. The berries, mixed with cedar-apples (the fleshy cones of eastern redcedar, p. 77) were sometimes taken to expel intestinal worms.

• Common winterberry leaves can be roasted until brown and then steeped in boiling water to make a pleasant-tasting hot drink. This was used as a substitute for black Oriental tea and was also said to act as a general tonic and to stimulate urination and sweating. Bark tea was used to treat fevers, liver problems and a variety of skin problems ranging from pimples to incipient gangrene.

Also Called: Michigan holly, black-alder, striped-alder, white-alder, false-alder, fever-bush.

Size and Shape: Tall shrubs or slender trees 10–15' tall; crowns rounded to oval; roots shallow.

Trunks: Short, up to 3" in diameter; mature bark thin, olive green to mottled bluish-gray, peeling in small pieces.

Branches: Stout, numerous; twigs slender, olive brown to gray, finely ridged, with wart-like pores (lenticels); buds about ⅛" long, round.

Leaves: Alternate, **deciduous**, simple; **blades thin to leathery,** dull dark olive green above with sunken veins, paler beneath with raised veins, **usually widest above midleaf,** 1⅛–4" long, pointed, **wedge-shaped at the base,** edged with **fine, incurved teeth tipped in tiny bristles that often point upward** (perpendicular to leaf surface); stalks purplish, hairy, grooved; leaf scars small, with 1 large vein scar; **leaves turn black with frost** and drop.

Flowers: Yellowish- to greenish-white, tiny; unisexual (rarely bisexual) with male and female flowers on separate trees; petals 4–8, **smooth-edged, fused at the base;** sepals 4–8, **fringed;** flowers 1–3 (female) or 2–10 (male) on short stalks (shorter than adjacent leaf stalks), in May–July (before leaves expand fully).

Fruits: Bright red to orange or rarely yellow, **berry-like drupes** with **smooth** (not grooved) **nutlets,** about ¼" thick, in lower leaf axils; seeds 3–5 per fruit; drupes mature in September–October, persist into winter.

Habitat: Swamps, ditches, damp shores, wet woods and bluffs.

Origin: Native.

Deciduous holly is a relatively fast-growing, short-lived species. It is too small to be of commercial value but is sometimes planted as an ornamental for its showy, red fruits. It is especially attractive in autumn, when the yellow leaves contrast with the scarlet "berries," and in winter, when the striking grayish bark and abundant fruits brighten a colorless landscape. These trees are usually trouble free and can grow well in poorly drained sites and rich garden soil. Several good cultivars have been developed, mainly for their ornamental fruit. These include 'Reed,' 'Sundance,' 'Warren's Red,' 'Council Fire' (scarlet fruits) and 'Byers Golden' (yellow fruits). The form *aurantiaca* has orange berries. • Branches with scarlet berries are sometimes gathered for use in Christmas decorations. • The sharp spur-branches provide protective cover and the persistent berries provide food for many songbirds and for game birds such as turkeys and quail. These bitter "berries" are not a favorite food, but when other fruits are limited, birds will flock to deciduous holly trees and strip them of their fruit. Whitetail deer and cattle often browse tender young shoots and leaves, sometimes leaving isolated shrubs contorted and flat-topped.

Also called: Swamp holly, possum-haw.

Size and Shape: Tall shrubs or trees up to 30–40' tall, with **milky sap;** crowns spreading, often dense.

Trunks: Short, single or clumped, 8–12" in diameter; bark light grayish brown, with small, warty pores (lenticels); wood yellowish-white, hard, heavy.

Branches: Moderately stout; twigs numerous, hairless, of **2 types: slender, silvery gray main branches, and stubby side-branches (spurs); buds light gray, ¹⁄₁₆" long,** with slender-pointed scales.

Leaves: Alternate, **deciduous,** simple, often clustered near twig tips; **blades not leathery,** hairless with impressed veins above, paler and slightly hairy beneath, 1¼–2¾" long, usually **widest above midleaf, rounded or notched at the tip, wedge-shaped at the base; teeth few, shallow, rounded;** stalks hairy, grooved; leaves yellow in autumn.

Flowers: Pale yellowish-green to whitish, about ¼" across; unisexual with male and female flowers on separate plants; sepals 4–5; petals 4–5; **stalks slender, without bracts;** flowers in small, tassel-like clusters (fascicles) of 6–11 on stubby side-branches, in April–May (with leaves).

Fruits: Orange to scarlet (rarely yellow), **berry-like drupes,** about ¼" across; seeds 4, each in an **irregularly grooved, ³⁄₁₆" long nutlet** shaped like an orange section; drupes **on ¹⁄₁₆–⁵⁄₁₆" stalks** in clusters of 2–5, mature in October, persistent.

Habitat: Swamps, moist, wooded slopes and bluffs.

Origin: Native.

These attractive, slow-growing, long-lived shrubs and trees are often planted as ornamentals. Hundreds of cultivars have been developed, and hardy selections can survive as far north as southernmost Canada. • Holly leaves remain green through the winter and are finally pushed off by new growth the following spring. The shiny, evergreen leaves and bright scarlet berries are widely used for Christmas decorations. Wild trees are often rare near cities because of Christmas demand. • After a hard freeze, the abundant fruits are a preferred food of many birds. • Although this is our largest native holly, it is still too small to produce wood of commercial value. The hard, fine-grained wood has been used for turning and for making small articles such as print blocks and novelty items. • American holly is the state tree of Delaware. • Historically, holly bark and roots were used in tonics and medicinal teas for treating chest problems, bloating and constipation. • **Caution:** These beautiful berries are mildly **poisonous** and could be dangerous to small children. Chewing only 10 berries can cause severe vomiting and diarrhea in an adult.

Size and Shape: Tall, bushy shrubs or small trees 40–50' tall, usually smaller; crowns narrow, pyramid-shaped, densely symmetrical in full sun.

Trunks: Straight, short, 1–3' in diameter, single or clumped; **bark light gray, rough with warty bumps,** up to ½" thick; wood nearly white, brown with age and exposure to air, tough, hard, fine-grained.

Branches: Short, slender; twigs green, with fine, rusty hairs, hairless with age; buds ⅛–⁵⁄₁₆" long, with narrow, overlapping, fringed scales, present at branch tips.

Leaves: Alternate, **evergreen,** simple; **blades dull yellowish-green** above, paler beneath, hairless, **stiff, leathery,** 1½–4" long, **with a stout spine tip** and 2 to several prominent, **spine-tipped teeth** per side (sometimes smooth edged on upper branches); leaves persist for 3 years.

Flowers: **Greenish-white to yellowish-green, pea-sized,** about ³⁄₁₆" across; unisexual with **male and female flowers on separate plants;** sepals and petals usually 4; stalks 2-bracted; **male flowers 3–12, in ½–1" long, tassel-like clusters** (short cymes) in leaf axils; **female flowers single** (sometime 2–3), in leaf axils; flowers in May–June (with new leaves).

Fruits: **Bright red to orange (rarely yellow) berry-like drupes,** ¼–½" across, round or slightly oblong; seeds 3 (rarely 3–8), each in a **grooved nutlet;** drupes mature in November, persist through winter.

Habitat: Rocky, wooded slopes.

Origin: Native.

Many sources report the "berries" of this tree were used by Native peoples for food, but details about the type of food and its preparation are lacking. Generally, this fruit is considered too sour for modern tastes. Descriptions range from spicy to extremely bitter. • **Caution:** The fruits are sometimes classified as **poisonous**. Some speculate that if the fruit was indeed used by Native peoples, it was probably for some evil purpose. • The buds and wood were used in medicinal teas to stimulate sweating and thus break fevers, hence the common name "feverbush." A branch tea, boiled to the consistency of syrup, was taken as a tonic. The stronger fruit was used to initiate vomiting and diarrhea and to expel intestinal worms. • Birds apparently eat the "berries" only when preferred foods are unavailable. They may be wise to stay away. The bark was used to make bird-lime, a sticky substance for ensnaring small birds. • *Nemopanthus*, from the Greek *nema*, "thread," *pous*, "foot" and *anthos*, "flower," alludes to the long, slender flower stalks. The specific epithet *mucronata*, "with a mucro or a short, sharp point," refers to the abruptly pointed leaves.

Also Called: Catberry, feverbush, wild holly, brick-timber • *N. mucronata*.

Size and Shape: Tall shrubs or small trees, up to 15' tall; crowns rounded; roots spreading, often forming dense colonies.

Trunks: Up to 3" in diameter; bark thin, smooth, gray, with pale, raised pores (lenticels).

Branches: Numerous, of **2 types: long, slender shoots** with scattered leaves, and **short, stout side-shoots** with crowded leaves; twigs smooth, purplish, gray with age; buds small, with a thick, slightly longer upper scale.

Leaves: Alternate, simple, early deciduous; blades thin, hairless, dark green above, grayish-green beneath, ¾–2" long, usually **abruptly sharp-pointed, smooth edged** or with a few small, sharp teeth, finely net-veined; **stalks slender, reddish to purplish,** ¼–¾" long; leaf scars triangular, with 1 vein scar.

Flowers: Yellowish- to greenish-white, small; unisexual (rarely bisexual) with **male and female flowers on separate trees**; petals 4, slender,

separate, about ¹⁄₁₆" long; **anthers <¹⁄₃₂" long;** flowers single (sometimes 2–3), on thread-like, ³⁄₈–¾" long stalks from leaf axils, in (May?) June–July (before leaves expand).

Fruits: Purplish-red to crimson (rarely yellowish), **berry-like drupes ¼–³⁄₈" long, on slender, brittle stalks at least 1" long;** seeds in smooth-sided (sometimes faintly ribbed) nutlets, 4–5; drupes mature and drop in July–September.

Habitat: Moist to wet sites, swamps, swales, woods and on streambanks.

Origin: Native.

227

Jesuit missionaries brought tree-of-heaven to England from China in 1751, and it was introduced to North America in 1874. • This hardy, smog-tolerant tree is planted as an ornamental and has become very well established in urban areas. It grows rapidly (up to 6–10' per season) and thrives in even the poorest, driest soils, adding green to city landscapes and producing oxygen for urban dwellers. Unfortunately, the leaves and male flowers have an unpleasant odor and the pollen can cause severe hay fever, so female trees are usually preferred. Also, the spreading roots can damage wells and drainage systems, and the wood is so brittle that snow, wind and even moderately heavy storms can bring down dozens of trees. • Escaped trees often take over clearings, producing impenetrable thickets from root suckers. Once established, the thickets are hard to eliminate, so many people regard tree-of-heaven as a troublesome weed rather than a gift from above. • This species is featured in Betty Smith's *A Tree Grows in Brooklyn*, a story about a young girl inspired by a tree's determination to survive. • Tree-of-heaven has very bitter bark, wood and seeds. The small glands on the leaf lobes give off an unpleasant odor when rubbed, hence the alternative name "stinking-ash."

Also Called: Copal tree, ailanthus, Chinese-sumac, stinking-ash • *A. glandulosa*.

Size and Shape: Trees 30–40' tall; crowns broad, rounded; roots spreading.

Trunks: Often short and clumped, 12–40" in diameter; young bark greenish-gray; mature bark gray, thin, with irregular vertical lines; wood pale yellow, soft, weak.

Branches: Few, stout, fragile; **twigs stout,** yellowish- to reddish-brown, with **prominent U-shaped leaf scars and pores** (lenticels); buds downy, hemispherical, 2–4-scaled, absent at branch tips.

Leaves: Alternate, deciduous, ill-smelling; compound, **pinnately divided into 11–41 leaflets; central stalks 10–30" long,** with swollen bases; leaflets glossy, dark green, paler beneath, **2–6" long, with a gland-tipped lobe (sometimes 2) near the base,** slender-pointed, **stalked;** leaves clear yellow in autumn.

Flowers: Yellowish-green, about ¼" across, 5-parted, unpleasant-smelling (especially males); unisexual (occasionally bisexual) with male and female flowers on separate trees; **flowers in erect, pyramidal, 4–12" long clusters** (panicles) at branch tips, in June–July (after leaves expand).

Fruits: Pale reddish- to yellowish-brown, **winged nutlets** (samaras), 1⅛–2" long, with a **seedcase at the center of a flat, spirally twisted wing, hanging in dense clusters;** seeds single; mature in October, persist into winter.

Habitat: Open, usually disturbed sites in woods, fields, and towns.

Origin: Introduced from northern China.

This popular, moderately fast-growing ornamental is valued for its feathery leaves and showy, long-lasting flower clusters. Mimosa-tree originated in subtropical and temperate Asia, and was first cultivated Europe in 1745. Today it is widely planted in the southern U.S. (north to Boston) and often escapes to grow wild. Although it is limited to areas outside the range of severe cold, it can withstand moderate frost (tolerant to –4°F) and a wide range of unfavorable conditions, including high pH, saline soil, drought and high winds. It has few diseases and insect pests. • The swollen area at base of each leaf and leaflet expands and contracts with changes in light, causing the leaflets to bend inward (folding or closing the leaf) or pull outward (opening the leaf). As light diminishes in the evening, the leaflet pairs fold together and the leaves droop. Young leaves are sometimes sensitive to touch, similar to those of sensitive-plants (*Mimosa* spp.). • In tropical Asia, the young leaves of mimosa-tree and other *Albizia* species are used for food. In Asia, the wood has been used for cabinet-making.

Also Called: Albizia, silk-tree.

Size and Shape: Small trees 20–40' tall; crowns broad, often umbrella shaped; roots suckering.

Trunks: To 20" in diameter; young bark with conspicuous pores (lenticels); mature bark blotchy thin; wood dark brown, fine-grained.

Branches: Wide-spreading; twigs stout, zigzagged, smell of green peas when broken, with **many conspicuous, pale pores** (lenticels); buds small, round, partly embedded, **superimposed,** absent at twig tips.

Leaves: Alternate, deciduous, 6–20" long, **feathery, twice pinnately divided,** with 5–12 pairs of branches with 15–30 pairs of leaflets, tipped with a spine (not a leaflet); leaflets dark green above, paler beneath, ¼–⅝" long, **strongly asymmetrical,** main vein near edge, curved and abruptly pointed at tip, with midrib protruding; **leaf scars 3-lobed,** with 3 bundle-scars.

Flowers: Lime green (flushing) to ivory to **rose pink,** bisexual; sepals 5, tiny, hairy; petals 5, ⅛–¼" long, inconspicuous; **stamens 15+, showy,** pink, 1–1½" long; pistil with a thread-like style longer than stamens; **flowers in fluffy, tasseled heads** 1–2" in diameter on hairy stalks in broad clusters (corymbs) at branch tips, in June–August.

Fruits: Yellowish-brown, **papery, flattened pods** (legumes), **4–8" long,** tapered at both ends, constricted or wrinkled between seeds; seeds 8–10, lustrous light brown, bean-like, about ⅜", not splitting open when mature.

Habitat: Roadsides and open, disturbed areas or thin woods.

Origin: Introduced from tropical Asia and Africa; occasional escape.

229

This fast-growing, drought-resistant tree, with its showy, yellow flower clusters, is widely planted as an ornamental shade tree. In China, goldenrain-tree was traditionally planted over the graves of scholars. It is especially beautiful in early summer, when it is one of the few trees flowering. The bright yellow blooms open a few at a time, so flowering is usually prolonged over a 2-week period. • Clusters of young, lime-colored, 3-sided pods add interest in summer, but these soon fade to brown. Fall color can vary from a beautiful golden yellow in good years to chartreuse or green in poor years. • In China, the showy yellow flowers were used to make yellow dyes and traditional medicines. • Goldenrain-tree was first introduced to North America in 1763. In some parts of the U.S., it has become an invasive weed that threatens native vegetation, but in Illinois it rarely escapes. Harsh winters from central Illinois north (USDA Zone 5) can severely damage these marginally hardy trees. • Cultivated trees are grown from seed or from root cuttings. Inflated seed capsules can be carried over the ground for great distances by the wind, eventually shattering and releasing the seeds. • The genus *Koelreuteria* is named in honor of German botany professor, Joseph Gottlieb Kölreuter (1733–1806). The species name *paniculata* refers to the showy, branched flowers clusters or "panicles."

Also Called: Varnish-tree, pride-of-India.

Size and Shape: Small, graceful trees 30–60' tall; crowns as broad as tall, rounded.

Trunks: Asymmetrical, irregular, single or clumped; bark silvery gray to light brown, with flat-topped ridges and shallow, reddish-brown furrows; wood lightweight but strong.

Branches: Few, stout; twigs stout, reddish-brown with many pale pores (lenticels), somewhat zigzagged; buds round, absent at branch tips.

Leaves: Alternate, deciduous, once or (usually) **twice pinnately divided,** with about 9 main divisions, each with 1–7 leaflets; leaflets pink at first, then green, broad-based, 1¼–3⅛" long, irregularly toothed or lobed; leaf scars shield-shaped; leaves turn yellow in autumn.

Flowers: Bright yellow, bisexual, **asymmetrical,** about ½" wide, with 4 inconspicuous sepals, 4 petals, 8 stamens, 1 superior pistil; **flowers in 8–16" long, hanging, branched clusters** (panicles) at branch tips, in July–September.

Fruits: Lime-green to reddish, papery, lantern-like capsules, 3-sided, 1½–2" long, 3-parted; seeds 1–3, black; pods pale brown when mature in autumn, persist into following spring.

Habitat: Disturbed sites.

Origins: Introduced from China, Korea and Japan; rare escape.

Common hop-tree is a short-lived, slow-growing species that is sometimes planted as an ornamental or hedge for its bright, shiny leaves and unusual clusters of persistent, buff-colored fruits. It is known to thrive well beyond its natural range and is hardy as far north as Lake Superior. This tree is fairly shade tolerant but flowers only in full sunlight. • The close-grained wood is fairly strong, but the trunks are too small to be of commercial use. • When bruised, all parts of hop-tree give off a distinctive, citrus-like odor that is generally considered disagreeable, though some people find it pleasant. • In earlier days, when bad-tasting medicines were considered best, bitter-tasting hop-tree juice was sometimes given as a substitute for quinine. The fruits have been used in beer as a substitute for hops (*Humulus* spp.), hence the name "hop-tree." • The flowers smell like rotting flesh and attract carrion flies, which carry pollen from one tree to the next. The fruits are seldom consumed by wildlife, but the trees can provide shelter for birds in otherwise open areas. • *Ptelea* was the Greek name for elm. It was transferred to the hop-tree genus by Linnaeus because of the resemblance of the fruit to that of elms.

Also Called: Wafer-ash, stinking-ash, three-leaved hop-tree • *P. angustifolia.*

Size and Shape: Small trees or tall shrubs 12–15' (occasionally to 25') tall; crowns irregular, rounded.

Trunks: Short, 3–6" in diameter; **young bark shiny, reddish-brown, with prominent pores** (lenticels); mature bark grayish, rough, scaly; wood yellowish-brown, heavy, hard.

Branches: Numerous, twisted, short; twigs yellowish- to **reddish-brown** with prominent pores (lenticels), **foul-smelling when bruised; pith** large, white; **buds woolly, rounded, tiny, sunken under leaf stalk bases,** absent at branch tips.

Leaves: Alternate (mostly), deciduous; compound, **divided into 3 leaflets; leaflets glossy, dark green above, paler beneath, speckled with tiny, translucent glands** (visible in front of strong light), ovate to elliptical, 2–4½" long, sharp-pointed with wedge-shaped bases, smooth-edged or faintly toothed; leaf stalks 2⅜–6" long; leaf scars horseshoe-shaped around buds.

Flowers: Greenish-white, foul-smelling, 4–5-parted; unisexual (occasionally bisexual) with male and female flowers on separate trees; petals hairy, about ¼" long; flowers in 1½–3" wide, **repeatedly branched clusters** (cymes) at branch tips, in May–July (after leaves expand).

Fruits: Buff-colored, **winged nutlets** (samaras) ¾–1" across, **with 2 seedcases surrounded by a flat, circular, net-veined wing; samaras hang in dense, stalked clusters,** mature in September–October, persist through winter.

Habitat: Open wood and sandy sites, including dunes.

Origin: Native.

Russian-olive is an attractive, silver-leaved shrub or small tree that is often planted as an ornamental. It is very hardy in cold climates and can resist drought, tolerate city smoke and grow on salty soil. Occasionally, Russian-olive can become a serious pest when it sends up suckers from spreading roots. • Although the fruits are rather mealy, they are sweet and edible. • Two East Asian species, **autumn-olive (*E. umbellata*,** also called Japanese silverberry), shown in pink/dark green (species overlap) on the map, and **long-stalk oleaster (*E. multiflora*),** shown in dark pink, sometimes escape to grow wild in Illinois. Both are shrubby trees up to 15' tall with long-stalked, pink to red "berries" and brown and silvery scales on leaves and twigs. Autumn-olive is distinguished by its relatively long corolla tube (longer than the calyx) and by its smaller (¼–⁵⁄₁₆" vs. ⅜–⅝") fruits with shorter (<⅜" vs. >⅝") stalks. Also, long-stalk oleaster leaves soon shed their scales and become green on top. In recent years, autumn-olive has become a serious invasive weed, especially in areas with nutrient-poor, sandy soils. Long-stalk oleaster is found only rarely. • Without flowers or fruits, Russian-olive could be mistaken for a willow, but willow leaves lack silvery scales, the leaf scars have 3 vein scars and the buds are 1-scaled.

Also Called: Oleaster.

Size and Shape: Small, slender trees or shrubs 15–35' tall; crowns dense, low, rounded.

Trunks: Often crooked or leaning; bark grayish-brown, thin, fissured, **shredding in strips.**

Branches: Usually spiny, erect or hanging; **twigs densely silvery with tiny scales,** some reduced to leafless, spine-forming shoots; buds small, ovoid, several-scaled, silvery.

Leaves: Alternate, in small clusters, simple, deciduous; **blades dull silvery green** with tiny scales and star-shaped hairs, leathery, narrowly oblong to lance-shaped, pointed, 1⅛–3" long, 3–8 times as long as wide; leaf scars with 1 dash-like vein scar.

Flowers: Yellow inside, silvery-scaly outside, fragrant, bisexual or unisexual, **bell-shaped,** about ⅜" **long,** with a short, tubular nectary around the style; petals lacking; sepals 4; flowers short-stalked, 1–3 at the base of new growth, in May–June.

Fruits: Yellow to brownish, **silvery-scaled, mealy, drupe-like "berries"** (enlarged hypanthium bases), elliptic-oblong, ⅜–¾" **long, tipped with sepals;** each contains a dry, smooth, about ¼" nutlet (achene) that encloses a single seed; "berries" mature in autumn, often persist through winter.

Habitat: Moist, open sites such as fields and riverbanks.

Origin: Introduced from Eurasia.

This fast-growing, moderately long-lived tree is an attractive ornamental with fragrant flowers, large leaves, excellent response to pruning and deep, spreading roots that make it wind-firm. • American basswood is one of our softest, lightest hardwoods, valued for use in hand carving and turnery. It has also been used for interior trim, veneer, plywood, cabinets, furniture, musical instruments, measuring sticks and pulp and paper. The odorless wood makes excellent food containers. • Native peoples and settlers soaked the inner bark in water to separate its tough fibers, which were then used to make ropes, nets, mats, shoes, clothing and thread. • Some tribes carved ritual masks on living trees, then split the masks away to hollow and dry the inside. If the tree survived, the mask was believed to have supernatural powers. • A hot bath with basswood (linden) flowers followed by a cup of linden-flower tea is said to soothe cold symptoms and enhance sleep. • A hairy variety, (*T. americana* var. *heterophylla*, also called white basswood or *T. heterophylla*), shown in pink/dark green (species overlap) on the map, is distinguished by its hairy leaf and flower stalks and white undersides of its leaves. • In North America, the native *Tilia* is called a "basswood," but in horticulture, other *Tilia* species are called "lindens" and in England, "lime-trees."

Also Called: American linden, whitewood, bee-tree, bast-tree, lime-tree, lime, spoonwood • *T. glabra.*

Size and Shape: Trees 60–80' tall; crowns regular, rounded; roots deep, wide-spreading.

Trunks: Straight, 16–50" in diameter; young bark pale, smooth; mature bark dark grayish-brown with blocky, narrow, flat-topped ridges; inner bark fibrous; wood pale reddish-brown, light, soft, uniform.

Branches: Numerous, spreading and upcurved to ascending and arching; twigs yellowish-brown, hairless, zigzagged; **buds plump, asymmetrical, 2–3-scaled,** hairless, about ¼" long, in 2 rows, absent at twig tips.

Leaves: Alternate, simple, deciduous; blades dull green, paler beneath with hairy vein axils, **heart-shaped, asymmetrical at bases,** abruptly slender-pointed, 3–7" long, palmately veined at base, **edged with coarse, sharp, gland-tipped teeth;** stalks almost half as long as blades; leaf scars semi-oval, raised, with 5–10 vein scars.

Flowers: Creamy-yellowish, about ½" across, fragrant, bisexual; flowers hang in loose, branched clusters **(cymes) on slender stalks from the lower midvein of prominent 4–5",** strap-like bracts; petals 5; sepals 5; flowers in clusters in axils of new leaves, in June–July (6–8 weeks after leaves expand).

Fruits: Brown-woolly, round, nut-like capsules, about ¼" across, 1-seeded; **in long-stalked clusters on strap-like bracts;** mature in September–October, persist through winter.

Habitat: Cool, moist, rich woods, often near water and mixed with other hardwoods.

Origin: Native.

This hardy European tree tolerates urban conditions well and has been planted since ancient times as an ornamental for its fragrant flowers, dense, deep green, neatly textured canopy and bright yellow autumn leaves. • In Saxon times, littleleaf linden was the dominant tree of many forests in England and Wales. Today, it is widely planted in North America, but in Europe the common lime (*T.* x *vulgaris* or *T. europaea*, a hybrid of *T. cordata* and another European species, *T. platyphyllos*, largeleaf lime) is preferred for landscaping. • The fine-textured, easily worked wood is ideal for carving and turning. Many of the intricate carvings of the famous English artist Grinling Gibbons (1648–1721) were made from this wood. Because linden wood does not warp, it is used for drawing boards and for the sounding boards and keys of pianos and organs. • The dried flowers are sometimes sold in health-food stores. They are used to make medicinal teas for stimulating sweating, enhancing resistance to infection and inducing sedation. • This shapely tree can become burred, sprouty and heavily branched with age. Some linden trees in English parks are more than 350 years old. • The specific epithet *cordata*, "heart-shaped," refers to the leaves.

Also Called: Small-leaved European linden, small-leaved lime.

Size and Shape: Trees 40–50' tall; crowns pyramidal to round; roots deep, spreading.

Trunks: Straight, 15–30" in diameter; young bark pale, smooth; mature bark dark grayish-brown, with blocky ridges; wood light, soft, even-grained.

Branches: Arching (typically) to spreading; twigs reddish-brown, soon hairless, **zigzagged; buds plump, asymmetrical, 2-scaled,** greenish-red, in 2 rows, absent at twig tips.

Leaves: Alternate, simple, deciduous; blades shiny, dark green, paler beneath, with rusty-hairy vein axils, **heart-shaped to nearly round, only slightly asymmetrical,** 1⅜–3" long, edged with **coarse, sharp, gland-tipped teeth;** stalks hairless; leaf scars semi-oval, with 5–10 vein scars; leaves pale yellow to tan in autumn.

Flowers: Greenish-yellow, fragrant, star-shaped, about ½" across, bisexual; petals 5; sepals 5; flowers spreading to erect in branched, 5–8-flowered, **1–2" wide clusters** (cymes) **on slender stalks from midveins of** 1⅜–3" **long, strap-like bracts,** in May–July (after leaves expand).

Fruits: Grayish to pale yellow, rusty-hairy, **nut-like capsules,** faintly ribbed (if at all), about ¼" long, 1-seeded, thin-shelled; **capsules hang in clusters from strap-like bracts,** mature in autumn, persist through winter.

Habitat: Disturbed, open sites.

Origin: Introduced from Europe; rare escape.

Black tupelo is an attractive shade tree often planted as an ornamental for its interesting form, abundant, bird-attracting, blue fruits and decorative leaves (shiny and dark green in summer; golden to brilliant scarlet, often blotched with green, in autumn). Black tupelo reaches the northern limit of its range in southern Michigan but is planted as a hardy ornamental farther north. • This tree rarely reaches commercial size, but over the years, its tough wood found many uses, especially when resistance to wear was important. Unusual items included pipes in a salt factory, hatters' blocks, pistol grips and even rollers for glass. • The fruits are too sour for human tastes, but they are an important food for many animals, including foxes, wood ducks, wild turkeys, pileated woodpeckers and large songbirds. A more southern species, **swamp tupelo** (*N. biflora,* also called swamp gum and *N. sylvatica* var. *biflora*), shown in dark green (species overlap) on the map, resembles black tupelo, with short (usually <1") leaf stalks and small (<⅝" long) fruits. Its flowers can be single (similar to water tupelo, p. 236) or in clusters of 2–3 (similar to black tupelo). Unlike black tupelo, swamp tupelo leaves are usually small (<2⅜" long) and always smooth-edged. Swamp tupelo is very rare in Illinois.

Also Called: Blackgum, sourgum, pepperidge.

Size and Shape: Trees 35–65' tall; crowns broadly elongated, often flat-topped.

Trunks: Straight, 4–16" in diameter; mature bark dark gray, with thick, irregular, blocky segments; wood fine-grained, hard, heavy, strong.

Branches: Crooked, horizontal, often drooping with upturned tips; twigs reddish-brown with grayish skin, long and slender or short and dwarfed; **pith with hard, greenish crossbars** in long-section; buds reddish-brown, hairy-tipped, ⅛–¼" long, **pointing outward.**

Leaves: Alternate, **clustered at shoot tips,** simple, deciduous; **blades shiny, dark green,** whitened beneath, tough, 2–4¾" long, **shape variable, generally widest above midleaf, abruptly pointed, tapered to a wedge-shaped base,** with smooth to slightly wavy edges (rarely irregularly coarse-toothed); stalks reddish; upper leaf surface golden to scarlet in autumn.

Flowers: Greenish-white, inconspicuous, tiny, unisexual (sometimes a few bisexual) with male and female flowers on separate trees; stalkless (female) or short-stalked (male); flowers in clusters (umbels), on hairy, ⅜–1½" long stalks, in April–June (after leaves expand).

Fruits: Blue-black, plum-like drupes, ⅜–½" long, with thin, oily flesh around a stone, in **clusters of 1–3, stalkless;** seeds single within indistinctly 10–12-grooved stones; fruit clusters **on stalks 1⅛– 2¼" long,** mature in October.

Habitat: Moist to wet, wooded sites; sometimes in drier upland forests.

Origin: Native.

235

Water tupelo is one of the most flood-tolerant trees in temperate North America. Flooded trees move oxygen to their roots through pores in the wood. This structure makes the wood very light and buoyant, so much so that water tupelo wood has been used for fishing floats. • Each spring, a blanket of cottony down covers new growth, tingeing the treetops of water tupelo stands white, giving it another common name, "cotton-gum." As leaves and branches mature, the down is gradually shed. • Water tupelo is seldom bothered by insects. Its greatest enemies are fire and fluctuating water levels. Fire easily breaches the thin bark, opening trees to fungal infections; both flooding and severe drainage can kill trees. • These long-lived trees do not flower for about 30 years, but once mature, they produce heavy crops almost every year. Although the fruits are eaten by small animals such as woodchucks, turkeys and various large songbirds, water tupelo is usually carried to new sites by water. Seedlings enjoy full sunlight in drowned sites where most other trees cannot survive. • Water tupelo wood has been used to make paneling, woodenware and crates. Old-timers chewed the twig tips to create a tuft of fibers used as tooth sticks (for cleaning teeth) or snuff dippers (for putting snuff in the mouth).

Also Called: Tupelo gum, cotton-gum, large tupelo.

Size and Shape: Trees to 100' tall; crowns narrow, oblong or cone-shaped.

Trunks: Straight, long, typically enlarged (buttressed) at the base, 3–4' in diameter; mature bark dark brown, ¼–½" thick, with small scales forming vertical ridges; wood light-brown to almost white, fine-grained, soft.

Branches: Short, stout, spreading; twigs stout, reddish-brown and hairy at first, smooth and brown with age; pith with crossbars in long-section; buds light reddish-brown, up to 1" long.

Leaves: Alternate, clustered at shoot tips, simple, deciduous; blades leathery, shiny and dark green above, paler with downy hairs and a whitish bloom beneath, 4–6" long, oblong to ovate, tapered to a pointed tip, smooth-edged or with a few irregular, coarse triangular teeth; stalks grooved, 1–2" long, hairy; yellow (occasionally scarlet) in autumn.

Flowers: Greenish-white, tiny; unisexual (sometimes a few bisexual) with male and female flowers on the same tree; male flowers in dense heads (umbels) at the tips of hairy, ¼–¾" long stalks; female flowers single on slender, ¾–1³⁄₁₆" stalks; flowers in April–May (as leaves expand).

Fruits: Dark purple-blue, plum-like drupes, ¾–1³⁄₁₆" long, with thin, oily flesh around a hard, obovate stone; seeds single inside the stone, spongy, with 8–10 narrow lengthwise ridges (wings); drupes single on slender stalks, mature and fall in September–October.

Habitat: Deep freshwater swamps.

Origin: Native.

236

lossy buckthorn was introduced to our continent from the Mediterranean region primarily as an ornamental. The cultivar 'Columnaris' (tall-hedge buckthorn) is popular in hedges and windbreaks. Glossy buckthorn is hardy throughout the state, and in some areas, it has become a serious, aggressive invader of wetlands. • The hard wood has been used for making shoe lasts, nails and veneers. Its charcoal was once highly prized for making gunpowder. • Buckthorns were long ago credited with protective power against witchcraft, demons, poisons and headaches, but glossy buckthorn's true value, as a laxative, was not recognized until the 1300s. Today, herbalists recommend a tea of glossy buckthorn bark as a laxative. In Europe, the bark is often included in commercial laxatives. • The fruits mature over several weeks, so green, red and black fruits can occur at the same time. Unripe "berries" produce a green dye, and the bark gives a yellow dye. • Birds eat glossy buckthorn fruits, which are **slightly poisonous** to humans, usually causing vomiting. • European buckthorn (p. 239) is distinguished by its spine-tipped branches, sub-opposite, finely toothed leaves and deeply grooved "seeds" (stones).

Also Called: European alder-buckthorn, European-alder, columnar buckthorn, fen buckthorn, arrow-wood, black-dogwood • *Rhamnus frangula.*

Size and Shape: Small trees or shrubs to 20' tall; crowns rounded, open; roots spreading, suckering to form dense colonies.

Trunks: Short; bark thin, with conspicuous, pale, elongated pores (lenticels); wood fine-grained.

Branches: Rather stout; twigs brown to gray, mottled with lenticels, minutely hairy, brittle; **buds brown, hairy, lacking scales.**

Leaves: Mostly alternate, simple, deciduous; blades glossy, green, with **5–10 conspicuous, parallel veins per side,** elliptical to ovate and widest above midleaf, 1⅛–3" long, ¾–2" wide, abruptly pointed, **smooth-edged** or slightly wavy-edged; stalks stout, 2⅜–4¾" long, with slender, ephemeral stipules; leaves yellow to red-tinged in autumn.

Flowers: Greenish-yellow, <¼" across, bisexual; petals 5, <1/16" long, with notched tips; sepals 5, with fused bases; flowers on slender, unequal, ⅛–⅜" long stalks, in clusters of 1–6 (umbels) in lower leaf axils, in May–July (after leaves expand).

Fruits: Green to red to purplish-black, berry-like drupes, about ¼" across; seeds single within smooth, nutlet-like stones, **2–3 stones per fruit;** fruit clusters mature in July–September.

Habitat: Moist to wet, typically disturbed sites in bogs and low woods.

Origin: Introduced from Eurasia and North Africa.

Carolina buckthorn is a slow-growing, usually short-lived shrub or tree that prefers rich limestone soils. It can be grown as a hardy ornamental well north of its natural range (USDA Zone 5). Plants are easily moved and also grow readily from fall-planted seeds. Carolina buckthorn tolerates sun or shade and grows on soils of almost any pH. Unfortunately, ice storms can take their toll, as brittle branches snap under heavy loads. • The sweet fruits are edible raw or cooked (see Caution) but were not widely used by people. However, many birds, including pileated woodpeckers, find them delicious. • Some tribes boiled the bark to make medicinal teas that acted as a strong laxative and also induced vomiting. Milder preparations are still used to relieve constipation, especially cases associated with nervous or muscular deterioration of the intestines. Fresh bark is too strong, so bark strips must be heat treated or dried for up to 2 years. • **Caution:** The bark can cause diarrhea and vomiting. Some sources report that the fruit also has this effect, but most say it is edible. Large amounts may be cathartic. • The name Carolina buckthorn is also applied to smooth southern-buckthorn (p. 205).

Also Called: Indian cherry • *Rhamnus caroliniana.*

Size and Shape: Tall shrubs or small trees 20–25' tall; crowns open, rounded.

Trunks: Short, straight, up to 1' in diameter; bark light gray, thin, smooth to slightly furrowed; wood light brown, hard, brittle.

Branches: Spreading, slender, **without thorns;** twigs slender, reddish-brown and hairy at first, gray and smooth with age; **buds hairy, tiny, without protective scales.**

Leaves: Alternate, **deciduous,** simple; blades thin, glossy and dark green above, paler beneath, hairless, with **8–10 pairs of impressed, parallel veins,** elliptical to oblong, **2–6" long,** less than ½ as wide, pointed at the tip, rounded at the base, **edged with tiny, often scattered, blunt teeth; stalks hairy, slender, ¼–¾" long;** leaves yellow (occasionally red) when shed in autumn.

Flowers: Greenish-yellow, tiny, bisexual; sepals 5, fused in a bell-shaped calyx; petals 5, inconspicuous, each wrapped around a stamen; stalks finely hairy, ⅛–¼"; flowers in tassel-like clusters (umbel-like cymes) of **3–8 at tips of 0–⅜" stalks** (shorter than adjacent leaf stalks) in leaf axils or along branchlets, in May–June (after leaves expand).

Fruits: Round, **berry-like drupes,** red at first, shiny and **black when ripe,** ¼–⅜" across, slightly fleshy, containing 3 (sometimes 2 or 4) **smooth (not grooved) stones;** seeds 1 per stone; dense fruit clusters mature in September–October.

Habitat: Moist, well-drained woods.

Origin: Native.

Buckthorns cannot be categorized neatly as alternate- or opposite-leaved. Most have alternate leaves, but European buckthorn is more or less opposite-leaved. • This small tree's hardiness, spiny branches, insect resistance and responsiveness to pruning have made it a popular hedge plant. European buckthorn escaped from cultivation many years ago in North America and has been widely dispersed by birds. It is now an aggressive, unwelcome invader that can choke out native woodland shrubs and herbaceous perennials. • The extremely unpleasant-tasting fruits are somewhat **poisonous** to humans and have a strong laxative effect. In 1650, European buckthorn syrup, which contained cinnamon, nutmeg and aniseed to cut the bitter flavor of the fruits, was included in the British pharmacopoeia. Buckthorn fruits are still recommended as a laxative and are listed in the U.S. National Formulary. • European buckthorn retains green leaves until late in the year. In autumn, such introduced species often stand out in sharp contrast to native plants, which shed their leaves promptly each fall.

Also Called: Common buckthorn, purging buckthorn, European waythorn, Hart's thorn, Carolina buckthorn.

Size and Shape: Shrubs or small trees to 20' tall; crowns rounded; roots spreading, suckering to form dense colonies.

Trunks: Short; bark grayish-brown with **elongated pores** (lenticels), thin, smooth, peeling in curly-edged sheets; wood fine-grained.

Branches: Stiff, **often spine-tipped;** twigs rigid, of 2 types: long, smooth, rather angled shoots, and short, warty shoots with crowded leaf scars and/or thorn-like tips; **buds hairless with blackish scales,** flat-lying.

Leaves: Mostly opposite, simple, late-deciduous; **blades dull dark green,** hairless, with **3–4 conspicuous, strongly upcurved veins per side,** minutely blunt-toothed, **broadly ovate to elliptical,** 1⅛–3½" long, **1–2 times as long as wide,** abruptly pointed, slightly folded and often curved back; stalks hairy, grooved.

Flowers: Greenish-yellow, <¼" across; functionally **unisexual** with male and female flowers on separate plants; petals 4, lance-shaped; sepals 4, fused; flowers on thread-like, unequal stalks, in compact clusters **(umbels)**, in leaf axils, in May–June (as leaves expand).

Fruits: Green to red to purplish-black, berry-like drupes, about ¼" across; seeds single within grooved, nutlet-like stones, usually **4 stones per fruit;** fruits in dense clusters, mature in August–September.

Habitat: Open, typically disturbed sites such as abandoned lots, open woodlands and roadsides.

Origin: Introduced from Europe.

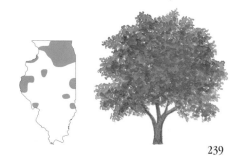

239

This attractive, exotic shrub is densely branched and responds well to clipping, so it is usually planted as a hedge or windbreak. In its native environment in the Himalayas, Dahurian buckthorn forms part of the forest understory, but in North America, it thrives in many different settings. Although it requires moist soil, this hardy tree can thrive on light, sandy soil to heavy clay, on acidic to basic (alkaline) substrates and in partial shade to full sun. • Exotic buckthorns are widely recognized as aggressive weeds, but they are still commonly sold as ornamentals, and there are few legal restrictions on their sale or propagation. Dahurian buckthorn is considered a noxious weed in Iowa and also appears on other weedy-plant lists. Although it is not as widely naturalized as some species, it has the potential to spread rapidly and should be avoided and extirpated. • The fruit is readily eaten and carried to new sites by birds. • Another small introduced tree, **Japanese buckthorn (*R. japonica*)**, shown in dark green (species overlap) on the map, is distinguished by its leaves, which are relatively fine-veined (5 or more veins per side), short-stalked (stalk less than ⅙ as long as blade) and slender-tipped (gradually tapered to a point). This attractive ornamental rarely escapes from cultivation in Illinois, but has been found in a disturbed, open site in DuPage County.

Also Called: *R. dahurica, R. citrifolia.*

Size and Shape: Tall shrubs 6–20' tall; crowns open, rounded.

Trunks: Single or clumped; bark gray-brown, often silvery, thin, with abundant **rough pores** (lenticels); wood red-brown with yellowish sapwood, moderately hard.

Branches: Spreading, slender, often **tipped with a short spine;** twigs flattened, grayish to red-brown, stiff, often with a whitish bloom; **buds with smooth, overlapping, red-brown scales.**

Leaves: Mostly opposite, deciduous, simple; blades hairless, yellow-green, with (3) 4–6 **veins** per side, oblong or ovate, widest above midleaf, 2¾–4" long, pointed, tapered to a **wedge-shaped base, edged with tiny** (15–25 per inch), **blunt teeth;** stalks hairless, grooved above; leaf scars broadly crescent-shaped; leaves brown in autumn.

Flowers: Greenish-yellow; functionally **unisexual** with male and female on separate plants; sepals 4, slender, about ⅛" long, spreading; petals 4, inconspicuous; stamens 4; **styles divided in 2;** flowers in **tassel-like clusters** (umbel-like cymes) **of 1–4** from leaf axils and/or along small branches, in May–June (after leaves expand).

Fruits: Semi-glossy, **dark purple to black, berry-like drupes,** widest above the middle, ¼–⅓" long, juicy, smooth; seeds in smooth, grooved, dull gray-brown stones about ¼" long, **2 per fruit;** fruits on ½" long stems, clustered in leaf axils or on short spur branches, mature in September.

Habitat: Disturbed sites, woodlands and savannas.

Origin: Introduced from northeast Asia (Siberia, northern China and Korea).

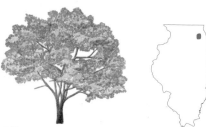

Key to the Dogwoods (Genus Cornus)

1a   Leaves alternate . . . . *C. alternifolia*, **alternate-leaf dogwood** (p. 242)

1b   Leaves opposite **2**

2a   Flowers tiny, in a compact cluster at the center, or 4 large, white, petal-like bracts forming a flower-like cluster (pseudanthium); individual fruits stalkless, in a compact cluster at the end of a slender stalk, red when ripe
. . . . *C. florida*, **eastern flowering dogwood** (p. 246)

2b   Flowers larger (about ⅛–¼" long), in open, widely branched, flat-topped clusters (cymes) without obvious bracts; individual fruits clearly stalked, variously colored **3**

3a   Upper leaf surface rough to the touch with tiny, stiff, erect hairs; fruits white to bluish . . **4**

3b   Upper leaf surface smooth to the touch, hairless or with soft, flat-lying hairs; fruits variously colored **5**

4a   Leaves with 3–5 veins per side; pith of old twigs usually brown
. . . . , ... *C. drummondii*, **roughleaf dogwood** (p. 244)

4b   Leaves with 6–8 veins per side; pith of old twigs white
. . . . *C. rugosa*, **roundleaf dogwood** (p. 244)

5a   Flowers yellow; mature fruits red
. . . . *C. mas*, ***Cornelian-cherry dogwood*** (p. 245)

5b   Flowers white; mature fruits white to bluish
. . . . *C. racemosa*, **gray dogwood** (p. 244)

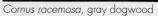
Cornus racemosa, gray dogwood   *C. florida*, eastern flowering dogwood

Dogwoods typically have opposite leaves, but this species is an exception to the rule. • Alternate-leaf dogwood and its cultivars are popular ornamental shrubs because of their profuse spring flowers, scarlet autumn leaves and purple, bird-attracting fruits. Also, these small trees have an unusual shape owing to their distinct layers of horizontal branches, giving rise to another common name, "pagoda dogwood." • The strong wood has no commercial value, but because it resists abrasion and withstands friction, the wood was used to make bearings and parts for mills. • The roots, mixed with vinegar, yield a light to dark brown dye. • Alternate-leaf dogwood is hardy throughout the state. It is not prone to serious diseases, but it is sometimes damaged by dogwood borer (*Synanthedon scitula*) and other insect pests. • The dry, bitter fruits provide food for grouse, pheasants, wild turkeys and squirrels. White-tailed deer browse the twigs and leaves. • The specific epithet *alternifolia* refers to the alternate leaves. • One leaf characteristic common to all dogwoods is that one can tear a leaf (gently, but completely) across the middle, but the latex in the veins holds the 2 halves together.

Also Called: Pagoda dogwood, green osier, blue dogwood, pagoda-tree.

Size and Shape: Small trees or large, straggly shrubs 12–25' tall; crowns flat, layered.

Trunks: Short, 2–6" in diameter; young bark greenish- to reddish-brown, thin, smooth; mature bark shallow-ridged; wood reddish-brown, heavy, hard, fine-grained.

Branches: Almost horizontal, with upcurved tips, **in tiers;** twigs shiny, reddish-green to purplish, with pores (lenticels), often with **1–2 side-branches** longer than the central shoot; pith white; buds shiny, chestnut brown, with 2 loose outer scales.

Leaves: Alternate (sometimes semi-opposite on short shoots), **clustered at branch tips,** simple, deciduous; blades green and hairless above, grayish and minutely hairy beneath, oval, with **4–5 parallel side-veins arched toward the tip,** 2–5" long, tapered to a point, **smooth- or slightly wavy-edged;** stalks ⅜–2⅜" long; **leaves red to yellow in autumn.**

Flowers: White or **cream-colored,** small, 4-parted, bisexual, numerous, on jointed stalks, in **irregular, 2–4" wide, rounded to flat-topped clusters** (cymes), in May–June (after leaves expand).

Fruits: Dark blue to bluish-black, berry-like **drupes,** about ¼" across, **on short, red stalks** in branched clusters; seeds single within egg-shaped stones; drupes mature in August–October.

Habitat: Rich, moist sites in woodlands and along streams.

Origin: Native.

**Opposite
Broad
Leaves**

Although gray dogwood is usually too small to be considered a tree, vigorous specimens can reach 15' in height. It is sometimes planted as a hardy ornamental, capable of tolerating a wide range of soil moisture conditions. It is easily transplanted and can be grown as a hedge or in dense masses. The shrubs are valued for their attractive, white, springtime flowers, followed by showy, red-stalked fruit clusters in late summer and autumn. • A similar species, **roundleaf dogwood (*C. rugosa*)** is a slightly smaller shrub (3–10' tall) with pale blue to grayish fruits and larger (2–5" long), broader (often almost round) leaves that have 7–10 (rather than 3–4) pairs of veins. • A more widespread species, **roughleaf dogwood (*C. drummondii*)**, shown in pink/dark green (species overlap) on the map, is found in open, often rocky sites, especially in the southern ³⁄₄ of Illinois. Like gray dogwood, this species has leaves with only 3–4 (rarely 5) veins per side, but its upper leaf surfaces are distinctly rough-textured and the pith of its twigs is usually brownish rather than white. • Some names in this genus are confusing. The specific epithet *racemosa*, "with racemes," refers to the panicle-like flower clusters that are somewhat longer than the broad cymes typical of this genus. The name *rugosa*, "wrinkled" or "rough," refers to the rough upper surface of the leaves. However, the common name roughleaf dogwood applies to *C. drummondii*, not *C. rugosa*.

Also Called: Northern swamp-dogwood, panicled dogwood • *C. foemina* ssp. *racemosa*.

Size and Shape: Shrubs 3–15' tall; crowns rounded; roots spreading, often forming thickets.

Trunks: Short; young bark greenish to tan to gray-brown; **mature bark gray,** smooth.

Branches: Numerous, paired; twigs slender, essentially **hairless,** more or less **2-ridged,** green to reddish at first, soon **light brown to gray with age;** pith white in new growth, **pale brown after 2–3 years;** buds small, scales meeting at edges (not overlapping).

Leaves: Opposite, simple, deciduous; blades dark grayish green, **smooth to touch above,** paler, minutely hairy and often whitened by minute bumps (papillae) beneath, ³⁄₄–4" long, wedge-shaped at base, slender-pointed; **smooth-edged, with 3–4 weakly parallel, arching side-veins;** stalks ¹⁄₄–¹⁄₂" long; **leaves red to purplish in autumn.**

Flowers: White or cream-colored, small, strongly convex, ill-scented, 4-parted, bisexual; petals 4, curved backward; **calyx lobes <¹⁄₃₂" long;** stamens 4; flowers in loose, 1¹⁄₈–2³⁄₈" **wide, rounded to pyramidal clusters** (panicles) on hairy, reddish, ³⁄₄–1" long stalks, in May–July.

Fruits: White (rarely pale gray to bluish), **berry-like drupes** about ¹⁄₄" across, **on bright red stalks** in branched clusters; seeds single, within egg-shaped, **pinkish stones;** drupes mature in July–September.

Habitat: Open, usually moist sites in woodlands, on shores and along roads.

Origin: Native.

Cornelian-cherry dogwood has been cultivated in Europe and Asia for centuries. It arrived in Britain before the 16th century, and then was introduced to Canada and the U.S. • This attractive shrub is planted for its early yellow blossoms and attractive, edible fruits. Old records suggest that Cornelian-cherry trees produced fruit much more prolifically in the past. Warmer summers may have allowed the fruit to set and ripen more frequently. Apparently, this was also the case with grapes. Today, several cultivars of Cornelian-cherry dogwood are available with leaves of different colors. • The edible drupes were traditionally made into preserves, jams, syrups and drinks. In ancient times, these fruits were also used in medicines for preventing dysentery and other bowel problems. • The common name "dogwood" is a corruption of "dagwood," from the Old English *dag*, "a sharp-pointed tool," because the hard, fine-textured wood of a European species (*C. sanguinea*) was used for making skewers. The ancient Persians, Greeks and Romans are said to have used Cornelian-cherry wood for making the shafts of javelins, spears and arrows. • *Cornus mas* is the type species for this genus — the one species that is permanently attached to the name *Cornus*. *Cornus* was derived from the Latin *cornu*, "horn," probably in reference to the hard wood.

Also Called: Cornel, Cornelian-cherry.

Size and Shape: Tall shrubs or small, bushy trees 10–25' tall, often pruned to tree form; crowns rounded.

Trunks: Single or clumped; slender; bark grayish, mottled, sometimes peeling in sheets; wood hard, strong, fine-grained.

Branches: Numerous; twigs red and green, hairy, ridged lengthwise; pith white; buds yellow, with 2 scales; flower buds spherical at tips of short side-branches.

Leaves: Opposite, deciduous, simple, green (even in late autumn); blades hairy above and beneath, ovate, 2–4" long, with (3) 4–5 pairs of **parallel side-veins arched toward the tip.**

Flowers: Pale yellow, about ³⁄₁₆" across, bisexual; 4 hairy, boat-shaped bracts, 4 stamens;

flowers several, in tassel-like clusters (umbels), in February–March (before leaves), soon shed.

Fruits: Bright red, cherry-like drupes, oblong, ½–¾" long; seeds 2; drupes single, mature in August–September.

Habitat: Disturbed sites.

Origin: Introduced from central and southeastern Europe and western Asia; occasional escape.

This fast-growing, short-lived tree is popular in southern parks and gardens. With its beautiful spring flowers, showy, bird-attracting fruits and red autumn leaves, eastern flowering dogwood is one of our finest native ornamental trees. However, its delicate flower buds are not frost hardy. Sadly, dogwood anthracnose (*Discula destructiva*) is rapidly eradicating eastern flowering dogwood in some regions. • The hard, strong wood has been used for golf-club heads, tool handles, rolling pins, weaving shuttles, spindles, small wheel hubs, barrel hoops and engravers' blocks. • Some tribes used the roots to make a scarlet dye for coloring porcupine quills and eagle feathers. The bark also yields a red dye. • Dried, ground bark was used as a quinine substitute for treating fevers. A bark decoction was used to treat mouth problems, and the fibrous twigs were used as chewing sticks (early toothbrushes), said to whiten teeth. • The drupes are not poisonous but are bitterly inedible when raw. Occasionally, they have been mashed, seeded and mixed with other fruits in jams and jellies. • Many birds and small mammals eat the bitter fruits.

Also Called: Arrow-wood, bitter red-cherry, common dogwood, white cornel, Florida dogwood, dogtree, great-flowered dogwood, Virginia dogwood.

Size and Shape: Small trees or tall shrubs 10–35' tall; crowns bushy, spreading, flat-topped; roots deep.

Trunks: Short, 4–12" in diameter; mature bark dark reddish-brown, deeply checked with 4-sided scales; wood white to brownish, tough, heavy and fine-grained.

Branches: Spreading in more or less horizontal tiers; twigs greenish to reddish with white hairs and pores (lenticels); flower buds stalked, dome-shaped, at twig tips.

Leaves: Opposite, usually 2–4 at branch tips, simple, deciduous; blades green above, grayish-green beneath, elliptical to oval, with **parallel veins arched toward the tip,** 2–6" long, narrow-pointed, **slightly wavy-edged;** leaves bronze to scarlet in autumn.

Flowers: Yellowish, tiny, 4-parted, bisexual; forming small, **dense, 20–30-flowered clusters at the center of 4 white or pinkish, petal-like bracts** (each ¾–2" **long** and tipped with a reddish notch); **pseudanthia** (clusters of flowers plus bracts) **resemble single, showy, 2–4" wide blooms** at branch tips; flowers in April–June (before leaves expand).

Fruits: Shiny, red, berry-like drupes ⅜–½" long, tipped with persistent sepals, with thin, mealy flesh around a stone, in **dense clusters of 3–6 or more on slender stalks;** seeds single within stones; undeveloped fruits often present; fruits mature in August–October.

Habitat: Moderately dry to moist sites in deciduous forests and ravines.

Origin: Native.

This native tree is too small to be commercially important. It is sometimes planted for its attractive autumn leaves and fruits, but European *Euonymus* species are more popular for landscaping. • Eastern wahoo bark was used in folk medicine as a tonic, laxative, diuretic and expectorant. Some Native tribes boiled the bark to make medicinal teas for treating problems of the uterus or eyes and for applying to facial sores. Various extracts, syrups and medicinal teas have been used over the years for treating fevers, upset stomachs, constipation, lung ailments, liver congestion and heart problems. Dried root bark was taken to relieve dropsy (fluid retention). The seed oil was used to induce vomiting and evacuation of the bowels, and the whole fruits were said to increase urine flow. In 1917, bark and root extracts we re reported to affect the heart much like digitalis, and wahoo became a popular heart medicine. By 1921, this species had been dropped as an official drug plant, although it remained in the U.S. National Formulary until 1947. • **Caution:** The fruits, seeds and bark of this tree are considered **poisonous**. The brightly colored fruits can tempt children. • Many species of birds eat these fruits and disperse the seeds.

Also Called: Burning-bush euonymus, spindle-tree • *E. atropurpureus.*

Size and Shape: Small trees or shrubs 10–15' tall; crowns rounded; roots spreading.

Trunks: Straight, often short or clumped, rarely up to 4" in diameter; bark greenish-gray, often streaked reddish-brown, thin; wood nearly white, hard, dense.

Branches: Spreading; twigs greenish, smooth, **somewhat 4-sided,** often with corky ridges below the buds; buds green, reddish-tinged, 6-scaled, about ⅛" long, flat-lying.

Leaves: Opposite, simple, deciduous; blades light green and hairless above, paler and **sparsely hairy beneath,** oblong-ovate to ovate or elliptical, 1½–5" long, ⅜–2" wide, **abruptly pointed, finely sharp-toothed;** stalks about ⅜" long; leaves red in autumn.

Flowers: Purplish-maroon, about ¼" across, bisexual; petals usually 4, wide-spreading; sepals usually 4, fused at the base; on slender stalks in branched, 5–18-flowered clusters (cymes) ¾–1½" wide; flower clusters on ¾–2" long stalks from leaf axils, in May–July (after leaves expand).

Fruits: Prominently 4-lobed capsules, pink to red or purplish when mature, ⅜–½" wide; hang on slender stalks; **seeds 4, each enclosed in a fleshy, bright red aril;** capsules hang on slender stalks, **split across the bottom to release seeds** in September, **empty capsules persist** into winter.

Habitat: Low, moist sites such as damp woods and streamside thickets.

Origin: Native.

European spindle-tree is planted as an ornamental for its red autumn leaves and fruits. • The dense, hard wood of this European species was once favored by carvers. It has also been used to make toothpicks, spindles, skewers, pipe stems and high-quality, easily erased art charcoal. Tanners valued the bark for preparing fine leather for gloves. • Herbalists and drug manufacturers used the bark, leaves and fruits of European spindletree as a strong laxative. Unfortunately, the medicine is rather too effective, causing drastic purging and pain in the colon. The U.S. Food and Drug Administration classifies this tree as dangerous. • *Euonymus*, meaning "well-reputed" or "famous," was euphemistically bestowed in recognition of the plant's toxicity. • **Winged burning-bush (*E. alata**, also called winged euonymus or *E. alatus*), shown in dark green (species overlap) on the map, is an Asian species that is used in horticulture and occasionally invades woodlands and untended yards. It is a tall (up to 23') shrub readily distinguished by the 2–4 conspicuous corky wings on its twigs and by its stalkless leaves, which turn bright red in autumn. • Eastern wahoo, the native *Euonymus*, is easily distinguished by its hairy lower leaf surfaces, bright red arils and maroon flowers.

Also Called: European euonymus, skewerwood, prickwood • *E. europaeus.*

Size and Shape: Small trees or tall shrubs up to 20' tall; crowns rounded; roots spreading.

Trunks: Straight, often short or clumped; bark greenish-gray, often reddish-streaked, thin; wood hard, dense.

Branches: Spreading; twigs greenish, smooth, **somewhat 4-sided; buds loosely 6-scaled,** about ⅛" long, **plump, not flat-lying,** present at twig tips.

Leaves: Opposite, simple, deciduous; **blades hairless,** green above, paler beneath, oblong-ovate to lance-shaped or elliptical, 1½–4¾" long, **abruptly pointed, finely toothed;** stalks <1" long; **leaves red in autumn.**

Flowers: Greenish to yellowish-white, about ¼" across, bisexual, 4 parted; petals usually 4, wide-spreading; sepals usually 4, fused at the base; flowers in loose, branched, 3–7-flowered clusters (cymes), on ¾–2" long, slender stalks from leaf axils, in May–June (after leaves expand).

Fruits: Prominently 4-lobed capsules, yellow, pink or red- to purple-tinged when mature, ⅜–½" wide; hang on slender stalks; **seeds 4, each enclosed in a fleshy, orange aril; capsules split open across the bottom to release seeds** in September, **empty capsules persist.**

Habitat: Low, moist sites, often in disturbed areas.

Origin: Introduced from Europe.

Although not widely grown as an ornamental, this shade-tolerant native shrub has been cultivated since 1640 for its attractive, dark green leaves, lightly fragrant flower clusters and distinctive, persistent fruits. The hanging clusters of unusual papery pods attract attention through much of the year. The pods, along with the striped, greenish branches, add interest in winter when the shrubs are leafless and loose seeds in the pods rattle in the breeze. Children sometimes like to crush the fresh pods to hear them pop. • The spreading roots send up suckers that may form thickets in open areas. In gardens, this tendency can cause problems when shoots appear in unwanted places. Otherwise, this attractive shrub is relatively maintenance free. It transplants easily and can be grown from cuttings or seeds. • The genus name *Staphylea* is derived from the Greek *staphyle*, "bunch of grapes," in reference to the hanging clusters of flowers. The specific epithet *trifolia* describes the 3-parted leaves. • When fruits and flowers are absent, American bladdernut may be confused with common hop-tree (p. 231). However, these two species are easily distinguished by examining their leaves and branches, which are opposite in bladdernuts and alternate in hop-trees.

Also Called: Tall bladdernut.

Size and Shape: Trees or shrubs to 20' tall; crowns rounded; roots spreading.

Trunks: Often clumped, up to 4" in diameter; young bark smooth, green, often with mottled stripes; mature bark gray to brown, becoming slightly ridged with pale, longitudinal stripes.

Branches: Erect, rather stiff; twigs stout, greenish, almost ringed at nodes, somewhat striped; buds egg-shaped, 2–4-scaled, paired at stem tips.

Leaves: Opposite, deciduous; compound, divided into **3 leaflets;** leaflets dark green and smooth above, paler and sparsely hairy beneath, 1½–4" long, pointed, finely sawtoothed; tip leaflet long-stalked, side-leaflets essentially stalkless; main leaf stalk 1⅛–4¾" long, with slender, ephemeral bracts at the base (2 stipules) and at the top (2 stipules below each leaflet); leaves green to pale yellow in autumn.

Flowers: Greenish-white, narrowly bell-shaped, about ⅜" long, bisexual, 5-parted; sepals nearly as long as petals; flowers **in nodding, branched, 1⅛–4" long clusters** (racemes) at branch tips, in April–May (just before leaves expand fully).

Fruits: Inflated, thin-walled, veiny capsules with 3 pointed lobes, green to yellowish-brown, 1⅛–2⅜" **long;** hang on slender stalks; seeds yellow-brown, bony, 1–4 per chamber, **rattling in ripe capsules;** capsules split open near tips in September, persist into winter.

Habitat: Moist, rich woods on floodplains and hillsides.

Origin: Native.

249

Horsechestnut is a hardy, moderately fast-growing tree often planted as an ornamental. It lives 80–100 years and can tolerate urban conditions, but its broad, domed canopy requires considerable space. • Horsechestnut is the "spreading chestnut tree" that Henry Wadsworth Longfellow wrote about. The large, sweeping branches tipped with showy, erect flower clusters suggest enormous candelabras. • The fruits and seeds have been used for centuries to treat colds, whooping cough, fever, rheumatism, backache, nerve pain and sunburn. Today, horsechestnut-seed preparations are sold in Europe and the U.S. for reducing inflammation and pain associated with varicose veins, ulcers, hemorrhoids and phlebitis. • **Caution:** The seeds, leaves and bark contain aesculin, a **toxic** alkaloid that can cause vomiting, stupor, twitching and even paralysis. Some sources report that horsechestnuts have been used as horse fodder, but most say these fruits are poisonous to livestock. • Horsechestnut trees produce good seed crops almost every year. The large, inedible fruits are generally shunned by wildlife, though squirrels occasionally eat the embryo stalks in the seeds. • The name "horsechestnut" reflects the similarity between these seeds and the edible seeds of chestnuts (*Castanea* spp., p. 117). Be careful never to confuse them.

Size and Shape: Trees 35–65' tall; crowns broad, rounded.

Trunks: Short, 12–32" in diameter; young bark dark gray-brown, smooth; mature bark fissured, scaly; wood pale, light, close-grained.

Branches: Ascending, then downcurved and finally upcurved at the tips; **twigs stout,** reddish-brown with white pores (lenticels), **unpleasant-smelling when bruised; buds shiny, dark brown, sticky, ¾–1½" long at twig tips,** smaller and paired below.

Leaves: Opposite, deciduous; compound, **palmately divided into 5–9 (usually 7) stalkless leaflets at the tip of a long stalk;** leaflets yellowish-green, widest above midleaf, gradually tapered to the base, 4–8" long; leaf scars large, horse-shoe-shaped; leaves rusty yellow in autumn.

Flowers: White to cream-colored, spotted with red and yellow, bell-shaped, ¾–1⅛" long; unisexual and bisexual flowers in each cluster; petals 5, unequal; flowers **in showy, erect, 8–12" long, cone-shaped clusters (panicles) at tips of branches,** in May–June (after leaves expand).

Fruits: Green to brown, spiny, leathery, round capsules, 2–2¼" across; hang in clusters; **seeds up to 2" across,** 1–2 (rarely 3) per capsule, smooth, **satin-shiny, mahogany brown with a rough, pale end;** capsules split lengthwise into 3 segments, drop in autumn.

Habitat: Disturbed sites in fields and woodlands.

Origin: Introduced from southeastern Europe; rare escape.

Illinois lies near the center of the range of this Midwestern species. Ohio buckeye is sometimes planted as an ornamental shade tree, and trees sometimes spread from cultivated parents. • The weak, uniform wood is easy to carve and resists splitting, so it was ideal for making artificial limbs. It has been also used as a source of paper pulp and for making woodenware, crates and troughs for collecting maple sap. Ohio buckeye was once a valuable timber tree in the U.S., but because of its increasing rarity, it now has little commercial importance. • **Caution:** Most parts of this tree, including the large seeds, contain the **toxic** alkaloid aesculin. Perhaps because of its toxicity, Ohio buckeye is relatively disease- and insect-free, and its fruits are seldom harvested by wildlife. However, squirrels sometimes eat the soft, young "nuts." • The name "buckeye" refers to the seeds, which somewhat resemble the eyes of deer, and this species is the official state tree of Ohio. • Horsechestnut (p. 250) is readily distinguished by its larger (4–8"), more numerous (usually 7), abruptly pointed leaflets and its sticky winter buds. • A distinctive variation with whitish bark and white lower leaf surfaces is sometimes recognized as a separate variety, **chalky buckeye (*A. glabra* var. *leucodermis*)**. Chalky buckeye is a rare inhabitant of Jackson County.

Also Called: Fetid buckeye.

Size and Shape: Trees 25–50' tall; crowns broad, rounded.

Trunks: Straight, 6–14" in diameter; young bark gray, smooth; mature bark dark gray-brown, with thick, scaly plates; wood pale, light, close-grained.

Branches: Slender, spreading to drooping, upcurved at tips; **twigs stout, reddish-brown, with orange pores** (lenticels), unpleasant-smelling when bruised; **buds ½–¾" long at twig tips, reddish, powdery-coated,** smaller and paired below.

Leaves: Opposite, deciduous; compound, **palmately divided into 5 (rarely 7) stalkless leaflets at the tip of a 4–6" long stalk;** leaflets bright or yellowish-green above, paler and hairy beneath, lance-shaped, **widest above midleaf,** gradually tapered to base, 2½–6" long, unevenly sharp-toothed; leaf scars large, horseshoe-shaped; leaves yellow to orange in autumn.

Flowers: Pale greenish-yellow, narrowly bell-shaped, ½–1⅜" long; unisexual and bisexual flowers in each cluster; petals 4, unequal, hairy; stamens 7, often twice as long as petals; flowers in **showy, erect, 4–6" long, cone-shaped clusters (panicles) at branch tips,** in April–May (after leaves expand).

Fruits: Yellowish-green, spiny, leathery capsules ¾–1⅛" across (rarely to 2"); **seeds satin-shiny, dark reddish-brown** with a rough, pale end, ¾–1⅜" across, 1 (rarely 2–3) per capsule; capsules split lengthwise into 3 segments, drop in September–October.

Habitat: Moist, rich forests, especially on floodplains.

Origin: Native.

R ed buckeye is a popular ornamental whose scarlet flower clusters are among the most beautiful produced by a temperate-zone tree. Dwarf forms and a yellow-flowered variety (**A. pavia** var. **flavescens**) are available in nurseries. • This hardy native species is cultivated north of its natural range, well into southeastern Canada (USDA Zone 4). Red buckeye thrives in heavy shade, but becomes much denser in sunny sites. Young plants especially need a cool, moist rooting zone. • Red buckeye is perhaps best known as a parent of **red horsechestnut (A. x carnea)**, a popular ornamental, created by crossing red buckeye and horsechestnut (p. 250). Red horsechestnut has the showy, scarlet flowers of red buckeye and the handsome foliage of horsechestnut. • The leaves and the fruits of red buckeye are **toxic**, so very few wild animals use this plant for food and few insect pests bother it. • A rare species, **sweet buckeye** (**A. flava**, also called yellow buckeye or *A. octandra*), shown in dark green (species overlap) on the map, grows in rich woods in Galatin County. Sweet buckeye is a canopy tree (up to 100' tall). Its May–June flowers have bell-shaped calyxes and yellow (sometimes red- or purple-tinged) petals edged with simple hairs. In contrast, red buckeye is a small, understory species that has April–May flowers with tubular calyxes and red petals edged with stalked glands.

Also Called: *A. discolor.*

Size and Shape: Tall shrubs or small trees, usually 10–20' tall; crowns open, rounded.

Trunks: Usually clumped, 4–12" in diameter; bark dark grayish-brown, smooth.

Branches: Large, erect, **paired;** twigs gray or brown, round; **buds not resinous-sticky,** paired, with overlapping, not prominently keeled scales.

Leaves: Opposite, deciduous, compound, 7–12" across, **palmately divided into 5** (rarely 7) **short-stalked leaflets** at the tip of a slender stalk; leaflets thin, **shiny and dark green above,** paler and smooth to finely woolly beneath, **2–6" long,** 1–1½" wide, **widest at or just above midleaf,** pointed, gradually tapered to a wedge-shaped base, finely toothed; leaf scars large, horseshoe-shaped; leaves red to orange (yellow) in early autumn.

Flowers: Bright red-purple or red-yellow, narrowly bell-shaped, 1–1½" long, with unisexual and bisexual flowers in each cluster; sepals 5, fused in a shallow-lobed, finely hairy (not glandular), red or yellow tube; **petals 4** (sometimes 5), unequal, **edged with stalked glands** near the base; stamens 6–8, projecting slightly; flowers **in showy, erect, 4–8" long, loose, cone-shaped clusters (panicles) at branch tips,** in April–May (after leaves expand).

Fruits: Egg-shaped, smooth, yellowish-green, leathery capsules 1³⁄₁₆–2³⁄₈" across; seeds 1–2, shiny, dark orange-brown with a rough, pale end, **1–2 per capsule;** capsules split lengthwise into 3 segments, drop in August.

Habitat: Rich, moist soil in woodlands.

Origin: Native.

Key to the Maples (Genus *Acer*)

1a Leaves compound, divided into 3–5 leaflets . . . . *A. negundo*, **Manitoba maple** (p. 260)

1b Leaves simple 2

2a Leaves deeply 3–5-lobed, otherwise smooth-edged or with a few coarse teeth, notches rounded 3

2b Leaf variously lobed, edged with many sharp teeth, notches pointed at the base and often toothed almost to the base 7

3a Flowers with conspicuous petals, borne on ascending, hairless stalks in elongated, stalked clusters; samaras with wings spreading at almost 180°; leaf juice milky 4

3b Flowers lacking petals, hanging on slender, hairy stalks in tassel-like clusters; samaras with wings spreading at less than 120°, often almost parallel; leaf juice clear. 5

4a Leaves relatively large (4–7" across) with sharp to slender pointed lobes . . . . *A. platanoides*, **Norway maple** (p. 256)

4b Leaves relatively small (2–4" across) with blunt to rounded lobes . . . . *A. campestre*, **hedge maple** (p. 259)

5a Leaf lobes blunt, rounded; bark pale and smooth (like that of a beech tree) . . . . *A. barbatum*, **southern sugar maple** (p. 254)

5b Leaf lobes sharp- to slender-pointed; bark dark and rough 6

6a Leaves mostly 3-lobed with drooping edges, smooth- or wavy-edged or with a few irregular, coarse teeth, green or brownish and more or less hairy beneath . . . . *A. nigrum*, **black maple** (p. 255)

6b Leaves mostly 5-lobed with flat (not drooping) edges, edged with regular, coarse, pointed teeth, pale and essentially hairless beneath . . *A. saccharum*, **sugar maple** (p. 254)

7a Leaves deeply cut into 5 or more coarsely toothed, relatively narrow lobes, with lobe bases usually narrower than the upper lobe 8

7b Leaves more shallowly cut into 3–5 parallel-sided to broadly triangular lobes, edged with regular, coarse to fine teeth. 10

8a Leaves cut more than halfway to the center into 5–9 lance-shaped lobes. . . . . *A. palmatum*, **Japanese maple** (p. 259)

8b Leaves cut less than halfway to the center in 5 broad lobes 9

9a Flowers with conspicuous petals, borne in elongated, stalked clusters, appearing after the leaves unfold; samaras maturing in mid- to late summer, wings spreading at <30°; leaves with coarse single teeth . . . . *A. pseudoplatanus*, **sycamore maple** (p. 256)

9b Flowers lacking petals, hanging on slender stalks in tassel-like clusters, appearing long before the leaves; samaras maturing in spring, wings spreading at about 90°; leaves with many double teeth. . . . . *A. saccharinum*, **silver maple** (p. 257)

10a Leaves narrowly triangular, longer than wide, with 2 small basal lobes and a large, coarsely toothed central lobe. . . . . *A. ginnala*, **Amur maple** (p. 259)

10b Leaves more rounded, usually about as wide as long, with 3 large lobes above midleaf and sometimes 2 smaller basal lobes . . . . *A. rubrum*, **red maple** (p. 258)

Fine-grained, durable sugar maple wood polishes well and sometimes has a beautiful wavy or speckled (bird's-eye) appearance. It is highly valued for flooring, furniture, veneer, paneling, plywood, sports articles, musical instruments, tool handles, spindles, cutting blocks and other items that require hard wood. In the past, the wood was used for plows, wagons and early wooden railway rails. • Settlers used potash-rich maple ashes as fertilizer. The ashes also have been used in soap and in pottery glazes. • "Sugaring off" was an important part of pioneer culture. Sugar maple sap was gathered in pails each spring and boiled over wood fires to produce maple syrup or sugar. The sap contains 2–6% sugar, so 30–40 quarts are required to produce a single quart of syrup. Today, vacuum plastic tubing carries sap from trees to processing sites where oil- or gas-powered evaporators reduce it to syrup for this multimillion dollar industry. • Severe declines in sugar maple numbers in parts of North America during the 1980s were caused by a combination of drought, cold winters, defoliation and acid rain. • A close relative, **southern sugar maple** (***A. barbatum***, also called *A. saccharum* var. *floridanum*), shown in dark green (species overlap) on the map, is a smaller tree that can tolerate hot, humid summers. It is distinguished by its smooth, pale gray bark and its smaller (usually <3") leaves, with blunt lobes and pale, usually hairy undersides.

Also Called: Rock maple, hard maple, bird's-eye maple, curly maple, sweet maple • *A. saccharaphorum.*

Size and Shape: Trees 65–100' tall; crowns rounded, broad; roots shallow, wide-spreading.

Trunks: Straight, 20–60" in diameter; mature bark dark gray, irregularly ridged, sometimes scaly; wood light yellowish-brown, hard, heavy.

Branches: Sturdy; twigs shiny, reddish-brown, hairless, straight; buds brown, faintly hairy, **sharply pointed, with 12–16 paired scales,** ¼–⅜" long at twig tips, smaller and paired below.

Leaves: Opposite, simple, deciduous; blades deep yellowish-green above, paler beneath, hairless, 3–8" long, with **5 palmate lobes** (occasionally 3) separated by rounded notches, edged with **a few irregular, blunt-pointed teeth;** stalks 1½–3" long; leaves yellow to bright red in autumn.

Flowers: Greenish-yellow, small; functionally unisexual, often with male and female flowers in mixed clusters on the same tree; petals absent; sepals 5; **flowers hang on slender, hairy, 1⅛–2¾" long stalks in tasseled clusters** (umbel-like corymbs) at or near branch tips, in April–May (before or as leaves expand).

Fruits: Green to brown **pairs of winged samaras,** ¾–1½" long, **U-shaped, with spreading to almost parallel wings shorter than the slender stalks; seedcases plump;** samaras hang in clusters, mature and drop in September–October.

Habitat: Rich, moist to mesic forests.

Origin: Native.

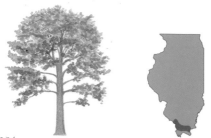

254

Black maple has strong, straight-grained, uniformly textured wood that is sold as "hard maple," a term applied to both black and sugar maple (p. 254). It is used for furniture, fixtures, farm tools, spindles, veneer, plywood, flooring, dies and cutting blocks. • The sap from black maple trees can be collected and used to make syrup and sugar. • Like sugar maple, black maple saplings are shade tolerant and can survive for many years in the forest understory until new openings provide the light necessary for them to shoot up quickly and take their place in the canopy. • Black maple and sugar maple hybridize frequently, producing offspring with intermediate characteristics. Some taxonomists classify black maple as a variety or subspecies of sugar maple. Black and sugar maples are distinguished by their leaves and bark. Sugar maple leaves are flat, deep yellow-green and hairless, and their central lobes are rather square, with parallel sides. Black maple leaves are drooping and deep green with velvety lower surfaces, and their central lobes tend to taper from the base. Sugar maple bark is grayish with loose-edged plates, whereas black maple bark is blackish-gray and more deeply furrowed.

Also Called: Black sugar maple, hard maple, rock maple • *A. saccharum* ssp. *nigrum*.

Size and Shape: Trees 65–100' tall; crowns broad, rounded.

Trunks: Straight, 20–48" in diameter; mature bark blackish-gray, with long, irregular, vertical ridges, sometimes scaly; wood pale yellowish-brown, heavy, hard.

Branches: Stout; twigs dull yellowish- to reddish-brown, stout, straight; buds dark grayish-brown, hairy, with paired scales, about ¼" long at twig tips, smaller and paired below.

Leaves: Opposite, simple, deciduous, **appearing wilted;** blades dark green above, densely **brownish-velvety beneath,** 4–6" long, with **3 palmate lobes** (sometimes 5 indistinct lobes) separated by **open, shallow notches,** edged with **a few irregular, blunt-pointed teeth;** stalks hairy; leaves yellow to brownish-yellow (seldom red) in autumn.

Flowers: Yellowish, small; unisexual with male and female flowers mixed or in separate clusters on the same tree; petals absent; sepals 5; **flowers hang on slender, hairy, ¾–2¾" long stalks, in tasseled clusters** (umbel-like corymbs) at or near branch tips, in May–June (before or as leaves expand).

Fruits: Green to brown **pairs of winged samaras, U-shaped with slightly spreading to almost parallel wings about as long as the slender, hairy stalks;** samaras about 1⅛" long; **seedcases plump;** samaras hang in clusters, mature and drop in October.

Habitat: Moist woods in bottomlands and along streams.

Origin: Native.

255

This popular ornamental shade tree can grow in polluted urban sites with compacted, nutrient-poor soils. It is more resistant than native maples to insects and fungal diseases. Norway maple usually produces abundant seed, and it can become an aggressive invader of natural vegetation. • Many cultivars of this beautiful, hardy species have been developed. The cultivar 'Schwedleri' (Schwedler maple), with its purplish-red spring leaves and bright orange-red to purple autumn foliage, has been planted in North America for over a century. 'Crimson King' boasts rich maroon leaves and is also very popular. Norway maple keeps its leaves about 2 weeks longer than native maples in the autumn. • Norway maple can be confused with sugar maple (p. 254), but Norway maple's dark green (vs. yellow-green) leaves have 5–7 (vs. 3–5), bristle-tipped (vs. blunt-pointed) lobes, milky (not clear) sap and turn only yellow (never red or orange) in autumn. • Another introduced European species, **sycamore maple (*A. pseudoplatanus*)**, shown in dark green (species overlap) on the map, is also widely planted in the state, but it rarely escapes. Sycamore maple is distinguished by its thicker, more wrinkled leaves, with white-hairy veins and numerous coarse teeth.

Size and Shape: Trees 40–65' tall; crowns dense, rounded, broad; roots spreading, fairly deep.

Trunks: Straight, 12–28" in diameter; bark very dark gray, with regular low, intersecting ridges, not scaly; wood pale, straight-grained, uniformly textured.

Branches: Sturdy, ascending to spreading; twigs straight, purplish-tinged to reddish-brown, hairless, with prominent pores (lenticels) and milky juice; buds purplish to reddish, plump, blunt, with **4–8 fleshy, paired scales, about ¼" long at twig tips,** smaller and paired below.

Leaves: Opposite, simple, deciduous, with milky juice; blades dark green, hairless, 3–6" long, 4–7" wide, with **5 (rarely 7) palmate lobes plus a few large, bristle-tipped teeth;** stalks long; leaves yellow to orange brown in autumn.

Flowers: Greenish-yellow, about ⅜" across, bisexual or male; petals 5; sepals 5; **flowers in erect, rounded clusters** (corymbs) at branch tips, in April–June (before or as leaves expand).

Fruits: Green to brown **pairs of winged samaras,** with **wings spreading at almost 180°;** samaras 1¾–2" long; **seedcases flat; samaras hang on slender stalks in clusters,** mature in September–October, often persist through winter.

Habitat: Roadsides, vacant lots and thickets.

Origin: Introduced from Europe and western Asia.

Although not as showy as most maples in autumn, this handsome, fast-growing, hardy tree is widely planted as an ornamental. However, silver maple requires considerable space and usually produces abundant seed and leaf fall each year. Also, its brittle limbs break easily, and its roots can spread aggressively to clog sewer pipes. • Silver maple has straight-grained, rather brittle wood that is sold as "soft maple." It is usually used where strength is not important, such as for inexpensive furniture, veneer, boxes, crates and pulp. • Several cultivars with deeply divided leaves have been developed and are propagated from cuttings. 'Laciniatum' or 'Wieri' (cutleaf silver maple) is especially popular. • Silver maple sap is only half as sweet as that of sugar maple (p. 254), but with patient boiling, it yields a delicious, pale syrup. • When felled, silver maple sends up vigorous shoots from dormant buds in the stump. Also, fallen branches can sprout roots and grow into new trees. • Many birds and small mammals such as grosbeaks and squirrels eat the abundant seeds. Silver maple trees commonly have hollow trunks that provide dens for squirrels, raccoons and other mammals, nesting cavities for wood ducks and other birds and hideouts for small children.

Also Called: Soft maple, white maple, river maple.

Size and Shape: Trees 65–100' tall; crowns broad, rounded, open; roots spreading, usually shallow.

Trunks: Short in open sites, taller in forests, 20–48" in diameter; young bark gray, smooth; **mature bark gray, often shaggy,** with thin strips that peel from both ends; wood pale, hard, heavy.

Branches: Sharply ascending, then arching downward to upturned tips; twigs shiny, hairless, unpleasant-smelling when broken; buds shiny, reddish, blunt, with 6–10 paired scales; flower buds plump, ringing the twigs.

Leaves: Opposite, simple, deciduous; blades light green above, **silvery white beneath,** 3–6" long, with **5–7 palmate lobes separated by deep, concavely narrowed notches, irregularly coarse-toothed;** stalks 3–4" long; leaves pale yellow to brown in October.

Flowers: Greenish-yellow or reddish, tiny; unisexual with male and female flowers in separate clusters on same or separate trees; petals absent; sepals 5; **flowers in dense, almost stalkless clusters** (umbels), in February–April **(long before leaves expand).**

Fruits: Yellowish-green to brownish **pairs of winged samaras with wings spreading at 90°,** often only 1 per pair maturing; **samaras 1⅛–2¾" long; seedcases ribbed; samaras hang on slender stalks in clusters,** mature and drop singly in late May–early June (as leaves expand fully).

Habitat: Moist to wet sites, usually near streams.

Origin: Native.

This attractive, red-tinged tree is widely planted as an ornamental for its red twigs, buds, flowers, young fruits and autumn leaves. Red maple is one of the first trees to flower each spring. It is an extremely variable species, with a wide range of ecological, morphological and cytological (cell structure) variations. Several cultivars have been developed that can endure urban conditions. • Red maple is often a succesful invader of recently cleared land and open forests. It grows quickly for the first 20–23 years and usually lives 75–100 years. If trees are cut, burned or otherwise damaged, they can sprout vigorously from the base. Most red maples produce both male and female flowers, but young trees occasionally have only one sex or the other. • Although red maple sap is only half as sweet as that of sugar maple (p. 254), it can be used to make syrup. • Red maple's straight-grained, uniform wood is sold as "soft maple" and has been used for pulp and for making crates, furniture, cabinets, veneer and flooring. • Pennsylvanian colonists made a dark red ink by boiling the bark, which also yields brown or black dyes with different mordants. • The abundant seeds are eaten by rodents, but white-tailed deer and rabbits often browse on the young shoots and leaves.

Also Called: Scarlet maple, soft maple, swamp maple, curled maple.

Size and Shape: Trees 50–80' tall; crowns dense, long, rounded; roots shallow, wide-spreading.

Trunks: Short in open sites, often branch-free for half its length in forests, 16–32" in diameter; young bark light gray, smooth; mature bark dark grayish-brown, scaly, with thin plates that peel from both ends; wood pale brown, heavy, hard, not strong.

Branches: Ascending; twigs shiny, reddish, hairless, not unpleasant-smelling; buds shiny, reddish, hairless, usually with 8 paired scales, blunt, about ⅛" long at twig tips, smaller and paired below; **flower buds usually ring dwarf twigs.**

Leaves: Opposite, simple, deciduous; blades light green above, whitish beneath, 2–6" long, with **3–5 palmate lobes separated by shallow, sharp notches, irregularly double-toothed;** stalks 2–4" long; leaves bright red, orange or yellow in autumn.

Flowers: Red to orange, short-stalked, about ⅛" across; unisexual, usually with male and female flowers on separate branches on the same tree; petals 5; sepals 5; **flowers in small, tassel-like clusters** (umbels), in March–April **(long before leaves expand).**

Fruits: Red, reddish-brown or yellow **pairs of winged samaras with wings spreading at 50–60°; slender-stalked; samaras ½–1⅛" long; samaras hang in clusters,** mature and drop singly in late May–early June (4–6 weeks after flowering).

Habitat: Cool, moist sites in low-lying forest swamps; sometimes on moderately dry, upland sites.

Origin: Native.

This popular ornamental tree is widely planted for its fragrant flowers, showy, reddish samaras and spectacular autumn foliage. Amur maple is one of the few maples with perfumed flowers and one of the best trees for fall color. • Amur maple is adapted to northern areas with relatively cool summers, and it tolerates dry conditions and partial shade. This hardy tree requires little maintenance. It can withstand heavy pruning and is often shaped into tree form. Maples should not be pruned until the leaves are fully expanded, because the heavy flow of spring sap causes excessive "bleeding" if trees are pruned too early. • Many exotic maples are grown as ornamentals and occasionally escape to grow wild. **Japanese maple (*A. palmatum*)**, shown in dark green (species overlap) on the map, is an Asian native that rarely exceeds 20' in height. It is easily identified by its distinctive leaves, which are cut more than halfway to the center into 5- 7 slender, pointed lobes. • **Hedge maple (*A. campestre*,** also called field maple), also in dark green on the map, is another small tree (usually 15–30' tall) that rarely escapes in Illinois. This European ornamental has small, blunt-lobed leaves. Like its cousin, Norway maple (p. 256), hedge maple has milky juice (latex), relatively late (May–June), showy flowers and samaras with wings spreading at almost 180°.

Size and Shape: Small trees or tall shrubs 13–20' tall; crowns rounded, shrubby and uneven when young; roots shallow.

Trunks: Usually clumped, sometimes pruned to a single stem; bark dark gray, scaly, fissured; wood pale, light, soft, weak.

Branches: Slender, often wand-like and arching; twigs slender, yellowish-brown, hairless, somewhat angled; buds reddish-brown to tan, with hairy-tipped scales.

Leaves: Opposite, simple, deciduous; blades glossy, deep green above, paler beneath, essentially **hairless with age,** 1⅛–4" long, narrowly triangular, 3-lobed (rarely undivided or 5-lobed) with **2 short, basal lobes and a large, central lobe, wedge-shaped notches, with irregularly double sharp-toothed edges;** stalks slender, 1⅛–1½" long; leaves brilliant red (sometimes yellow or orange) in autumn.

Flowers: Pale yellow to creamy white, fragrant, about ¼" long; petals 5, inconspicuous; sepals 5; **flowers in drooping clusters** (corymbs) at branch tips, in May–June (as leaves expand).

Fruits: Scarlet or pinkish-brown pairs of dry samaras with **inner edges of wings almost parallel;** samaras ¾–1" long, hairless; **samaras in hanging clusters,** mature in July–August, often persist into winter.

Habitat: Yards, ditches, fence lines and other open, disturbed sites.

Origin: Introduced from Manchuria and Japan.

259

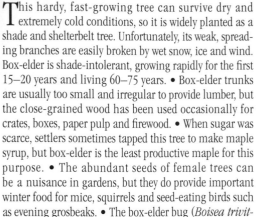

This hardy, fast-growing tree can survive dry and extremely cold conditions, so it is widely planted as a shade and shelterbelt tree. Unfortunately, its weak, spreading branches are easily broken by wet snow, ice and wind. Box-elder is shade-intolerant, growing rapidly for the first 15–20 years and living 60–75 years. • Box-elder trunks are usually too small and irregular to provide lumber, but the close-grained wood has been used occasionally for crates, boxes, paper pulp and firewood. • When sugar was scarce, settlers sometimes tapped this tree to make maple syrup, but box-elder is the least productive maple for this purpose. • The abundant seeds of female trees can be a nuisance in gardens, but they do provide important winter food for mice, squirrels and seed-eating birds such as evening grosbeaks. • The box-elder bug (*Boisea trivittata*) is a widespread pest that can occur in large numbers in urban areas where box-elder is common. • This maple could be mistaken for an ash (*Fraxinus* spp., pp. 262–66), but ash trees usually have more numerous (5–9), smooth-edged or regularly toothed leaflets. Also, ash leaf scar ends are well separated (not meeting), ash samaras are single with symmetrical wings and ash seedcases are smooth.

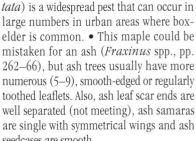

Also Called: Western box-elder, ashleaf maple, Manitoba maple.

Size and Shape: Trees 35–65' tall; crowns broad, uneven, open; roots widely spreading, mostly shallow.

Trunks: Usually short, 12–32" in diameter; young bark light grayish-brown, smooth; mature bark darker grayish-brown, with narrow, interlacing ridges; wood nearly white, soft, weak.

Branches: Spreading, crooked; **twigs shiny or waxy-powdered,** brown to greenish-purple, smooth; buds dull red, finely white-hairy, blunt, with 2–6 paired scales, about ¼" long at twig tips, flat-lying or hidden by leaf stalk bases below.

Leaves: Opposite, deciduous; compound, **pinnately divided into 3–5 leaflets** (sometimes 7–9 with rapid growth); leaflets yellowish-green above, grayish-green beneath, **2–4¾" long, irregularly coarse-toothed or shallow-lobed; leaf scars meeting around twigs;** leaves yellow in autumn.

Flowers: Pale yellowish-green, tiny; unisexual with male and female flowers on separate trees; petals absent; sepals 5; male flowers hang on hairy, thread-like stalks in loose bundles (umbels); female flowers short-stalked along a central axis in nodding clusters (racemes); flowers in April–May (as or before leaves expand).

Fruits: Green to pale brown **pairs of winged samaras,** with **wings usually spreading at <45°;** samaras 1⅛–2" long; **seedcases wrinkled, elongated,** pointed; **samaras hang in elongated clusters,** mature in autumn, may persist through winter.

Habitat: Low, moist woods, usually near water or on floodplains.

Origin: Native.

Key to Genera in the Olive Family (Oleaceae)

1a Leaves pinnately divided into leaflets; fruits slender, long-winged samaras
. . . . *Fraxinus*, **ash** (key to species, see below)

1b Leaves simple; fruits not samaras **2**

2a Individual flowers small, inconspicuous, without petals, usually unisexual; fruits spindle-shaped to ellipsoidal drupes . . . . *Forestiera*, **swamp-privet** (p. 268)

2b Individual flowers showy, with a 4–lobed, trumpet-shaped corolla, bisexual; fruits rounded drupes or capsules **3**

3a Leaves tapered to a wedge-shaped base and short (<$^3/_8$") stalk; flowers white, $^1/_8$–$^1/_4$" across, in 1–3$^1/_2$" long clusters; fruits berry-like drupes. . . . . . . *Ligustrum*, **privet** (p. 269)

3b Leaves squared to notched at the base, with $^3/_8$–$^3/_4$ long stalks; flowers deep purple to (occasionally) white, about $^3/_8$" across, in 4–8" long clusters; fruits woody capsules
. . . . *Syringa*, **lilac** (p. 267)

Key to the Ashes (Genus *Fraxinus*)

1a Leaflets smooth-edged, sometimes with a few faint, irregular, blunt teeth; samaras with cylindrical seedcases winged on the upper part only (not to the base) **2**

1b Leaflets regularly (sometimes faintly) toothed above the middle; samaras various **3**

2a Wings extending about $^1/_3$ of the way down the seedcases; leaflets 2$^3/_8$–6" long, lower leaf surfaces pale green, essentially hairless and dulled by many minute bumps
. . . . *F. americana*, **white ash** (p. 262)

2b Wings extending over halfway down the seedcases; leaflets 5–10" long, lower leaf surfaces pale yellowish-green, soft-hairy and lacking minute bumps
. . . . *F. profunda*, **pumpkin ash** (p. 264)

3a Leaves divided into 5–9 leaflets, distinctly paler beneath; seedcases cylindrical, winged on the upper part only (not to the base), tapered to the base; calyx visible at the base of each samara; uppermost side-buds close against the branch-tip bud
. . . . *F. pensylvanica*, **red ash** (p. 263)

3a Leaves divided into 7–13 leaflets, green above and below; seedcases flattened, winged to the blunt base; calyx minute, not visible on each samara; uppermost side-buds clearly separated from the branch-tip bud **4**

4a Twigs 4-sided, with 4 corky ridges; bark soft and velvety; leaflets stalked
. . . . *F. quadrangulata*, **blue ash** (p. 266)

4b Twigs round; bark firm and hard; leaflets stalkless . . . . *F. nigra*, **black ash** (p. 265)

Fraxinus profunda, pumpkin ash

F. quadrangulata, blue ash

White ash is the main source of commercial ash, a tough, shock-resistant wood highly valued for hockey sticks, baseball bats and tennis rackets. It is also used for tool handles, boats, barrels, casks, ladders and furniture veneer. In earlier days, plowing implements and airplane and automobile frames were made of ash wood. White ash also makes excellent fuel, comparable to oak and hickory. • Some tribes used the bark to produce a yellow dye. • Ash leaf juice has been recommended for soothing mosquito bites and bee stings. • The colorful autumn leaves, slender, graceful shape and neatly patterned bark make white ash an attractive ornamental. • In some parts of North America, white ash populations have undergone a progressive dieback called "ash yellows," leaving trees more susceptible to insects or disease. As well, the emerald ash borer (*Agrilus planipennis*) now threatens to devastate Illinois' white and green ashes. • Wood ducks, quail, wild turkeys, grouse and songbirds feed on the seeds. • The genus name *Fraxinus* is derived from the Greek *phraxis*, "hedges," because European ashes were often used in hedges. "White" refers to the silvery to pale gray leaf undersides, twigs and bark.

Also Called: American ash, Canadian white ash, Biltmore ash • *F. bilimoreana*.

Size and Shape: Trees 35–80' tall; crowns pyramidal; roots usually moderately deep.

Trunks: Straight, long, 20–40" in diameter; **mature bark grayish, with narrow, intersecting ridges in regular diamond patterns;** wood light brown, straight-grained, heavy, hard.

Branches: Long, stout, ascending to spreading; **twigs hairless,** shiny, developing a waxy, grayish skin, stout; buds reddish-brown with a soft, granular surface, 2–6-scaled; **tip buds reddish-brown,** broadly pyramidal, ¼–½" long, flanked by a smaller bud on each side.

Leaves: Opposite, deciduous, 8–16" long; compound, **pinnately divided into 5–9 (usually 7) similar leaflets;** leaflets dark green above, dull, **whitish beneath, with tiny bumps** (papillae), essentially hairless, ovate to oblong, 2⅜–6" long, on ¼–½" long stalks, abruptly sharp-pointed, **smooth-edged or with a few rounded teeth; leaf scars raised, U-shaped; leaves yellow or bronze-purple in autumn,** leaflets shed singly.

Flowers: Purplish to yellowish, tiny; unisexual with male and female flowers on separate trees; petals absent; sepals minute; flowers in compact clusters along twigs, in April–May (before leaves expand).

Fruits: Pale green to yellowish, **slender, winged nutlets** (samaras), 1–2" long, with **a long wing enclosing the upper ⅓ of each cylindrical seedcase; hang in long clusters;** seeds single; samaras mature in August–September, persist into winter.

Habitat: Upland woods with well-drained soils.

Origin: Native.

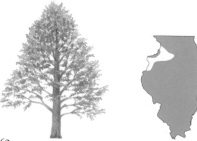

A fast-growing, hardy tree, red ash is often planted as an ornamental, but it can become invasive in urban landscapes. • The tough wood of red ash is not as strong as that of white ash (p. 262), but it is marketed under the same name and has been used for canoe paddles, baseball bats, tennis rackets, snowshoe frames, tool handles and picture frames. • Red ash bark produces a red dye, and the wood ashes provided potash. • The abundant seeds provide important autumn and winter food for quail, wild turkeys, cardinals and finches, as well as for squirrels and other rodents. • *F. pennsylvanica* is a widely distributed and variable species. In the past it was divided into 2 varieties—the typical var. *pennsylvanica*, with hairy leaflets, twigs and flower and fruit stalks, is called **red ash,** and the essentially hairless var. *subintegerrima* is called **green ash**. Red ash is the most typical form in the East, and green ash is the most common ash on the prairies, but both are the same species. • It is fairly easy to identify a tree as an ash, but much more difficult to determine which species. Ashes with hairy twigs include red ash, blue ash (p. 266) and pumpkin ash (p. 264), whereas green ash, white ash (p. 262) and black ash (p. 265) have hairless twigs.

Also Called: Rim ash, soft ash, green ash • *F. lanceolata.*

Size and Shape: Shrubby to medium trees 35–50' tall, variable; crowns irregular, rounded; roots shallow.

Trunks: Usually straight, 12–24" in diameter; bark grayish-brown, often reddish-tinged, flaky, with **irregular, shallow ridges in diamond-shaped patterns;** wood light grayish-brown, straight-grained, heavy, brittle.

Branches: Stout, ascending to spreading; **twigs stout, often hairy;** buds reddish-brown, hairy, 4–6-scaled, pyramidal, ⅛–⅜" **long, slightly longer than wide at branch tips, with a smaller bud on each side.**

Leaves: Opposite, deciduous, 10–12" long; compound, **pinnately divided into 5–9 (usually 7) leaflets;** leaflets yellowish-green above, paler beneath, oval, 3–6" long, taper-pointed, **shallow-toothed above the middle, borne on short, narrowly winged stalks;** leaf scars semi-circular; leaves yellowish-brown in autumn, leaflets shed singly.

Flowers: Purplish to yellowish, tiny; unisexual with male and female flowers on separate trees; petals absent; sepals minute; **flowers in many-flowered, compact clusters along twigs,** in April–May (before or as leaves expand).

Fruits: Pale green to yellowish, **slender, winged nutlets** (samaras), 1⅛–2⅜" long, **with a long wing enclosing the upper 1/2 or more of each cylindrical seedcase;** wings often with notched tips; seeds single; **samaras hang in long clusters,** mature in September, persist into winter.

Habitat: Moist to wet sites in hardwood forests.

Origin: Native.

263

Pumpkin ash is a native tree of the southeastern U.S. and reaches the northwestern limit of its range in southern Illinois. • The wood of all ash species except black ash (p. 265) is sold as "white ash." Pumpkin ash has no commercial value because of its scarcity. Although the wood is inferior to that of white ash (p. 262), it has been used for crates, railway ties, veneer, pulp and fuel. • Ash samaras are dispersed by wind and water. The seeds require exposure to cool, moist conditions for several months before they germinate. • Many small birds and mammals eat the seeds, and white-tailed deer browse on the twigs and leaves. Pumpkin ash snags provide nest sites and dens for cavity-dwelling birds and small mammals. • Gall gnats sometimes cause the male flowers of ash trees to develop abnormally into galls, which stay on the trees for several months. • The specific epithet *profunda* means "deep" or "profound" and refers to the swampy habitat of this species. • The leaves and fruits of pumpkin ash are distinctly larger than those of our other ashes. The leaves can grow to 18" long, with leaflets up to 10" long. The samaras average 2⅛" in length and ⅜" in width.

Also Called: *F. tomentosa.*

Size and Shape: Trees up to 100' tall; crowns narrow, oval; roots spreading, shallow.

Trunks: Straight, single, usually **buttressed;** mature bark grayish, **with thin, intersecting ridges in regular diamond patterns;** wood grayish-brown, straight-grained, hard.

Branches: Straight; **twigs downy,** grayish-brown, stout; **buds broadly pyramidal at branch tips;** bud scales paired, soft, **granular-textured.**

Leaves: Opposite, deciduous, 8–18" long; compound, **pinnately divided into 5–9 (usually 7) similar leaflets; central stalks woolly;** leaflets dark green above, **paler yellowish-green and soft-hairy beneath,** 3–6" long (rarely longer), lance-shaped to elliptical, taper-pointed, often unequal at the base, smooth-edged (or nearly so), **on wingless stalks ⅜–½" long;** leaf scars broadly U-shaped.

Flowers: Tiny; unisexual with male and female flowers on **separate trees;** petals absent; sepals 1/16–⅛" long; flowers in compact, many-flowered clusters, in early spring (before leaves expand).

Fruits: Pale green to yellowish, **winged nutlets** (samaras), single, slender, often widest above the middle, **1½–3" long,** with **tiny sepal remnants** at the base and a **wing extending over halfway down each thick, cylindrical seedcase;** wings round or notched at the tip; seeds single; **samaras hang in long clusters,** mature in autumn, persist into winter.

Habitat: Deciduous swamp forests.

Origin: Native.

This shade-intolerant, moisture-loving tree can tolerate standing water for many weeks. Usually it grows in mixed stands with other moisture-loving trees such as black spruce (p. 75), eastern white-cedar (p. 78) and silver maple (p. 257). • Black ash produces good seed crops irregularly, sometimes at intervals of up to 7 years. Fallen seeds lie dormant for a season before germinating. • Black ash wood is much softer and heavier than that of white ash, but it has been used for interior trim, furniture, cabinets and veneer. The wood is also very flexible and can be permanently bent, so it was favored for snowshoe frames and canoe ribs. When soaked and pounded, the logs separate readily along their annual rings into thin sheets. Long strips from these sheets were used for making barrel hoops and for weaving baskets and chair seats. • The wood ashes are rich in potash. • Hanging on branches through winter or buried under snow, the seeds provide important food for wild turkeys, grouse and small mammals. White-tailed deer and moose often browse new growth heavily. • This tree is easily recognized in winter by its soft, pale gray bark and blue-black buds. In most ashes, the tip bud is at least as wide as long, but in this species it is slightly longer than wide.

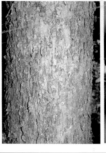

Also Called: Swamp ash, hoop ash, basket ash, water ash.

Size and Shape: Trees 35–65' tall; crowns narrow, open; roots very shallow, spreading.

Trunks: Slender, often bent, 12–24" in diameter; **young bark light gray, soft, corky-ridged, easily rubbed off by hand;** mature bark scaly; wood grayish-brown, coarsely straight-grained, heavy, tough.

Branches: Coarse, ascending; **twigs stout, soon dull gray, hairless; buds blackish-brown, pointed,** 6-scaled; **tip bud pyramidal, ¼–⅜" long,** typically ⅛–⅜" **above 2 smaller side-buds.**

Leaves: **Opposite,** deciduous, **10–16" long;** compound, pinnately divided into 7–11 similar leaflets; leaflets dark green, hairless (except for **reddish-brown fuzz at base**), elongated-ovate, 2¾–5½" long, slender-pointed, finely sharp-toothed, stalkless; leaf scars large, rounded; leaves reddish-brown in autumn, drop as whole leaves.

Flowers: Purplish, tiny; on hairless stalks, mostly bisexual, sometimes unisexual, with 1, 2 or 3 flower types on a single tree; petals absent; sepals minute; stamens 2; flowers in compact, branched clusters (panicles) along twigs and at branch tips, in May–June (before leaves expand).

Fruits: Pale green to yellowish, **winged, slender nutlets** (samaras) 1–1¾" long, with **broad, often twisted wings encircling flattened seedcases;** wings with round or notched tips; seeds single; **samaras hang in long clusters,** mature in August–September, sometimes persist through winter.

Habitat: Open, cool, wet sites in woodlands.

Origin: Native.

This unusual ash is native to the east-central U.S. and is very rare near its northern limit in Michigan, Wisconsin and Ontario. • Blue ash is sometimes planted as an ornamental shade tree. It grows quickly and can live 125–150 years. • Although blue ash is now of little commercial value because of its scarcity, its wood, sold as "white ash," has been used in sporting goods, agricultural tools, furniture, flooring and interior trim. Blue ash wood is durable, though somewhat brittle, and it has distinctive rings of large pores, which are laid down each spring. • The species name *quadrangulata* means "4-angled" and refers to the 4 corky ridges on the twigs. This characteristic distinguishes blue ash from all other ashes. Another unique feature is the sticky sap from the inner bark, which turns blue when exposed to air, hence the common name. • To produce a blue dye, the bark is chopped into pieces and steeped in boiling water. The mixture is then boiled down to concentrate the color. • The unusual scaly bark of blue ash is also distinctive. On older trees, the loose, hanging plates bring to mind the bark of shagbark hickory (p. 108).

Size and Shape: Trees 35–65' tall; crowns narrow, rounded, often irregular.

Trunks: Straight, slender, 6–20" in diameter; mature bark grayish, shaggy with loose, scaly plates; **inner bark blue when exposed to air;** wood yellowish-brown, coarse-grained, hard, heavy.

Branches: Spreading, short, stout; **twigs conspicuously 4-sided, with 4 corky ridges,** rusty-hairy; buds dark brown, hairy, 6-scaled, about ¼" long; **branch tip bud slightly flattened, with a smaller bud on each side.**

Leaves: Opposite, deciduous, **8–16" long;** compound, **pinnately divided into 5–11 similar leaflets;** leaflets dark yellowish-green, paler beneath, hairy in main vein axils or hairless, lance-shaped, 3–5½" long, taper-pointed, with asymmetrical bases, slender-stalked, coarsely toothed; leaf scars oval to crescent-shaped, with an upcurved line of bundle scars.

Flowers: Purplish, tiny, **bisexual;** petals absent; sepals minute, soon shed; flowers on hairless stalks, in compact, many-flowered, branched clusters (panicles), in March–April (before leaves expand).

Fruits: Green to yellowish, **winged nutlets** (samaras), with a **broad, often twisted wing enclosing each flattened seedcase, oblong-lance-shaped,** 1–2" long; wings with rounded or (usually) notched tips; **bases lack sepal remnants;** seeds single; **samaras hang in loose clusters,** mature in September–October.

Habitat: Low, moist, wooded sites; occasionally on limestone cliffs.

Origin: Native.

This tough immigrant is one of the most commonly planted flowering shrubs in North America. Hundreds of cultivars have been developed. • Lilacs bloom for about 2 weeks in spring, but hot weather shortens the flowering period, and hot sun may fade the flowers. • The fragrance of lilac bouquets can fill a room. To make bouquets last longer, cut flowers just as they are starting to open and bash the woody stem ends with a hammer or immerse them in boiling water for a few seconds. Most such bouquets will last 7–10 days. • Lilac flowers can be eaten raw in fruit salads, crystallized with a coating of beaten egg whites and sugar or added to batter for fritters. • **Japanese-tree lilac** (*S. reticulata* **ssp.** *pekinensis*, also called *S. pekinensis*), is a taller (20–30') variety that occasionally grows wild. It blooms later than most lilacs (early summer) and produces abundant clusters of cream-colored blooms. However, the tiny flowers are long, narrow trumpets with a musky (rather than perfumed) fragrance. Japanese-tree lilac is resistant to powdery mildew, scale insects and borers and does not spread via suckers. Many popular cultivars have been developed. • The name *Syringa*, from the Greek *syrinx*, "pipe," refers to the hollow branches.

Size and Shape: Shrubby trees or tall shrubs 10–25' tall; crowns rounded; roots spreading, often sending up suckers to form thickets.

Trunks: Usually clumped, small; bark grayish, thin, flaky with age.

Branches: Numerous; twigs olive green with prominent pores (lenticels), round, ¼" or more thick, stiff, soon hairless; buds green or brown, hairless, broadly egg-shaped, with 3–5 pairs of fleshy scales, usually paired at twig tips.

Leaves: Opposite, simple, deciduous; blades dull dark green, paler beneath, **ovate to heart-shaped, 2–5" long,** pointed, smooth-edged, with squared or notched bases; stalks slender, ¾–1⅛" long; leaf scars with 1 horizontal vein scar; leaves yellow to brownish in autumn.

Flowers: Purple, pink or white, fragrant, about ⅜" across, bisexual; **petals 4,** widely spreading, bases fused in a ⅜" long tube; sepals 4, fused at the base, glandular-hairy; stamens 2; flowers **in dense, conical, usually paired clusters (panicles) 4–8" long,** at the tips of previous year's branches, in May (as leaves expand).

Fruits: Green to brown, **leathery to woody,** hairless, flattened, **pointed capsules** ⅜–½" long; seeds 4 per capsule; capsules mature in August, persist through winter.

Habitat: Roadsides, disturbed sites and shores.

Origin: Introduced from southeastern Europe.

Eastern swamp-privet is rarely cultivated, but this attractive shrub deserves consideration as an ornamental wildlife plant. Female plants attract many birds with their fruits, and male plants make beautiful ornamental shrubs, covered with masses of yellow flowers each spring. • Eastern swamp-privet can be propagated from seed or by layering. Seeds sown straight from the bush usually germinate almost immediately, but if gardeners want to determine the sex of a tree before planting, it is best to layer the lower branches of older shrubs. For maximum fruit production, a few male trees should be planted among the females. For purely ornamental purposes, banks of male shrubs may be preferred. Abundant fruit production can create a mess on sidewalks and patios. • Eastern swamp-privet is the hardiest member of this small (about 20 species), relatively unknown genus. The trees often flourish in areas that are flooded for most of the growing season. Cultivated specimens are excellent by ponds and streams, but also do well in less soggy (but not dry) conditions.

Also Called: Adelia.

Size and Shape: Tall shrubs or trees 20–30' tall; crowns irregular, picturesque.

Trunks: Short, 8" in diameter; mature bark smooth, grayish, thin, slightly furrowed with age; wood yellowish-brown, heavy, soft, weak.

Branches: Stiff, spreading at right angles, somewhat spiny; twigs bright green to yellowish brown, darker with age, hairless; buds tiny, egg-shaped, pointed, with overlapping scales.

Leaves: Opposite, deciduous, simple; blades smooth, hairless, yellowish green above, paler

beneath, ovate to elliptical, 1–4½" long, 1–1½" wide, gradually tapered at both ends, edged with a few scattered teeth above midleaf; stalks slender, ¼–½" long; leaves green when shed in autumn.

Flowers: Tiny, greenish-yellow, usually unisexual (occasionally some bisexual) with male and female flowers on separate trees; male flowers nearly stalkless, in tiny, tassel-like clusters (umbel-like panicles) that may look like single, many-stamened flowers; female flowers stalked, in wide-branching, ½–¾" clusters (panicles); flowers scattered along twigs in March–April (before leaves expand).

Fruits: Dry, purplish-black drupes, thin-fleshed, spindle-shaped and curved when young, slender-ellipsoidal when mature, ½–¾" long, slightly flattened; seeds 1 (rarely 2) within a hard stone; mature in summer.

Habitat: Swamps, streambanks and low woods, often along rivers.

Origin: Native.

Many cultivars of this popular hedge plant have been developed, some with golden or variegated leaves. With their numerous, resilient twigs, these bushy shrubs take pruning and shaping well. • **Caution:** Children have been poisoned by eating the fruits, but no deaths have been documented. • The leaves and bark were boiled to make astringent, bitter, medicinal teas for treating stomach ulcers and diarrhea and for stimulating appetite and improving digestion. These decoctions were also used as a gargle and mouthwash and as a wash for skin problems and ulcerated ears with offensive discharges. • The seeds are widely disseminated by birds. • Another privet, introduced from Japan, occasionally grows wild in disturbed sites in the state. **Bluntleaf privet (*L. obtusifolium*,** also called border privet), shown in dark green (species overlap) on the map, is readily distinguished by its hairy twigs and leaves. It also has large (⅛") anthers that are mostly hidden within the flower and therefore much less conspicuous. Border privet flowers are relatively large (about ¼" long), and their petals are fused for ⅔ of their length. • Privets produce mazes of tangled, intertwining, leafy branches that shoot out in all directions, hence the expression "mad as a privet hedge."

Also Called: Common privet, primwort, print, skedge, skedgewith.

Size and Shape: Tall shrubs or small trees, 6–15' tall; crowns broad, rounded.

Trunks: Short, clumped; young bark thin, gray.

Branches: Numerous, paired; twigs slender, greenish, initially light brown, with tiny, curled hairs, gray and **hairless with age;** pith white; buds egg-shaped, with overlapping scales.

Leaves: Opposite, simple, variably evergreen; blades dark green above, paler beneath, firm, moderately thick, **hairless,** elliptical to lance-shaped or ovate, 1⅛–2⅜" long, **smooth-edged,** obscurely veined; stalks ⅛–⅜" long; leaf scars elliptical; leaves long-lived, eventually shed before spring.

Flowers: White, showy, with a heavy fragrance, broadly funnel-shaped, ⅛–¼" across, **bisexual; petals 4,** about ⅛" long, **fused for ½ their length or less,** spreading at the tips;

sepals 4, small, fused into unlobed cups; **stamens 2,** attached to the petals, **tipped with ¹⁄₁₆" long anthers, shorter than the petals; flowers in dense, 1⅛–2⅜" long, minutely hairy, branched clusters** (panicles) at branch tips, in June–July.

Fruits: Lustrous, **black, berry-like drupes,** about ¼" across, **firm;** seeds 1–4 per fruit, each in a hard stone; drupes mature in August–September, often persist on shrubs until spring.

Habitat: Dry to damp, often disturbed sites.

Origin: Introduced from the Mediterranean region of southern Europe and North Africa.

This popular ornamental shade tree is culti-vated around the world for its beautiful sprays of purple flowers. Empress-tree originated in China and Korea, but it has been grown in Japan and Europe for hundreds of years. It arrived North America in 1834. Today it grows wild throughout much of the southeastern U.S. • Cold is a limiting factor. Buds develop in summer and lie dormant until the following spring, so early frosts and cold winters can cause severe damage. • In warmer regions, this beautiful tree often becomes a troublesome weed. Sizable colonies can develop along roads and streams, as abundant seeds travel considerable distances on wind or water, and cut or damaged trees quickly send up vigorous shoots. • **Caution:** Empress-tree contains potentially **toxic** compounds. • In China, Empress-tree has been credited with almost magical preservative abilities, capable of preventing skin from wrinkling and hair from turning gray. The leaf juice was used to treat warts, leaf tea provided a footbath, and leaves fried in vinegar were poulticed on bruises. • The genus name honors Anna Paulowna, (1794–1865), daughter of Czar Paul I of Russia and Queen Consort to King William II of the Netherlands.

Also Called: Royal paulownia, foxglove-tree.

Size and Shape: Trees 30–60' tall; crowns round.

Trunks: To 4' in diameter; young bark with large, pale pores (lenticels); mature bark dark brown, thin, flaky; wood very lightweight, soft when cut, hard when dry.

Branches: Stout, spreading; **twigs hollow** in 2nd year (except at joints and scattered between nodes); **buds embedded in bark,** absent at twig tips.

Leaves: Opposite, deciduous, simple; blades finely hairy above, densely gray-velvety beneath with star-shaped and branched hairs, **6–12" long (24" on vigorous shoots), heart-shaped** or 3–5-sided, larger leaves often 3- or 5-lobed; **stalks up to 8" long**.

Flowers: Violet purple, funnel-shaped, fragrant, finely hairy outside, **1½–2¾" long,** tubular, with 5 unequal lobes forming **2-lips,** perfect; upper petals bent backward; lower lobes spreading; calyx thick, woolly, unequally 5-lobed; stalks densely woolly; flowers numerous, in **branched, candelabra-like clusters (panicles) up to 14" long,** at branch tips, in April–May **(before leaves expand).**

Fruits: Green to brown, densely glandular-hairy, **egg-shaped, leathery to woody capsules, usually 1–2" long** and 1" wide, abruptly sharp-pointed; seeds numerous, tiny, winged, striped; capsules erect, split in 2 in autumn, persist through winter.

Habitat: Roadsides and open woods.

Origin: Introduced from China via Japan.

Northern catalpa is cultivated for its showy flowers and large, tropical-looking leaves. It responds well to pruning and can be shaped into a small, dense, round tree that does not flower. Unfortunately, the weak branches often break during storms. • Catalpa wood is weak and light but slow to rot in soil. This fast-growing tree is sometimes grown in dense plantations to produce fence posts and telephone poles. Catalpa wood is also used occasionally in inexpensive furniture. • Northern catalpa flowers at about 15 years of age and produces large seed crops every 2–3 years. Bees and a variety of night-flying moths pollinate the beautiful flowers, producing conspicuous seedpods that are of little value to wildlife. • The generic name *Catalpa* was adapted from a Native name used by tribes in Carolina; *speciosa* means "beautiful" or "showy." • **Southern catalpa (*C. bignonioides*)**, shown in pink/dark green (species overlap) on the map, is native to the southeastern U.S. It does not grow naturally in Illinois, but it is widespread in the state because of its popularity as an ornamental. Compared to northern catalpa, southern catalpa is a smaller tree (30–50' tall), with smaller (about ⅛" wide), more numerous flowers and narrower (¼–⅜" thick) capsules. Its short-pointed leaves have an unpleasant odor when crushed.

Also Called: Catawba, cigar-tree, hardy catalpa, Indian bean-tree, western catalpa.

Size and Shape: Trees 35–65' tall; crowns narrow to broad, rounded.

Trunks: Short, 8–16" in diameter; mature bark dark reddish-brown, with large, irregular, thick scales; wood light brown, soft, coarse-grained.

Branches: Stout, spreading; twigs stout, blunt-tipped; buds 6-scaled, ⅛–¼" long, absent at branch tips.

Leaves: Opposite or whorled, simple, deciduous, **odorless;** blades firm, yellowish-green above, paler and soft-hairy beneath, with clusters of **dark, nectar-producing glands in vein axils, heart-shaped, slender-pointed, 4–12" long,** usually smooth-edged; stalks 4–6¼" long; leaf scars rounded, with a ring of vein scars; leaves blackened by first frost.

Flowers: White with yellow stripes and purple spots in the throat, bell-shaped, 2-lipped, showy, 2–2¾" **across,** bisexual; petals fused in a tube, with 5 spreading, frilly lobes; sepals greenish-purple, fused, irregularly split; **flowers in erect, branched, 4–8" long clusters** (panicles) at branch tips, in May–June (after leaves expand).

Fruits: Green to dark brown, cylindrical **capsules 10–20" long, about ½" thick,** hang in clusters of 1–3; **seeds numerous, flat, ¾–1⅛" long, with 2 blunt, hair-tipped, papery wings;** pods mature in early autumn, **persist through winter,** split open lengthwise in spring.

Habitat: Low woods in bottomlands.

Origin: Native.

In the past, bitter buttonbush bark and twigs were used in remedies for kidney stones, gallstones, coughs, fevers, asthma and loss of appetite. Buttonbush was also used to treat malaria, probably because it resembles its relative, quinine tree (*Cinchona pubescens*), a known source of quinine. In the 1800s, some pharmaceutical companies marketed buttonbush extract as a tonic, fever-reducer, laxative and diuretic. In folk medicine, the bark was chewed to relieve toothaches and bark tea was used to wash inflamed eyes; leaf tea was taken to relieve cramps, fevers, coughs, kidney stones, palsy, pleurisy and toothaches; and the flowers and leaves were made into a fragrant syrup that was taken as a mild tonic and laxative. More recently, analysis of buttonbush glycosides failed to explain past uses, and its medicinal value is now considered doubtful. • This attractive shrub has potential as an ornamental in low, moist to wet sites. It is easily propagated and tolerates a range of habitats. Buttonbush also produces a large amount of nectar, which attracts numerous small butterflies. • **Caution:** The leaves are **poisonous** to livestock, but white-tailed deer are said to browse the foliage and young twigs. Waterbirds, especially mallards, and shorebirds feed on the seeds, and dense buttonbush thickets make excellent protected nesting sites.

Also Called: Honey-balls, globe-flower, pond dogwood, pin-ball, little snowball.

Size and Shape: Tall shrubs or small trees 5–15' tall; crowns open, irregular; roots spreading, suckering.

Trunks: Clumped, often leaning, about 4" in diameter; mature bark dark brown to blackish, with broad, scaly ridges; wood pale red-brown, fine-grained, heavy, hard.

Branches: Paired or in 3s; twigs reddish to yellowish, essentially hairless, with vertical pores (lenticels); pith large, yellowish; buds small, embedded in bark, absent at twig tips.

Leaves: Opposite or in whorls of 3, simple, deciduous; blades glossy and dark green above, paler beneath, 2½–6" long, smooth-edged; stipules tiny, single; stalks stout, grooved; leaf scars small, semicircular; leaves drop over winter.

Flowers: Fragrant, creamy white, bisexual, funnel-shaped, about ¼" long, tipped with 4 small petal lobes, with a thread-like style and 4 stamens projecting from the mouth, stalkless, numerous (100–200), mixed with club-shaped bracts in dense, spherical heads, ¾–1⅛" wide; heads on upright stalks 1¼–2½" long, in June–August.

Fruits: Reddish-green to deep red-brown, narrowly pyramidal capsules, about ¼" long, tapered to the base, in dense, rough, ½–¾" balls; seeds oblong, hanging, 2–4 per capsule; capsules split from the base into 1-seeded segments in September–October.

Habitat: Wet sites on shores and in swamps and thickets.

Origin: Native.

Key to Genera in the Honeysuckle Family (Caprifoliaceae)

1a Leaves pinnately divided into 5–7 leaflets . . . . ***Sambucus*, elder** (p. 279)
1b Leaves with a single blade (simple) **2**

2a Leaves lance- to egg-shaped, gradually tapered to a long, slender point
. . . . ***Lonicera*, honeysuckle** (p. 278)
2b Leaves ovate to almost round, sometimes maple leaf–like, with 3 palmate lobes, abruptly
sharp-pointed or blunt . . . . ***Viburnum*, viburnum** (key to species, see below)

Key to the Viburnums (Genus *Viburnum*)

1a Leaves maple leaf–like, with 3 palmate lobes and palmate veins, smooth-edged or coarsely
toothed; outer flowers sterile, very showy, with greatly enlarged petals **2**
1b Leaves ovate, not lobed, regularly saw-toothed; outer flowers similar to inner flowers . . . **3**

2a Glands on leaf stalks mostly higher than wide, stalked, with rounded tops
. . . . ***V. trilobum*, American highbush-cranberry** (p. 277)
2b Glands on leaf stalks wider than high, sessile (not stalked), with concave tops
. . . . ***V. opulus* var. *opulus*, European highbush-cranberry** (p. 277)

3a Flower and fruit clusters with branches arising from the tip of a slender, ¼–2" long stalk; leaf
stalks not grooved and winged; plants usually small (<4 m tall) and shrubby. **4**
3b Flower and fruit clusters stalkless or short (<¼") stalks, with branches arising directly from
the leaf axils. **5**

4a Lower leaf surfaces with tiny, star-shaped hairs (at least when young); winter buds naked;
stones 3-grooved . . . . ***V. lantana*, wayfaring-tree** (p. 276)
4b Lower leaf surfaces without tiny, star-shaped hairs, sometimes with minute, red-brown scales;
winter buds with 2 outer scales; stones not grooved . . . ***V. nudum*, witherod** (p. 274)

5a Leaf tips abruptly narrowed to a tapered point; leaf stalks with wavy, often down-rolled wings
. . . . ***V. lentago*, nannyberry** (p. 274)
5b Leaf tips blunt or slightly pointed; leaf stalks with or without wings **6**

6a Leaves shiny, with reddish-woolly stalks and lower veins; leaf stalks winged; buds reddish-
woolly . . . . ***V. rufidulum*, southern blackhaw** (p. 275)
6b Leaves dull, essentially hairless but sometimes with brown, mealy scales; leaf stalks narrowly
winged or wingless; buds not reddish-woolly
. . . . ***V. prunifolium*, smooth blackhaw** (p. 275)

Viburnum lantana, wayfaring-tree

V. lentago, nannyberry

This hardy, fast-growing shrub is often planted as an ornamental for its showy, fragrant flowers, attractive fruits and reddish winter twigs. Nannyberry is extremely hardy and can be cultivated as far north as northern Canada (USDA Zone 2). It takes pruning well and can be shaped into a handsome hedge, but invasive root suckers can cause problems. In the wild, nannyberry spreads rapidly by vigorous roots and shoots to form thickets. • The fruits are edible and have a sweet, raisin-like flavor. "Berries" can be eaten straight from the branch or cooked and seeded to make jams and jellies. The sweet pulp is often mixed with tart fruits to sweeten fruit stews and sauces. • Nannyberries provide food for wild turkeys, grouse, pheasants and many songbirds, which disperse the seeds. • **Smooth blackhaw** (p. 275) is very similar to nannyberry, but its leaves are blunt to broadly pointed (not slender-pointed), and the leaves on flowering branches are smaller (1–2" long). Also, its leaf stalks usually lack wings. • The names *viburnum* (from the Latin *viere*, "to link") and *lentago* (from the Latin *lentus*, "pliant") both refer to the supple twigs.

Also Called: Sweet viburnum, blackhaw, wild raisin, sheepberry.

Size and Shape: Small trees or shrubs 10–25' tall; crowns irregular, broadly rounded; roots shallow, spreading, suckering.

Trunks: Slender, crooked, 4–8" in diameter, usually clumped; mature bark grayish-brown to reddish, with small, irregular scales; wood dark reddish-brown, hard, heavy, fine-grained.

Branches: Few, arching, stout, tough; twigs becoming purplish-brown, slender, smooth, with round pores (lenticels), **unpleasant-smelling** when bruised; **buds slender, brownish-gray, granular, lacking scales, with 2 immature leaves visible,** bulbous-based and ½–1⅛" long at branch tips, smaller below.

Leaves: Opposite, simple, deciduous, with an **unpleasant odor** when bruised; **blades hairless,** lustrous, deep yellowish-green, slightly paler and **speckled with brown dots beneath,** ovate to oval, 2–4" long, abruptly tapered to a **slender point,** edged with fine, sharp, incurved teeth; stalks grooved, **clearly winged** with a narrow, irregular extension of the blade.

Flowers: Creamy white, pleasant-smelling, bisexual, ¼" across, 5-parted; numerous, in **round-topped, wide-branching clusters** (cymes); flower clusters stalkless, **2–5" across,** at branch tips, in late May–early June (as or after leaves expand).

Fruits: Bluish-black, berry-like drupes with a **whitish bloom,** ¼–½" long, thin-fleshed, **on reddish stems, in open, branched clusters;** seeds single, in a black, flattened stone; drupes mature and drop in August–September.

Habitat: Wet, rich sites near water, along forest edges, by roadsides and in thickets.

Origin: Native.

Smooth blackhaw is occasionally planted as an ornamental, though it is not as popular as nannyberry (p. 274). • The sweet, edible berries can be eaten raw or added to baking and desserts. Wizened or dried "berries" look and taste like raisins, hence another common name "wild raisin." • **Caution:** Large amounts of fruit can cause nausea and other unpleasant symptoms. Too many seeds were said to cause constipation. • The leaves were sometimes used to make a pleasant tea. • Smooth blackhaw has also been called "crampbark," because its bark was commonly used in medicinal teas for relieving menstrual cramps. Bark preparations were also given to women threatened with miscarriage or suffering from other pregnancy discomforts. Research has shown that smooth blackhaw bark contains at least 4 substances that help to relax the uterus and relieve muscle spasms. • **Southern blackhaw (*V. rufidulum*,** also called rusty blackhaw or rusty nannyberry), shown in pink/dark green (species overlap) on the map, is a closely related species with similar, broadly pointed leaves and essentially stalkless flower clusters. It is distinguished by the reddish, woolly hairs on its buds and leaf stalks and by its shiny leaf blades.

Also called: Blackhaw, nannyberry, wild raisin.

Size and Shape: Small trees or tall shrubs 10–25' tall; crowns irregular, broadly rounded.

Trunks: Short, crooked, to 10" in diameter, usually clumped; mature bark reddish-brown, with shallow furrows between flat, irregular plates; wood reddish-brown, hard, strong.

Branches: Stout, spreading; **twigs slender, spine-like,** sometimes brownish-mealy at first (**not red-woolly**), grayish-brown and smooth with age; **buds slender, covered with 2 scales,** about ½" long (flowers) at branch tips, ¼" long (leaves) below, often finely reddish-hairy.

Leaves: Opposite, simple, deciduous; blades papery, **dull dark yellowish-green,** paler beneath, **hairless, oblong to egg-shaped or almost round,** widest at or above midleaf, **widely pointed or blunt-tipped,** 1–3" long, 1–1¾" wide, **finely sharp-toothed; stalks slender,** rarely margined, ¼–½" long, smooth, not rolled.

Flowers: Creamy white, ¼–¾" across, 5-parted, bisexual, numerous; flowers in **stalkless, round-topped, wide-branching clusters** (cymes) 2–4"

across, with 3–4 main branches (rays), at branch tips, in April–June (a little before, as or just after leaves expand).

Fruits: Bluish-black, berry-like drupes, with a whitish bloom, ⅜–½" long, tipped with a persistent calyx; seeds single, in an oval stone with 1 flat and 1 slightly rounded side, scarcely grooved; **drupes in open, branched clusters** mature and drop in September.

Habitat: Woodlands and thickets in bottomlands and on slopes.

Origin: Native.

275

This shrub is widely planted as an ornamental for its showy flowers (lasting about 2 weeks), attractive foliage (deep green in summer, purplish to scarlet in autumn) and attractive fruits (initially pinkish-white, becoming rose, red, purple and finally black). It is a tough, low-maintenance plant that resists most insects and diseases, tolerates dry soils and spreads readily via seeds and suckers. • The very hard wood of wayfaring-tree has been fashioned into mouthpieces for tobacco pipes. • Although the fruits are too astringent to be edible raw, they make wonderful jams and jellies. Mature fruits were once used to make ink. • The distinctive, star-shaped hairs on the lower leaf surfaces help to protect the leaves from insects and disease and conserve moisture. • **Downy arrowwood (*V. molle*,** also called softleaf arrowwood), shown in pink on the map, is a rare native species with similar, unlobed leaves and broad flower clusters. However, downy arrowwood leaves have simple (unbranched) veins that extend to the leaf teeth, long (2–5 cm) stalks and (usually) stipules.

Also Called: Wayfaring viburnum.

Size and Shape: Small trees or large shrubs to 13' tall; crowns dense and rounded; roots spreading.

Trunks: Slender, usually clumped; mature bark grayish-brown, scaly.

Branches: Wide-spreading, tough, thick; twigs yellowish-gray with dense, star-shaped hairs; buds grayish, with yellowish-white hairs, lacking scales, with 1–2 pairs of immature leaves visible; flower buds large, wider than long, surrounded by 2 young leaves.

Leaves: Opposite, simple, deciduous; blades dull dark green above, grayish with dense, star-shaped hairs beneath, 2–5" long, prominently veined, appearing wrinkled and leathery, ovate, short-pointed to blunt-tipped, rounded to slightly notched at the base, sharp-toothed; stalks 3/8–1 1/8" long, hairy; leaves deep red in autumn.

Flowers: Creamy white, sweet-smelling, 5-parted, 1/4–3/8" across, bisexual; numerous, in short-stalked, flat-topped, 2–4" wide clusters (cymes); flower clusters with star-shaped hairs, at branch tips, in May–June.

Fruits: Coral red to black, berry-like drupes, slightly flattened, about 3/8" long, fleshy, in flat-topped clusters; seeds single, in a flattened stone with 3 grooves on 1 side; drupes mature August–September.

Habitat: Roadsides, fence lines and deciduous woods and thickets.

Origin: Introduced from Europe and western Asia.

American highbush-cranberry fruits are boiled and strained to make jellies and jams. The fruits smell a bit like dirty socks, but their flavor isn't bad. Lemon or orange zest helps eliminate the odor. • The "berries" make an excellent winter-survival food because they remain above the snow and are sweeter after freezing. • The bark has been used to treat menstrual pains, stomach cramps, aching muscles, asthma, hysteria and convulsions. • **European highbush-cranberry (*V. opulus* var. *opulus*)**, also called Guelder-rose, shown in pink/dark green (species overlap) on the map, is a European introduction that frequently escapes cultivation. It is distinguished by its bristle-like leaf stipules, bitter fruits and the saucer-like glands at the tops of its leaf stalks. American and European highbush-cranberries intergrade and are often placed in the same species. • Another 3-lobed species, **mapleleaf viburnum (*V. acerifolium*)**, is a common smaller shrub (usually under 6' tall) with less conspicuous flower clusters that lack showy, sterile blooms. When not in flower, mapleleaf viburnum is distinguished by its downy, resin-dotted lower leaf surfaces, silky-hairy twigs and its distinctive blue-black fruits.

Also Called: Native highbush-cranberry, American cranberrybush, cranberry viburnum • *V. opulus* var. *americanum*, *V. opulus* ssp. *trilobum*.

Size and Shape: Tall shrubs or small trees to 15' tall; crowns open, irregular; roots spreading.

Trunks: Upright, less than 4" in diameter; mature bark grayish.

Branches: Few, arching; twigs thick, gray, hairless; buds plump, paired at branch tips, reddish, with 2 fused scales.

Leaves: Opposite, simple, deciduous; blades dark green and hairless above, paler and smooth or thinly hairy beneath, **maple leaf–like,** 1½–4¼" long and wide, **deeply cut into 3 spreading, pointed lobes,** sparsely coarse-toothed (rarely smooth-edged); **stalks grooved, with 1–6 club-shaped glands at the top** (near the blade) and 2 slender, thick-tipped stipules at the base.

Flowers: White, 5-parted, bisexual, of 2 types: **small, fertile flowers at the cluster center,** and larger (½–1" wide), flat, sterile flowers around the outer edge; flowers numerous, in **flat-topped, wide-branching, 2–6" wide clusters** (cymes); flower clusters on ¾–2" long stalks at branch tips, in late June–July (after leaves expand).

Fruits: Juicy, red to orange, berry-like drupes, about ⅜" across; **hang in branched clusters;** seeds single, within a flattened stone; drupes mature in August–September, often persist into winter.

Habitat: Moist, rich sites near water and in cool woodlands.

Origin: Native.

This handsome shrub is cultivated for its showy flowers and fruits. The fruits are most striking in late fall, when they stand out in contrast to the dark, glossy leaves. • A hardy Asian species originally from Manchuria and Korea, Amur honeysuckle is highly adaptable and seems able to thrive in a variety of environments, ranging from sunny, urban, high-stress sites to deep, shady forests. Amur honeysuckle has almost no insect or disease pests in North America, and it can tolerate many adverse conditions, including restricted root zones, drought, heat, salt spray and heavy browsing. Consequently, this fast-growing shrub has become a very nasty invader, rapidly spreading into areas where it is not wanted and often displacing native plants from their natural habitats. Amur honeysuckle is now scattered throughout Illinois and is becoming an increasingly aggressive, exotic weed. • The berries attract squirrels and numerous songbirds, which then carry the seeds to new sites. • **Caution:** These fruits should be treated with care. Although the fruits of some Asian honeysuckles are edible, most European species have poisonous fruits that cause digestive, nervous and heart disorders, and occasionally death. Unfortunately, some toxic fruits are sweet and pleasant tasting, so they present an even greater risk.

Size and Shape: Tall shrubs to 15' tall; crowns broad, spreading, vase-shaped; roots shallow.

Trunks: Erect to spreading; bark relatively light brown with **low, interconnecting ridges, not peeling off in layers.**

Branches: **Arched** to spreading, often in almost horizontal tiers; **twigs pale brown, striped** to lightly furrowed; buds paired.

Leaves: **Opposite,** deciduous, simple; blades glossy, dark green, egg-shaped to broadly lance-shaped, 1¼–3¼" **long, tipped with a long, slender point, tapered to the base,** downy on both surfaces (at least on veins), smooth-edged, short-stalked; green to chartreuse in autumn, appear early and drop late.

Flowers: **White** (ivory to cream with age), fragrant, bisexual, funnel-shaped, **2-lipped** with a broad, 4-lobed upper lip and narrow lower lip, ½–¾" **long, 2 per stalk;** petals 5, fused into a short tube at the base, spreading at tips; sepals 5, tiny, fused; stamens 5; **styles hairy;** stalks <¼" long, shorter than adjacent leaf stalks; **flowers in twin pairs** (4 per joint) from upper leaf axils in May–June.

Fruits: Fleshy, **dark red berries, on very short stalks;** seeds few; berries mature in September, **persist** into winter.

Habitat: Swampy to upland, open or wooded areas, often in disturbed areas.

Origin: Introduced from northeastern Asia.

The juicy fruits of common elderberry have been used to make jelly, jam, preserves and wines. • **Caution:** The leaves, bark and roots of elders contain cyanide. Raw berries may cause vomiting, though cooking destroys the toxins. • Historically, the bark and leaves were used to "cleanse the system." Bark peeled downward was believed to stimulate bowel movements, whereas bark peeled upward would cause vomiting. No matter how you peel it, the bark usually acts both ways at once. • Flower clusters have been used to make healing salves, and hot flower tea is taken to stimulate sweating and relieve rheumatism and cold and flu symptoms. • A widespread native species, **red-berried elderberry (*S. racemosa*,** also called *S. pubens*), shown in dark green (species overlap) on the map, is distinguished by its fewer (5–7, usually 5) leaflets and by the dark brown (not white) pith of its twigs. Its relatively elongated flower clusters develop in May–June (with the leaves) and the bright red, inedible fruits mature in early summer. • The European **black elderberry (*S. nigra* ssp. *nigra*)** has been shown to stimulate the immune system and prevent viruses from invading respiratory tract cells. An Israeli study of the drug Sambucol found that 20% of flu sufferers felt better within 24 hours, 73% improved in 2 days and 90% felt cured in 3 days. Sambucol has been found to inhibit many viruses, including herpes and even HIV.

Also Called: Common elder, American elder, white elder • *S. nigra* ssp *canadensis, S. canadensis.*

Size and Shape: Shrubs or small trees 6–13' tall, foul-smelling when bruised; crowns irregular; roots shallow, suckering to form thickets.

Trunks: Short, up to 1½" in diameter; bark thin, gray to yellowish-brown, with raised pores (lenticels), furrowed with age.

Branches: Opposite, few; twigs stout, essentially **hairless,** soft, **scarcely woody,** with widely spaced, swollen joints; **pith large, white** (sometimes brown at edges); buds egg-shaped, ¹⁄₁₆–⅛" long, with paired, overlapping scales.

Leaves: Opposite, deciduous, 4–12" long; **compound,** pinnately divided into **5–11 (usually 7) leaflets;** leaflets lustrous green above, paler beneath, 2–6" long, slender-pointed, rounded and slightly uneven at the base, **sharply toothed,** short-stalked; lowermost leaflets sometimes divided into 2–3 parts; leaf scars triangular with 5 vein scars.

Flowers: White, heavily scented, bisexual, 5-parted, star-shaped, about ⅛" across; flowers in **flat-topped, clusters (cymes) 2–7" wide,** in June–July (after leaves expand).

Fruits: Purplish black (rarely red, green or yellow), **berry-like drupes,** with red juice, about ¼" across, on rose red stalks, **in large, flat-topped clusters; seeds 3–5,** in small, yellowish stones; drupes mature in August–October.

Habitat: Moist sites in woods, meadows and along roads.

Origin: Native.

This graceful, lacy native of eastern Asia is a popular ornamental shade tree, valued for its broad canopy, glossy leaves, picturesque branching and deeply grooved, corky bark. It is also pest free and hardy, capable of growing as far north as USDA Zone 3b. Trees grow best in full sun on moist, well-drained sites, but they can also tolerate drought, alkaline soils, poor drainage, soil compaction and pollution. • The dark, aromatic fruits can litter driveways and sidewalks, so many people plant male trees. 'His Majesty' and 'Macho' are popular male cultivars that produce no fruit litter or weedy seedlings. • Amur corktree is easily transplanted or grown from seed. More desirable forms (usually male trees) are propagated using softwood or heeled, semi-ripe cuttings in summer and root cuttings in late winter. Amur corktree is recommended for planting in buffer strips around parking lots and along highway medians. It is also used as a residential shade tree in gardens and parks and along streets, but its spreading roots and broad crowns require space. • The bark was used traditionally and is still sold commercially in remedies for treating acne, sores and other skin problems. Corktree bark also produces a bright yellow dye.

Also Called: Chinese corktree.

Size and Shape: Aromatic trees 25–50' tall; crowns open, usually **wider than high**, 40–60' across, rounded to vase-shaped; roots spreading.

Trunks: Short, 1–2' (rarely 3') in diameter; bark pale yellowish-gray, deeply furrowed with **thick, corky ridges,** soft to touch (like cork); inner bark bright yellow; wood yellowish-brown, ring-porous.

Branches: Spreading; twigs yellowish, coarse, with prominent pores (lenticels); **buds with 2 hairy, immature leaves, lacking scales, hidden under leaf stalk bases.**

Leaves: Opposite, deciduous, 8–15" long, compound, **pinnately divided into 5–13 leaflets;** central stalk woolly; leaflets **glossy, dark green with translucent dots,** pale and grayish beneath, hairless except for leaf edges and base of main vein, narrowly ovate, tapered to point, ¼" long, smooth edged and undulate; **leaf scars horseshoe-shaped,** with 3 groups of vein scars, encircling buds; leaves bronze to clear yellow when shed in late summer.

Flowers: Yellowish-green, about ¼" long; unisexual with **male and female flowers on separate trees;** flowers insignificant, in erect, branched clusters (panicles) 2–3½" long at branch tips, in May.

Fruits: Blue-black, berry-like drupes with a strong turpentine scent, about ⅜" across; seeds 5, each in a small, hard stone; stalk short; drupes in broad, rounded to flat-topped clusters; mature in early summer, sometimes persist into winter.

Habitat: Open, disturbed sites.

Origin: Introduced from northern China and Japan; rare escape.

Illinois Arboreta & Herbaria • Appendix

Arboreta

Chicago
Chicago Botanic Gardens

Elmhurst
Wilder Park Conservatory

Evanston
Ladd Arboretum and Nature Center

Glen Oak Park
Luthy Memorial Botanic Garden

Lisle
Morton Arboretum

Normal
Fell Arboretum, Illinois State University

Palos Heights
Lake Katherine Nature Preserve

Peoria
Forest Part Nature Center

Rockford
Klehm Arboretum/Ecology Center

Skokie
Emily Oaks Nature Center

Springfield
Abraham Lincoln Memorial Garden

Urbana
University of Illinois at Urbana-Champaign
Arboretum

Wheaton
Cantigny Gardens

Herbaria

Carbondale
Southern Illinois University Herbarium

Champaign
Illinois Natural History Survey Herbarium
Collection

Chicago
Field Museum Herbarium
Chicago Botanic Garden
Notebaert Nature Museum, Chicago Academy
of Science

DeKalb
Northern Illinois University, Department of
Biological Sciences

Lisle
Morton Arboretum Herbarium

Springfield
Illinois State Museum Collections

Urbana
University of Illinois

A mounted and labeled herbarium
specimen

Glossary

Page numbers indicate where terms are illustrated.

achene: a small, thin-walled, dry fruit containing a single seed (p. 286)

acorn: the hard, dry nut of oaks, with a single, large seed and a scaly, cup-like base (p. 286)

adventive: introduced but only locally established in the wild, if at all; compare "naturalized"

adventitious: growing from unusual places, e.g., roots growing from stems

aggregate fruit: a fruit produced by two or more pistils of a single flower, sometimes appearing to be dense clusters of many tiny fruits (e.g., a raspberry) (p. 286); compare "multiple fruit"

alternate: attached singly, neither paired nor whorled (p. 284); compare "opposite," "whorled"

angiosperm: a plant with ovules/seeds enclosed in an ovary/fruit; a flowering plant, member of the Magnoliophyta; compare "gymnosperm"

annual ring: the wood laid down in a single year, visible (in cross-section) as a ring because of alternating layers of earlywood and denser latewood (p. 16)

anther: the pollen-bearing part of a stamen (p. 20)

arboretum [arboreta]: a place where trees and other plants are cultivated for their beauty and for scientific and educational purposes (see appendix, p. 281)

aril: a specialized covering attached to a mature seed (p. 286)

armed: bearing prickles, spines or thorns (p. 284)

ascending: oriented obliquely upward (p. 15)

axil: the angle between an organ (e.g., a leaf) and the part to which it is attached (e.g., a stem) (p. 17)

axis [axes]: the main stem or central line of a plant or plant part

bark cambium: see "cork cambium"

bark: the protective outer covering of the trunks and branches of a woody plant, composed of dead, corky cells and produced by the cork cambium; in the broadest sense, bark includes all tissue from the phloem outward (pp. 16, 17)

bast: see "phloem"

berry: a fleshy fruit developed from a single ovary and containing one to several seeds (p. 287)

bisexual: with both male and female sex organs; also called "perfect"; compare "unisexual"

blade: the broad, flat part of an organ (e.g., of a leaf or petal) (p. 289)

bloom: a whitish, waxy powder on the surface of some leaves and fruits

board foot [board feet]: a cubic measure for lumber, equivalent to that of a board measuring 12 inches by 12 inches by 1 inch

bole: the section of a trunk below the crown (p. 15)

bract: a small, specialized leaf or scale (p. 285)

Compound leaves

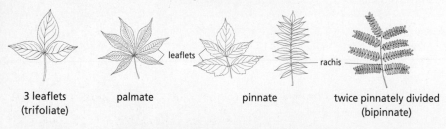

3 leaflets (trifoliate)   palmate   leaflets   pinnate   rachis   twice pinnately divided (bipinnate)

Simple leaves: lobes and teeth

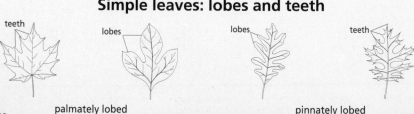

teeth   lobes   lobes   teeth

palmately lobed   pinnately lobed

bud: an undeveloped stem, branch, leaf or flower, usually covered by protective scales (pp. 17, 288)

bur: a barbed or bristly fruit (or compact cluster of fruits) designed to stick to passing animals (p. 286)

callus: a small, firm thickening or protuberance

calyx [calyxes, calyces]: the outer (lowermost) circle of floral parts composed of separate or fused segments called sepals, which are usually green and leaf-like (p. 19); compare "corolla"

cambium: a thin layer of cells responsible for producing new xylem and phloem cells or new bark cells (see "cork cambium") and thereby controlling stem growth (p. 16)

canopy: see "overstory"

capsule: a dry fruit produced by a compound ovary and splitting open at maturity (p. 286)

carpel: the female unit of reproduction in a flower, formed from a modified leaf and consisting of a stigma, style and seed-bearing ovary; compare "pistil" (p. 286)

catkin: a dense spike or raceme of many small, unisexual flowers that lack petals but usually have a bract (pp. 285, 286)

chlorophyll: the green pigment that allows plants to manufacture carbohydrates through photosynthesis

ciliate: edged with cilia; fringed

cilium [cilia]: a tiny, eyelash-like structure, usually part of a fringe

clone: the offspring produced vegetatively (asexually) by a single individual

compound: composed of two or more smaller parts, such as leaves consisting of several leaflets (p. 282), flower clusters consisting of smaller groups, ovaries consisting of two or more carpels, or substances formed by the chemical union of two or more ingredients; compare "simple"

cone: a reproductive structure with overlapping scales or bracts arranged around a central axis, usually woody when bearing seeds and non-woody when bearing pollen (pp. 18, 285)

conifer: a cone-bearing shrub or tree

coniferous: cone-bearing (e.g., coniferous trees) or composed of coniferous trees (e.g., coniferous forests)

cork cambium: thin layer of living cells located on the inner side of the bark and responsible for producing new bark cells (p. 16)

corolla: the circle of floral parts second from the outside, composed of separate or fused segments called petals; usually conspicuous in size and color but sometimes small, reduced to nectaries or absent (p. 19); compare "calyx"

corymb: a flat- or round-topped, branched flower cluster in which the outer (lower) flowers bloom first (p. 285)

cotyledon: a leaf of the developing plant (embryo) within a seed; a seed leaf

Leaf shapes

needles linear linear-oblong oblong lance-shaped, widest above midleaf (oblanceolate) lance-shaped (lanceolate) ovate ovate, widest above midleaf (obovate)

single teeth

sheath

elliptical oval round (orbicular) heart-shaped (cordate) broadly triangular (deltate) triangular

double teeth

Glossary

cross-pollination: the transfer of pollen from the anthers of one flower to the stigma of another flower on a different plant; compare "self-pollination"

cross-section: a slice or fragment cut and viewed at right angles to the main axis; compare "long-section"

crown: the leafy head of a tree or shrub (p. 15)

cultivar, abbreviated **cv.:** a cultivated plant variety with one or more distinct differences from the species; e.g., *Acer platanoides* is a botanical species, of which 'Crimson King' is a cultivar

cuticle: a waxy layer covering the outer surface of a-stem of leaf

cyme: a flat- or round-topped flower cluster in which the inner (upper) flowers bloom first (p. 285)

DBH: trunk diameter at breast height or diameter at 4½ feet from the ground (p. 15)

deciduous: shed after completing its normal function, usually at the end of the growing season; compare "persistent"

dehiscent: splitting open along slits or via pores to release seeds

dioecious: with male and female flowers or cones on separate plants (p. 285); compare "monoecious"

disjunct: separated, referring to plant or animal populations located a significant distance from all other populations of the same species

double-toothed: edged with large teeth bearing smaller teeth (p. 283); compare "single-toothed"

drupe: a fruit with an outer fleshy part covered by a-thin skin and surrounding a hard or bony stone that encloses a single seed, e.g., a plum (p. 287)

dwarf shoot: see "spur-shoot"

earlywood: pale, relatively large-pored wood produced by rapid growth early in the growing season (p. 16); also called "springwood"

ellipsoid: a three-dimensional form in which every plane is an ellipse or a circle

embryo: an immature plant within a seed

endangered: threatened with immediate elimination through all or a significant portion of a region

evergreen: always bearing green leaves

extinct: a species that no longer exists anywhere

extirpated: formerly native to a region, now no longer existing there in the wild but still found elsewhere

family [families]: a group of related plants or animals forming a taxonomic category ranking below order and above genus

fertile: plants capable of producing viable pollen, ovules or spores; soil rich in nutrients and capable of sustaining abundant plant growth

fetid: with a strong, offensive odor

filament: the stalk of a stamen, usually bearing an anther at its tip (p. 19)

fleshy: succulent, firm and pulpy; plump and juicy

flora: the plants that are representative of a certain region or period; also a comprehensive treatise or list that includes all such plants

flower: a specialized shoot of a plant, with a shortened axis bearing reproductive structures (modified leaves) such as sepals, petals, stamens and pistils

follicle: a dry, pod-like fruit, splitting open along a single line on one side (p. 286)

fruit: the seed-bearing organ of an angiosperm, including the ripened ovary and any other structures that join with it as a unit (pp. 286, 287)

functionally unisexual: having both male and female parts (sometimes appearing bisexual), but with organs of only one sex maturing to produce reproductive cells

Leaf/branch attachment

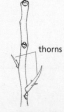

thorns

whorled   spiraled   opposite   alternate   armed

generic name: the first part of a scientific name, denoting the genus to which the species belongs; e.g., *Abies* in *Abies balsamea*

genus [genera]: a group of related plants or animals constituting a category of biological classification below family and above species

germinate: to sprout

girdle: to remove a ring of bark and cambium around a trunk, thereby stopping the transport of water and nutrients and killing the tree

gland: a bump, appendage or depression that secretes substances such as nectar or oil (p. 289)

glandular-hairy: with gland-tipped hairs

glandular-toothed: with gland-tipped teeth (p. 289)

gymnosperm: a plant with naked ovules/seeds (i.e., not enclosed in an ovary); a conifer, a member of the Pinophyta; compare "angiosperm"

hardwood: a broad-leaved, deciduous tree (occasionally evergreen elsewhere) belonging to the angiosperms or Magnoliophyta; compare "softwood"

haw: the fruit of hawthorns, a small, berry-like pome containing 1–5 bony nutlets (p. 287)

heartwood: the darker, harder wood at the center of a trunk, containing accumulations of resin and other compounds and therefore unable to transport fluids (p. 16)

herbarium [herbaria]: a large collection of dried plant specimens that have been mounted, labelled and filed systematically (see appendix, p. 281)

husk: the dry, often thick, outer covering of some fruits (p. 286)

hybrid: the offspring of two kinds of parents (usually parents from different species)

hybridization: the process of creating a hybrid

hypanthium [hypanthia]: a ring or cup around the ovary formed by fused parts of the sepals, petals and/or stamens

imperfect: see "unisexual"

introduced: brought in from another region (e.g., Europe), not native

key: see "samara" (p. 287)

latewood: the relatively small-pored wood produced by slow growth toward the end of the growing season (p. 16); also called "summerwood"

layering: a form of vegetative reproduction in which branches droop to the ground, root and send up new shoots

leader: the uppermost shoot of a tree

leaf scar: the mark left on a stem where a leaf was once attached (pp. 17, 288, 289)

leaflet: a single part of a compound leaf (p. 282)

legume: a pod-like fruit characteristic of the pea family (Fabaceae or Leguminosae), typically splitting down both sides (p. 286)

lenticel: a slightly raised pore on root, trunk or branch bark (p. 17)

Cones and flower/fruit clusters

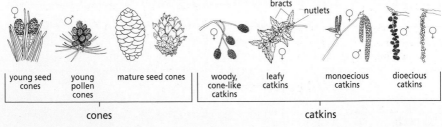

bracts nutlets

| young seed cones | young pollen cones | mature seed cones | woody, cone-like catkins | leafy catkins | monoecious catkins | dioecious catkins |

cones | catkins

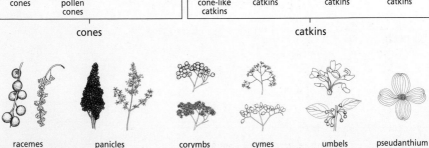

racemes | panicles | corymbs | cymes | umbels | pseudanthium

285

Glossary

lobe: a rounded division, too large to be called a tooth (p. 282)

long-section: in full, "longitudinal section"; a slice or fragment cut and viewed parallel to the main axis; compare "cross-section"

membranous: in a thin, usually translucent sheet; like a membrane

midvein: the middle vein of a leaf (p. 289)

monoecious: with male and female parts in separate flowers or cones on the same plant (p. 285); compare "dioecious"

multiple fruit: a dense cluster of many small fruits, each produced by an individual flower (e.g., a mulberry) (see below); compare "aggregate fruit"

naked: exposed, not covered by scales, hairs or other appendages

native: indigenous to a region, having evolved there as part of an ecosystem over a long period of time; compare "naturalized," "introduced"

naturalized: well established in the wild, but originally introduced from another area; compare "adventive," "native"

nectar: the sweet liquid secreted by a nectary, usually serving to attract pollinators

nectary: a nectar-secreting gland, usually in a flower

net-veined: with a network of branched veins; also called "reticulate"

node: the point where a leaf or branch attaches to a stem; a joint (p. 288)

nut: a dry, thick-walled, usually one-seeded fruit that does not split open when mature (see below)

nutlet: a small, nut-like fruit (p. 285)

opposite: situated directly in front of one another (e.g., stamens opposite petals) or directly across from each other at the same node (e.g., leaves, branches) (p. 284); compare "alternate," "whorled"

ovary: the organ containing the young, undeveloped seed(s), located at the base of the pistil and maturing to become all or part of the fruit (p. 19)

overstory: the uppermost stratum of foliage in a forest, the forest canopy; compare "understory"

ovoid: a three-dimensional, egg-shaped form that is broadest below the middle

ovule: an organ that develops into a single seed after fertilization (p. 19)

palmate: with three or more lobes or leaflets arising from one point, like fingers of a hand (p. 282); compare "pinnate"

panicle: a branched flower cluster in which the lower blooms develop first (p. 285)

perfect: see "bisexual"

perianth: a flower's petals and sepals collectively

persistent: remaining attached after its normal function has been completed; compare "deciduous" (p. 287)

Fruits

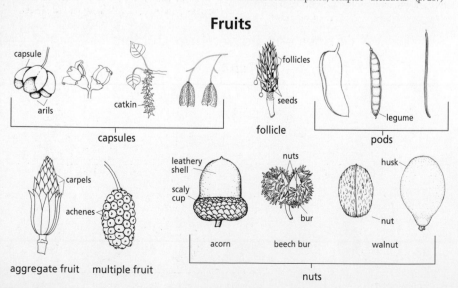

286

petal: a segment of the inner whorl (corolla) of the perianth, usually white or brightly colored (p. 19)

phloem: a thin layer of vascular tissue located between the bark and the wood, responsible for transporting nutrients (e.g., sugars) produced by the tree to its living tissues (p. 16); also called "bast"

photosynthesis: the process by which plants manufacture carbohydrates using chlorophyll, carbon dioxide, water and the energy of the sun

pinnate: with branches, lobes, leaflets or veins arranged on both sides of a central stalk or vein, feather-like (p. 282); compare "palmate"

pioneer species: a colonizer of sites in the early stages of succession (e.g., sites that have been burned, cleared or otherwise disturbed)

pistil: the female part of a flower, composed of single or fused carpels (p. 19)

pith: the soft, spongy centre of a stem or branch (pp. 17, 288)

pod: a dry fruit that splits open to release seeds (p. 286)

pollard: a tree with a small, dense crown produced by cutting branches almost back to the trunk; also to prune a tree in this severe manner

pollen: tiny, powdery grains containing the male reproductive cells that fertilize the ovule

pollen cone: a cone that produces pollen, i.e., a male cone (p. 285); compare "seed cone"

pollination: the transfer of pollen from male to female reproductive organs, leading to fertilization

pome: a fleshy fruit with a core (e.g., an apple); comprises an enlarged hypanthium around a compound ovary (p. 287)

pseudanthium [pseudanthia]: a compact cluster of tiny flowers and associated bracts resembling a single large flower (p. 285)

raceme: an unbranched cluster of stalked flowers on an elongated central stalk, in which the lowest flowers bloom first (p. 285)

rachis [rachises]: the main axis of a compound leaf or flower cluster (p. 282)

rare: existing in low numbers and/or in very restricted areas in a region

ray: a ribbon-like group of cells visible as a radial line in wood (viewed in cross section), responsible for transporting water and nutrients across trunks or large branches

respiration: the act of taking in oxygen and producing carbon dioxide through oxidation

rib: a prominent, usually longitudinal vein

runner: a slender, prostrate, spreading branch, rooting and often developing new shoots and/or plants at its nodes or at the tip

samara: a dry, winged, one-seeded fruit that does not split open at maturity; may be single (e.g., ashes) or paired (e.g., maples) (p. 287); also called "key," especially for the ashes and maples

sap: the mineral- and sugar-containing solution that circulates through a plant via the xylem and phloem

Fruits

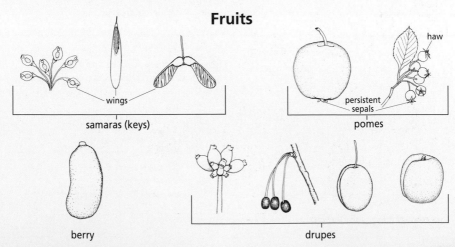

samaras (keys)

wings

pomes

persistent sepals

haw

berry

drupes

Glossary

sapwood: the paler, softer, outer wood of a trunk, still capable of transporting fluids (p. 16)

scale: a small, flat structure, usually thin and membranous (pp. 17, 18)

scar: the mark left on a stem by a fallen leaf, scale or fruit (pp. 17, 288, 289)

scurfy: covered with tiny scales

seasonality: the timing of biological events (e.g., leaf growth, flower development) during the year

seed: a fertilized ovule, containing a developing plant embryo along with nourishing tissue (usually) and a protective covering or seed coat (pp. 18, 286)

seed cone: a cone that produces seeds, i.e., a female cone (p. 285); compare "pollen cone"

self-pollination: the transfer of pollen from the anthers to the stigma of the same flower, or from one flower to another flower on the same plant; compare "cross-pollination"

sepal: a segment of the outer whorl (calyx) of the perianth, usually green and leaf-like (pp. 19, 287)

sexual reproduction: producing offspring through the union of female and male cells, as in the fertilization of the egg cell in an ovule by a pollen grain; compare "vegetative reproduction"

sheath: a tubular organ surrounding or partly surrounding some part of a plant (e.g., the base of a bundle of pine needles) (p. 283)

shrub: a perennial, woody plant, usually less than 15 feet tall and bushy with several small (typically less than 3 inches wide) main stems originating at or near the ground; compare "tree"

simple: in one piece, undivided; describes leaves not divided into separate leaflets (though sometimes deeply lobed); describes fruits derived from a single ovary; compare "compound"

single-toothed: edged with simple teeth, that is, teeth not bearing smaller teeth (p. 283); compare "double-toothed"

softwood: a needle-leaved, coniferous, normally evergreen tree (deciduous in larches) belonging to the gymnosperms or Pinophyta; compare "hardwood"

species [species], abbreviated **sp.** [spp.]: the fundamental unit of biological classification; a group of closely related plants or animals ranked below genus and above subspecies and variety

specific epithet: the second part of a species' scientific name, distinguishing that species from other members of the same genus; e.g., *balsamea* in *Abies balsamea*

spreading: diverging widely from the vertical, approaching horizontal (p. 15)

springwood: see "earlywood"

spur-shoot: a short, compressed branch, developing many closely spaced nodes (p. 288); also called a "dwarf shoot"

stamen: the male organ of a flower, usually comprising a pollen-bearing anther and a stalk called a filament (p. 19)

staminate: with stamens

sterile: lacking viable pollen, ovules or spores

stigma: the tip of the female organ (pistil) of a flower, designed to catch and hold pollen (p. 19)

stipule: a bract-like or leaf-like appendage at the base of a leaf stalk (p. 289)

stoma, stomate [stomata]: a tiny pore in the plant "skin" (epidermis), bounded by two guard cells that open and close the pore by changing shape; gas exchange takes place through a plant's stomata

stone: the tough, bony centre of some fruits (e.g., drupes), enclosing and protecting a seed

style: the narrow middle part of a pistil, connecting the stigma and ovary (p. 19)

subspecies, abbreviated **ssp.:** a naturally occurring, regional form of a species, often geographically isolated from other subspecies but still potentially

Twig parts

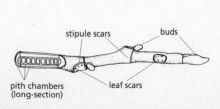

stipule scars
buds
pith chambers
(long-section)
leaf scars

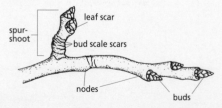

leaf scar
spur-shoot
bud scale scars
nodes
buds

interfertile with them; a ranking between species and variety in biological classification

succulent: fleshy, soft and juicy; also refers to a plant that stores water in fleshy stems or leaves

sucker: a vertical vegetative shoot growing from an underground runner or from spreading roots (p. 15)

summerwood: see "latewood"

synonym: an alternative name for a plant; usually a scientific name that has been rejected because it was incorrect or was misapplied

taproot: a root system with a prominent main root that extends vertically downward and bears smaller side roots (p. 15)

taxon [taxa]: a taxonomic group or entity (e.g., a genus, species or variety)

taxonomy: the orderly classification of organisms based on similarities and differences believed to reflect natural evolutionary relationships; also the study of these systems of classification

tepal: a sepal or petal, when these structures are not easily distinguished

terminal: located at the tip

threatened: likely to become endangered in a region unless factors affecting its vulnerability are reversed

tooth [teeth]: a small, often pointed lobe on the edge of a structure such as a leaf (pp. 282, 283, 289)

tree: an erect, perennial, woody plant with a definite crown reaching over 15 feet in height, and with a trunk (or trunks) reaching at least 3 inches in diameter; compare "shrub"

trifoliate: divided into three leaflets (p. 282)

trunk: the main stem of a tree or shrub, composed mainly of dead, woody cells covered by a thin layer of living tissues under a protective covering of bark (pp. 15, 16)

umbel: a round- or flat-topped flower cluster in which several flower stalks are of approximately the same length and arise from the same point, like the ribs of an inverted umbrella (p. 285)

understory: the lower stratum of foliage in a forest, located below the forest canopy; compare "overstory"

unisexual: with one set of sex organs only, either male or female; also called "imperfect"; compare "bisexual," "functionally unisexual"

variety, abbreviated **var.:** a naturally occurring variant of a species; ranked below subspecies in biological classification

vascular: pertaining to the conduction of substances such as sap or blood within the body of an organism; see also "vein," "xylem," "phloem"

vegetative reproduction: producing offspring from asexual parts (e.g., rhizomes, leaves) rather than from fertilized ovules (seeds); compare "sexual reproduction"

vein: a strand of conducting tubes consisting of xylem and phloem, especially if visible on the surface (e.g., on a petal or leaf) (p. 289)

vein scar: the mark left on a stem where a vein was once attached (p. 17)

whorl: a ring of three or more similar structures (e.g., leaves, branches or flowers) arising from one node

whorled: arranged in whorls (p. 284); compare "alternate," "opposite"

wing: a thin, flattened expansion on the side(s) or tip of an organ (e.g., on a fruit or twig) (pp. 18, 287)

wood: the tough, fibrous material forming the greater part of the trunks, branches and roots of trees and shrubs; composed mainly of cellulose and lignin

xylem: a vascular tissue, consisting mainly of tubes of hollow dead cells joined end to end, that conducts water and minerals and provides support; makes up the wood in trees and shrubs (p. 16)

Leaf parts

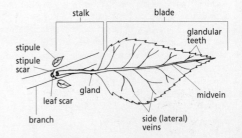

stalk   blade

glandular teeth

stipule

stipule scar

gland

leaf scar

branch

midvein

side (lateral) veins

References

Barnes, B. V. and W. H. Wagner. 1981. *Michigan Trees*. University of Michigan Press, Ann Arbor, Michigan.

Benvie, S. 1999. *The Encyclopedia of Trees: Canada and the United States*. Key Porter Books: Toronto, Ontario.

Blackburn, B. 1952. *Trees and Shrubs in Eastern North America*. Oxford University Press, New York.

BONAP. 2001. *A Synonomized Checklist of the Vascular Flora of the United States, Canada and Greenland*. Biota of North America Program of the North Carolina Botanical Garden and Museum Informatics Project website at http://www.mip.berkeley.edu/query_forms/browse_checklist.html. University of California, Berkeley, California.

Britton, N. L. and A. Brown. 1913. *An Illustrated Flora of the Northern United States and Canada*. Dover Publications, New York.

Campbell, C. S., F. Hyland, et al. 1975. *Winter Keys to Woody Plants of Maine*. University of Maine Press, Orono, Maine.

Chicago Botanic Garden. 1996. *Trees*. Pantheon Books, New York.

Core, E. L. and N. P. Ammons. 1958. *Woody Plants in Winter*. The Boxwood Press, Pittsburgh.

Couplan, F. 1998. *The Encyclopedia of Edible Plants of North America*. Keats Publishing, New Canaan, Connecticut.

Crellin, J. K. and J. Philpot. 1989. *A Reference Guide to Medicinal Plants. Volume II: Herbal Medicine Past and Present*. Duke University Press, Durham, North Carolina.

Dirr, M. A. 1990. *Manual of Woody Landscape Plants*. Stipes Publishing Company, Champaign, Illinois.

Duke, J. A. 1997. *The Green Pharmacy*. Rodale Press, Emmaus, Pennsylvania.

Duncan, W. H. and M. B. Duncan. 1988. *Trees of the Southeastern United States*. University of Georgia Press, Athens, Georgia.

Edlin, H. 1978. *The Tree Key: A Guide to Identification in Garden, Field and Forest*. Charles Scribner's Sons, New York.

Elias, T. S. 1989. *Field Guide to North American Trees*. Grolier Book Clubs, Danbury, Connecticut.

Erichsen-Brown, C. 1979. *Use of Plants for the Past 500 Years*. Breezy Creeks Press, Aurora, Ontario.

Farrar, J. L. 1995. *Trees in Canada*. Fitzhenry and Whiteside, Markham, Ontario.

Fernald, M. L. 1950. *Gray's Manual of Botany*. American Book Company, New York.

Flint, H. L. 1983. *Landscape Plants for Eastern North America*. John Wiley and Sons, New York.

Foster, S. and J. A. Duke. 1990. *Field Guide to Medicinal Plants: Eastern and Central North America*. Houghton Mifflin, Boston.

Gleason, H. A. and A. Cronquist. 1991. *Manual of Vascular Plants of Northeastern United States and Adjacent Canada*. New York Botanical Garden, Bronx, New York.

Gorer, R. 1976. *Trees and Shrubs: A Complete Guide*. David and Charles Publishers, Vancouver, B.C.

Grieve, M. 1931. *A Modern Herbal*. Jonathan Cape, Harmondsworth, Middlesex, England. Republished in 1976 by Penguin Books.

Grimm, W. C. 1962. *The Book of Trees*. Stackpole, Harrisburg, Pennsylvania.

Grimm, W. C. 1966. *Recognizing Native Shrubs*. Stackpole, Harrisburg, Pennsylvania.

Hole, L. 1997. *Lois Hole's Favourite Trees and Shrubs*. Lone Pine Publishing, Edmonton, Alberta.

Holmgrem, N. H. 1998. *Illustrated Companion to Gleason and Cronquist's Manual*. New York Botanical Garden, Bronx, New York.

Hosie, R. C. 1969. *Native Trees of Canada*. Canadian Forest Service, Queen's Printer, Ottawa, Ontario.

Hottes, A. C. 1952. *The Book of Trees*. A. T. De La Mare Company, New York.

Hutchens, A. R. 1991. *Indian Herbalogy of North America*. Shambhala Publications, Boston.

Huxley, A., M. Griffiths, et al., Eds. 1999. *The New Royal Horticultural Dictionary of Gardening*. Groves Dictionaries, New York.

Hyams, E. 1965. *Ornamental Shrubs for Temperate Zone Gardens*. A. S. Barnes and Company, New York.

Illinois Department of Natural Resources. n.d. 2006. *Endangered and Threatened Species List*. Office of Resource Conservation, Illinois Department of Natural Resources website, http://dnr.state.il.us/espb/datelist.htm. Accessed 05 March 2007.

Illinois Foresty. 2006. *Illinois Forest Facts*. University of Illinois Extension. http://web.extension.uiuc.edu/forestry/il_forest_facts.html. Accessed 26 March 2007.

ITIS, N. A. 2003. *ITIS Integrated Taxonomic Information System*. U.S. Department of Agriculture website, http://www.itis.usda.gov/. Accessed 27 March 2007.

Johnston, A. 1987. *Plants and the Blackfoot*. Lethbridge Historical Society, Lethbridge, Alberta.

Kartesz, J. T. and C. A. Meacham. 1999. *Synthesis of the North American Flora*. North Carolina Botanical Garden, University of North Carolina, Chapel Hill, North Carolina.

Kershaw, L. J. 2001. *Trees of Ontario*. Lone Pine Publishing, Edmonton, Alberta.

Lacey, L. 1993. *Micmac Medicines: Remedies and Recollections*. Nimbus Publishing Limited, Halifax, Nova Scotia.

Lauriault, J. 1992. *Identification Guide to the Trees of Canada*. Canadian Museum of Nature, Ottawa, Ontario.

Little, E. L. 1980. *The Audubon Society Field Guide to North American Trees: Western Region*. Alfred A. Knopf, New York.

Little, E. L. 1996. *The Audubon Society Field Guide to North American Trees: Eastern Region*. Alfred A. Knopf, New York.

Lust, J. 1974. *The Herb Book*. Bantam Books, New York.

Marles, R. L., Christina Clavelle, et al. 2000. *Aboriginal Plant Use in Canada's Northwest Boreal Forest*. UBC Press, University of British Columbia, Vancouver, B.C.

References

Medsger, O. P. 1966. *Edible Wild Plants*. Collier-Macmillan Canada Ltd., Toronto, Ontario.

Mitchell, A. and J. Wilkinson. 1982. *The Trees of Britain and Northern Europe*. Wm. Collins, Sons and Co., London.

Mitchell, A. 1987. *The Guide to Trees of Canada and North America*. Prospero Books, Kansas City, Missouri.

Mohlenbrock, R. H. and D. M. Ladd. 1978. *Distribution of Illinois Vascular Plants*. Southern Illinois University Press, Carbondale, Illinois.

Mohlenbrock, R. H. 2002. *The Vascular Flora of Illinois*. Southern Illinois University Press, Edwardsville, Illinois.

Mozingo, H. 1987. *Shrubs of the Great Basin*. University of Nevada Press, Reno, Nevada.

MuseumLink Illinois. 2000. *Illinois Forests*. Illinois State Museum. http://www.museum.state.il.us/muslink/forest/htmls/intro.html. Accessed 26 March 2007.

Naegele, T. A. 1996. *Edible and Medicinal Plants of the Great Lakes Region*. Wilderness Adventure Books, Davisburg, Michigan.

Peattie, D. C. 1966. *A Natural History of Trees of Eastern and Central North America*. Houghton Mifflin Company, Boston.

Peirce, A. 1999. *The American Pharmaceutical Association Practical Guide to Natural Medicines*. Stonesong Press, William Morrow and Company, New York.

Peterson, L. A. 1977. *A Field Guide to Edible Wild Plants of Eastern and Central North America*. Houghton Mifflin, Boston.

Petrides, G. A. and O. Petrides. 1992. *A Field Guide to Western Trees*. Houghton Mifflin, Boston.

Petrides, G. A. and J. Wehr. 1998. *Eastern Trees*. Houghton Mifflin, Boston.

Phillips, R. 1978. *Trees of North America and Europe*. Pan Books, London.

Phillips, D. H. and D. A. Burdekin. 1992. *Diseases of Forest and Ornamental Trees*. MacMillan Press, London.

Phipps, J. B. and M. Muniyamma. 1980. A taxonomic revision of Crataegus Rosaceae in Ontario. *Canadian Journal of Botany* 58: 1621–1699.

Preston, R. J., Jr. 1989. *North American Trees*. Iowa State University, Ames, Iowa.

Reader's Digest. 1981. *Field Guide to the Trees and Shrubs of Britain*. Reader's Digest Association, London.

Reader's Digest. 1986. *Magic and Medicine of Plants*. Reader's Digest Association, Montreal, Quebec.

Rehder, A. 1951. *Manual of Cultivated Trees and Shrubs Hardy in North America*. Macmillan, New York.

Robertson, K. R. 2004. *List of Woody Plants Native or Naturalized in Illinois*. Illinois Natural History Survey, Champaign, Illinois.

Rosendahl, C. O. 1955. *Trees and Shrubs of the Upper Midwest*. University of Minnesota Press, Minneapolis.

Smith, N. F. 1995. *Trees of Michigan and the Upper Great Lakes*. Thunder Bay Press, Lansing, Michigan.

Soper, J. H. and M. L. Heimburger. 1961. *100 Shrubs of Ontario*. Ontario Department of Commerce and Development, Toronto, Ontario.

Soper, J. H. and M. L. Heimburger. 1982. *Shrubs of Ontario*. Royal Ontario Museum, Toronto, Ontario.

Spangler, R. L. and J. Ripperda. 1977. *Landscape Plants for Central and Northeastern United States Including Lower and Eastern Canada*. Burgess Publishing, Minneapolis.

Sternberg, G. and J. Wilson. 2004. *Native Trees of North American Landscapes*. Timber Press, Portland, Oregon.

Stokes, D. W. 1981. *The Natural History of Wild Shrubs and Vines: Eastern and Central North America*. Harper and Row, New York.

Swink, F. and G. Wilhelm. 1979; 1994. *Plants of the Chicago Region*. Morton Arboretum, Lisle, Illinois.

Trelease, W. 1931. *Winter Botany*. Dover Publications, New York.

Viertel, A. T. 1970. *Trees, Shrubs and Vines*. Syracuse University Press, Syracuse, New York.

Vines, R. A. 1977. *Trees of East Texas*. University of Texas Press, Austin, Texas.

Voss, E. G. 1972. *Michigan Flora. Part I: Gymnosperms and Monocots*. University of Michigan Herbarium, Ann Arbor, Michigan.

Voss, E. G. 1985. *Michigan Flora. Part II: Dicots Saururaceae-Cornaceae*. University of Michigan Herbarium, Ann Arbor, Michigan.

Voss, E. G. 1996. *Michigan Flora. Part III: Dicots Concluded*. University of Michigan Herbarium, Ann Arbor, Michigan.

White, J. H. and R. C. Hosie. 1968. *The Forest Trees of Ontario*. Ontario Department of Lands and Forests, Toronto, Ontario.

Woods, Alan J., Omernik, James M., Pederson, Charles L., and Moran, Brian C. 2006. *Level III and IV Ecoregions of Illinois*. United States Environmental Protection Agency. http://www.epa.gov/wed/ecoregions/il/il_eco_desc.pdf. Accessed 27 March 2007.

Index

Index

Index

Index

Index

Index

About the Author

An avid naturalist since childhood, Linda Kershaw focused on botany at the University of Waterloo, earning her masters degree in 1976. Since then she has worked as a consultant and researcher in northwestern Canada and as an author and editor in Edmonton, while pursuing two favorite pastimes—photography and illustrating. Linda hopes that her books will help people to appreciate the beauty and fascinating history of plants and to recognize the intrinsic value of nature's rich mosaic.

Author photo: Peter Kershaw